The Women's Movement

The Women's Movement against Sexual Harassment recounts the story of how a diverse grassroots social movement placed sexual harassment on the public agenda in the 1970s and 1980s. The collaboration of women from varying racial, economic, and geographic backgrounds strengthened the movement by representing the experiences and perspectives of a broad range of women, and incorporating their resources and strategies for social change. Black women; middle-class feminists; women breaking into construction, coal mining, and other nontraditional occupations; and women in pink-collar and working-class white-collar jobs all helped to convince governments to adopt public policies against sexual harassment in the United States. Based on interviews and voluminous original research, this book is the first to show how the movement against sexual harassment fundamentally changed American life in ways that continue to advance women's opportunities today.

Carrie N. Baker is a Visiting Assistant Professor of Women's Studies at Smith College, on leave from Berry College, where she is an Assistant Professor in the Program for Women and Gender Studies and Sociology. She holds a B.A. in philosophy from Yale University and a J.D. and Ph.D. in women's studies from Emory University. Dr. Baker was Editor-in-Chief of the *Emory Law Journal* while attending law school and later served as law clerk to United States District Court Judge Marvin Shoob in Atlanta. Dr. Baker's primary areas of research are women's legal history, gender and public policy, and women's social movements. Her work has been published in *Feminist Studies, Women in Politics,* the *Journal of Women's History, NWSA Journal,* the *Journal of Law and Inequality, Emory Law Journal,* and *Women and Social Movements in the United States.* Dr. Baker is a member of the National Women's Studies Association and the American Sociological Association.

The Women's Movement against Sexual Harassment

CARRIE N. BAKER

Smith College

1/10

CAMBRIDGE
UNIVERSITY PRESS

CAMBRIDGE UNIVERSITY PRESS
Cambridge, New York, Melbourne, Madrid, Cape Town, Singapore, São Paulo, Delhi

Cambridge University Press
32 Avenue of the Americas, New York, NY 10013-2473, USA

www.cambridge.org
Information on this title: www.cambridge.org/9780521879354

First published 2008

Printed in the United States of America

A catalog record for this publication is available from the British Library.

Library of Congress Cataloging in Publication Data

Baker, Carrie N.
  The Women's movement against sexual harassment / Carrie N. Baker.
    p. cm.
  Includes bibliographical references and index.
    ISBN 978-0-521-87935-4 (hardback) – ISBN 978-0-521-70494-6 (pbk.)
  1. Sexual harassment of women – United States – History – 20th century.
  2. Feminism – United States – History – 20th century.   3. Sexual harassment of women – Law
  and legislation – United States.   4. Women's rights – United States.   I. Title.
  HQ1237.5.U6B35 2008
  305.420973'09047–dc22   2007028242

ISBN 978-0-521-87935-4 hardback
ISBN 978-0-521-70494-6 paperback

Contents

Figures

Acknowledgments

I have vivid memories of October 1991, during my first year of law school, sitting in the student lounge watching Anita Hill on television testify in excruciating detail before the Senate Judiciary Committee about her experiences of sexual harassment while working for Supreme Court nominee Clarence Thomas a decade prior at the Equal Employment Opportunity Commission (EEOC). The year before, when I was a graduate student at the same institution, the issue had arisen closer to home when a senior member of the law school faculty departed, allegedly with a golden parachute, after students had staged a walkout from classes because the administration had repeatedly failed to act on student complaints of sexual harassment against him. Then the Tailhook scandal broke out. Seemingly out of nowhere, the issue of sexual harassment was all over the headlines and on the minds of everyone, everywhere. I wondered why sexual harassment had suddenly become such a big deal. Where did it come from? What was sexual harassment, and what was the law? Had sexual harassment always been around, and, if so, how had women dealt with it in the past? These and other questions set me on a path to explore the social movement against sexual harassment that emerged in the 1970s and brought the issue to the Supreme Court in the 1980s. This book is the result of that exploration.

Many people helped me along the way. I would like to thank everyone who read drafts of this manuscript and provided guidance and encouragement during the research and writing of this book, especially Mary Odem, Beth Reingold, Mary Radford, Cherrie Granrose, Mindy Wilson, and John Salatti. Many people associated with libraries, collections, and archives around the country have assisted me with this project. In particular I would like to thank David Hopson, Elaine Bailey, and Kathy Jiang at the Barnard Center for Research on Women; Deborah Richards at the Arthur and Elizabeth Schlesinger Library on the History of Women in America at Radcliffe College; and Aaron Mooney at Emory University's Woodruff Library. My appreciation also goes to Yolanda Wu at NOW Legal Defense and Education Fund, Terri Witherspoon at

Equal Rights Advocates (ERA), and Frances Hart at the EEOC for digging through old files for me. I offer heartfelt thanks to the many wonderful women who provided me with interviews and access to their private papers, including Karen Sauvigné, Freada Klein, K. C. Wagner, Susan Meyer, Lynn Rubinett, Nadine Taub, Peggy Crull, Anne Simon, Maudine Rice Cooper, Katherine Mazzaferri, Joan Grafff, Trudy Levy, and Nan Stein. For financial support I thank Emory University's Institute for Women's Studies and the Graduate School of Arts and Sciences, Emory Women's Club, the Woodrow Wilson Foundation, and Berry College. I would like to thank my editor, Lewis Bateman, at Cambridge University Press, as well as the anonymous reviewers who provided very helpful comments. I also thank Diane Land, Amy Summerlin, and Darla Fox at Berry College for editorial support. Finally, I thank my family, especially Harvey Hill, who throughout the research and writing of this book generously offered his support and encouragement.

I dedicate this book to all the courageous women who spoke up and broke the silence.

Organizational Abbreviations

AASC	Alliance Against Sexual Harassment, Cambridge, MA
ACLU	American Civil Liberties Union, New York, NY
CASH	Committee on Sexual Harassment, Columbus, OH
CEP	Coal Employment Project, Oak Ridge, TN
CETA	Comprehensive Employment Training Act
CLUW	Coalition of Labor Union Women, New York, NY
DOL	Department of Labor, Washington, D.C.
EEOC	Equal Employment Opportunity Commission, Washington, D.C.
ERA	Equal Rights Advocates, Inc., San Francisco, CA
HAP	Human Affairs Program, Cornell University, Ithaca, NY
IUE	International Union of Electrical, Radio & Machine Workers, Pittsburgh, PA
LCCRUL	Lawyer's Committee for Civil Rights Under Law, Washington, D.C.
LSCRRC	Law Students Civil Rights Research Council, New York, NY
MALDEF	Mexican-American Legal Defense & Education Fund, San Francisco, CA
MSPB	Merit System Protection Board, Washington, D.C.
NOW	National Organization for Women, Washington, D.C.
NOWLDEF	NOW Legal Defense & Education Fund, New York, NY
OBAW	Organization of Black Activist Women, Washington, D.C.
OCR	Office of Civil Rights, Department of Education, Washington, D.C.
OFCCP	Office of Federal Contract Compliance Programs, Washington, D.C.
OPM	Office of Personnel Management, Washington, D.C.
UAW	United Auto Workers, Detroit, MI

WAJE	Women's Alliance for Job Equity, Philadelphia, PA
WLDF	Women's Legal Defense Fund, Washington, D.C.
WOASH	Women Organized Against Sexual Harassment, Berkeley, CA
WOW	Women Office Workers, New York, NY
WREE	Women for Racial and Economic Opportunity, New York, NY
WWU	Working Women United, Ithaca, NY
WWUI	Working Women United Institute, New York, NY
WWI	Working Women's Institute, New York, NY

Introduction: Enter at Your Own Risk

In March 1975, a group of feminist activists in Ithaca, New York coined the term "sexual harassment" to name something they had all experienced but rarely discussed – unwanted sexual demands, comments, looks, or sexual touching in the workplace. The experience they wanted to spotlight was one that women in this country had faced since colonial times. Seventeenth-century indentured servants, eighteenth-century black slaves, nineteenth-century factory workers, and twentieth-century office workers all shared the experience of having fended off the sexual demands of those wielding economic power over their lives – masters, overseers, foremen, and supervisors.[1]

Women responded to workplace sexual coercion in a myriad of ways, often submitting, but also resisting. Some escaped the situation, others tried using official channels to stop the abuse or seek relief from its effects, and yet others joined together to protest sexual coercion by their employers. Escape was the only option for many female slaves, who had little power to resist their owner's sexual advances, no legal recourse, and no home outside their owner's reach. In her 1861 autobiography, *Incidents in the Life of a Slave Girl*, Harriet Jacobs described her escape from a master who "began to whisper foul words in [her] ear" when she was fifteen.[2] Domestic servants who could afford to do so escaped the sexual abuse of employers by leaving their jobs. In 1874, Louisa May Alcott published an account of how at the age of eighteen she had left a job as a domestic servant because her employer assigned her backbreaking work after she refused his sexual advances.[3]

Women sometimes turned to governmental authorities for help. Although colonial courts heard charges against masters for "violating" female servants, making "forcible attempts" on their chastity, and exhibiting "lewd behavior," victims rarely gained relief.[4] In cases when a servant ended up pregnant, courts sometimes required masters to pay a fine or give security to maintain the child.[5] However, indentured servants did not have easy access to the judicial system, and their direct dependence on those who assaulted them often dissuaded them from taking action. When former slaves registered charges of sexual abuse by white men with the Freeman's Bureau, an agency set up after emancipation to assist blacks, they seldom obtained relief.[6] Sometimes, women sued their employers for assault or for monetary damages when they became pregnant.[7] In 1908, a young immigrant woman sued her employer, a saloon-keeper, because he "abused her shamefully and then turned her out when he found that she was to become the mother of his illegitimate child," but she lost her case.[8]

Women also resisted sexual coercion in the workplace collectively. In Chicago, at the turn of the century, Grace Abbot formed immigrant protective organizations with a primary goal of protecting immigrant girls from lecherous employers.[9] Later, tradeswomen formed groups to fight sexual abuse in the workplace. In 1914, a group of women in the needle trades formed the Young Ladies Educational Society to support each other in resisting the sexual advances of their employers.[10] A major goal of the Working Women's Society, a forerunner of the Women's Trade Union League, was to protect working women from unwanted sexual advances by supervisors.[11] Sexual abuse of workers sometimes became an issue that sent unions out on strike. One of the issues in a 1937 strike at the Chevrolet-Flint Plant in Michigan was sexual abuse, after a large number of female workers had to go to the county hospital to be treated for venereal disease traced to a single foreman. A worker recalled, "Those were the conditions that young women had to accept in order to support their families. Sometimes they earned just enough to provide food for the family and they couldn't lose their jobs because nobody else in the family had a job."[12]

Despite their resistance, women often were blamed for sexual abuse because of their presence in the workplace, which was thought to provoke uncontrollable male lust or to reflect women's promiscuous nature. The nineteenth-century white middle-class ideal of "true womanhood" required women to guard their purity and deny knowledge of sexuality. To admit a sexual incident blemished a woman's character, which silenced many. Women were traditionally classified as respectable or not respectable, and for a woman to enter the workplace was to forfeit respect.[13] Working women were often characterized as enticing their employers and later becoming prostitutes. If the sexual abuse of female workers was acknowledged at all, it was considered a moral issue, and concern focused on the moral degradation of the women targeted. During industrialization, when women began entering mills and factories in large numbers, sexual behavior in the workplace was framed as a social problem – one of vice, not economic coercion. Concern for the moral conditions of women's employment led to official investigations by the federal government in 1887 and again in 1911. A 1911 Bureau of Labor Statistics study of the relation between occupations and the criminality of women warned, "Wherever the sexes work indiscriminately together great laxity obtains."[14]

Beginning in the nineteenth century, however, female social reformers shifted the terms of the debate by characterizing working women as victimized by male lust and seduction rather than being promiscuous seducers themselves.

Although they identified the problem to be male sexual aggression and violence, their solutions often restricted women socially and economically by rigidly enforcing sex-segregated workplaces and strong cultural taboos against sexual mixing. Reformers fought for protective labor legislation to shield women from workplace sexual abuse. They expressed concern for the "physical and moral safety" of women in the workplace. Unions, protective associations, and settlement house organizations were at the forefront of the drive for protective legislation for women workers. Reformers believed that limiting women's hours, banning night work, and prohibiting women from certain occupations would help to shield women from sexual abuse.[15] But these social reformers still characterized the problem of sexual coercion in the workplace primarily as one of moral degeneration, not economic abuse.

During the second wave of the women's movements in the 1970s, a grassroots movement against sexual harassment emerged, which framed workplace sexual abuse in new ways. For those with backgrounds in the rape crisis movement, sexual coercion in the workplace was an issue of violence against women. For others, sexual harassment was a form of sex discrimination in employment and a violation of women's civil rights. This book charts the evolution of sexual harassment from a private indignity women suffered silently to an issue of public concern and debate. This transformation occurred as a result of women speaking out – a few women took legal action, others began talking about their experiences with each other – and then women collectively began to recognize sexual harassment as a widespread and systemic problem. This gathering chorus of women's protests soon began to resound in the larger society.

The movement against sexual harassment emerged from multiple feminisms – the grassroots activism of diverse groups of women – and the resulting public policy reflected this diverse participation. The activists' experiences of harassment and strategies to combat it were fundamentally shaped by their gender, race, and class identities. African-American women brought most of the precedent-setting lawsuits. They filed employment discrimination complaints with equal employment offices in the early 1970s, turning to civil rights organizations for assistance. The early sexual harassment plaintiffs were the first to conceptualize sexual harassment as sex discrimination under Title VII of the Civil Rights Act, thus fundamentally shaping the movement against sexual harassment by grounding it in Title VII sex discrimination law.

White middle-class feminists also made significant contributions to the movement against sexual harassment and were similarly shaped by their identities and backgrounds. Two of the first organizations to work on sexual harassment, Working Women United in Ithaca, New York, and Alliance Against Sexual Coercion in Cambridge, Massachusetts, were founded by white middle-class women with experience in the women's movement. These women used feminist theory to analyze sexual coercion in the workplace and used the tools and resources of the women's movement to raise awareness of the problem through speak-outs, surveys, newsletters, and the media. Feminist attorneys litigated most of the early sexual harassment cases and actively participated in developing public policy on sexual harassment. By the end of the 1980s, a wide range of mainstream feminist organizations were working on the issue.

The third important group to shape the movement against sexual harassment was working-class women in nontraditional and blue-collar occupations, who advocated for broadening the definition of sexual harassment to include hostile environment harassment. In the late 1970s, a diverse array of women began to break into traditionally male fields like construction and coal mining. In unions and on the job, women experienced male hostility to their presence in these nontraditional work settings. Male supervisors and co-workers subjected them to sexual abuse and even physical violence in order to push them out of the workplace. The women used the resources of their unions and employee associations to raise awareness about sexual harassment and develop strategies to combat it. They also urged courts and policymakers to broaden their definitions of sexual harassment to include not just sexual demands by a supervisor of a subordinate employee, but hostile environment harassment, both sexual and nonsexual, not only just from supervisors but from co-workers as well. Blue-collar women brought several precedent-setting lawsuits, and they participated in and influenced organizations that fought sexual harassment, including Working Women United Institute and Alliance Against Sexual Coercion.

Finally, women working in female-dominated "pink-collar" occupations and working-class "white-collar" jobs were involved at every stage of the movement against sexual harassment, filing lawsuits, raising public awareness of the issue, and fighting for better treatment in the workplace. Flight attendants, clerical workers, and other women in female-dominated occupations, who had organized against sex discrimination in the workplace since the mid-1960s, turned to the issue of sexual exploitation of women in the workplace in the early 1970s. Through groups like Stewardesses for Women's Rights and the National Association of Working Women, these women fought for the need to be treated as professionals rather than sex objects.

Through the use of social movement theory, this book seeks to understand how the movement against sexual harassment emerged and thrived in the 1970s and 1980s. Social movements are usually defined as a mixture of informal networks and formal organizations outside of conventional politics that make clear demands for fundamental social, political, or economic change and utilize unconventional or protest tactics. Social movements function at multiple levels: the microlevel of individual activists and their interactions, the meso level of groups and institutions and their interactions, and the macrolevel, where these individuals, groups, and institutions function as a coherent whole to create societal change. Activism against sexual harassment emerged from an array of grassroots locations around the country, including from individual women filing lawsuits to the formation of organizations to combat harassment, ultimately converging at the national level in the 1980s. The movement against sexual harassment was not only rooted in the civil rights and women's movements, but was also influenced by the student movements of the 1960s, the sexual revolution, the gay and lesbian rights movement, and the labor movement. This movement resulted from formal and informal resources mobilized from these other movements, including most importantly, the civil rights legal framework and the women's movement's network of rape crisis centers and feminist attorneys. The movement took advantage of the political opportunities available at the time – progressive judicial appointees of presidents Kennedy and Johnson and the legacy of the Warren Court's advancement of individual rights, as well as the government agencies developed to advance equal employment opportunity and human rights in the wake of the civil rights movement. Finally, activists against sexual harassment developed a shared understanding of the issue that legitimated and motivated collective action. They tapped into the tension between women's increasing need to enter the workplace (and stay there) and many men's tendency to view women through the lens of sexuality. They also tapped into the tension between the emerging feminist demand that women should be able to control their bodies, particularly their sexuality, and women's experience of sexual coercion in the workplace.[16] This book seeks to understand the movement against sexual harassment by analyzing the relationship between the movement's internal dynamics and its external context – how the political and social context shaped the movement's collective identity, its forms of collective action, and the meanings and structures it created to effect social change.[17] In order to understand this complex mix of factors that creates a social movement, this study draws on many stories of grassroots activists and "acts by individuals and small groups in everyday life as part of a struggle for social change."[18] It also emphasizes how intersections of race, class, and gender shaped the movement. Finally, this book seeks to understand how the movement effected both policy change and cultural change over time.

This story of the early movement against sexual harassment challenges the standard conceptualization of the feminist movement as primarily white and middle-class. This whitewashed version of the movement has obscured much of the complexity of the second wave of the women's movements. Recent scholarship has explored this complexity, such as the work of Maria Bevacqua on rape, Premilla Nadasen on welfare rights, Dennis Deslippe and Dorothy Sue Cobble on working-class women, Winifred Breines on the relation of white and black women in the women's liberation movement, and the works of Kimberly Springer, Benita Roth, and Nancy MacLean on Black and Chicana feminisms.[19] This scholarship reveals that the second wave of the women's movements was a diverse movement, and there were a number of issues that drew diverse women into collaborative activism. Sexual harassment was an important issue to women because it affected so many, so often, across race and class lines, and was rooted in fundamental concerns about economic survival and basic personal integrity. Not surprisingly, the fight against sexual harassment brought women together across differences to fight a common problem. This book demonstrates how the movement against sexual harassment arose from multiple locations, from diverse political communities, and how structural and

PART I

RAISING THE ISSUE OF SEXUAL
HARASSMENT

Articulating the Wrong: Resistance to Sexual Harassment in the Early 1970s

Resistance to sexual harassment emerged in the form of several lawsuits filed around the country, under Title VII of the Civil Rights Act of 1964. Sexual harassment litigation was a battleground on which traditional notions that women belonged in the private sphere and entered the public sphere at their own risk struggled with feminist notions that women were entitled to participate fully in the public sphere. Since the founding of the United States, the law enforced male dominance and female subordination by excluding women from the public sphere of the marketplace and government and refusing to intervene in disputes arising in the domestic sphere. Women could not vote, serve on juries, or testify in court. Under the legal doctrine of coverture, inherited from English common law, a woman's legal identity merged into her husband's upon marriage. Married women could not control their property, sue or be sued, or enter into a contract in their own names, and a woman's husband controlled any wages she earned. The doctrine of marital unity also gave men control over their wives' bodies so the state rarely interfered in ongoing family relationships, even in cases of battery and rape.[1]

By custom, as well, women were largely excluded from public life. In the early nineteenth century, the social ethic of domesticity shaped the lives of white middle-class women, excluding them from participation in the workplace. The ideology of domesticity distinguished between home – the locus of tranquility, rest, and familial love associated with women – and the public life of business and politics associated with men.[2] This ideology, however, often did not reflect the lives of poor women and women of color, who had no choice but to work outside of their homes. Many women, as domestic servants in particular, straddled the line between the public and the private spheres.[3] The influence of this ideology of domesticity on the law, however, powerfully shaped all women's lives by limiting women's participation in the public sphere and denying legal relief for harms arising in the private sphere.

Courts in the United States consistently used the public/private ideology when adjudicating legal cases brought by women. Courts upheld laws excluding women from the public sphere, including protective labor laws that limited women's participation in the workplace and laws that allowed women to be excluded from armed combat, refused credit, excluded from trade unions and professional associations, and denied public accommodations and membership in business clubs.[4] Courts often refused to adjudicate cases involving violence or coercion in intimate relationships or cases involving sexual behavior, which was associated with the private sphere. In the early 1970s, when women began to bring sexual harassment cases before federal courts, they encountered the ongoing legacy of the public/private ideology in courts' refusal to grant relief.

However, social mores were changing, and activists built upon these changes to convince courts, and the public, to take women's concerns seriously. Over the course of the twentieth century, American society saw a decline of Victorian ideas about men's sexual aggressiveness being natural and unchanging. By the 1960s, the sexual revolution led to increasing openness about sexuality in the culture at large.[5] This enabled women to question the inevitability of men's sexual behavior in the workplace and to begin to articulate opposition to this behavior. Another change that contributed to the rise of a movement against sexual harassment was a decline in the notion of men's entitlement to a family wage and women's entitlement to economic support from men, a change that strengthened women's claim to full participation in the workplace.[6] This movement also resulted from an increasing reliance on the state and law to solve problems. The civil rights movement had successfully challenged school segregation in *Brown v. Board of Education*, and the women's movement had challenged sex discriminatory laws and obstacles to birth control using the Bill of Rights. Following this legacy, activists against sexual harassment turned to the law and the courts to challenge sexual coercion in the workplace.

The movement against sexual harassment emerged out of the social movements that were challenging the status quo in the early 1960s, including the civil rights movement, the new left and antiwar movements, the labor movement, and the women's movements. In the 1960s and 1970s, dramatic social, political, and legal changes transformed women's lives in the United States. The publication of Betty Friedan's *The Feminine Mystique* in 1963 raised the problem of middle-class women's lack of fulfilling roles and responsibilities in American society, galvanizing women across the country to demand expanded roles. Middle-class women were much more likely to find themselves in the workforce as these decades progressed, particularly before marriage and after divorce, as the average age of first marriage rose and the divorce rate doubled between the early 1960s and the mid-1970s.[7] Women were having fewer children and were more able to control when they had their children because of FDA approval of the Pill in 1960, for the first time giving women a highly effective method of pregnancy prevention that they controlled, and the Supreme Court's legalization of abortion in 1973. Women's increasing control over their reproductive lives freed them to engage more fully in the workplace. As a result, women's participation in the civilian labor force jumped from 37.7% in 1960 to over

51% in 1980. Women moved into new types of jobs, entering traditionally male fields in higher numbers, such as mining, construction, and law, and they began to move up from the bottom rungs of the employment ladder.[8] Because more women were in the workplace, and working in a wider variety of occupations, workplace equality became an increasingly compelling issue.

The first advancements in women's workplace rights occurred during the Kennedy administration. After Kennedy was elected in 1960, he appointed a Presidential Commission on the Status of Women, chaired by Eleanor Roosevelt. In 1963, the Commission issued a detailed report describing widespread gender discrimination in the United States, including discrimination in employment, unequal pay, lack of social services such as child care, and continuing legal inequality. As a result, Kennedy signed a presidential order prohibiting the civil service from discriminating on the basis of sex in hiring for career positions. Congress then passed the Equal Pay Act in 1963, prohibiting sex-based pay discrepancies in most jobs, and in 1964 passed Title VII of the Civil Rights Act, prohibiting employment discrimination on the basis of race, color, national origin, religion, and sex. The failure of the government to enforce Title VII's prohibition of sex discrimination in the workplace led to the formation in 1966 of the National Organization for Women (NOW), which became a leading women's rights advocate in the second wave of the women's movements. Herman Edelsberg, the first executive director of the federal enforcement agency for Title VII, the EEOC, told reporters at his first press conference that he and other men at the EEOC thought men were entitled to have female secretaries, and he publicly labeled the sex provision of Title VII "a fluke conceived out of wedlock."[9] The EEOC virtually ignored the sex discrimination provision of Title VII, leading Betty Friedan, Pauli Murray, Sonia Pressman, and others to form NOW to fight for an expansive definition of sex-based discrimination under Title VII.[10] Later, NOW would raise the issue of sexual exploitation on the job after National Airlines initiated a $9.5 million advertising campaign that required female cabin crew to wear buttons saying "Fly Me." The first all-female national organization of flight attendants, Stewardesses for Women's Rights, and NOW denounced the advertising campaign, staged protests, and worked with female flight attendants to file suit against National Airlines and Continental to stop the "sexploitation" of women in the workplace.[11]

The women's movement quickly expanded to focus on a wide range of issues, including health, abortion, rape, domestic violence, and sexuality. In the late 1960s, the women's liberation movement emerged, posing a radical challenge to patriarchy and male domination in society. Consciousness-raising groups brought women together to analyze the problems they faced, leading to the creation of groups like Redstockings, Cell 16, The Feminists, The Combahee River Collective, and New York Radical Women, and women began to produce manifestos, newsletters, music, and art to express their ideas. Women's bookstores began popping up all over, facilitating communication among women. A major focus of radical feminist activism was men's sexual exploitation of and violence against women, as well as women's sexual autonomy and pleasure, especially with other women. In 1968, radical feminists protested the sexual objectification of women in the Miss America pageant in Atlantic City, where they crowned a live sheep and tossed girdles, bras, curlers, and issues of the *Ladies Home Journal* in a "freedom trashcan." The Boston Women's Health Book Collective formed in 1969, and soon published the first edition of *Our Bodies, Our Selves* to educate women about their bodies and health. The same year, feminists held the first abortion speak-out in New York, thereby fueling the reproductive rights movement. In 1971, feminists in New York held the first speak-out and conference on rape, launching the feminist antirape movement, which created rape crisis centers across the nation, raised public awareness through guerrilla actions and Take Back the Night marches, taught self-defense classes, and fought for rape law reform. The battered women's movement, also formed in the early 1970s, established hundreds of shelters and crisis centers around the country. Women articulated their identities not only as women, but also as members of other social groups, resulting in a range of feminist movements, including Black feminism, Chicana feminism, and lesbian feminism.[12] This activism contributed to women's growing sense of their rights to economic opportunity and bodily self determination, creating a foundation from which the movement against sexual harassment sprung.

In response to this growing movement, women's rights were significantly enhanced in the 1970s. In 1972, Congress passed the Equal Employment Act and the Educational Amendments to the Civil Rights Act, strengthening laws against sex discrimination in employment and prohibiting sex discrimination in education under Title IX, which later became the foundation for activism against sexual harassment in education. In 1976, Congress passed the Pregnancy Discrimination Act, prohibiting employment discrimination against pregnant women. By 1977, thirty-five states had ratified the Equal Rights Amendment, which Congress had passed in 1972. During this time, the Supreme Court also significantly enhanced women's legal rights. In 1973, the Supreme Court established a woman's right to abortion in *Roe v. Wade* and handed down several decisions under the Equal Protection Clause that invalidated sex-discriminatory laws. In the 1976 case of *Craig v. Boren*, the Supreme Court formulated a new standard of review under the Equal Protection Clause – intermediate scrutiny: classifications by sex had to serve important governmental objectives and be substantially related to achievement of those objectives.[13] In these cases, the court moved toward abandoning the traditional view that women were primarily homemakers and mothers operating within the private sphere.[14] Out of this social, political, and legal context emerged resistance to workplace sexual harassment.

The earliest activists against sexual harassment framed their resistance within the rubric of Title VII of the Civil Rights Act of 1964, which was the crowning achievement of the civil rights movement and resulted from an outpouring of citizen support in response to the violent treatment of peaceful black protesters in 1963 and 1964. Title VII prohibited employment discrimination

based on race, color, national origin, religion, and sex. African-American activists had used Title VII in the courts to challenge workplace race discrimination, including racial harassment.[15] Title VII began as a race discrimination
statute to which an amendment to prohibit sex discrimination was added on the
floor of the House at the last minute.[16] Representative Howard W. Smith of
Virginia, an 80-year-old former judge who was once described as "one of the
leading reactionaries of the twentieth-century House of Representatives,"[17]
introduced the amendment after several weeks of debate, the day before the
final vote was taken, and there were no hearings and little serious discussion of
the amendment. Southern members of Congress generally supported the
amendment in an attempt to defeat the underlying legislation. Norbert Schlei,
a senior official in the Justice Department who was in the House gallery on the
day the sex discrimination amendment was discussed, commented, "'They
thought it was a joke. They didn't think there was any discrimination against
women that mattered. They were laughing down on the floor as they were
talking about it.'"[18] Although there was much levity in the brief debate on
the amendment, there was also some serious discussion of the amendment,
largely offered by some of the few female members of Congress at the time.[19]
In the House, the combined votes of the Southern legislators opposed to the Act
as a whole and the advocates for women's equality led to the passage of the
amendment to prohibit sex discrimination by 168 to 133.[20] The Civil Rights
Act, as well as other federal, state, and local laws passed to promote equality,
resulted in a network of equal employment opportunity offices and agencies
throughout the federal government, as well as human rights commissions at the
state and local levels. These new laws and the infrastructure created to imple-
ment them provided the movement against sexual harassment an "existing
organizational space and collective identity" to challenge sexual coercion in
the workplace.[21]

EARLY SEXUAL HARASSMENT CASES

Six cases, filed between 1971 and 1975, led the legal effort against sexual
harassment in the 1970s and set the framework for the movement against
sexual harassment. These cases heavily influenced the development of the
law and of public opinion, as they were widely discussed in the media and
among legal scholars and feminists.[22] The women in these cases made the novel
argument that a male employer who fires a woman for refusing his sexual
advances has discriminated against her based on sex and therefore, has violated
her civil rights guaranteed by Title VII. In other words, these cases asked federal
courts to interpret Title VII to prohibit sexual harassment. At the time these
women filed their cases, there were no legal precedents for this interpretation of
Title VII.

A diverse group of women from around the country working for both public
and private employers brought these lawsuits. Plaintiffs in three of the six
cases were young African-American women, two of whom were harassed by

African-American men while working for federal agencies in Washington, D.C. that addressed race discrimination issues. These women were familiar with discrimination law and the mechanisms for legal redress because of their understanding of race discrimination. Two of the African-American women initially filed their complaints as race and sex discrimination claims. All six cases involved a male supervisor firing or forcing out a female subordinate employee after she rejected his sexual advances.

The facts of these cases reveal the sexist atmosphere many women faced in the workplace in the early 1970s. Diane Williams, who brought the first successful sexual harassment lawsuit, *Williams v. Saxbe*, was a young African-American woman working as a public information specialist with the Justice Department's Community Relations Service (CRS), which mediated racial tension in troubled communities. Williams alleged that her black male supervisor, Harvey Brinson, who was married with four children, attempted to date her between January and July of 1972, but that she repeatedly refused. Williams alleged that there was a great deal of dating going on at CRS between the single female employees and the married male supervisors, especially Brinson, who she said had a "notorious reputation for dating his staff members."[23] According to Williams, women who acquiesced on such dates received better work assignments and promotions from the male supervisors. Williams alleged that because she resisted Brinson's attempts he "began a process of fault finding" with her. He criticized her work habits in general and her attitude toward him in particular. He subjected her to "oral and written attacks both professional and personal" and threatened her with transfer or termination. Eventually in September 1972, Brinson fired Williams, allegedly for poor performance. Paulette Barnes, who brought the precedent-setting case of *Barnes v. Train*, was a twenty-eight-year-old African-American mother of three working as an administrative assistant in the Office of Equal Opportunity of the Environmental Protection Agency. Barnes alleged that, within a week of starting her job at the EPA in July 1971, the African-American male director of her office, Norris Snydor, "began a campaign to extract sexual favors" from her by repeatedly inviting her out for social activities after hours, making sexual remarks to her, and suggesting that he would promote her if she had a sexual affair with him. Barnes resisted, telling Sydnor that she wanted their relationship to be strictly professional and her employment status to be based on her work performance. Barnes alleged that Snydor then began a "conscious campaign" to belittle and harass her and to strip her of her job duties. Snydor allegedly denied her a promised promotion, abolished her job, and reassigned her to a position of lesser responsibility. Her former position was subsequently reinstated and filled by a white woman at a much higher salary level. The third African-American plaintiff, Margaret Miller, worked as a proofing machine operator at Bank of America in California. Miller alleged that her white male supervisor, Kimberly Taufer, dismissed her when she rebuffed his sexual advances. Miller alleged that her supervisor appeared uninvited at her home on November 22, 1974 with a bottle of wine in hand and said, "I've never felt this way about a black chick before" and that he would get her "off the machines" if she would cooperate with him sexually. When she refused his advances, he fired her.[24]

The plaintiffs in the other three cases were white women harassed by white men. Jane Corne and Geneva DeVane were technical writers at Bausch and Lomb's Pima County office in Arizona. They alleged that their white male supervisor, Leon Price, made repeated verbal and physical sexual advances to them and to other female employees in the office and that he favored women who agreed to his sexual demands. Corne and DeVane, who did not, eventually found working for Price so onerous that they left their jobs. Darla Jeanne Garber, a twenty-five-year-old white female secretary working at Saxon Business Products, Inc., in Fairfax, VA, alleged that Saxon's white male branch manager, John Johnson, fired her after she rebuffed his sexual advances. According to Garber, Johnson started showing up at her apartment after hours and then began "hassling and frightening" her. She told him to stop coming over, that she was not interested in him, but he persisted. When she started dating another employee, Garber alleged that Johnson got mad, threatened to fire her, and said that she "would either go out with him or no one." In the middle of December 1974, about six months after she started working at Saxon, Garber again refused to have sex with Johnson and he fired her shortly thereafter. Finally, Adrienne Tomkins, a white female stenographer working for Public Service Electric and Gas Company in Newark, NJ, alleged that on October 30, 1973, her white male supervisor, Herbert D. Reppin, asked her out to lunch, purportedly to discuss her employment prospects with the firm. At lunch, Tomkins reported, he gave her an "ultimatum to engage in an affair with him or lose my job." In her complaint, Tomkins alleged that he said to her: "I want to lay you," "I can't walk around the office with a hard-on all the time," and "This is the only way we can have a working relationship." When Tomkins refused, Reppin grabbed her arm and said, "You're not going anywhere. You're going with me to the 13th floor" of the hotel. He also warned, "Don't go to anyone for help because I have something on all of them, all the way to the top, and they're not going to do anything to help you." He then forcibly held her and kissed her, but eventually let her go. Tomkins complained to the company and was transferred, but to a less desirable position. She alleged that because of her complaints she was subjected to disciplinary layoffs, threats of demotion and salary cuts, and was ultimately fired on January 7, 1975.[25]

With no obvious avenues for recourse, these women reached out to what seemed their only option – the equal employment offices. Barnes initially contacted an EEO counselor at the EPA, who said that her experience was not sex discrimination but advised her that she could file a race discrimination claim because she was replaced by a white woman, which she did in December 1971. Williams also sought the advice of an EEO counselor and filed a formal charge of sex discrimination with the Justice Department on September 13, 1972. The other plaintiffs filed charges with the EEOC, Miller for race and sex discrimination and the others for sex discrimination. Corne and DeVane filed their charges on October 12, 1973, Tomkins on August 19, 1974, and Garber on January 8, 1975.

When these early plaintiffs sought counsel, they found civil rights and feminist attorneys in their communities. Both Barnes and Williams found civil rights attorneys through the Lawyers' Committee for Civil Rights Under Law (LCCRUL), a private organization in Washington, D.C., that had a well-established reputation for handling civil rights and employment discrimination cases. Barnes hired Warwick R. Furr II, a Washington civil rights attorney who shared office space with a LCCRUL volunteer. Williams hired Michael Hausfeld, a young attorney in private practice who had experience handling civil rights cases. In two other cases, the plaintiffs retained explicitly feminist lawyers. Corne and DeVane retained civil rights attorney Heather Sigworth, and Tomkins retained Nadine Taub, who was a law professor and the director of the Women's Rights Litigation Clinic at Rutgers Law School in Newark, NJ. Both Miller and Garber retained employment discrimination attorneys, Stuart Wein and Elaine Major, respectively.[26] In all cases, the plaintiffs were represented by civil rights attorneys and feminist attorneys practicing alone or in small law firms, whereas the defendants were represented by government attorneys, in-house counsel, and lawyers from large established law firms, a David and Goliath-like matchup.

The parties' arguments in these cases centered on whether the alleged conduct was private behavior, as the defendants contended, harking back to the early perception of sexual harassment as a moral issue, or an economic issue that impaired women's participation in the workplace, as the plaintiffs contended. In *Barnes*, the government argued that Barnes had not made out a case of sex discrimination because her sex was "merely a natural incident to a desire for a heterosexual affair." The government's lawyer noted that Barnes did "not contend that her difficulties were caused by prejudice against women in certain job positions, or because of stereotypes as to proper sexual roles." He concluded that there was "a clear distinction between discrimination based on sex and ill-will based on refusal to engage in sexual intercourse."[27] Barnes' attorney, Warwick Furr, responded by pointing out the economic impact on women of sexual advances in the workplace, which he described as an "invidious and recurrent problem which causes economic hardship and embarrassment to many women each day." Furr further argued that the discrimination arose out of stereotypes as to proper sexual roles, "from preconceived notions that women are to be regarded as sex objects and that therefore decisions concerning their employment status are routinely made on non-job-related bases." Furr concluded that Title VII "'intended to strike at the entire spectrum of disparate treatment of men and women resulting from sex stereotypes'" and to eliminate "'irrational impediments to job opportunities and enjoyment which have plagued women in the past.'"[28]

As government lawyers had argued in *Barnes*, in *Williams* they argued that the "plaintiff was allegedly denied employment enhancement not because she was a woman, but rather because she decided not to furnish the sexual consideration claimed to have been demanded. Therefore, plaintiff is in no different class from other employees, regardless of their gender or sexual orientation, who are made subject to such carnal demands."[29] The government argued that there was no employer policy or regulation supporting the alleged discrimination and that Brinson's conduct was an "isolated personal incident" that should not be the courts' concern. On behalf of Williams, Michael Hausfeld argued that the testimony showed that "it was a company-wide practice and policy for the married male supervisors at CRS to date the unmarried black women" and reward compliant females with favored treatment.[30]

The Organization of Black Activist Women (OBAW), a Washington, D.C.-based women's group, supported Williams by filing a "friend of the court" brief on her behalf.[31] Members of the group were outraged that the agency that was supposed to be defending people's rights was violating them. The brief was written by Maudine Rice Cooper, who later became President of the Greater Urban League of Washington, D.C., and Benjamin L. Evans. In a newspaper article reporting on the brief, Cooper cited statistics and facts that demonstrated black women were particularly vulnerable to sexual harassment. Cooper noted that one of every five black families was headed by a woman, that two of every three poor black families were headed by a woman, that young minority women were particularly vulnerable to low wages and unemployment, that black women did not have needed child care, and that the unemployment rate for nonwhite women had traditionally been twice that of white women. She also argued that "the pecking order for salaries is white men, first; black men, second; white women, third; and black women, fourth."[32]

The plaintiffs in *Corne* also received outside support, when the EEOC filed a strongly worded brief on January 17, 1975 – the EEOC's first appearance in a sexual harassment case. The defendants' attorneys in the case had argued that Corne and DeVane did not allege "disparate treatment due to their sex" but merely alleged "advances from a man to a woman." The EEOC, in a brief submitted by EEOC attorneys Beatrice Rosenberg, Charles Reischel, and Josephine A. Trevathan, countered that Price's sexual advances were "obviously directed toward [the plaintiffs] because they were female. Indeed, more clearly sexually motivated conduct could not be alleged." The EEOC argued that Title VII prohibits "irrational impediment to job opportunities" and "no more irrational, or unwarranted, a condition of employment . . . can be imagined." The argument continued, "the choice between frequent unsolicited sexual advances and being unemployed has a significant and clearly unwarranted effect on employment opportunities. . . . If Title VII does not provide such elementary protection against sexually motivated conduct, its promise to women is virtually without meaning." The EEOC concluded that the company violated Title VII by failing to ensure that its supervisors did not "utilize the power they are thus granted to discriminate in violation of Title VII."[33]

The defendants in *Tomkins* argued that the conduct at issue was not gender-based, but was personal sexual conduct that Title VII was not intended to prohibit. In their brief, the defendants meticulously avoided using the phrase "sex-based," but instead used "gender-based." They argued that "gender" had no relevance to the dispute: "the fact that Tomkins was a woman was incidental to the issue."[34] According to the defendants, the dispute had to do with "personal relationship and sexual desires," not stereotypes limiting women's employment opportunities. They argued that the class of people affected was not "women" but "those not willing to furnish sexual consideration." They continued, "the party making formal demands could have been either male or female with homosexual, heterosexual, or bisexual tendencies," so "the class allegedly discriminated against is not defined by gender but rather it includes all those who were made subject but refused to submit to the carnal demands."[35] In conclusion, the defendants argued that the "court should not be concerned with the social life of the company employees or their personal relationships or encounters" and should decline to "act as a social arbiter as to all aspects of employee conduct."[36]

In response, Nadine Taub argued on behalf of Tomkins that sexual harassment was sex discrimination because it was based on stereotypes of women as "sex objects" and that employer tolerance of sexual harassment had a disparate impact on women. On the issue of employer liability, Taub argued that Public Service Electric and Gas knew or should have known about the harassment of Tomkins but did nothing to assist her and in fact retaliated against her. According to Taub, "regardless of the fact that the conduct arises from the personal proclivity of the offending employee," Public Service Electric and Gas had a duty to stop the harassment, redress the injury done, punish the harasser, and prevent future harassment. She also advocated for a subjective test of harassment, one "depending on the subjective appraisal of the complaining employee rather than upon the intent of the actor,"[37] the first appearance of an issue that would later make it all the way up to the Supreme Court.[38]

In all of the cases except *Williams*, the judges denied relief, concluding that the alleged misconduct was a private matter, not employment-related, and not sex discrimination for which employers should be liable. One judge described the case as a "controversy underpinned by subtleties of an inharmonious personal relationship," perhaps "inexcusable" but not "an arbitrary barrier to continued employment based on sex."[39] Another described the harasser's conduct as "nothing more than a personal proclivity, peculiarity, or mannerism . . . satisfying a personal urge . . . with no relationship to the nature of the employment."[40] A third judge stated, the "attraction of males to females and females to males is a natural sex phenomenon and it is probable that this attraction plays at least a subtle part in most personnel decisions." In addition, the court ruled that the alleged behavior, which he described as "isolated," fell within the employer's policy prohibiting "moral misconduct."[41] Another judge stated, "the abuse of authority by supervisors of either sex for personal purposes is an unhappy and recurrent feature of our social experience," but that the "sexually motivated assault" amounted to a "physical attack motivated by sexual desire on the part of a supervisor and which happened to occur in a corporate corridor rather than a back alley."[42] The courts characterized the conduct as purely sexual and motivated only by sexual desire. By portraying the conduct as natural, personal, sexually motivated behavior, the judges obscured the underlying power dynamics of the behavior – the abuse of authority and the economic coercion involved.

The judges also argued that the behavior was not motivated by gender. One judge stated that "in this instance the supervisor was male and the employee was female. But no immutable principle of psychology compels this alignment of parties. The gender lines might as easily have been reversed, or not even crossed at all. Although sexual desire animated the parties, or at least one of them, the gender of each is incidental to the claim of abuse."[43] Completely contrary to the evidence in the record, the judge suggested that the victim may have been motivated by sexual desire too. Another judge reasoned that the plaintiff "was discriminated against not because she was a woman but because she refused to engage in a sexual affair with her supervisor."[44] Another judge said that it would be "ludicrous" to rule that Title VII prohibited "the sort of activity involved here" because "if the conduct complained of was directed equally to males, there would be no basis for the suit."[45] These courts ignored or denied the social reality that women were usually the targets of this behavior, not men.

The judges further argued that treating sexual harassment as sex discrimination would "open the floodgates of litigation," overwhelming the court system and inviting a lawsuit for every sexual indiscretion in the workplace. One judge expressed concern that there "would be a potential federal lawsuit every time any employee made amorous or sexually oriented advances toward another." According to the judge, "the only sure way an employer could avoid liability to such charges would be to have employees who were asexual."[46] Another judge warned, "it is conceivable under plaintiff's theory that flirtations of the smallest order would give rise to liability."[47] A third judge argued,

"if the plaintiff's view were to prevail, no superior could, prudently, attempt to open a social dialogue with any subordinate of either sex. An invitation to dinner could become an invitation to a federal lawsuit if a once-harmonious relationship turned sour at some later time. And if an inebriated approach by a supervisor to a subordinate at the office Christmas party could form the basis of a federal lawsuit for sex discrimination if a promotion or a raise is later denied to the subordinate, we would need 4,000 federal trial judges instead of 400."[48]

Tapping into traditional stereotypes, the judges assumed that women would bring lawsuits in retaliation for affairs gone bad or based on trivial occurrences and used this assumption to deny relief in clearly egregious cases.

By contrast, in the first successful sexual harassment case decided on April 24, 1976, *Williams v. Saxbe,* Judge Charles Richey characterized the behavior of Williams' supervisor as a serious, employment-related, gender-based civil rights violation.[49] Whereas denials of other claims focused on the plaintiffs' refusal of sexual advances and only briefly mentioned that the plaintiffs lost their jobs, Judge Richey focused on the harasser's retaliatory actions and their impact on Williams. Judge Richey described how Williams was harassed and humiliated by Brinson's "unwarranted reprimands, refusal to inform her of matters for the performance of her responsibilities, refusal to consider her proposals and recommendations, and refusal to recognize her as a competent professional in her field."[50] Judge Richey ruled that Brinson's conduct was not an isolated personal incident but "created an artificial barrier to employment which was placed before one gender and not the other, despite the fact that both genders were similarly situated."[51] Judge Richey dismissed the "fear that the courts will become embroiled in sorting out the social life of the employees of the numerous federal agencies," arguing that whether the conduct was a policy or practice of the employer or a non-employment-related personal incident was a factual question to be determined by the fact-finder.[52]

Judge Richey also argued that Title VII did not require the allegedly discriminatory practice to be applicable to only one of the genders, based on the characteristics that were peculiar to that gender. The important factor, according to Judge Richey, was whether the conduct was applied to one gender and not the other, despite the fact that the genders were similarly situated. Judge Richey analogized the facts of Williams' case to employer policies barring women with preschool age children or married women, both of which the Supreme Court had ruled discriminatory. In a footnote, which later received much critical attention, Judge Richey rejected the argument that whether conduct was discriminatory would depend upon the "sexual preference" of the supervisor, but he did note that a finding of discrimination could not be made if the supervisor was bisexual and made sexual advances toward both genders.[53] Judge Richey ruled in favor of Williams and later awarded her damages in the amount of $16,251.33 in back pay and interest. The government appealed Judge Richey's decision to the D.C. Circuit Court of Appeals.

Whereas before this decision the media had paid only minimal attention to the issue of sexual harassment, including the earlier cases denying relief, the press extensively covered Judge Richey's groundbreaking decision in *Williams v. Saxbe*, often ridiculing and mocking him. Although much of the publicity about the case was negative, media coverage of this precedent-setting case served to raise awareness about the issue of sexual harassment. The Associated Press and United Press International broke the story the day the case was decided, April 20, 1976. On April 21, over fifty newspapers around the country from over twenty states picked up the story, including major newspapers such as the *New York Times, Wall Street Journal, Washington Post, Atlanta Constitution, Los Angeles Times,* and *Houston Chronicle.*[54] Coverage continued in the days that followed, and numerous editorials appeared, largely critical of Judge Richey's decision. The critical editorials focused on Judge Richey's footnote referring to bisexuality.

The most widely reprinted editorial was by Art Buchwald of the *Los Angeles Times.* Buchwald's editorial appeared in over forty newspapers around the country between April 27 and May 3, 1976.[55] The editorial began by sarcastically describing Judge Richey's decision as one of the most important legal decisions of the last fifty years because the ruling "sets new guidelines for how bosses can behave during and after office hours all over the country." Focusing on the footnote suggesting that harassment by bisexual supervisors would not violate Title VII, Buckwald recounted a fictional conversation of a boss, Mr. Novak, a female employee, Miss Roseberry, with whom Mr. Novak seeks a sexual relationship, and Mr. Callihan, Novak's legal foil. Novak invites Roseberry on a date but also brings Callihan in order to avoid a lawsuit. When Novak compliments Roseberry about her sweater, he also compliments Callihan about his shirt. Novak asks both employees to stay late, takes them both out to dinner at a small French restaurant, and then takes them both to Roseberry's apartment afterward. When Callihan objects and says he's tired, Novak replies,

"'Who isn't tired? You think it's fun having to worry about being sued every time I take someone from the office out to dinner? You can take Miss Roseberry anywhere you want to. But if I take her I have to take you, too. I don't make that kind of money, Callihan.'
'I guess it does take the fun out of being a boss, Mr. Novak.'
'Oh, forget it. Why don't you get into something more comfortable, Miss Roseberry? . . . You too, Callihan.'
'Why me, Mr. Novak?'
'Because, dammit, it's the law!'"

This editorial, which appeared across the country, often in the style section of newspapers, trivialized Judge Richey's decision.[56]

Editorials also appeared in several other newspapers, such as the *Los Angeles Times*, *Wall Street Journal*, *Dallas Times Herald*, and *Dallas Morning News*.[57] On April 26, an editorial in the *Los Angeles Times* entitled, "Sex Rears Its Mixed-Up Head" reflected the recurrent viewpoint that sexual harassment was simply a matter of bad manners, having no deeper social or economic causes or implications. Describing Judge Richey's decision as "lively," the editorial focused on the footnote mentioning bisexuality. Suggesting that the lawyers "drop their lawbooks momentarily to consider the dispute in a wider context," the editorial asked, "Why must the clanking machinery of the law have to be set in motion to resolve problems in human relations that could be settled by the simplest code of ethical conduct?"[58] On April 27, the *Wall Street Journal* editorial, reprinted in several newspapers, was entitled "The Law and Threats to Virtue" and criticized Judge Richey for his decision. Focusing in particular on the issue of bisexual harassment, the editorial chided, "Judge Richey's opinion would suggest that there are some situations where a little discrimination might still be a good thing."[59] Condemning Judge Richey's decision as "grotesque," Dick Hitt of the *Dallas Times Herald* focused almost entirely on Richey's footnote about bisexuality. Describing the decision as "the Richey Ruling on how bisexual bosses may be insulated from sex discrimination suit," Hitt argued that Richey had "carved [bisexuality] in stone" and suggested that progressive companies "may even now be appointing a vice president in charge of Promiscual Equality."[60] Jim Wright of the *Dallas Morning News* described Judge Richey as "the creative jurist, who recently laid down the first federal guidelines for office hanky-panky." According to Wright, the "chief significance" of the decision was that "the so-called Sexual Revolution is over." He declared, "Judge Richey has done more than any man since Cotton Mather to detour society off the primrose path." Similar to Hitt, Wright trivialized the decision by focusing on Richey's footnote on bisexuality, ruminating about how a particularly resourceful boss might engage in nondiscriminatory lechery. He then concluded, "Judge Richey, in brief, did for the conduct of office hanky-panky what other judges and federal guideline writers have previously done for the conduct of business: he didn't actually make it a crime; he just wrapped it in so many miles of ridiculous red tape that it no longer seems worth the trouble."[61] Discussion of the case appeared not only in print media but on television as well.[62] The media coverage of this case was notable for its volume, reflecting how the issue had hit a nerve, and its negativity toward Judge Richey's decision, reflecting male editorial writers' resistance to the idea that sexual harassment was a serious issue. Similar to the district court judges that ruled against women in all of the other early cases, these writers believed that sexual harassment was a personal problem, not a discriminatory employment practice.

The revolutionary ruling in *Williams v. Saxbe* resulted from the efforts of two principled and determined individuals – Diane Williams and Judge Charles Richey. Judge Richey was known for his independence and his "passion for doing justice."[63] He grew up during the Depression in Delaware, Ohio, the only child of parents who were Ohio Wesleyan University professors – his mother taught Latin and his father taught physics and math. He was raised as a Democrat, but his maternal grandparents were Republicans, and he switched parties after law school, when he got a job as legislative counsel for Congresswoman Frances P. Bolton, a Republican from Ohio, who was later one of the supporters of the amendment to Title VII to prohibit sex discrimination. A friend of Vice President Spiro T. Agnew, Judge Richey was appointed to the bench in 1971 by President Richard Nixon. Judge Richey was known as a judicial maverick, who throughout his career ruled in favor of individual rights. For example, in 1974, he ruled that Vietnam Veterans Against the War could demonstrate on the Mall in Washington. Out of concern for the religious rights of those who came before him in court, Judge Richey, despite his strict Methodist upbringing, replaced the 200-year-old oath that witnesses usually take in federal courts with his own version, which contained no religious references and dispensed with the Gideon Bible. He was also known for using sex-neutral terms when discussing statutes that used exclusively male language, and he served on the Task Force on Gender, Race, and Ethnic Bias for the District of Columbia.

Like Judge Richey, Diane Williams exhibited a passion for justice, but also a dogged persistence. Williams embarked upon her case without legal precedents and endured years of complicated litigation, which caused her financial hardships and psychological distress. From the time she first brought her EEO complaint in September 1973 until the final resolution of her case in June 1981, Williams pursued her charges of sexual harassment in the face of unlikely odds and at great personal sacrifice. When testifying about her experience at the first congressional hearings on sexual harassment in 1979, Williams described sexual harassment as "a very emotional experience, a very degrading experience, a very humiliating experience." She testified about the "emotional trauma that has been wreaked upon me in the last seven years we have been litigating the case." She chastised the Justice Department for "capriciously and vexatiously pursuing litigation" in the case. In particular, she condemned the department for bringing her mother into the controversy. The Justice Department had deposed her mother as a witness, questioning her as to Williams' social activities. Williams explained, "she virtually has had to serve as my alibi to attest to the fact that no, I did not go out two or three times a week; no, I am not the disco queen of this city; and no, I didn't have a personal relationship or an affair with" her supervisor. She claimed the government was trying to make her out to be a "loose woman." She testified she felt as though she were the defendant, like women who complain of sexual assault. She described the atmosphere at the agency as a game among the executive level staff, who were all male: "which one was going to be able to take Diane Williams out first and which one of them was going to be able to take her to the poshest restaurant in town."[64]

During the course of the lawsuit, Williams became an advocate against sexual harassment, discussing her case with the media and testifying at congressional hearings on sexual harassment. Her case bounced up and down the administrative and judicial systems, all the way up to the United States Circuit Court of Appeals, for close to eight years before she was vindicated. Her perseverance finally paid off not only in a personal victory but in establishing an important legal precedent and raising awareness of the issue of sexual harassment. The case of *Williams v. Saxbe* was a significant legal breakthrough for sexual harassment victims. Judge Richey's April 1976 ruling was cited widely and discussed in legal briefs, law reviews, and feminist literature on sexual harassment. This case gave feminists attorneys a legal peg on which to hang their hats when appealing the early cases denying relief to sexual harassment victims.

The early cases denying relief and the media coverage of the *Williams* case show that women faced an uphill battle to convince people that sexual harassment was a serious problem. But these early cases laid the groundwork for the emerging movement against sexual harassment by framing the issue of sexual harassment as an issue of employment discrimination and a violation of Title VII of the Civil Rights Act. The individual women around the country who brought these early sexual harassment cases tapped into resources developed by the civil rights and women's movements – the theories and precedents of employment discrimination law, as well as the networks of attorneys knowledgeable about and willing to take on these cases. These cases broke new ground by focusing on the economic consequences of sexual coercion in the workplace and linking these consequences to discriminatory attitudes of male supervisors. Even before feminist activists had coined the term "sexual harassment," the courageous women who brought these suits conceived of sexual coercion in the workplace as sex discrimination and brought lawsuits, despite terrible odds.

Several of the women who filed the earliest sexual harassment cases were African-American women whose backgrounds in the civil rights movement gave them an understanding of discrimination law that they applied to the issue of sexual harassment. In the *Williams* case, the Organization for Black Activist

Women framed the issue within an intersectional analysis of racism and sexism by highlighting black women's economic vulnerability to sexual harassment. The intersectionality of race and sex manifested most clearly in the interracial harassment case of Margaret Miller, but also shaped the responses of Paulette Barnes and Diane Williams to intraracial harassment in federal government agencies designed to combat race discrimination. The irony of experiencing sexual harassment in agencies set up to advance civil rights from those commissioned to end discrimination added insult to injury that motivated Paulette Barnes and Diane Williams to fight back. Relying upon racial harassment cases, they framed the issue of sexual harassment as a civil rights violation.

Echoing the separate spheres ideology, five of the six older white male judges dismissed these cases because they understood sexual harassment to be private sexual misconduct that could not rightly be seen as the responsibility of employers to prevent.[65] They characterized the alleged behavior as natural, personal, sexually motivated, and gender-neutral, a characterization that obscured the underlying power dynamics of the behavior – the abuse of authority and the economic coercion involved. Judges "privatized" the harassment by focusing on individual actors and their intent and ignoring the impact of this behavior on women's participation in the workplace. But the presence of Judge Richey on the federal bench was a political opportunity – his concern for and involvement in furthering individual rights enabled him to understand Diane Williams' perspective and rule in her favor, creating an important legal precedent. The women who lost their cases appealed, seeking the aid of feminist attorneys from public interest law firms, and relying upon the work of feminist activists, who in the 1970s began to raise public awareness about sexual coercion in the workplace. The next chapter will describe the emergence of two organizations founded specifically to fight sexual harassment and how the work of these organizations contributed significantly toward the effort to convince judges that sexual coercion in the workplace was a serious violation of women's civil rights, not just a personal problem.

2

Speaking Out: Collective Action against Sexual Harassment in the Mid-1970s

Collective action against sexual harassment was rooted in the women's movements, emerging at the intersection of activism against employment discrimination and feminist opposition to violence against women. The issue of sexual harassment brought together two of contemporary women's deepest, most troubling concerns – their desires for an unbiased workplace and their fears of male sexual aggression. Activists within the women's movements formed two organizations that focused primarily on sexual harassment in employment and that were heavily responsible for generating the movement against sexual harassment in the 1970s – Working Women United in Ithaca, New York, which later relocated to New York City and became Working Women's Institute (WWI), and the Alliance Against Sexual Coercion (AASC) in Cambridge, Massachusetts. The founders of these organizations were influenced by the early lawsuits and, in turn, their success in raising awareness of sexual harassment buttressed the appeals in these cases. These new organizations not only relied on existing organizations and networks, but also generated new networks and framed the issue of sexual harassment as an important feminist issue. This nascent movement engaged in initial "interpretive processes" that allowed them "to reject institutionalized routines and taken for granted assumptions about the world and fashion new world views and lines of interaction."[1]

WORKING WOMEN UNITED

The formation of Working Women United in the spring of 1975 was inspired by the case of Carmita Wood. Wood, a forty-four-year-old mother of four, had been denied unemployment compensation after she resigned as an administrative assistant to a Cornell professor because she had become physically ill from the stress of fending off his sexual advances.[2] Wood had begun working at Cornell University in 1966, had an outstanding work record, and was promoted to be the first female administrative assistant at Cornell's Laboratory of Nuclear Studies in 1971. According to Wood, shortly after she began working in the lab, a well-known physicist named Boyce McDaniel began to sexually harass her. Wood described McDaniel as a "dirty old man" who did not want her on the job and who treated women as "second-class citizens, and inferior beings."[3] Wood reported that McDaniel constantly made "palpably sexual gestures" – he would "lean against her, immobilizing her between his own body and the chair and desk," he would "never look her in the eye but instead move his eyes up and down her body below the neck," and he would "stand with his hands shaking in his pockets and rock against the back of a chair, as if he were stimulating his genitals."[4] The most egregious incident occurred at a Christmas party in December 1973. McDaniel repeatedly asked Wood to dance with him. She refused, but he insisted. According to Wood, "he pulled me out on the dance floor, he took his hand, and pulled up all of my clothes, and exposed my bare back to everyone." Another time McDaniel put his hand on her bottom at an office party. Wood explained that McDaniel "never looked at a woman, except from the neck down."[5]

Wood and other women in the lab complained about McDaniel's behavior to the Executive Officer of the Nuclear Laboratory, Henry Doney, whose response, unfortunately, reflected the typical attitude of the times that sexual harassment was a personal problem. Doney told the women that they were "capable of taking care of themselves" and suggested that they "try not to get into those situations."[6] To escape the harassment, Wood consciously avoided McDaniel, including using the stairs instead of the elevator, wearing pants so he could not stare at her legs, telling her secretary she did not want to be alone with him, and trying to transfer to another job away from him. Shortly after the Christmas party incident, McDaniel went on leave for a semester, but as his return drew closer, Wood developed severe neck pain and numbness in her shoulder and arm caused by anxiety over his impending return. Wood resigned in June 1974, before McDaniel returned, and her pain subsided.

After unsuccessfully searching for another job, Wood filed for unemployment compensation in December 1974. Her claim was denied, and she asked for a hearing. At the February 1975 hearing, she called two witnesses to confirm her story, one of whom testified that McDaniel was condescending toward women and another who testified that he had once made a pass at her in an elevator and would often stare suggestively at women. Wood also testified that McDaniel inappropriately touched female employees in the office. Wood's claim was again denied on March 7, 1975. The hearing officer held that her reasons for leaving her job did not amount to "good cause" because they were "personal" and "noncompelling."[7]

Not willing to give up, Wood sought support from the women's section of the Human Affairs Program (HAP) at Cornell University, which was staffed by three committed feminist activists. Established in response to student uprisings in the late 1960s, HAP offered public-interest-oriented courses that involved community fieldwork on topics such as prison reform, urban redevelopment, and money and banking. HAP established a women's section in the fall of 1974 and hired Lin Farley as director. A former Associated Press reporter, Farley was a longtime activist in radical feminist politics and was a member of the Furies, a radical lesbian collective in Washington, D.C. She had testified at the 1971 New York Radical Feminist Conference on Rape and later moved to New York City, where she joined Lesbian Feminist Liberation.[8]

In January 1975, Farley recruited two friends to work with her at HAP, Susan Meyer and Karen Sauvigné. Meyer had grown up near New York City and graduated from the University of Michigan in 1968. An antiwar activist in college, she worked with Students for a Democratic Society and later participated with Sauvigné in a Quaker training workshop on community organizing and nonviolent community dispute resolution. When she moved back to New York City, Meyer continued to participate in leftist political activity. She taught English as a second language and did some organizing in the Hispanic community in Brooklyn. She also participated in consciousness-raising groups, came out as a lesbian, and became active in radical feminist politics. Meyer was part of the *Rat* collective in New York, an underground radical feminist newspaper, and worked with Lesbian Feminist Liberation as head of the media committee.[9] Meyer had met Farley in the early 1970s, and they later worked together at Lesbian Feminist Liberation.[10]

Sauvigné also grew up near New York City and, like Meyer, had been an antiwar activist as a student. She graduated from Montclair College in 1970 and then worked on a master's degree in history at Rutgers. In the early 1970s, Sauvigné participated in consciousness-raising groups and became active in radical feminist politics, joining New York Radical Feminists. She worked on the issues of rape and marriage and became familiar with the analysis of the role of sexual violence in women's oppression. Sauvigné worked at the American Civil Liberties Union, including the Women's Rights Project while the future Supreme Court Justice Ruth Bader Ginsburg was there, and for the Law Students Civil Rights Research Council (LSCRRC), gaining a legal background, fundraising experience, and contacts that she would later find very useful in organizing against sexual harassment. Meyer and Sauvigné met during the summer of 1974 while the Lesbian Feminist Liberation and New York Radical Feminists were collaborating in political organizing to try to raise women's visibility at the annual gay pride march in New York City. In their activism in the early 1970s, Meyer and Sauvigné learned about feminist theory on rape and domestic violence, which later helped them articulate the issue of sexual harassment. At HAP, Meyer and Sauvigné shared the job of Research Director, assisting students with research on community organizing.[11]

When Carmita Wood sought help from HAP, Farley, Meyer, and Sauvigné immediately offered their support. The issue of sexual coercion on the job had come up in Farley's class on women and work in the fall of 1974. Because of a scarcity of analytical literature on women and work, Farley had turned to consciousness-raising: women in the class talked about their experiences as women on the job. It soon became apparent to Farley that "each one of us had already quit or been fired from a job at least once because we had been made too uncomfortable by the behavior of men."[12] According to Sauvigné,

Lin's students had been talking in her seminar about the unwanted sexual advances they'd encountered on their summer jobs. And then Carmita Wood comes in and tells Lin *her* story. We realized that to a person, every one of us – the women on staff, Carmita, the students – had had an experience like this at some point, you know? And none of us had ever told anyone before. It was one of those *click, aha!* moments, a profound revelation.[13]

Sauvigné explained, "We began talking to all the women we knew and pretty much everyone could recount a story of how they quit or lost a job sometime in their life because of failing to go along with unwanted sexual advances. It was beginning to seem to us that it was an incredibly widespread phenomenon."[14] While she was in graduate school, Sauvigné herself had been fired from a job as a cocktail waitress when she refused her bosses' sexual advances, and Susan Meyer was sexually harassed while working as an office manager in New York City.[15]

The women quickly recognized that sexual harassment was an "important issue to develop in the feminist movement," and they attacked the problem legally and politically.[16] First, they located attorneys for Wood. Sauvigné contacted Karen DeCrow, the President of NOW, who lived in nearby Syracuse, and whom Sauvigné knew from her work with ACLU and LSCRRC. DeCrow located two feminist attorneys to represent Wood's appeal – Maurie Heins and Susan Horn from Syracuse. Although Wood's case did not involve Title VII, the women at HAP immediately realized the potential of Title VII for combating sexual harassment. In a March 28, 1975, letter to Heins, Sauvigné argued that Title VII should protect women from sex-based intimidation on the job. An April 5, 1975 news article in the *Ithaca Journal* quoted Farley making the same point. Sauvigné attempted to find other people working on the issue. Using mailing lists from ACLU and LSCRRC, she sent a letter to female lawyers and law students asking them if they had any cases involving sexual harassment, and she surveyed women's organizations about the issue. She did not receive many responses, but she did receive one from Catharine MacKinnon, whom Sauvigné knew because MacKinnon had been an LSCRRC intern. Sauvigné had first met MacKinnon in 1974 when Sauvigné and Meyer were visiting Farley in Ithaca, and MacKinnon passed through town as a traveling folk singer. Sauvigné also contacted the EEOC to get information about the case of *Corne v. Bausch and Lomb* and subsequently discussed the case with Heather Sigworth, the attorney for Corne and DeVane in Arizona.

In addition to organizing legal support for Wood, the women at HAP sought to generate political support by forming a working women's organization, which they called Working Women United (WWU), and planning a speak-out in order to break the silence. At the time, Cornell planned to close HAP in 1976 because the leftist social protests that had led to its opening had subsided. So the HAP Director and Advisory Board fully supported the HAP staff in building groups in the community that would endure. Sauvigné, Meyer, and Farley hoped the speak-out would help create such an organization. According to Sauvigné, the speak-out was a "mechanism for public consciousness raising," with which she was familiar from her work with New York Radical Feminists. In her letter to Heins, Sauvigné explained, "we hope to politicize the issue and begin to ease up women's self-consciousness about speaking about it. I think that sexual abuse on the job is an issue very much akin to rape and we will need to do a lot of consciousness-raising to free women up to talk about it."

But, first, "it" would need to be named and defined. In the weeks since Carmita Wood had approached HAP, the women had used a variety of phrases, including "sexual abuse," "sexual coercion," "sexual intimidation," and "sexual harassment." Farley, Sauvigné, Meyer, and several other women agreed to sit down and decide upon a single term, one that included not only blatant examples of sexual abuse but also more subtle behaviors. They were primarily focused on sexual behavior by a male toward a female in the workplace, not on nonsexual gender-based hostility of the kind blue-collar women were subjected to once they began to break into traditionally male occupations at the end of the 1970s. At a meeting at the HAP offices, the women made a collective decision to use the term sexual harassment because it conveyed the broad array of conduct they intended to include.[17] They used the term in an April 3, 1975, press release, and soon thereafter it began appearing in press coverage of the issue.

A broad cross-section of working women in Tomkins County, NY, attended a meeting on April 2, 1975, launching a campaign to expose the problem of sexual exploitation of women on the job. Wood and twenty-three-year-old Janet Oestreich were among those who described their experiences of sexual harassment. A press release HAP issued the next day quoted Oestreich, who had been sexually harassed by customers when she was a waitress, as saying, "I feel very strongly that this subjugation of working women to the power of men who have economic control over them must be stopped!" In the same press release, Farley explained the purpose of the upcoming speak-out:

When women came forward to tell their stories about rape and abortion it culminated in changes in the New York State rape laws and in a landmark Supreme Court decision. It took women telling the untold truth about our lives to show how widespread and damaging these problems really are to activate these changes. Sexual exploitation of working women needs the same exposure. That's the purpose of the speak-out.

Farley, Meyer, and Wood were quoted in numerous local newspapers, including the *Ithaca Journal, Ithaca New Times,* and *Cornell Daily Sun*.[18]

In the month before the speak-out, WWU members engaged in several actions to raise public awareness about sexual harassment and publicize the event. Carmita Wood published an opinion editorial about sexual harassment in a local newspaper and wrote a letter to the editor on behalf of WWU, announcing their campaign and encouraging participation at the speak-out.[19] WWU members appeared on several local television programs discussing sexual harassment, and two local radio stations ran stories about Carmita Wood's case and the upcoming event.[20] In hopes of gaining broad community participation, WWU members leafleted the town's three big factories, Ithaca Gun,

Morse Chain, and National Cash Register, and distributed flyers at the town's banks. According to Sauvigné, however, many of the posters were ripped down, and women working at the factory experienced heightened harassment because of them. WWU also encouraged NOW's national president, Karen DeCrow, to visit Ithaca to promote the speak-out. In a news report in the *Ithaca Journal*, DeCrow hailed the speak-out, saying, "It's about time. This is one of the few sexist issues which has been totally in the closet. . . . As we begin to speak out about such indignities, we realize that this is not a personal problem, but rather a class problem, which we as females share."[21] DeCrow also publicized the issue around the country in her work for NOW.

WWU promoted the issue beyond Ithaca as well. On April 21, Farley traveled to New York City to testify about sexual harassment before the New York City Human Rights Commission, which was chaired by Eleanor Holmes Norton, who would later play a key role in shaping federal policy on sexual harassment. Norton was conducting hearings on patterns of discrimination faced by women in blue-collar and service industry jobs. According to Farley, Norton "treated the issue with dignity and great seriousness." In response to Farley's testimony, the commission drafted a standard clause for affirmative action agreements addressing "unfair abuse of sexual privacy." Enid Nemy, a reporter covering the hearings for the Family/Style section of the *New York Times*, heard Farley's testimony and convinced her editor to send her to Ithaca to research the issue of sexual harassment.[22]

On the afternoon of Sunday, May 4, in the pouring rain, 275 women showed up at the Greater Ithaca Activities Center for the sexual harassment speak-out sponsored by WWU, HAP, and the Ithaca chapter of NOW. About twenty women – young and old, black and white, and from a variety of occupations – testified passionately about the devastating impact of sexual harassment on their lives. They included Carmita Wood, Wood's daughter Angela Faust, Wood's co-worker Connie Korbel, three waitresses, a mailroom clerk, a factory shop steward, a secretary, an assistant professor, and an apprentice filmmaker. The women testified about "crude propositions to barter sex for employment, physical overtures and masturbatory displays, verbal abuse and hostile threats that appeared patently designed to intimidate a woman and drive her out of her job."[23] They described their feelings of self-blame, shame, and fear and described sexual harassment as "dehumanizing." They recognized sexual harassment as an abuse of power and as a structural condition of the workplace. They expressed feelings of relief at being able to talk about their experiences, with one of the women describing her testimony as a "catharsis." No press was allowed, but the sponsors held a press conference the next day. All the local radio and television stations and all the local newspapers covered the event. Afterward, Sauvigné said the speak-out had been "awesome and powerful and well beyond our wildest expectations."[24]

Aside from generating publicity, the speak-out also began the process of developing more detailed information about the extent of sexual harassment. During the event, Meyer distributed a survey she had developed with Diedre

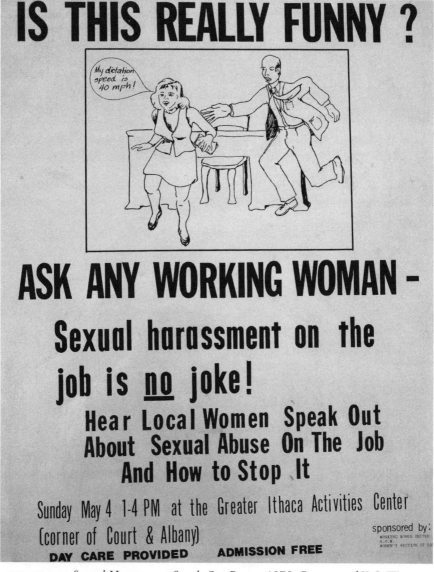

FIGURE 2.1. Sexual Harassment Speak Out Poster, 1975. Courtesy of K.C. Wagner

Silverman, a social scientist at Ithaca College, asking women about their experiences with sexual harassment.[25] The survey defined sexual harassment as "any repeated and unwanted sexual comments, looks, suggestions, or physical contact that you find objectionable or offensive and causes you discomfort on your job." Of the 155 women responding, 7 out of 10 reported experiencing sexual harassment. Those reporting harassment included teachers, factory workers, professionals, waitresses, clerical workers, executives, and domestics. The women reported feeling angry, upset, frightened, and guilty about the harassment. Only 18% had complained through established channels, and in half of those cases nothing was done. In a third of the cases where women complained, the woman experienced negative repercussions such as increased workload and complaints about the quality of their work. Ninety-two percent of the women surveyed considered sexual harassment a serious problem.[26] Although this survey was not scientific, it was the first of its kind and for years was widely cited in legal proceedings, law review articles, and mass media reports as evidence of the serious impact of sexual harassment on women. It also inspired many other studies of sexual harassment.

After the speak-out, forty women met and officially launched WWU. WWU members hoped to encourage collective action, including unionization, and aspired to be like 9-to-5 in Boston, an organization of female office workers and part of the burgeoning movement to organize working women. In August 1975, recognizing the need to do research and public education on the issue of sexual harassment, WWU members created a separate organization, Working Women United Institute (WWUI), which was incorporated as a 501(c)(3) non-profit organization "to engage in research, education, and litigation on issues of concern to working women." According to Sauvigné, they modeled themselves after the ACLU by creating a nonprofit organization separate from the membership organization that could engage in political activities. Sauvigné's contacts at the ACLU helped WWUI to become established, including consulting on organizational development and tax-exempt status, as well as providing office space and equipment for part of one summer. WWUI sought to assist women both locally and nationally through a three-part system: a research component, a legal resource component, and an information/referral and public education component. Susan Meyer was the Executive Director and Karen Sauvigné was the Program Director. WWUI's Board of Advisors included Eleanor Holmes Norton, NOW President Karen DeCrow, author Susan Brownmiller, and New York Congress member Elizabeth Holtzman. The Board of Advisors also included Alice Cook and William Foote Whyte from Cornell's School of Industrial and Labor Relations.

In the summer of 1975, WWU was extremely active. General membership meetings were held monthly, with attendance ranging from twenty to thirty women and membership swelling to sixty-five in September 1975. Numerous committees, concerned with a range of topics from legal grievances to fundraising, began to meet regularly. WWU members immediately began researching targets for political actions and began collecting information about local corporations' treatment of women. They continued to field calls from the media and produced a film on sexual harassment, "Working Women's Dilemma," which was aired on local television. They also worked on developing the organization, including building membership, creating a structure, and obtaining office space.

Their first newsletter, *Labor Pains*, appeared in August 1975, infused with a spirit of enthusiastic and inclusive sisterhood. The eleven-page newsletter, addressed "the problems and concerns of working women," encouraged all types of women to participate in the activities of WWU and welcomed a "variety of views." According to one article, "Working Women United includes women from grandmothers to granddaughters, college professors to factory workers, radicals to conservatives." In an article on the next page entitled "Our First Issue," WWU members envisioned the newsletter as "a place where waitresses, college professors, and factory workers can all learn from one another; we may find that we have more in common than suspected at first."[27] The newsletter attempted to create a sense of community and shared purpose among women, but also to educate and inform them about the issue of sexual harassment. It included articles on sex discrimination in the workplace generally, but focused on sexual harassment. Several articles offered support to victims by sharing stories of sexual harassment, discussing ways to fight back, and encouraging victims to contact WWUI. The front-page article, reporting on the "historic" May 4 Sexual Harassment Speak-Out, recounted the stories of several of the women who spoke and commended them for their courage. Carmita Wood wrote a piece entitled "Woman Alone" about her experience of being a controversial figure because she publicly challenged sexual harassment in the workplace. The newsletter also reported on harassment charges brought in other parts of the country by a police officer in Los Angeles and a woman employed at a fire department in Gainesville, Florida. Another article reported on national support for raising the issue of sexual harassment, citing the work of New York City Human Rights Commissioner Eleanor Holmes Norton, Congresswoman Bella Abzug, and Karen DeCrow, President of NOW, who was reportedly "traveling around the country telling audiences about the exciting work WWU is doing and the importance of the issue of sexual harassment on the job."[28] The newsletter also announced more than nine membership and committee meetings and a men's support group to discuss issues of sexual harassment and discrimination.

The activities of WWU led to the first national press coverage of sexual harassment in August 1975, when the *New York Times* published Enid Nemy's story.[29] The article was syndicated nationally, appearing in more than a dozen newspapers around the country, including the *Philadelphia Bulletin* and *Chicago Tribune*. According to Sauvigné, "Nemy's story put sexual harassment on the map." The story, despite appearing in the family and style section, provided a serious, well-researched, and thorough treatment of the issue of sexual harassment. Nemy quoted feminist activists Farley, DeCrow, and Meyer, government officials, including Norton, and several sexually harassed women, including two WWU members, Oestreich and Korbel. Farley said that workplace sexual harassment was "extremely widespread," citing the speak-out survey, but often "treated as a joke." The article described WWU as having "launched a campaign to expose the problems of sexual exploitation of women on the job." Nemy discussed potential legal remedies at the local, state, and federal level. Norton stated that New York was drafting a standard clause for affirmative action agreements addressing "unfair abuse of sexual privacy."

The Director of the Unemployment Insurance Division of the New York State Department of Labor was also quoted, saying sexual harassment was good cause for leaving a job. On the federal level, the article reported that the EEOC had filed a brief supporting the plaintiffs in the appeal of *Corne v. Bausch and Lomb*. The article also discussed the experiences of five sexually harassed women, three of whom were from Ithaca, one from New York City, and one from Washington, D.C. They experienced harassment in varied occupations – waitressing, nursing, and real estate. One woman, Jan Crawford, reported that her supervisor demanded sex "after making it clear he didn't approve of women working outside the home." The article resulted in a "tidal wave of response from women across the country."[30] WWU received "enthusiastic letters of support and encouragement, as well as donations from across the nation."[31] This article led to other media outlets taking up the issue of sexual harassment.

A *Wall Street Journal* article on sexual harassment in January 1976, written by Mary Bralove, also treated the issue with great seriousness.[32] The article recounted several stories of sexually harassed women, who were "boldly speaking out and seeking protection against unwanted sexual advances by bosses or clients." The article mentioned United Nations' employees publicly airing harassment charges, the Los Angeles Screen Actors Guild's recently established morals complaint bureau, student pressure to include curriculum on harassment at Simmons College's Graduate Program in Management, the work of the City of New York Commission on Human Rights, and the WWU speak-out and survey. On the law, the article mentioned the EEOC brief filed in the *Corne* appeal and also interviewed Linda Singer, the attorney who represented Paulette Barnes in the appeal of the district court's dismissal of her case. In the same month that the *Wall Street Journal* article appeared, *Redbook* magazine published a questionnaire on sexual harassment in the workplace.[33] According to the article, the purpose of the survey was "to have a reliable and factual basis on which to judge the problem" and "to amass a significant body of information about sexual harassment." Nine thousand women responded to the survey, 88% of whom reported experiencing sexual harassment. The results were published in the November 1976 issue of *Redbook*. The issue also attracted the attention of television producers. In February and March of 1976, the local affiliate of CBS in New York broadcast a series of news programs on sexual harassment at work.

The first critical voice to emerge in the popular press was Rhoda Koenig in the February 1976 issue of *Harper's Magazine*.[34] Her scathing opinion piece came in response to Enid Nemy's article in the *New York Times*. Describing sexual harassment as "sex in the office" and "flirtation," Koenig trivialized the issue by commenting that "a lot of women would feel deprived without a reasonable quota of sexual harassment per week." She condemned feminists for characterizing women as "helpless victims" and "miserable and weak" and for perpetuating the "myth of women as oppressed." She argued that feminists, "with jesuitical ingenuity, . . . go about convincing white, middle-class college-educated women that society has done them wrong, like the snake-oil salesman whose suggestible listeners began to feel all the symptoms of sciatica, dropsy, and the botts." She added, "for persons who do feel guilt at being dissatisfied, feminism offers absolution." As opposed to the feminist characterization of men as aggressive, Koenig argued that men were "more like shy woodland creatures, fawns peeping through the thicket of masculine self-protection." Ironically, she predicted that "sexual harassment probably won't make its way onto the picket lines or the evening news," and "antiharassment forces will [never] work up enough steam to roll over the rest of us." This early media coverage began the process of raising awareness of sexual harassment.

Despite their successes in bringing the issue to national attention, WWU disbanded after they published their last newsletter in the Spring of 1976. According to Sauvigné, Ithaca's demography led to WWU's demise. Most of the working women in Ithaca either worked in blue-collar jobs at the three big factories in town – Morse Chain, Ithaca Gun, and National Cash Register – or they worked in pink-collar jobs at Cornell, the town's biggest employer. At first, women from both groups were involved in WWU. Carmita Wood was able to draw in women from Cornell, such as Connie Korbel, but after she lost her appeal in October of 1975, she was no longer involved. For a while, a local letter carrier, Jean McPheeters, served as chair of WWU and inspired blue-collar women to become active. But when McPheeters stepped down to become head of her union, participation from local blue-collar women waned. WWU sought to gain a broader base in the community but was dominated by college students and was closely associated with HAP and Cornell. Students were very active and enthusiastic in the organization, but everyone knew that to the extent that Cornell students had blue-collar jobs, they were temporary. The social distance created by this disparity tended to drive blue-collar women away.

WWUI, however, continued to work on sexual harassment. In February 1976, Sauvigné obtained funding to hire Drs. Harriet Connolly and Judith Greenwald from City University of New York to write a grant application to the National Institute of Mental Health (NIMH) for funding a major research project on sexual harassment. The application, submitted in the summer of 1976, proposed to study "sexual interaction at work" by interviewing 150 women and 50 men in order to "generate objective parameters by which sexual harassment can be differentiated from other forms of social interaction occurring within the informal structure of the workplace." Many individuals and groups supported this application, including Eleanor Holmes Norton, Elizabeth Holtzman, Patricia Schroeder, Susan Brownmiller, Shirley Chisholm, District 65 of the Distributive Workers of America, the National Congress of Neighborhood Women, and the NAACP Legal Defense Fund. NIMH approved the proposal but did not fund it because Connolly and Greenwald decided they wanted to conduct the study through the City University of New York rather than with WWUI, leading to a dispute between WWUI and the grant writers about who owned the project.

In addition to working on the NIMH grant, WWUI assisted attorneys working on sexual harassment cases. Greg Finger, from the Center for Constitutional Rights, suggested that WWUI establish a brief bank to "prevent people from having to reinvent arguments." Sauvigné immediately began to collect pleadings, briefs, and opinions in sexual harassment cases, which they provided to attorneys for the cost of copying and mailing. In the process, WWUI began to build a network of attorneys knowledgeable about sexual harassment. During this time, Meyer and Sauvigné also spoke on sexual harassment to a variety of groups, including students, lawyers, and working women, and they promoted the results of their survey on sexual harassment.

In mid-1976, Farley had a falling out with Meyer and Sauvigné. Tension had begun even before the speak-out and escalated in 1976. In early 1976, Farley had asked WWUI to sign over to her the releases from the speak-out participants so she could use their testimony in a book. At the May board meeting, the women came to an agreement whereby Farley could use the testimony but would "make every effort possible in all publications to cite the existence of the Institute, its purpose and its projects, its past and its future."[35] A contract was apparently drafted but never signed. Farley also sided with Connolly and Greenwald in their dispute with WWUI about ownership of the NIMH grant proposal. As a result of these conflicts, Farley parted ways with the Institute[36] and left the Human Affairs Program at the end of the 1976 school year when Cornell terminated the program. After twenty-seven rejections, she published her book on sexual harassment with McGraw-Hill Book Company in 1978. In the book, Farley never mentioned WWU and only briefly mentioned the work of Sauvigné and Meyer in her preface, where she described the "origin of the issue."[37]

In June 1977, in search of a better place to run a national organization, conduct research, and obtain funding, Meyer and Sauvigné moved WWUI to New York City, to the basement of Central Presbyterian Church at Park Avenue and 64th Street, and they decided to focus exclusively on sexual harassment. The Institute's first grant application to the Ms. Foundation was rejected for not addressing a "bread-and-butter issue," but the Foundation later gave the Institute its first grant for $3,000.[38] Both Sauvigné and Meyer volunteered their time. Sauvigné worked part-time at the College for Human Services while Meyer drove a cab. In its first few years, the Institute worked to raise awareness of sexual harassment through the media and public speaking, provided information and referrals to sexually harassed women, built a resource library and a legal brief bank, conducted research on sexual harassment, and supported public policy initiatives. Meyer and Sauvigné also tried to get other feminist organizations to work on the issue. They experienced resistance at first because the movement had so many other priorities, but they were soon able to convince others of the importance of the issue.

Just as WWU began with the May 4 speak-out in Ithaca, WWUI's rebirth in New York City was launched in October 1977 by a speak-out cosponsored with *Ms.* magazine, which did a cover story on sexual harassment in the November issue. About 200 women attended the four-hour event on Saturday,

October 22, at the Community Church of New York on the Lower East Side. Speakers included Meyer and Sauvigné, Gloria Steinem, Jill Goodman of the ACLU Women's Rights Project, Robin Morgan, and Karen Lindsey, a writer for *Ms.* Ten women presented prepared testimony, including Adrienne Tomkins, Freada Klein, and Farley, and many more women spoke during an "open mike" period. The speak-out received television and newspaper coverage. In addition to a November cover story in *Ms.*, which mentioned the work of the Institute and gave contact information, many other magazines and newspapers ran stories on sexual harassment around this time and mentioned the work of Meyer and Sauvigné, including a *New York Times* article.[39] Meyer and Sauvigné began to appear regularly on television and radio shows, including *Good Morning America*, the *Phil Donahue Show*, and the *Mike Douglas Show*.[40] For this groundbreaking work, Meyer and

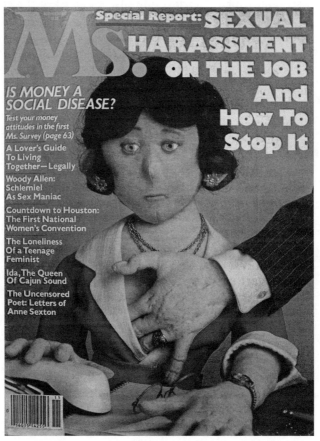

FIGURE 2.2. Ms. Magazine Cover, November 1977. Courtesy of Ms. Magazine

Sauvigné received the Mademoiselle Award in 1977. They also began to attend more speaking engagements, including speak-outs, and conducted workshops on sexual harassment for harassed women, private corporations, foundations, unions, the government, and voluntary organizations. Through these activities, the Institute sought to "alter popular consciousness about sexual harassment."[41]

Due to this exposure, the Institute began receiving hundreds of letters and phone calls a week from sexually harassed women seeking advice. In response, Meyer and Sauvigné built an extensive network of organizations and individuals around the country interested in helping sexually harassed women. Using a large map of the United States and color-coded pushpins to track resources, they referred sexually harassed women to crisis counselors and lawyers. In the summer of 1978, they established a National Information and Referral Service with the help of a $6,500 grant from the New York Foundation. The service provided emotional support, advice on how to handle sexual harassment, information about local laws, and referrals to attorneys and crisis counselors. The Institute also established a Legal Project, which kept track of sexual harassment litigation and maintained a "brief bank." The project built a network of more than 300 attorneys to which to refer sexually harassed women. Meyer and Sauvigné began testifying as expert witnesses in sexual harassment cases and lobbying for legislative changes. In 1977, the Institute helped to develop and promote legislation in New York that expanded unemployment compensation law to cover sexual harassment by defining harassment based on age, race, creed, color, national origin, sex, or disability as "good cause" to leave one's job voluntarily, allowing the victim to collect unemployment benefits.

The Institute continued to conduct research on sexual harassment. Meyer and Sauvigné recruited Peggy Crull in late 1977 to assist with the NIMH grant, but when that fell through, she began to conduct other research for the Institute. At the time, Crull was completing a doctorate in developmental psychology at Columbia University's Teacher's College and taught psychology of women at Lehman College. Crull had been active in the women's movement, starting a feminist research group at Columbia, participating in consciousness-raising through New York Radical Feminists and Marxist Feminist Group 2, and working with the Committee on Abortion Rights and Against Sterilization Abuse. The Institute's early research included a survey of state fair employment practice agencies to see how they dealt with sexual harassment and a study of questionnaires sent to women who had contacted the Institute for help.[42] They also contacted hundreds of women's organizations asking for case studies and other information about sexual harassment.[43] In 1978, the Institute changed its name from WWUI to Working Women's Institute (WWI) because WWU no longer existed. WWI worked for the next several years to increase public awareness of sexual harassment, to support victims of harassment emotionally and legally, and to conduct research to better understand sexual harassment.

ALLIANCE AGAINST SEXUAL COERCION

The Alliance Against Sexual Coercion (AASC) was the other organization formed in the mid-1970s that made pioneering efforts to help victims of sexual harassment and raise public awareness of the issue. AASC was a grassroots service-oriented organization that grew out of the rape crisis movement and characterized sexual harassment as an issue of violence against women. AASC members produced some of the first in-depth theoretical analyses of sexual harassment, locating the roots of sexual harassment not only in sexism, but also in classism and racism. They also developed a broad range of strategies to address the problem, calling not only for legal redress, but for collective organizing and direct action.

AASC was founded in Cambridge, MA, in June 1976 by Freada Klein, Lynn Wehrli, and Elizabeth Cohn-Stuntz.[44] Each of these women had extensive experience working on the issue of rape and first became aware of the issue of sexual harassment while working at the Washington, D.C., Rape Crisis Center. Klein had worked with the Bay Area Women Against Rape, one of the first rape crisis centers in the United States, while earning her bachelor's degree in criminology at University of California at Berkeley. In the summer of 1974, she moved to Washington, D.C., to do national political work and to start graduate work in women's studies at George Washington University. While in D.C., she worked with the Washington, D.C., Rape Crisis Center and was a founding member of the Feminist Alliance Against Rape, a national network of rape crisis centers that published a bi-monthly newsletter. She also worked with Prisoners Against Rape in Lorton, VA, a self-help and education group for prisoners who had raped and been raped. Klein was invited to participate in making a documentary film of interviews with convicted rapists at the Lorton prison, called "Rape Culture" and produced by Cambridge Documentary Films. As a result, Klein began traveling on a regular basis to Cambridge and also collaborated with the *Our Bodies, Our Selves* collective on the rape chapter in a mid-1970s edition. Klein eventually moved to Cambridge. Wehrli, in addition to volunteering at the Washington, D.C., Rape Crisis Center, also worked with the Feminist Alliance Against Rape and taught a course on Rape and U.S. Institutions at the Women's School. Wehrli moved to Boston to enter MIT's master's program in urban planning. Cohn-Stuntz, who graduated from Smith College, had written her senior thesis on the emotional reactions of women to rape. She was a psychiatric social worker in D.C. and volunteered at the Washington, D.C., Rape Crisis Center. Cohn-Stuntz moved to Cambridge because her husband was going to Harvard Business School.

While at the Washington, D.C., Rape Crisis Center, Klein and others on the hotline shift had received phone calls from women experiencing severe sexual coercion on the job. Realizing the unique legal and emotional problems of women sexually assaulted by their bosses and co-workers, Klein knew that neither rape crisis centers nor working women's organizations provided services that addressed these women's needs. Once in Cambridge, Klein contacted Cohn-Stuntz and Wehrli, and they established the Alliance Against Sexual Coercion as a collective with the goal of eliminating workplace sexual harassment. To avoid expending energy applying for grant money to pay their salaries, the members earned their livelihoods elsewhere but put their major energies and commitment into AASC. Several Boston-area organizations supported AASC, including 9-to-5, the Cambridge Rape Crisis Center, and Transition House (a battered women's shelter).

From its inception in June 1976, AASC provided crisis intervention counseling, but in the first year, members focused mostly on intensive research into understanding sexual harassment and developing ways to deal with it. In August, AASC surveyed more than 200 rape crisis centers and working women's groups about employment-related sexual assault. Every group that responded had received these types of calls, but few of them had information on the issue, and none of them had programs to assist victims.[45] Originally, AASC focused on developing a sexual harassment protocol for rape crisis centers with the hope that the centers would take on this issue, but it soon became clear that rape and sexual harassment were very different issues. In the fall of 1976, AASC published its first position paper, written by Klein and Wehrli, and Wehrli completed one of the earliest in-depth theoretical studies of sexual harassment in the form of a master's thesis at MIT entitled *Sexual Harassment at the Workplace: A Feminist Analysis and Strategy for Social Change*, which documents AASC's early theoretical analysis of the issue. In December 1976, AASC organized a strategy meeting of women from local feminist organizations to come together and share their ideas on how to respond to the issue most effectively. AASC also spread the word by helping to organize and participating in the first Take Back the Night march in Boston in 1977.

In AASC's first position paper, Klein and Wehrli emphasized employers' power over women and the serious economic implications of sexual coercion for women. Like WWUI, AASC conceptualized the issue solely in terms of sexual conduct and expressions. AASC defined sexual coercion to include "verbal harassment or abuse, subtle forms of pressure for sexual activity, as well as rape and attempted rape" and noted that co-workers and clients, as well as employers, could threaten women's jobs. Making parallels to rape, they argued that silence was often very destructive to women's emotional well-being and that laws were inadequate. They argued that the issue "provides us a way to extend the women's movement" and that it stood "at the crossroads of two important women's organizing trends – workplace and antirape organizing."[46]

Wehrli's master's thesis developed what she called a "dominance" theory of sexual harassment. She argued that sexual harassment in the workplace was both an expression of and a means of perpetuating the unequal power relationships between men and women and between employers and employees. Wehrli argued that the extent to which dominance is exercised through sexual harassment depended on social conditions, personal choice, and threats to dominance. Social conditions included differences in socialization of males and females, males' greater access to instruments of power, the absence of sanctions, high unemployment, and women's historically marginal position in the labor market. Threats to dominance included an active feminist movement and the entrance of women into traditionally male fields. In the face of these threats, argued Wehrli, men were more likely to actively reassert their dominance by sexually harassing women. Wehrli argued that dominance took a sexual form because of the predominant view of women as sexual objects and the strong cultural associations between dominance, masculinity, and sexual prowess. Wehrli rejected alternative explanations of sexual harassment as a deviant act, as biologically determined, as fun or bribery, or as a transitional phenomenon. Arguing that the root of sexual harassment was unequal power relationships based on racism, sexism, classism, and other forms of dominance, Wehrli concluded by proposing strategies for social change, suggesting eliminating the cultural and social supports of dominance – hierarchy in the workplace and socialization of men to dominate and women to submit. More concretely, she suggested the development of sanctions against perpetrators of sexual harassment, support systems for its victims, educational programs on sexual harassment, and further research on the problem.[47]

In June 1977, AASC began providing a broad range of services to victims of sexual harassment, including emotional support, legal information and referrals, unemployment eligibility information, vocational and educational counseling referrals, and rap groups. AASC operated a telephone hotline for sexually harassed women.[48] AASC focused on workplace sexual harassment but also was concerned about other forms of harassment and later became very involved with sexual harassment in education. In addition to offering assistance to individuals, AASC assisted women's groups in other communities to develop similar services and conducted educational programs, seminars, and workshops on sexual harassment. AASC sought to serve as a clearinghouse for cases and additional information involving sexual harassment. Klein described AASC's goal in the November 1977 *Ms.* cover story on sexual harassment: "I hope this becomes a large movement – like rape, like battered women – because it's also an issue of violence against women. To have services, resources, and options available in every community throughout the country would be the greatest thing that could happen."[49] The *Ms.* cover story led to an explosion of calls to AASC from sexually harassed women and from the press, as it had for WWUI. Many other magazines and newspapers then discussed the work of AASC. By 1979, AASC could support itself from fees collected from literature, speaking, and training.[50]

Despite their decision not to become a research-focused organization, AASC members published prolifically on sexual harassment, including both resource materials and theoretical analyses. Their informational brochures, myth and fact sheets, and other informational resources significantly increased public awareness of the issue. By informing and educating women about sexual harassment, these publications contributed toward creating a sense of community among women who were opposing sexual harassment. In 1977, AASC produced a well-researched and theoretically sophisticated twenty-three-page informational brochure on sexual harassment written by Rags Brophy, Mary Bularzik, Martha Hooven, Freada Klein, Liz Cohn-Stuntz, and Lynn Wehrli and printed with a grant from Wellesley College's Center for Research on Women in Higher Education and the Professions. AASC sent this brochure out as part of an informational packet that included a flyer for outreach purposes, a small information card designed for leaving with women who were harassed, AASC's first position paper, and sample letters to send to harassers in both educational and workplace contexts.[51] The brochure included both practical advice for sexually harassed women and a far-reaching critique of U.S. culture and the capitalist economic system. AASC argued that sexual harassment was a form of violence against women that reflected and reinforced women's subordinate status in society. Described as a "highly effective tool of social control," violence against women resulted from "our country's history of relying upon violence as a method of problem solving" and from the fact that "men are socialized to dominate women through the use and threat of violent behavior."[52] They argued that men sexually harass women whom they see as threats to their masculinity, power, or economic status. Furthermore, both the unequal status of workers and employers as well as the unequal status of men and women reinforced each other in cases of sexual harassment: "Sexist attitudes, along with racist and classist beliefs, are vital parts of the U.S. economic system. Not until an egalitarian and democratic work structure is established will sexual harassment be eradicated."[53] The brochure described women's economic vulnerability in the labor force, their long history of sexual harassment in the United States, and the psychological effects of sexual harassment. On the practical side, the brochure contained a section on "myths and facts" about sexual harassment and a section on legal options, including a discussion of Title VII, state human rights laws, occupational safety and health codes, rape statutes, and unemployment insurance. Finally, the brochure ended with a description of the work of AASC. The illustrations in the brochure showed women in clerical, construction, and janitorial jobs.

In addition to developing resource materials, AASC members regularly published articles on sexual harassment, which developed the themes that appeared in the 1977 brochure. These publications often appeared in a newsletter published by the Feminist Alliance Against Rape, for which Freada Klein continued to serve as staff. In mid-1978, Feminist Alliance Against Rape joined with AASC and the National Communication Network, a grassroots organization focusing on battered women, to publish *Aegis, A Magazine on Ending Violence Against Women*. Reflecting their roots in the rape crisis movement, AASC members often characterized sexual harassment as an issue of violence against women.[54] They drew upon the feminist critique of rape in developing their critique of sexual harassment, regularly making parallels between sexual harassment and rape, and also "wife-beating." For example, they argued that sexual harassment was not a sexually motivated act but was an "assertion of power expressed in a sexual manner."[55] In 1978, Freada Klein noted that the responses to the issue of sexual harassment in 1978 were the same as those to rape in 1972 – "'How do you know it's a problem?' or 'women only file complaints when an affair has gone bad' or 'women make false charges of sexual harassment.'" According to Klein, "the repetition of these old myths reflects the depths of sexism's stronghold on our culture and the inability of most people to extend the information that challenges rape myths to the myths about sexual harassment."[56]

Many of the publications of AASC members placed sexual harassment within a broader critique of capitalism, patriarchy, and racism. AASC member Martha Hooven and Nancy McDonald, who worked at the Washington, D.C., Rape Crisis Center, argued in a 1978 article in *Aegis* that capitalism contributed to the proliferation of sexual harassment because the conditions of work under capitalism made women vulnerable to sexual harassment. They argued, "capitalism feeds on sexism and racism." They suggested that ending sexual harassment might require abolishing capitalism.[57] In late 1978, Martha Hooven and Freada Klein published an article in *Aegis* entitled, "Is Sexual Harassment Legal?", which was deeply pessimistic about the ability of government and the legal system to treat women and people of color fairly. Hooven and Klein explained that AASC did not seek to pass new laws against sexual harassment because they believed that "the legal system oppressed women and was racist and classist. They argued, "it is doubtful that enforcement of [a new law] will differ greatly from usual enforcement practices – i.e., a married middle-class white woman, if harassed by a man with less societal status, will probably receive benefits; while a poor, Third World, or lesbian woman, particularly if harassed by a 'respectable' man, may find compensation under this new law difficult to obtain."[58] Also, they noted that legal remedies only addressed harassment after the fact, and they sought to prevent harassment before it occurred. Instead, they sought to use existing laws and provide public education and support services for victims of sexual harassment. According to Hooven and Klein, the primary benefit of a new law would be as a form of public education, rather than for its deterrent effect: "more women will be encouraged to speak out about their victimization and the chances for finding workplace support are increased."[59]

Although Hooven and Klein did seek to redefine and enforce existing laws to protect women from sexual harassment, they hesitated to rely exclusively on the legal system because they feared co-optation: "winning reforms may gradually take the place of working for the ultimate goal of eliminating sexual harassment."[60] They did not believe legal victories alone would eradicate the causes of sexual harassment. Instead, they supported tactics such as public education to change attitudes about women and the inequality of power between women and men. They also advocated "extralegal" activities, like picketing harassers' places of employment, surveying workplaces for prevalence of harassment, leafleting women's bathrooms at work as a warning to other women, and negotiating with personnel departments, unions, or workplace associations for policies against harassment and for grievance procedures.

Insofar as Hooven and Klein sought to redefine existing laws, they sought civil institutional liability rather than individual criminal liability against the harasser because they believed that working at the institutional level was more effective than working at the individual level. Furthermore, they opposed using criminal laws because they believed that the criminal justice system discriminated on the basis of race and class and those criminal penalties were more destructive than helpful. They argued, "prison dehumanizes people; it does not 'rehabilitate.'" [61] Finally, they argued that workplace harassment should be viewed as an occupational hazard and regulated by the Occupational Safety and Health Administration.

WWUI and AASC first learned of each other around the time that *Ms.* magazine made sexual harassment their cover story. The article described WWUI as "A National Resource" and AASC as "the first grassroots group devoted to offering services to victims of sexual harassment at work." [62] Representatives from the organizations met in April 1978 and discussed working together on several projects, including a film on sexual harassment, an annotated bibliography on sexual harassment, joint fundraising efforts, speak-outs, and starting other groups. The organizations agreed not to compete for grants, and they agreed to mention each other when talking to the media "so that the media wouldn't zero in on one person and encourage a hierarchical order that we are working against." [63] Although the organizations shared ideas and podiums, they did little else together. The film was never made, and each organization published its own bibliography. [64] According to Sauvigné, not only was it difficult to collaborate long distance, but the organizations were very different, and there was some competitive tension between them. AASC grew out of rape crisis work, was direct-service-oriented, and made a significant contribution to feminist theory on sexual harassment. WWUI, on the other hand, grew out of working women's activism and was focused on developing legal remedies for sexual harassment and on educating the public about the issue.

In addition to WWUI and AASC, which focused exclusively on sexual harassment, other groups began to work on the issue of sexual harassment in the mid-1970s. Inspired by the WWU survey, several surveys on sexual harassment began to appear. A New York City group called Women Office Workers (WOW), formed in the summer of 1975, surveyed fifteen thousand women later that year about their working conditions, including sexual harassment. One-third of the respondents said that they had been the object of "direct sexual harassment." [65] In October of 1975, WOW held a hearing and speak-out at the YWCA's Central Branch to address major issues affecting female office workers. Several speakers testified about their experiences of sexual harassment. In September of 1976, WOW organized a protest of a sexy secretary joke told on New York Telephone's Dial-a-Joke. The same year, the *Redbook* survey appeared and was followed by several others showing high rates of sexual harassment. A naval officer in Monterey, California used the *Redbook* survey to poll women on his base about sexual harassment and found that 81% experienced some form of sexual harassment. Also in 1976, the United Nations Ad Hoc Group on Equal Rights for

Women surveyed 875 men and women and found that half of the women surveyed reported sexual harassment.[66] These were the first of many surveys on sexual harassment conducted by advocacy groups, governments, and social scientists in the years following. Although these early surveys did not use scientific sampling, they showed that many women were experiencing sexual harassment. The WWU and *Redbook* surveys in particular were widely cited through the end of the decade to prove the prevalence of sexual harassment. The feminist press regularly began to cover the issue of sexual harassment in 1975 and 1976, particularly *Sister Courage, Majority Report, Womanpower,* and *Quest: A Feminist Quarterly.* These early publications and studies began the process of reframing the issue of sexual coercion in the workplace as a violation of women's civil rights.

The groundbreaking efforts of WWU and AASC spurred a movement that by the end of the 1970s would proliferate around the country and would challenge sexual exploitation in the workplace. Feminist activism in the mid-1970s created physical and intellectual spaces for women to speak out about sexual coercion on the job. Similar to abortion, rape, and domestic violence, speaking out about sexual harassment legitimized women's feelings of violation. Naming "sexual harassment" created a cognitive category that made the conduct visible, enabling women to share their pain and express their outrage.[67] Activists drew upon theory of the various social movements of the day to analyze sexual coercion in the workplace and to articulate the phenomena as an important feminist issue. Using feminist theories on rape, legal theories of race and sex discrimination in employment, as well as feminist critiques of patriarchy, racism, and capitalism, they argued that sexual harassment was a form of male domination and amounted to sex discrimination in the workplace. They also drew upon feminist theory advocating women's sexual autonomy and right to control their bodies.

The issue resonated with women because it spoke to the changing reality of women's lives. Women were more likely to find themselves in the workplace and more likely to be dependent on their income for survival because of the changing economic and demographic landscape. The country was shifting from a manufacturing economy that could provide jobs paying a family wage to a service economy with many lower-paying jobs and opportunities for women. Demographic factors also contributed to women's increasing participation in the workplace – older age at first marriage, fewer children, increasing likelihood of divorce, and higher rates of single parenthood. These factors, paired with an increasing standard of living and greater consumption expectations, meant that women were more likely to be in the workplace and were more likely to depend on their income from their labor force participation. This new reality of women's lives came into direct conflict with traditional attitudes toward women in the workplace – that they were working for pin money and not supporting a family, as well as attitudes that sexualized women. In the context of the civil rights and women's movements of the day, which advocated justice and equal opportunities for all, as well as the sexual revolution that affirmed individuals' rights to sexual autonomy, the issue of sexual harassment in the workplace resonated deeply with women. For women of color, whose experiences of racism had often been sexualized, the new civil rights framework became an opportunity to resist both racism and sexism in the workplace.

The strength of this emerging movement grew from its diversity, which provided a range of resources to the effort. Women working in different parts of the women's movements participated – feminists with backgrounds in radical feminism and the lesbian rights movement, the more liberal NOW, the antirape movement and socialist feminism, as well as the civil rights movement. Bringing to the issue a rich mix of backgrounds, perspectives, skills, and resources, these activists crafted a solid foundation for the movement against sexual harassment. Activists used the resources of the women's movements, publishing articles in feminist newsletters and magazines and using the growing network of rape crisis centers to spread the word. They used women's movement strategies, such as speak-outs, surveys, myth/fact sheets, and media work. They also used the fruits of the civil rights movement, testifying before the New York Civil Rights Commission and drawing on the resources of the ACLU and the LSCRRC. This combination of efforts proved to be a very effective means of legitimating the issue, motivating collective action, and raising awareness about sexual harassment. Increased awareness of the issue began to change public attitudes, and the attitudes of judges, about sexual coercion in the workplace. In the appeals of the early sexual harassment cases, feminist attorneys would build upon this increased awareness as they would attempt to convince judges that sexual harassment was illegal sex discrimination.

3

A Winning Strategy: Early Legal Victories against Sexual Harassment

By the late 1970s, when federal circuit courts were hearing the appeals of the early cases denying sexual harassment claims, the climate was right for a change in court opinion. By then, feminists had succeeded in raising awareness of sexual harassment, developing stronger networks, and generating influential research and analysis of the issue, all of which contributed significantly to convincing courts that sexual harassment was a serious violation of women's civil rights. Feminists' efforts, growing media coverage of the issue, and the more progressive makeup of the appellate courts ultimately led to victory for each of the plaintiffs of the early sexual harassment cases. In overturning every case that denied relief and ruling in favor of the sexually harassed women, appellate courts agreed that Title VII prohibited *quid pro quo* sexual harassment, where a supervisor fires a subordinate employee for refusing to comply with sexual advances. In addition to the workplace cases, a district court ruled for the first time in *Alexander v. Yale* that federal law prohibited *quid pro quo* sexual harassment at educational institutions. These landmark rulings resulted from the joint efforts of individual women filing suits and the collective activism against sexual harassment.

Feminist attorneys and activists had developed a network that could now support the women appealing their cases. The plaintiffs turned to feminist attorneys to represent them on appeal. In *Barnes v. Train*, Linda Singer, a feminist lawyer well connected with other feminist attorneys, represented Paulette Barnes on appeal before the D.C. Circuit.[1] Singer, a 1968 graduate of George Washington University Law School, practiced civil rights law with the firm of Kurzman and Goldfarb in Washington, D.C., where she became a partner in 1972. In the early 1970s, she volunteered at the Women's Legal Defense Fund (WLDF), which referred the *Barnes* case to her. In *Miller v. Bank of America*, Mary Dunlap, a 1971 graduate of the University of California's Boalt Law School in Berkeley, represented Margaret Miller on appeal. Dunlap was co-founder of Equal Rights Advocates (ERA) in San Francisco, a public interest law firm engaged in litigation and education to further equal rights for women.

In *Tomkins* and *Corne*, the feminist attorneys – Nadine Taub and Heather Sigworth, respectively – who had represented the plaintiffs before the district court represented them on appeal as well. Like Singer, Taub had extensive connections with other feminist lawyers, contacts she used to recruit *amicus curiae* support for Tomkins. In *Corne*, Jane Corne and Geneva DeVane's attorney, Sigworth, was a feminist civil rights attorney and a founding member of the local chapter of NOW in Tucson, Arizona.[2] Other feminist attorneys filed supporting briefs on behalf of sexual harassment plaintiffs in *Miller v. Bank of America* and in *Tomkins v. Public Service Electric and Gas*. In *Miller*, Vilma S. Martinez and Linda Hanten of the Mexican-American Legal Defense and Education Fund (MALDEF) submitted a brief on December 20, 1976, in support of Margaret Miller's appeal to the Ninth Circuit. MALDEF took a particular interest in this case because it addressed the intersection of race and sex discrimination. In *Tomkins*, MALDEF and ERA joined forces to file a brief in September 1977 in support of Adrienne Tomkins' appeal to the Third Circuit.

Feminist attorneys working on these early cases and activists against sexual harassment shared information, discussed strategy, exchanged briefs, and gave each other moral support. In 1975, Karen Sauvigné of WWU talked with Sigworth about the *Corne* case. When Taub began working on the *Tomkins* case, she contacted WWUI for information and assistance. Through this contact, Taub found out about other sexual harassment cases elsewhere in the country. Taub collaborated with Dunlap of ERA and Martinez and Hanton of MALDEF on the *Tomkins* appeal and discussed the *Alexander* appeal with Freada Klein of AASC. Dunlap and Taub cited the WWU survey of sexual harassment in their appellate briefs in *Miller* and *Tomkins*, and the plaintiff's attorneys in *Alexander* cited later WWI studies.[3] In this way, feminist activists made groundbreaking progress in the fight against sexual harassment in the workplace and at educational institutions.

SEXUAL HARASSMENT IN THE WORKPLACE

The challenge for this informal network of feminist attorneys and activists was to convince courts that sexual harassment was not a personal problem but a serious barrier to women's equal employment opportunity. To do so, feminists made not only legal arguments but also economic, sociological, and historical arguments in their appellate briefs. Their arguments drew upon feminist research and theory showing that sexual harassment was a widespread and devastating phenomenon that denied women equal employment opportunity. A primary argument of the plaintiffs was that sexual harassment was based on sex and therefore constituted sex discrimination. Several argued that sexual harassment was based on the stereotype of women as sex objects. For example, in *Barnes*, the plaintiff's attorney, Linda Singer, argued that sexual harassment assumed that women workers were "sexual fair game, and passive, willing recipients of the sexual advances of their male supervisors."[4] Singer argued that coercive sexual advances in the workplace had a disparate impact on women because the vast majority of supervisors in the federal government were male and the majority of lower-level employees were female. Therefore, women were more likely to be subject to the sexual demands of their supervisors than men. Similarly, Nadine Taub argued in *Tomkins* that women were statistically more likely to be subject to harassment because they were more likely to be subordinate to male bosses than men were to be subordinate to female bosses. Finally, Taub contended that women were more emotionally and psychologically vulnerable to sexual harassment than men because women had a long history of sexual abuse.

Another important strategy that plaintiffs used to frame sexual harassment as sex discrimination was to analogize sexual harassment to racial harassment. They argued that if Title VII prohibited harassment based on race, national origin, and religion, it should also prevent harassment based on sex. These plaintiffs cited *EEOC v. Rogers* and other cases and EEOC decisions confirming that employers had a duty to maintain an atmosphere free of racial intimidation and insult. In *Corne*, Sigworth argued that denying her clients' claim would mean "women would be a less protected class than the parallel protected classes based on race, national origin, and religion."[5] In Nadine Taub's comparison of race and sex discrimination in *Tomkins* , she argued that "a supervisor's sexual advances coupled with threats of job reprisals give rise to a far more debilitating and intimidating work environment than does a supervisor's use of racial epithets or derogatory ethnic jokes."[6] MALDEF argued in *Miller* that Title VII covered not only isolated and distinguishable events such as hiring, firing, and promotion but also "inherently demeaning behavior" directed against members of a protected class.

Taub's brief in *Tomkins* was the first to provide a detailed discussion of analogous racial harassment cases. Taub cited Judge Irving Loeb Goldberg's ruling on racial harassment in *EEOC v. Rogers*, noting that Congress intended to define discrimination in the "broadest possible terms" to include the psychological as well as economic benefits of employment. Quoting *Rogers*, she argued that Title VII covered not only the bread-and-butter issues but more subtle "nuances and subtleties of discrimination," which could "so debilitate a minority employee's psychological and emotional well-being as to result in a barrier to employment." She then cited another racial harassment case, *Gray v. Greyhound Lines*, to argue that Title VII guarantees a work environment free from an atmosphere of discrimination, including psychological harm resulting from isolation on the job. Finally, she discussed the 1972 EEOC ruling that an employer's referring to his adult African-American female employees as "girls" constituted both racial and gender discrimination because of the "repellant historical images the term understandably evokes."[7]

The *Tomkins* case is also significant because it was the first time public interest organizations officially filed supporting briefs in a sexual harassment case and the first time explicitly sociological arguments were made in the briefs filed in such a case. Taub recruited a joint *amicus curiae* brief from ERA and

MALDEF. The EEOC also filed an amicus brief. At oral argument, according to Taub, "we packed the courtroom with students."[8] In the appellate brief, filed on March 24, 1977, Taub used a wide range of sources, including Kate Millett's *Sexual Politics* and the *Statistical Abstract* of the U.S. Census Bureau, to argue that the socialization of men and women as well as women's history of sexual abuse made women more vulnerable to sexual harassment than men. Taub noted that men in society have the exclusive social right to initiate sexual interaction with others. Citing *Amy Vanderbilt's Etiquette*, Taub noted that in areas such as dancing and dating, males do the asking and females do the refusing. She added, "[it] is relatively 'normal' for males to seek sexual access to females who are their subordinates."[9] This gendered socialization, she argued, made women more likely than men to be the target of sexual harassment. She also argued that sexual harassment was a "reminder, a badge or indicia, of the servile status women have suffered in former societies and from which they are now trying to free themselves."[10] Citing Susan Brownmiller's *Against Our Will*, she recounted men's sexual dominance over women in "primitive societies" based on physical force and in the industrial era based on economic wealth and power. Although the twentieth century had brought tremendous change, she argued, "to make a woman's advancement on the job depend on her sexual acquiescence is to resurrect her former status as man's property or plaything."[11] Taub argued that allusions to sexual availability have an especially pejorative meaning for women, noting the tremendous number of sexually derogatory words in the English language. She argued that sexual harassment "strikes a particularly painful chord for women," citing and discussing the *Redbook* and the WWI surveys on sexual harassment.

ERA and MALDEF also made sociological arguments in *Tomkins* in an *amicus curiae* brief filed on September 1, 1977. They contended that women historically had to "submit their bodies to sexual use in order to keep their jobs, or advance in their work." They quoted socialist Emma Goldman from her 1917 book *The Traffic in Women*, in which she said, "Nowhere is woman treated according to the merit of her work, but rather as a sex. It is therefore almost inevitable that she should pay for her right ... to keep a position in whatever line, with sex favors."[12] They argued female employees were treated as a "possession of the 'boss,' ... reminiscent of the plight of the black female slave," citing Gerda Lerner's *Black Women in White America*, and Patricia Hill Collins' article "A Conflict Theory of Sexual Stratification." Noting that both racial and sex-based discrimination shaped the experiences of minority female employees, they quoted historian Eleanor Flexner on how female slaves faced "hazards peculiar to her sex" because they had "no defenses against the sexual advances of the white man." They concluded by condemning the "foul history of economic exploitation of women of all races."[13]

While plaintiffs significantly broadened their original arguments before the appellate courts, defendants essentially repeated the same assertions they had made before the lower courts. First and foremost, defendants argued that the alleged conduct was not based on sex because the women were terminated for rejecting the advances of their supervisors, not because they were women. They argued that the conduct was personal and had nothing to do with employer policies or practices. Despite their arguments that the conduct at issue was an isolated, personal indiscretion, defendants also argued that courts would be flooded with cases if they were to allow such claims, warning that opening the "floodgates" to litigation would make federal courts a "social arbiter" in the workplace. Echoing the traditional distrust toward rape victims, this argument assumed that women would lie about sexual harassment, or that they would assert "subjective" claims based on trivial occurrences in the workplace. By characterizing women's grievances as personal and trivial, defendants sought to relegate sexual harassment to the private sphere, as simply a matter of "bad manners," not worthy of judicial attention.

At the appellate level, as in the lower courts, the identities of the judges in these early cases were telling. Whereas the district court judges had been mostly older white male Nixon appointees, the appellate judges were more diverse and more liberal. In the substantive rulings in favor of sexual harassment plaintiffs, the judges writing the decisions were appointed by President Johnson and, in one case, President Kennedy. Only four of the twelve appellate court judges were Nixon appointees. Of the remaining judges, five were appointed by President Johnson and the other three were appointed by presidents Eisenhower, Kennedy, and Truman.[14] The appellate court judges were also more religiously and racially diverse than the lower court judges. Whereas all of the district court judges were Protestant, two of the appellate court judges were from other religious traditions – one was Jewish and one was Catholic. Judge Robinson, who wrote *Barnes,* the first case to establish an appellate-level precedent in favor of a sexual harassment plaintiff, was African-American. The more liberal appellate court judges provided a political opportunity for activists against sexual harassment.

The plaintiffs' arguments prevailed in the appellate courts, but only two courts provided their reasoning in written opinions. In June 1977, the Circuit Court of Appeals for the District of Columbia provided the first extensive appellate-level analysis of the issue of sexual harassment in the case of *Barnes v. Costle.* As fate would have it, the appellate panel hearing Barnes' appeal consisted of Judge Spottswood W. Robinson III, a long-time civil rights attorney and activist, Judge David Bazelon, known as an activist liberal judge, and Judge George E. MacKinnon, a moderate Republican and father of Catharine MacKinnon, who at the time the *Barnes* case was under consideration was working on the issue of sexual harassment as a law student at Yale.[15] In Judge Robinson's strongly worded opinion, the court ruled that sexual harassment was sex discrimination in violation of Title VII. On the pivotal issue of whether the alleged discrimination was based on sex, Judge Robinson wrote that it was "plainly based on appellant's gender" because the supervisor would not have sought sex from any male employee, noting that there was no indication that he was "other than heterosexual." Judge Robinson then continued,

But for her womanhood ... her participation in sexual activity would never have been solicited. To say, then, that she was victimized in her employment simply because she declined the invitation is to ignore the asserted fact that she was invited only because she was a woman subordinate to the inviter in the hierarchy of agency personnel ... no male employee was susceptible to such an approach by appellant's supervisor.[16]

For the first time, a court acknowledged the power dynamics that shaped women's experience of sexual harassment in the workplace. In addressing the district court's statement that the controversy was merely an "inharmonious personal relationship," Judge Robinson noted that employers were liable for discriminatory practices of supervisory personnel, even when the conduct was a "personal escapade rather than an agency project," and that Title VII prohibited discrimination against individuals, even though less than all the employees of the claimant's gender were affected. In conclusion, Judge Robinson noted that Congress intended to outlaw "any and all sex-based discrimination," and that Title VII must be construed liberally and given an "interpretation animated by the broad humanitarian and remedial purposes" of the Act. Finally, he quoted Judge Goldberg from *EEOC v. Rogers* that "'seemingly reasonable practices of the present can easily become the injustices of the morrow.'"

The *Barnes* case was highly influential in the development of sexual harassment law. Over the years, this decision has been cited by many courts and discussed in hundreds of law review articles and legal treatises.[17] The case was significant for several reasons. First, it was the first thorough treatment of the issue by a federal appellate court. Second, the Circuit Court of Appeals for the District of Columbia was the most influential federal intermediate appellate court in the country at the time. Finally, Judge Robinson's forceful language left no room for doubt that sexual harassment was sex discrimination that was prohibited by Title VII. *Barnes* was covered extensively in the press, inspiring sarcastic editorials. One commentary appearing in the *Washington Star* and reprinted in William F. Buckley's *National Review*, asked "how are we going to breed more little bureaucrats if the court rules that a he-bureaucrat cannot make time with a she-bureaucrat?"[18] The *Barnes* case eventually settled for $18,000 in back pay and attorney fees. Barnes remained with the EPA for a while, never advancing in salary, but later became a federal air traffic controller.[19]

The Third Circuit Court of Appeals in Philadelphia was the other appellate court to issue a detailed written opinion upholding a sexual harassment claim under Title VII. The appellate panel hearing *Tomkins v. Public Service and Gas Co.* included Judge Ruggero John Aldisert, Judge Max Rosenn, and Judge Leonard I. Garth. Judge Aldisert, a Roman Catholic of Italian descent, was appointed to the court of appeals in 1968 by President Lyndon Johnson. Judge Rosenn, a Nixon appointee, was Jewish and in the 1950s served as the Chair of the Board of Directors of the Anti-Defamation League. Judge Garth was appointed to the federal district court in 1970 and then elevated to the appellate court in 1973 by President Richard Nixon. On November 23, 1977, these judges reversed Judge Stern's dismissal of Tomkins' sexual harassment suit. The Court first reasoned that the alleged facts "clearly demonstrate an incident with employment ramifications," pointing to Tomkins' allegation that her employer either knowingly or constructively made acquiescence in her supervisor's sexual demands a necessary prerequisite to the continuation of, or advancement in, her job. The Court then ruled that the conduct was based on sex, citing the reasoning of *Williams v. Saxbe* that the discriminatory practice need not be peculiar to one gender or directed at all members of a sex. Finally, the Court rejected Judge Stern's concern about opening the "floodgates of litigation" by arguing that the plaintiff still had the burden to prove her case and that the traditional judicial mechanisms would separate the valid from the invalid complaints. Issued one month after the highly-publicized WWUI/*Ms.* speak-out in New York City, the judges' decision to rule in favor of Tomkins likely was influenced by the resulting media coverage of sexual harassment generated by feminist activism. The *Tomkins* case eventually settled out-of-court for $20,000 plus attorney's fees and court costs. In addition to paying monetary damages, Public Service Gas and Electric agreed to notify every nonunion employee in writing of their rights under Title VII, to set up a review panel to hear all sexual harassment charges, to show a film explaining Title VII to all employees, to distribute a pamphlet on how to file a complaint, and to reinstate Tomkins' personnel file to what it was prior to the initial incident. *Tomkins* was widely cited by courts over time and was extensively discussed in law review and in the media.[20] The first successful district court case, *Williams v. Saxbe*, was also affirmed on appeal in 1978, but the case was remanded to the district court for a new trial. At trial, Judge Richey issued a decision in favor of Williams and awarded her $14,821.65 in damages as well as over $70,000 in attorney's fees and costs. The government appealed the amount of the attorney's fees and the parties eventually settled this issue out of court. Williams later went to law school and became a lawyer.[21]

Garber, Barnes, Tomkins, and *Williams* established a strong precedent for the legal principle that sexual harassment was sex discrimination prohibited by Title VII. Feminist arguments convinced the courts to take the issue seriously and treat workplace sexual harassment as employment discrimination. The courts did not discuss the plaintiff's sociological arguments supporting the claim that sexual harassment had a disparate impact on women, but *Barnes* acknowledged that sexual harassment was rooted in a workplace hierarchy that subordinated women. With four federal circuit courts of appeals having affirmed the basic principle that sexual harassment was sex discrimination, no further courts ruled against sexual harassment plaintiffs on this basic principle, although they often disallowed less clear-cut claims. In just a few years, feminists had overcome significant negative precedent on the issue of sexual harassment. By representing plaintiffs and participating as *amicus curiae*, feminists made a broad range of arguments to convince appellate courts to overturn the lower court cases dismissing claims of sexual harassment plaintiffs and to rule that sexual harassment was sex discrimination in violation of Title VII.

In the late 1970s, several other lower courts around the country ruled that Title VII prohibited sexual harassment. On September 9, 1977, before the *Tomkins* appellate decision but after the *Barnes* and *Corne* appellate decisions, a federal district court in Michigan ruled in *Munford v. James T. Barnes and Company* that *quid pro quo* sexual harassment was sex discrimination in violation of Title VII. In that case, Maxine Munford, a young black woman working as an assistant collections manager, alleged that her white male supervisor discharged her after she refused to engage in sexual relations with him. Munford, represented by a friend of a friend, Thomas H. Oehmke, who had just started a private law practice, filed suit on October 27, 1976, stating claims for sex and race discrimination under Title VII and several state law claims. The trial court allowed Munford's sex discrimination claim to go to trial, but it dismissed her race discrimination claim before trial, stating that "nothing presented to this Court even faintly suggests racial overtones to this incident."[22] At trial, Munford lost her sex discrimination claim.[23] On appeal to the Sixth Circuit, Jan Leventer of the Women's Justice Center represented Munford, and two *amicus curiae* briefs were filed by the Metropolitan Detroit Branch of the American Civil Liberties Union and the Women Lawyers Association of Michigan.

Before both the trial court and appellate courts, Munford's attorneys presented to the courts race-based sociological arguments in a way that had never before been done in sexual harassment cases. At oral arguments before trial, Oehmke contended that statistical sociological studies showed that Munford was more likely to be a victim of sexual harassment because she was black. The court rejected this legal theory on the ground that statistical evidence was admissible in individual actions only where the statistics were evidence of the intent or motive of the specific employer, which the court said was not so in this case. For similar reasons, the court subsequently barred two expert witnesses from testifying at trial. The two experts, a sociologist and a socioanthropologist, were prepared to testify as to the historical interaction between white males and black females, particularly where the white male was in a position of authority over the black female. The Sixth Circuit Court of Appeals also rejected these arguments. Despite this eventual defeat, Maxine Munford raised public awareness about the issue of sexual harassment in Michigan by testifying at public hearings on sexual harassment and by making several appearances on Michigan radio and television talk shows, thereby inspiring the first statewide movement against sexual harassment.[24]

By the end of the 1970s, while the Supreme Court had yet to rule on the issue, district courts across the country, including Maryland, Alaska, and Colorado, had established the basic principle that Title VII held employers responsible if they tolerated sexual demands made by supervisory employees of their subordinates who then suffered tangible harm, such as termination or denial of a promotion. Beyond this narrow scenario, however, courts were reluctant to go. For example, courts applied a very narrow standard of employer liability. In the 1979 case of *Ludington v. Sambo's Restaurants, Inc.*, a Wisconsin district court dismissed a sexual harassment claim on the grounds that the plaintiffs failed to allege that their employer sanctioned the harassment by supervisory employees, despite the fact that the plaintiffs complained to the home office and were then fired. The court stated, "Title VII is directed at acts of employment discrimination and not at individual acts of discrimination."[25]

In addition to a narrow interpretation of employer liability, courts denied relief under Title VII for those who suffered sexual harassment without tangible harm. This type of harassment, later called hostile environment sexual harassment, involved women subjected to a hostile working environment but who did not suffer any tangible adverse employment consequences such as termination or demotion. In the 1978 case of *Neely v. American Fidelity Assurance Company*, an Oklahoma district court ruled that, despite a supervisor's continuous sexual conduct toward his subordinate employees, Title VII had not been violated because the employer "had a strictly-enforced policy against sexual harassment," it did not know of the alleged harassment, and the plaintiff did not suffer any tangible employment consequences. The court's factual findings indicated its narrow understanding of sexual harassment liability under Title VII. The court found that between 1969 and 1974 the supervisor made sexual remarks, told dirty jokes, exhibited pictures of sex activity, and "affectionately" touched the shoulders of several female employees, including the plaintiff. The court put "dirty" in quotations but not "affectionately," and the employer policy that the court described as "strictly-enforced" was unwritten. Despite these findings, the court concluded that the supervisor's acts were "personal acts," not "conditions of employment" to which the plaintiff was required to submit in order to maintain her job. The court did not describe how the plaintiff might have escaped the conduct. The court repeatedly emphasized that the supervisor never intended to be offensive or abuse female employees. Furthermore, after describing in detail the plaintiff's "mental breakdowns, depression, and attempted suicides" and a failed relationship she had with another man, the court concluded without explanation that there was "no credible evidence that [the supervisor's] conduct in any way caused plaintiff's breakdowns and depression."[26] On even more egregious facts, a District of Columbia court in 1979 denied a hostile environment sexual harassment claim in the case of *Bundy v. Jackson*, where a young black woman working at the D.C. Department of Corrections was continuously pressured to have sex with her supervisors but did not suffer any tangible employment harm.[27] Not until the 1980s would courts begin to hold that Title VII prohibited sexual harassment without tangible job consequences.

The EEOC, however, was moving more quickly toward prohibiting this kind of harassment. In August 1977, the commission issued its first ruling on a harassment case involving sexual behavior other than sexual propositioning by an employer. In that case, a woman employed as a "lobby hostess" was required to wear a sexually revealing costume and act in a sexually provocative manner, which made her the target of lewd comments and sexual propositions from men. In her initial interview, she was ordered to remove her slacks so her employer could see her legs. When she reported the harassment, her employer laughed and suggested the uniform be made more revealing. When she refused to wear the costume, she was discharged. Defining "sexual harassment" as "conduct which injects sexual stereotypes into the work environment"[28] and citing the *Williams* case, the EEOC ruled that the employer had discriminated against the woman on the basis of her sex in the terms and conditions of employment in violation of Title VII. The decision noted that the costume was not necessary for the performance of the employer's business and that the costume, in fact, inhibited rather than facilitated the woman's performance of her duties. This decision was an indication of the future direction the EEOC and the courts would take on the issue of sexual harassment.

SEXUAL HARASSMENT IN EDUCATION

Women sought legal relief from sexual harassment not only in the workplace, but also at educational institutions. In 1977, in what turned out to be only a preliminary victory, a Connecticut district court in the case of *Alexander v. Yale* became the first court in the country to rule that sexual harassment of a student by a teacher was sex discrimination in violation of Title IX of the Education Amendments of 1972, a federal law amending the Civil Rights Act to prohibit sex discrimination in educational institutions receiving federal money.[29] This case, a class-action suit brought by students and a professor who alleged that they were directly and indirectly victimized by sexual harassment, galvanized students around the country, stimulating widespread concern about sexual harassment of students by professors.[30]

The case grew from efforts of the Yale Undergraduate Women's Caucus to raise awareness about the problem of sexual harassment of women students by male professors. The purpose of the caucus, formed in September 1974 shortly after Yale began admitting women, was to promote the position of women at Yale through educational, cultural, and political actions. Caucus members formed a Grievance Committee in March 1977 to investigate sexual harassment of students at Yale and to petition the school to establish an official grievance procedure specifically for sexual harassment. One of the students leading the investigation, Ann Olivarius, contacted the New Haven Law Collective, a feminist community-based law practice, in the spring of 1977 because she feared she might become the target of a defamation lawsuit by one of the accused professors. A university administrator had told Olivarius that she was courting litigation and that the university would not support her if she were sued. Feminist attorney Anne Simon, a 1976 Yale Law School graduate, had opened the New Haven Law Collective in the fall of 1976 with several recent graduates of Yale Law School, including Judith Burton, Kent Harvey, Rosemary Johnson, and Catharine MacKinnon. Indicating that it would be better to be a plaintiff than a defendant, Simon and others at the collective suggested that Olivarius file a sex discrimination lawsuit. Olivarius brought the idea back to the women in the caucus, who then talked to other undergraduates who had experienced sexual harassment. Several women and one male faculty member eventually decided to file a sexual harassment case against Yale.[31]

The case, *Alexander v. Yale*, was filed as a class action suit on July 7, 1977 by three students and one faculty member – Ronnie Alexander, Lisa Stone, Ann Olivarius, and John Winkler. Two other students, Margery Reifler and Pamela Price, were added later, on December 7, 1977. Ronnie Alexander alleged that her teacher made sexual demands of her, leading her to leave his field of study. Lisa Stone alleged that she suffered "great emotional distress" by learning that another woman student was the "subject of sexual pressures and attentions from" a male university employee. John Winkler, a male faculty member, alleged that an "atmosphere of distrust" of male professors had hampered his teaching efforts. Ann Olivarius alleged that as a member of the Undergraduate Women's Caucus she was rebuffed by Yale when she attempted to press the sexual harassment complaints of several other students. Margery Reifler alleged she was humiliated, distracted from her studies, and denied "recognition" by a coach who harassed her when she was manager of an athletic team. Reifler did not report this incident to Yale. Pamela Price, who was black, alleged that one of her white male professors, Raymond Duvall, offered to give her an "A" in his International Relations class in exchange for sexual compliance. Price alleged she received a "C" when she refused her professor's sexual demands. Price complained to Yale officials but nothing was done.

The Caucus Grievance Committee worked to generate financial, political, and moral support for the lawsuit by sponsoring discussion sessions, distributing fact sheets, conducting a collegewide petition drive, organizing a faculty support committee, and soliciting support from campus organizations. Members of the committee wrote articles and editorials for university and community newspapers, appeared on radio and television talk shows, and spoke to groups in the community and at other colleges. The committee, along with the New Haven Law Collective, issued numerous press releases during the course of the lawsuit and distributed personal statements by the plaintiffs in the case. To raise funds, the committee sold T-shirts, sponsored benefit performances and speeches with speakers such as Robin Morgan and Marge Piercy, and solicited funds from foundations and individuals. In addition to the caucus, the Council of Third World Women at Yale became very involved, especially as the trial approached and the students began negotiating with the university about adopting sexual harassment grievance procedures.[32] In *Alexander v. Yale*, the plaintiffs alleged that Yale discriminated against them on the basis of sex by refusing to adopt procedures to handle complaints of sexual harassment. Magistrate Arthur H. Latimer, who issued a written opinion on December 21, 1977, dismissed most of the claims because the alleged harm was too "tenuous," but he allowed Price's claim to go forward to trial. Citing *Barnes v. Costle*, Judge Latimer held that conditioning academic advancement upon submission to sexual demands constituted sex discrimination in education and that a university may be held responsible for condoning or ratifying the discriminatory conduct by refusing to investigate.[33]

Later, Judge Ellen Bree Burns tried Price's case and ruled in favor of Yale on July 2, 1979. Judge Burns, who had been appointed to the federal bench by President Jimmy Carter in 1978, found that "the alleged incident of sexual proposition did not occur" and that Price's grade of "C" did not reflect consideration of any factor other than academic achievement.[34] Judge Burns agreed that Yale's procedures for handling complaints of sexual harassment were inadequate but refused to enjoin Yale to establish a different procedure because Price was no longer at Yale so the relief was moot.

On appeal, Taub, Simon, and Elizabeth Schneider of the Center for Constitutional Rights, represented the plaintiffs, who were also supported by several women's advocacy groups.[35] The Second Circuit panel hearing the case consisted of Judge Joseph Edward Lumbard, a former prosecutor appointed to the Second Circuit by President Dwight D. Eisenhower in 1955, Judge William Hughes Mulligan, an Irish Catholic Republican appointed to the Second Circuit by President Richard Nixon in 1971, and Judge Adrian Anthony Spears, appointed to the United States District Court for the Western District of Texas by President John F. Kennedy in 1961 and sitting on the Second Circuit by designation. On September 22, 1980, the Second Circuit affirmed both Judge Burns' decision and Magistrate Latimer's dismissal of the other plaintiffs.[36]

Reflecting the fact that sexual harassment was now a topic of public concern, *Alexander v. Yale* received national press coverage in newspapers and magazines.[37] The coverage, however, often trivialized sexual harassment. For example, the *New York Times* published an editorial by Russell Baker on July 26, 1977, shortly after the case was filed, entitled "The Courts of First Resort," in which Russell criticized the Yale women for bringing the suit. Russell characterized the alleged harassment as a "nuisance" and a matter of bad manners. Rather than resorting to the "ponderous and expensive machinery of the courthouse," Russell suggested "quicker and cheaper ways of making professors mind their manners," like calling on the services of a "robust father... carrying a shotgun," "a large brother or boyfriend," or simply by using a "hat pin" or "a few simple words thrust neatly into his vulnerable asininity."[38] A similar sentiment was expressed by a Yale University official quoted in a *New York Times* article reporting on the case: "if women students aren't smart enough too know how to outwit some obnoxious professor, they shouldn't be here in the first place."[39] A few weeks after the Russell editorial appeared, *Time Magazine* ran a short article entitled, "Bod and Man at Yale," describing the lawsuit and reporting statements by the attorneys on both sides. In the article, Yale attorney, Jose Cabranes, denounced the suit as "reckless and obviously designed to attract maximum publicity for groundless charges."[40]

Not all of the press coverage was negative, however. On January 14, 1978, *The Nation* ran an extensive article written by Anne Nelson on sexual harassment at Yale. Nelson provided a detailed and relatively sympathetic description of the case, placing the issue of sexual harassment in the larger context of coeducation at Yale. Nelson described the resistance to coeducation at Yale and the resulting tension for women entering that "bastion of male supremacy." Noting that "political ardor of any kind is considered a little old-fashioned these days," she described Yale students as tending to regard the plaintiffs as "agitators and publicity seekers." She criticized the plaintiffs for rushing into the legal process and for releasing the names of the faculty members cited in the complaint. However, Nelson was also critical of Yale for hiding behind a façade of procedure in its legal defense and for not dealing with the clearly existing problem of sexual harassment at Yale: "it's puzzling that Yale, with its mammoth administrative system for dealing with every other aspect of university life, doesn't take the simple action of setting up [a sexual harassment] procedure."[41] A couple of months later, another magazine, the *Yale Graduate Professional*, published an even more in-depth account of the lawsuit against Yale. This article traced the issue of sexual harassment at Yale from 1971 to 1977, quoting Yale students, faculty, and administrators.[42] The feminist press, as well, covered the case.[43]

Although the issue of race was largely ignored in the reported decisions and in the press, this issue permeated the students' discussions of sexual harassment.[44] Pamela Price and other women spoke out about the racial overtones of the case. In a press release issued in December 1977, Price wrote, "Black women have always been sexually harassed, have often protested it, and have been ignored even more thoroughly than white women." Abbe Smith, head of the Yale Undergraduate Caucus Grievance Committee, commented, "We hope the courage of this black woman will encourage others, who may feel that women's issues have been defined in terms of the experiences of white women, to join the fight."[45] In a statement issued after Magistrate Latimer's December 21, 1977 decision, Price characterized her experience of sexual harassment as "racist sexual discrimination." She argued that the poor grade she received was based on a "historical conception of the relationship between my racial heritage and my sexuality."[46] In a statement issued in January 1978, Alexander, Price, and Linda Hoaglund of the Yale Undergraduate Women's Caucus protested the court's focus on "legal technicalities" instead of the humiliation and anguish women suffer in their experiences of sexual harassment. Asserting their right to control their lives, the women noted that for black women "this struggle is compounded by the realities of racism in America today."[47] In a March 1978 letter soliciting support for the case, Phyllis Crocker said of Price, "because she is a black woman, her complaints were not only viewed as inconsequential, but were ignored more blatantly than complaints of white women." This argument was also made in one of the "fact sheets" distributed by the caucus.[48] Later Crocker argued that the case "unites black and white women against a common expression of their subordination."[49] In a press release issued in July 1978, after Judge Burns ruled against Price, Simon stated, "By focusing on the individuals rather than on Title IX, the judge reduced the case to a black woman's accusation and a white man's denial of improper sexual conduct, with all too predictable results." According to Simon, racism "had something to do with how Yale treated not only Price but the case."[50]

Alexander v. Yale was significant in several regards. First, despite Price's eventual defeat, the December 1977 lower court decision in *Alexander v. Yale* established a precedent that sexual harassment of students by professors violated Title IX's prohibition of sex discrimination in educational institutions. This legal precedent, however, did not have much impact until 1994 when the Supreme Court ruled that victims of sexual harassment could sue schools for monetary damages under Title IX.[51] Second, the case inspired a movement against sexual harassment in education. According to Simon, in contrast to the failure of the press to understand sexual harassment as sex discrimination, the notion "just spread like wildfire" among students. The women involved in the lawsuits, both the students and their attorneys, worked to raise awareness of the issue by speaking to student groups on other campuses, speaking at conferences on the issue, and sharing materials relating to the case. This led to a huge push for sexual harassment grievance procedures all over the country. Students around the country formed organizations to combat sexual harassment, surveyed students on sexual harassment, and brought lawsuits against colleges and universities.[52] Soon schools around the country began to develop and adopt policies and procedures to address sexual harassment on campus. Finally, the extensive press coverage of the case increased public awareness of sexual harassment in educational institutions and stimulated discussion of the issue.

By the mid-1970s, the civil rights and women's movements had generated a network of attorneys skilled at using Title VII to combat employment discrimination. The WLDF, Equal Rights Advocates, the Women's Rights Litigation Clinic at Rutgers Law School, the Mexican American Legal Defense Fund, the Women's Justice Center, the New Haven Law Collective, the Center for Constitutional Rights, and others provided resources to which sexual harassment activists and early plaintiffs turned for support in appealing the early cases. Activists and attorneys created networks and collaborations that generated an effective strategy to convince courts to rule in favor of sexual harassment plaintiffs. The activists proved the seriousness of the problem through surveys, which the attorneys then presented to the appellate court judges. Making sociological and historical arguments, and relying on racial harassment law under Title VII, the attorneys were able to reframe the issue of sexual coercion in the workplace. These activists also took advantage of the political opportunity presented by a more diverse and progressive appellate court bench.

As a result, sexual harassment jurisprudence underwent a shift that employment discrimination law had made a few years earlier. In the late 1960s, the Civil Rights Act had brought about a new realization of the extent of job discrimination. This realization was explained in a 1970 Senate Committee report:

In 1964, employment discrimination tended to be viewed as a series of isolated and distinguishable events, for the most part due to ill will on the part of some identifiable individual or organization.... This view has not been borne out by experience. Employment discrimination, as viewed today, is a far more complex and pervasive phenomenon. Experts familiar with the subject generally describe the problem in terms of "systems" and "effects" rather than simply intentional wrongs.[53]

Judges initially viewed sexual harassment as merely a personal problem, an "isolated and distinguishable event," the result of an individual actor, a bad egg, the office wolf. With time, however, courts began to recognize that employer tolerance of sexual harassment affected women as a class, creating barriers to equal employment opportunity. Feminist advocacy on sexual harassment together with larger cultural and legal shifts occurring in the 1970s, including Supreme Court jurisprudence and congressional actions expanding equal rights for women, provided fertile grounds for the development of this recognition. Courts had come a long way by accepting the basic principle that sexual harassment was sex discrimination.

These early sexual harassment cases were also significant in that they document the changing perceptions of women in the 1970s. Defendants' arguments that prevailed in the lower courts characterized sexual harassment as an insignificant, personal problem. These arguments assigned a low value to female participation in the workforce and assumed both the propriety of male sexual initiative and the untrustworthiness of female complainants. The power of defendants' arguments lay in the traditional association of women with the private sphere and the concomitant notion that women entered the public sphere at their own risk. Plaintiffs and their feminist attorneys, on the other hand, argued for the women's right to full and equal participation in the workforce. They were able to convince courts that sexual harassment was not just a personal problem but had a devastating impact on women in the workplace, sufficient to warrant judicial intervention. These early cases were revolutionary in that they affirmed women's right to participate in the public sphere as equal to men's. But the movement's framing of the issue was fundamentally shaped by the external context and drew upon both oppositional and dominant beliefs.[54] The movement chose strategies and arguments that were most likely to convince judges to rule in their favor. The Title VII framework that required the claimant to prove that they were a member of a protected class encouraged movement participants to frame the issue of sexual harassment as a gender-based harm – a violation of women by men. Activists characterized women as the victims – particularly vulnerable because of social, economic, and cultural factors – and men as perpetrators, a dichotomy the movement would later abandon when the issue of same-sex harassment arose in the 1990s.[55] This gendered framing of the issue, however, was critical to the successful articulation of sexual harassment as a Title VII violation in the late 1970s.

The scope of the early sexual harassment decisions, however, was narrow. They covered only *quid pro quo* sexual harassment – where a supervisor fires a subordinate employee who has refused his sexual advances. Several courts held that harassment resulting in intangible harm, such as a hostile working atmosphere, was not sex discrimination. This narrow definition of sexual harassment was soon challenged by women working in nontraditional and blue-collar fields. As women began to break into these fields as a result of anti-discrimination and affirmative action laws, they encountered harassment designed to push them out of male-dominated working environments. Women working in construction, mining, and other traditionally male occupations began to raise concerns about what came to be known as hostile environmental sexual harassment, the new frontier of sexual harassment activism.

PART II

GROWTH OF A MOVEMENT AGAINST
SEXUAL HARASSMENT

4

Blue-Collar Workers and Hostile Environment Sexual Harassment

In the late 1970s, while feminist activism was raising public awareness of sexual harassment and appellate courts were ruling in favor of victims, women were breaking down occupational barriers. Antidiscrimination laws and the resulting affirmative action programs encouraged more women to enter traditionally male-dominated workplaces and occupations. As women began breaking into these masculine domains, they experienced a range of harassing behavior. Much of the harassment consisted of sexual graffiti, dirty jokes, repeated propositioning, and even sexual assault. Marian Swerdlow, a subway conductor in New York City in the late 1970s, described, "the first few months on the job, I got propositioned so consistently that I finally joked about giving a civil service exam for the position, with a filing fee and a physical."[1] Judy Jarvela, who worked at Eveleth Mines in Minnesota, repeatedly found semen on the clothes in her locker, and co-worker Diane Hodge reported that her foreman came up from behind her and grabbed both her breasts in front of her co-workers.[2]

But often the harassment experienced by women in nontraditional occupations had nothing to do with sex, but was an attempt to discourage women from staying in the trades because they were taking a "man's" job. Women were subject to isolation, work sabotage, severe verbal abuse, and physical violence. Rose Melendez, a police officer in San Francisco, had male co-workers who would not speak with her and ignored her like she wasn't there. One day a co-worker drove Melendez to a secluded area, pulled a gun on her, pointed it directly at her, and said "I just want to see how fast you women cops can run." Sometimes women experienced dangerous work sabotage. Pat Crull, a carpenter in California, described how "my [co-workers] gave me the hardest tasks they could find and then sat back to watch me struggle. Once I was assigned to carry four-hundred-pound steel beams with a guy who was about six feet tall and weighed about three hundred pounds. I was five-foot-two and weighed about a hundred and twenty-five pounds." Crull explained, "because I was older, I was rarely seen as a sex object in the way that the younger women were. They had to deal with the 'come fuck me' kind of harassment while I had to deal with the 'she can't do it' kind of harassment." Mary Ruggiero, an aircraft welder in New Jersey, reported that a male co-worker "cut the chain holding up a big motor mount I was welding. It fell down on me and burned my arm to the bone." Sue Doro, a machinist in Milwaukee, described how a co-worker sabotaged her machine: "Dick would loosen stuff on it, which could kill you. Like, he would loosen a big drill, a huge part. If it's not right, and it hits, it will shatter in your face. Safety glasses wouldn't help; you'd be real cut up. He did stuff like that."[3]

In response, women working in construction, coal mining, fire fighting, law enforcement, and other nontraditional occupations across the country organized against sexual harassment. As with the African-American women who brought many of the first sexual harassment cases, the working environments, backgrounds, and identities of blue-collar women in male-dominated fields shaped their experiences of sexual harassment and their strategies and resources for addressing the problem. Through unions and employee associations, blue-collar women urged courts and policy-makers to broaden their definitions of sexual harassment to include not just sexual demands by a supervisor of a subordinate employee, but also hostile environment harassment – when supervisors or co-workers create a hostile working environment through sexual or nonsexual behavior aimed at creating an intimidating or offensive environment for women. This activism occurred simultaneously but usually independently from other antisexual harassment activism until at the very end of the 1970s when activists converged in Washington to testify about sexual harassment before Congress.

Blue-collar women working in male-dominated fields influenced the development of public policy on sexual harassment. Their activism led to the first federal regulations on sexual harassment. Blue-collar women won several precedent-setting hostile environment sexual harassment lawsuits, thereby establishing legal prohibitions against this conduct. By sharing stories that clearly demonstrated the fundamentally abusive nature of sexual harassment, blue-collar women significantly enhanced public understanding of sexual harassment – that it was motivated not by sexual desire but by men's desire to keep women subordinate in the workplace and that it, therefore, was a serious problem that harmed women on the job.

WOMEN IN CONSTRUCTION

Women breaking into the construction trades won the first federal regulations to limit harassment on the job. Seeking access to jobs in the industry, they turned to federal Executive Orders 11246 and 11375, which prohibited federal contractors from discriminating on the basis of sex. In response to two lawsuits brought by female construction workers protesting hiring practices and harassment of women in the industry, the Department of Labor (DOL) proposed regulations requiring federal construction contractors to hire more women and to ensure a workplace free of "harassment, intimidation, and coercion."[4]

The first lawsuit originated at a May 1975 nationwide meeting of women working in the construction industry in Washington, D.C. Katherine Mazzaferri, who was the Director of Litigation at the League of Women Voters Education Fund, and Joan Graff, a founder of Equal Rights Advocates (ERA), Inc., in San Francisco, convened the meeting, which was sponsored by the Education Fund's Litigation Division and funded by a grant from the Ford Foundation.[5] At the meeting, the women discussed problems of hiring, retention, and harassment in the construction industry, and they decided to bring a lawsuit under federal affirmative action law to gain access to the construction trade. After the meeting, Mazzaferri and Graff traveled around the country interviewing potential plaintiffs. According to Mazzaferri, "they were just incredible women. The stuff they had to go through was just awful and they were real pioneers."[6]

A year later, Mazzaferri, Graff, and Trudy Levy of the League of Women Voters Education Fund filed a lawsuit on behalf of several women's organizations and individual plaintiffs against the DOL to enforce Executive Orders 11246 and 11375.[7] The plaintiffs included Advocates for Women in San Francisco, Women in Trades in Seattle, and United Trade Workers Association in Tacoma, Washington, all of which helped women get jobs in the construction industry. The individual plaintiffs were from San Francisco, Seattle, Tacoma, and Fairbanks, Alabama. In addition to Mazzaferri, Graff, and Levy, Judith Lichtman of the WLDF and Lois Schiffer of the Center for Law and Social Policy provided legal assistance. Around the same time, a similar case arose challenging the Washington, D.C., affirmative action plan.[8] The plaintiffs included several individuals and two organizations, Women Working in Construction and Wider Opportunities for Women, both Washington, D.C.-based nonprofit organizations, working to expand employment opportunities for women, especially in skilled nontraditional employment, and focusing on federal employment policy. D.C. attorneys Lynn Cunningham and Susan Shapiro represented the plaintiffs at first, but the League took over the case in June 1977, and the two cases were joined. When Mazzaferri and Levy left the League in 1978, attorneys Marcia Greenberger and Margaret Kohn of the Center for Law and Social Policy took over the cases.

The plaintiffs in these cases sought to rectify the near total exclusion of women from the construction industry, and the issue of harassment was a key component of their argument. The complaint asked the DOL to set hiring goals and timetables for women in the industry, arguing that the scarcity of women on job sites fostered harassment against women and caused them psychological injury. The plaintiffs' affidavits testified that their male co-workers ostracized and scrutinized them. The women described experiencing "verbal assaults by hostile male co-workers," including sexist jokes and sexual allusions, which alienated and isolated them on the job. The plaintiffs' attorneys also filed a petition with the DOL seeking affirmative action in federally funded apprenticeship programs.[9]

The plaintiffs began to make headway in 1976 after a meeting with DOL Secretary Ray Marshall, a Carter appointee. Carin Clauss, the Solicitor of

Labor, set up the meeting at Mazzaferri and Graff's request and also brought in Alexis Herman, who was Director of the Women's Bureau and was committed to helping women gain access to nontraditional jobs. On April 21, 1977, Marshall met with several plaintiffs, their attorneys, and representatives from several activist organizations.[10] At the meeting, the plaintiffs described the ordeals they experienced working on federal construction sites. One woman, Libby Howard, described the obscene graffiti campaign waged against her for more than five years while she worked as one of just a few women on a work crew of 2,000. Marshall was moved by what he heard, and from then on he, the plaintiffs, and their attorneys had discussions on how to create a meaningful resolution to the problem.

Later in 1977, Marshall held DOL hearings on women in construction in Baltimore and heard testimony of many egregious examples of physical violence, threats, and sexual harassment against female construction workers. A representative from Women Working in Construction testified that she was badly hurt when working as an apprentice after her foreman forced her to ascend a rickety scaffold, in spite of her protests, and the scaffolding collapsed. Anna Ramos of the Chicana Service Action Center in Los Angeles told DOL officials of three cases involving violence against female construction workers in California, including one woman whose thumbs were smashed after she refused to quit a job. Women also testified that male co-workers made crude remarks, gestures, and pranks and used pornography to drive women from the workplace.[11]

The primary opposition to the plaintiffs' demands came from the contractors and administrators in the Department of Labor's Bureau of Apprenticeship and Training, which was the "voice" of unions and apprenticeship programs. They argued that women could not do the work, that they were not interested in doing the work, and that they would not stay on the job. The plaintiffs found a male witness to counter these arguments. John Heneghan, Director of the Office of Civil Rights Maritime Administration of the U.S. Department of Commerce, enforced Executive Orders 11246 and 11375 in regard to women construction workers at shipyards. Heneghan gave an affidavit saying that female construction workers at the shipyards were incredibly reliable, competent, and committed to their jobs. According to Mazzaferri, this testimony was a turning point in the case.

In August and September 1977, in response to the lawsuit, the DOL proposed regulations setting goals and timetables for federal construction contractors and apprenticeship programs. Many women's groups submitted comments on the proposed regulations, including from the plaintiffs in the two lawsuits. Marshall met with the plaintiffs and their attorneys again on October 4, 1977. On April 7, 1978, the DOL adopted the final regulations on women in construction and shortly thereafter published the final regulations on women in apprenticeships.[12] In addition to setting hiring goals and timetables for women in construction and in apprenticeship programs, the regulations required employers to ensure and maintain a working environment free of harassment, intimidation, and coercion and required contractors to assign two or more women to each construction project if possible. The guidelines also required contractors to ensure that all foremen, superintendents, and other on-site supervisory personnel were aware of and carried out the contractor's obligation to maintain a harassment-free working environment, "with specific attention to minority or female individuals."[13] An employer violating these regulations could be forced to give the victim back pay, vacation time, seniority, medical and psychiatric expenses, and other damages. Companies with significant government business, $50,000 or more annually, were required to prepare written procedures addressing harassment, and this information had to be given to the workers. Companies not adhering to these rules could be permanently forbidden from holding federal contracts. The lawsuits were finally settled in December 1978. The DOL agreed to conduct outreach programs for women, to establish a monitoring committee to measure the implementations and effectiveness of the regulations, and to maintain records of compliance reviews and complaints against federal construction contractors.[14]

The regulations were not enforced, however. In 1979, Women's Work Force, a national network of women's employment programs established by Wider Opportunities for Women, formed a national, industry-wide task force to monitor and assess construction contract compliance. In 1980, the group received grants from the Edna McConnell Clark and Robert Sterling Clark Foundation to conduct a monitoring project in conjunction with the Center for National Policy Review. The report, published in 1982, found that noncompliance with federal regulations was common and that sexual harassment was pervasive and often used to discourage women from construction trades employment. The Office of Federal Contract Compliance Programs defended itself by saying it had limited staff and that contractors were resistant. The head of DOL's Office of Federal Contract Compliance during the Carter Administration, Weldon Rougeau, reported after leaving office that companies "would promise anything to get us off their backs but never actually do anything."[15] The problem of slack compliance monitoring was compounded by the fact that few women filed complaints for fear of retaliation and increased harassment. The Wider Opportunities for Women report concluded, "Women are *not welcome* in construction trades. Women *do not belong* in the construction trades."[16] Despite the high level of noncompliance, Joan Graff believes that the regulations had a significant impact because they were "the first in a long series of steps that legitimized [nontraditional] jobs for women." The regulations were an "important public pronouncement" that women could do the work; they "shifted public opinion and expectation about who could and should be able to do [nontraditional] jobs."[17]

DOL later adopted regulations specifically addressing coercive sexual advances by employees of federal construction contractors. On December 28, 1979, DOL proposed regulations prohibiting sexual advances by persons who are in a position to affect the employment opportunities of those targeted, as well as prohibiting employment decisions based on sexual favors.[18] During the public comment period, DOL received twenty-eight comments from women's groups and contractors on this proposal. Women's groups, including ERA, argued that the regulation should address harassment by co-workers, clients, and customers and that contractors should be required to have policies against harassment. Contractors opposed the proposed liability standard that an employer would be liable if it knew or should have known of the harassment. Some contractors thought the DOL should not get into this area at all. DOL redrafted the regulations to make them consistent with the EEOC guidelines on sexual harassment and issued the final rule on December 30, 1980.[19] The regulations were supposed to take effect January 30, 1981, but the Reagan administration took office and froze the implementation of new regulations. The regulations were proposed again in largely the same form on August 25, 1981, but they have never been adopted as a final rule.[20]

WOMEN COAL MINERS

Women working in the coal mining industry also went to courts in the late 1970s to get federal relief from discrimination and harassment. In May 1978, women coal miners represented by the Coal Employment Project (CEP), an Oak Ridge, Tennessee-based grassroots group of women organized in 1977 to help women break into coal mining, filed a complaint with the Department of Labor against Consolidated Coal Company of Pittsburgh (CONSOL), the largest coal company in the United States. The plaintiffs, employed at Shoemaker coal mine in Benwood, West Virginia, alleged that they suffered sex discrimination and harassment in the mines. In response, the Department of Labor initiated a federal investigation of the entire coal mining industry. In 1978, a settlement in the case provided for hiring quotas, back pay, and affirmative action programs to protect women miners from discrimination and harassment underground. This lawsuit increased the number of female coal miners. According to federal statistics, the number of women miners jumped from none in 1972 to 992 in 1977 to 2,940 in 1979, at which time 11.4%of all entry-level miners hired as underground coal miners were women. As women began to enter mining toward the end of the decade, sexual harassment became a pressing issue and a priority for CEP.[21]

Female coal miners experienced pervasive, and often violent, sexual harassment. Coal mining had a strongly fraternal culture, with men closely bonded because of the danger of the work and families of men – fathers, sons, and brothers – working together. On the other hand, women coal miners were often hesitant to report harassment because they lived in small towns where they knew their fellow miners and they felt isolated from supportive social networks. When women began to enter the mines, male miners revived a traditional initiation rite, which had more or less been discontinued by the 1970s, of stripping and greasing new miners. In a 1977 case before the Kentucky Commission on Human Rights, miner Frieda Myers won a $2,000 conciliation agreement from Peabody Coal Company, the largest coal company in the country, for humiliation and embarrassment because she was stripped and greased by her male co-workers. Peabody agreed to issue a policy statement to "adopt safe working conditions for all employees and particularly to insure that female employees shall not be subjected to abuse, insult, or injury related to their sex."[22] A second form of harassment women miners experienced occurred during what were otherwise routine searches for cigarettes or other smoking materials as workers entered the mines. Women complained that they were searched "differently" from men and that they were touched inappropriately. A third form of harassment occurred when men drilled holes in women's bathhouses on company grounds to peep at the women showering and dressing.

In response, female coal miners used some of the same techniques used by women in other parts of the country to combat sexual harassment – they met at conferences and shared their stories through newsletters, which enabled them to create a sense of a shared community suffering from a systemic problem. As did activists in Ithaca and Cambridge, New York City, and Washington, D.C., female coal miners gathered together or used newsletters to share their stories. CEP reported hearing isolated stories about sexual harassment in 1978. At the first National Conference of Women Coal Miners in June 1979, sexual harassment was only mentioned "in whispers, in corners here and there." Women were too embarrassed, ashamed, and isolated to report sexual harassment, feeling that they had somehow provoked the behavior. Shortly after the conference, however, an anonymous woman's first person story about sexual harassment appeared in the newsletters of the United Mine Workers of America and the CEP. More women began to contact CEP with their stories of harassment, expressing relief that the subject was out in the open. At a November 1979 conference of women miners sponsored by the United Mine Workers of America in Charleston, West Virginia, women miners for the first time spoke openly about sexual harassment.

The Second National Conference of Women Coal Miners in May 1980 was a "major turning point, when 'things really came out of the woodwork.'"[23] Sexual harassment emerged as a major theme of the conference. CEP offered a sexual harassment workshop, which was packed to capacity both times it was offered. In the workshops, women told their stories of sexual harassment in coal mines, describing their fear, guilt, and hesitance to tell others. One woman exclaimed, "At last! Somebody else has been going through all this! I thought it was just me!"[24] The women miners passed several resolutions on sexual harassment. They asked CEP to conduct a study of sexual harassment in coal mines and to produce a brochure about women's legal rights. They resolved to ask unions and employers to adopt policies against sexual harassment and incorporate information about the issue into training sessions. They also asked CEP to produce information to send to new miners about the issue, to post on bulletin boards, and to distribute through newsletters.

Similar to activists in other areas of the country, CEP researched women's experiences using surveys and interviews and developed statistical information to support their sexual harassment complaints and educate themselves and the public. CEP surveyed women miners in ten states[25] about their experiences of sexual harassment and published the results in 1981 showing rampant and violent sexual harassment in coal mines. Fifty-four percent of women miners were propositioned by bosses at least once, seventy-six percent were propositioned by co-workers, and seventeen percent had been attacked physically.[26] To assist women miners, CEP provided counseling and support, including writing letters to employers on behalf of sexually harassed women. CEP published a brochure and a booklet on sexual harassment in coal mining. CEP also established support services for women in rural and mountain communities, who were particularly vulnerable because of their isolation. CEP formed a "buddy system" to connect women miners with women in nearby communities who were considering a career in mining. This program became known as the Coal Mining Women's Support Team.[27] These organizations not only supported female coal miners directly but also worked to advance policy on sexual harassment. In June 1980, Pat Baldwin, a miner and head of the Western Kentucky Women's Support Team, testified before the Kentucky Commission on Human Rights at a hearing on sexual harassment. In April 1981, Baldwin and CEP's Director Betty Jean Hall, an attorney, testified at hearings on sexual harassment before the Senate Committee on Labor and Human Resources in Washington, D.C. At these hearings, Baldwin and Hall worked to raise awareness about hostile environment harassment experienced by female coal miners.

UNION WOMEN

Unionized women in other industries also worked to combat sexual harassment, though their efforts were complicated by the collective nature of the unions. In the late 1970s, when only about 11% of female workers belonged to unions and another 5% were in employee associations, labor unions generally showed little interest in sexual harassment when female union members raised the issue. According to an early publication, unions worried that the issue might "divide the working class."[28] In particular, unions discouraged women from filing grievances against other union members. Sometimes harassed women would file grievances with employers, and unions would come to the defense of men disciplined by employers for sexual harassment. A 1981 study of arbitration and sexual harassment found twenty-four reported sexual harassment arbitration cases between 1965 and 1981, most of which were initiated by unions representing men disciplined by employers for harassment.[29] Despite this resistance, women associated with labor unions began to work on the issue of sexual harassment and, in some cases, were able to get unions to act on charges of sexual harassment. Female union members fought sexual harassment by supporting victims, surveying union members, distributing information about sexual harassment, and providing educational programs. The American Federation of State, County, and Municipal Employees formed a Women's Rights Committee in 1978 that trained stewards and union leadership in techniques for responding to sexual harassment complaints. In 1981, the Federation published a handbook on sexual harassment, which included sample contract language and policy statements.[30]

The American Federation of Government Employees supported victims of sexual harassment at Fort Wainwright in Fairbanks, AK, at the Johnson Space Center in Houston, TX, and at a Social Security Administration Office in San Francisco, and conducted workshops on sexual harassment. In Massachusetts, the Women's Committee of Local 201 of the International Union of Electrical Workers began working on the issue of sexual harassment after a black woman was raped by a white man in a bathroom at a General Electric plant.[31] The union surveyed women workers about sexual harassment and assault in the workplace and incorporated workshops on sexual harassment into its regularly scheduled business meetings. Several female union members published articles on sexual harassment in union publications.[32] Other female union members participated in shaping public policy on sexual harassment by testifying on sexual harassment at federal hearings, including representatives of the United Auto Workers, the Industrial Union of Electrical, Radio and Machine Workers, the Coalition of Labor Union Women, the American Federation of Government Employees, and Federally Employed Women.

In some cases, unions took a firm stand against sexual harassment. In June of 1979, representatives from several unions testified about sexual harassment before the National Commission on Unemployment Compensation in Washington, D.C., including Michigan United Auto Workers (UAW) member Tamara Bavar, Assistant General Counsel of the International Union of Electrical, Radio and Machine Workers (IUE), Barbara Somson on behalf of IUE and the Coalition of Labor Union Women, and Vincent R. Sombrotto, President of the National Association of Letter Carriers, AFL-CIO. In 1979, the President of the Michigan State AFL-CIO testified at public hearings on sexual harassment in the workplace in Grand Rapids, Michigan. The UAW were particularly active on the issue of sexual harassment. In 1979, UAW won specific clauses on sexual harassment in contracts with Ford and Chrysler. The Ford contract confirmed that sexual harassment charges were subject to grievance procedures and committed the union and the company to investigate sexual harassment through the Fair Employment Practices Committees. Chrysler agreed to issue a policy statement to its management informing them that sexual harassment would not be tolerated. In 1981, under the leadership of Douglas Fraser, UAW issued a strong and clear policy statement against sexual harassment, deploring harassment as "a serious obstacle to the achievement of full employment opportunity for workers of both sexes." UAW also supported an individual woman in a landmark sexual harassment case in Michigan, where Fayette Nale, a member of Local 400 in Utica, MI, won $187,032 from Ford Motor Company for sexual harassment in 1981. The UAW committeeperson at the plant, Jerry Sudderth, supported Nale when he first learned about the harassment in 1974, meeting with the plant superintendent and labor-relations personnel to tell them to stop harassing Nale and subsequently protesting Ford's firing of Nale. Sudderth later

provided decisive testimony at the trial of Nale. In another case, a union supported female auto workers in Massachusetts.[33]

In 1979, female UAW members in Michigan surveyed workers about sexual
harassment and testified on sexual harassment at federal hearings about unemployment compensation. Three UAW members, Elissa Clarke, Jane Slaughter,
and Enid Eckstein, contributed to a handbook on sexual harassment for the
Labor Education and Research Project in Detroit, MI, published in June 1980.
The pamphlet was cowritten with Connye Harper, an attorney and founder of
the Women's Justice Center, and Rita Drapkin, who was a member of the
Teamsters and founder of Cleveland, Ohio-based Hard Hatted Women, which
supported women in skilled trades and nontraditional jobs.[34] The handbook
gave practical advice on how to combat sexual harassment on the job, within
unions, and at educational institutions.

Sexual harassment was a key issue in several strikes in the late 1970s. For
example, in October 1979, fourteen hundred workers walked out at Simpson
Plywood in Washington State to protest sexual harassment of female members
of the International Woodworkers of America. Supervisors had asked female
job applicants if they wore bras, asked them to take off their blouses, and asked
them if they were willing to have sex with their supervisors. The strike was
called because one woman was fired after filing sex discrimination charges with
the Washington Human Rights Commission and the EEOC. The strike spread
to Simpson plants in California and eventually involved more than three thousand workers. In Mississippi, members of the International Chemical Workers
Union struck against Sanderson Farms, a chicken processing plant, over low
pay, unsafe working conditions, racism, and sexual harassment.[35]

Women fought hard to get unions to address their concerns about sexual
harassment. By the early 1980s, some unions and employee associations began
to respond to women's demands for change by issuing policy statements against
sexual harassment, advocating for sexual harassment clauses in union contracts, and educating workers about sexual harassment and sexism as a preventative measure. Union women, however, continued to encounter resistance
within unions and expressed concern themselves that management would selectively enforce prohibitions of sexual harassment against workers they dis-
liked because of their race or class, union activity, or political views.[36]

HOSTILE ENVIRONMENT LAWSUITS

In the late 1970s and early 1980s, women working in a broad range of nontraditional fields, including janitors, security guards, police officers, and assembly-line workers, began to build the case for broadening the definition of sexual
harassment beyond *quid pro quo* sexual harassment to cover the conditions of
the workplace. The EEOC ruled on several hostile environment cases in the
early 1970s, but the federal courts did not begin to entertain these suits until the
late 1970s.[37] Only a couple of courts in the 1970s ruled in favor of plaintiffs
bringing cases involving allegations of hostile environment sexual harassment.

In the 1977 case of *Macey v. World Airways*, a federal trial court in California allowed a Title VII case in a hostile environment harassment case that did not involve sexual conduct. The plaintiff, who was the first female electrician ever hired by World Airways, met resistance from male co-workers who resented her intrusion and responded with disparaging remarks and refusal to help her learn her job.[38] In 1978, in the case of *Kyriazi v. Western Electric Company*, a female engineer won a co-worker harassment case brought under section 1985 of the 1871 Civil Rights Act and state tort law. In that case, Kyriaki Cleo Kyriazi, who was a Greek immigrant, was an engineer at a Western Electric plant in Kearny, NJ. Kyriazi's male co-workers ridiculed and harassed her, speculating about her virginity and circulating an obscene cartoon of her. She complained to her supervisors, but they refused to stop the harassment and required her to seek psychiatric help. When she formally complained of discrimination, they fired her. The court ruled in favor of Kyriazi, becoming the first court to recognize that a sexually hostile working environment was discriminatory sexual harassment.[39]

An African-American factory worker from Minnesota won another important early co-worker harassment case brought under state law. In 1980, the Minnesota Supreme Court ruled that an employer was liable under the state Human Rights Act for tolerating co-worker sexual harassment in the case of *Continental Can Company v. Minnesota*. Willie Ruth Hawkins was one of two women working at the Eagan, MN, plant of Continental Can Company. Starting in December 1974, three of Hawkins's white male co-workers repeatedly made explicit sexually derogatory remarks and verbal sexual advances to Hawkins and touched her sexually. One of her co-workers, Cliff Warling, said to Hawkins that he "wished slavery days would return so that he could sexually train her and she would be his bitch," making reference to the movie *Mandingo*.[40] Warling and other male co-workers told her that "a female has no business in a factory" and "if a female would work [in] a factory, she has to be a tramp."[41] Hawkins repeatedly complained to her supervisor, but Continental took no action. One supervisor told Hawkins that there was nothing he could do and that she had to expect that kind of behavior when working with men.

In October 1975, the harassment escalated to physical violence. Warling approached Hawkins from behind while she was bending over and grabbed her between the legs. Hawkins complained immediately, but again Continental took no action. A few days later, Hawkins' husband came to the plant and confronted Warling, who denied the incident. When Mr. Hawkins returned later that evening to escort his wife home, they discovered that her car headlights were broken. Relations between Hawkins and her co-workers deteriorated further, culminating in a co-worker threatening Willie Ruth Hawkins with a gun in front of her children. The Hawkinses solicited the support of New Way Community Center and the Urban League, who threatened boycotts and adverse publicity if Continental did not take action. At that point, Continental suspended two of the harassers and held a plant meeting and informed all employees that Continental would not tolerate verbal or physical sexual harassment and discrimination. Fearing for her safety, Hawkins did not return to work after October 16 and was terminated from employment on December 5, 1975.

Hawkins filed a sex discrimination charge with the Minnesota Department of Human Rights on October 20, 1975. After she won before a hearing examiner, Continental appealed to a Minnesota district court, which reversed and dismissed Hawkins' complaint. Hawkins appealed to the Minnesota Supreme Court. NOWLDEF and WWI filed an amicus brief in this case. The Supreme Court ruled that verbal and physical sexual harassment by fellow employees was sex discrimination prohibited by the Minnesota Human Rights Act. The Court discussed Title VII sexual harassment jurisprudence but found these cases distinguishable because they all involved *quid pro quo* supervisory harassment. The Court then turned to racial harassment cases, finding them factually more similar to Hawkins' case. The Court also relied on the EEOC interim guidelines. The Court held that Minnesota's prohibition on sex discrimination included hostile environment sexual harassment by co-workers affecting the conditions of employment and that employers were liable when they knew or should have known of the employees' conduct and failed to take timely and appropriate action. The Court awarded Hawkins $5,000 in back pay and ordered Continental Can to stop discriminating on the basis of sex and to take prompt and appropriate action to address future instances of workplace sexual harassment.

Although plaintiffs won relief for co-worker sexual harassment in these early cases brought under state law, they were less successful invoking Title VII protection in federal lawsuits. Two decisions in the late 1970s denied relief under Title VII for sexual harassment by a co-worker. In the 1978 case of *Pantchenco v. C. B. Dolge Company*, a federal district court in Connecticut held that sexual harassment by a co-worker was not sex discrimination.[42] Similarly, in the 1978 case of *Smith v. Rust Engineering Company*, a federal district court in Alabama dismissed the sexual harassment claim of a woman subjected to repeated sexual demands by a co-worker on the grounds that compliance with these advances was not an expressed or implied requirement for keeping her job.[43]

Federal courts also denied Title VII relief for hostile environment harassment by supervisors in the case of *Bundy v. Jackson*. Sandra Bundy was a Vocational Rehabilitation Specialist with the District of Columbia Department of Corrections, responsible for finding jobs for former criminal offenders. Bundy alleged that her rejection of unsolicited and offensive sexual advances from several supervisors in her agency caused them to delay or block promotions to which she was entitled. Bundy was a young black woman who had participated in the civil rights movement in the 1960s. She attended marches and demonstrations and helped to organize a union whose demands included an end to racial segregation of the work force. When Bundy complained of sexual harassment in her workplace, her black co-workers disapproved and criticized her for bringing her lawsuit. Black women in her office avoided her. Bundy was hurt, but she continued with her lawsuit because, as she said at the time, "I wouldn't

FIGURE 4.1. Sandra Bundy, 1979. Photo by Gerald Martineau/Washington Post

be able to make a living, if I didn't. I wouldn't be able to protect my children. I wouldn't be able to keep my sanity."[44] The trial judge, United States District Court Judge George Hart Jr., who was appointed by President Dwight D. Eisenhower in 1958, ruled against Bundy, despite his finding that "improper sexual advances to female employees [was] standard operating procedure, a fact of life, a normal condition of employment" at the Department of Corrections.[45] In particular, Judge Hart found that four of Bundy's supervisors, all of whom were black men, routinely and graphically demanded sexual favors in calls to her home as well as in office confrontations. Bundy complained repeatedly to her supervisors, but they merely harassed her further. One supervisor to whom she reported harassment responded "I want to take you to bed myself" and "any man in his right mind would want to rape you."[46]

However, because Bundy did not complain until two years after the sexual advances began, Judge Hart found that she "did not appear to consider [the sexual advances] unusual or highly improper and insulting" and that she did not appear to take such actions seriously. He suggested that Bundy made a formal complaint not because the sexual advances bothered her but "primarily as a means of obtaining advancement." Similarly, he found that Bundy's supervisors did not take her rejections seriously and that they "did not consider plaintiff's rejection of their improper sexual advances as a reason or justification for harassing the plaintiff or of otherwise taking adverse action against her. It was a game played by the male superiors – you won some and you lost some. It was not a matter to be taken seriously." Judge Hart found Bundy's supervisors had independent, legitimate reasons for delaying and denying the promotions, so he denied relief. Judge Hart held that sexual harassment did not in itself represent discrimination absent any tangible economic effects. Bundy appealed, but it wouldn't be until the early 1980s, after the EEOC issued guidelines defining sexual harassment to include hostile environmental sexual harassment under Title VII, that federal courts would begin to offer relief for hostile environment sexual harassment.

In the late 1970s, blue-collar women joined the growing chorus of voices speaking out against sexual harassment, but they spoke with a distinct voice and made a distinct contribution to the growing movement against sexual harassment. Building on feminist understandings of sexual harassment, blue-collar women articulated their experiences of harassment – co-workers' misogynist, often violent, behavior designed to push women out of traditionally male fields. They reframed this behavior as a form of sexual harassment and argued that this behavior violated women's civil rights. Blue-collar women urged courts and federal policy-makers to broaden their understandings of sexual harassment to include hostile environment sexual harassment. They also urged feminist activists to include the issue of hostile environment harassment in their advocacy work. Working individually, or in local and regional groups such as Women in Trades, Women Working in Construction, CEP, Chicana Service Action Center, and in unions, grassroots activists collaborated with feminist attorneys in national organizations, such as the League of Women Voters, ERA, and NOW Legal Defense and Education Fund. While working-class women often did not share the same concerns as middle-class feminists, sexual harassment was an issue of cross-class concern that generated collaborative activism among women.[47]

To combat sexual harassment, blue-collar women engaged in many of the same strategies used by activists in Ithaca, Cambridge, and Washington, D.C. – such as surveys, newsletters, speak-outs, and support groups. But working-class women were able to draw upon other resources available to them as a result of their status as members of unions and employee associations, and they used the resources of these organizations to advance their agendas. They also took advantage of the political opportunities provided by newly formed governmental agencies to protect civil rights, like the Kentucky Human Rights Commission, or progressive Carter appointees in the Department of Labor who were committed to advancing affirmative action and sympathetic individuals in the federal government, like Alexis Herman of the Women's Bureau. By raising the issue in new contexts and pushing to broaden the scope of sexual harassment, blue-collar women made a significant contribution to building a persuasive argument that sexual harassment was a serious civil rights issue that government policy-makers should address. This broader articulation of the issue also contributed toward expanding participation in the movement. By the end of the 1970s, more and more women around the country were working on the issue of sexual harassment.

5

Expansion of the Movement against Sexual Harassment in the Late 1970s

By the late 1970s, the idea that sexual harassment was a serious problem took root. As the federal government and the courts were beginning to affirm women's complaints that sexual harassment was a legitimate, systemic, and serious workplace problem, an activist movement was growing to include women and organizations from around the country. WWI and the AASC entered their heyday and were joined by a broad array of organizations representing diverse constituencies, including public interest law firms, public policy groups, political organizations, working women's organizations, unions, government-sponsored women's commissions, and student groups. These varied organizations became aware of each other, influenced each other, and began to work together to achieve social change. Thousands of women began to turn to these organizations for support, sharing their stories, ideas, and resources and receiving information, counseling, referrals, and legal advice and representation. Some organizations lobbied governments to pass legal prohibitions and encouraged employers to adopt policies and procedures and to offer training on the issue. Others engaged in outreach and public education to raise awareness of sexual harassment, including publishing brochures and handbooks on the issue and stimulating press coverage. Several organizations offered sexual harassment training to women's organizations, community groups, government agencies, and private employers. These activities were all part of a growing movement against sexual harassment.

This movement developed theories about the meanings, origins, and functions of sexual harassment and disseminated their views by influencing media coverage of the issue. Articles about sexual harassment proliferated in feminist, academic, and legal journals. In addition to studies and analysis produced by members of AASC and WWI, three books appeared on the issue in the late 1970s, all written by feminist activists. These works, which argued that sexual harassment was a serious, widespread, and devastating phenomenon for women, contributed significantly to the development of feminist understanding and analysis of sexual harassment. Through this work, feminist activists placed the issue of sexual harassment squarely within the larger feminist struggle to eliminate sexism throughout society. As the growing movement gained media attention for the issue of sexual harassment, this coverage often incorporated feminist understandings of the issue. Particularly due to their influence on the media, feminists fueled and fundamentally shaped this public discussion of the issue. Their characterization of sexual harassment as a serious abuse of power with a disparate and devastating impact on women permeated the discourse, which would eventually influence the development of public policy on sexual harassment.

PROLIFERATION OF FEMINIST ACTIVISM

WWI in New York City continued to play a central role in fighting sexual harassment.[1] The Institute grew significantly in the late 1970s and early 1980s, funded by several large grants from the New York Foundation, Exxon, and the Ford Foundation, and a large number of medium-sized grants, several from church organizations. The Institute's operating budget grew from $20,000 in 1978 to $75,000 in 1979 to $105,000 in 1980 to $131,000 in 1981. At its peak in the early 1980s, the Institute had a staff of five full-time employees and several part-time employees and a budget of more than $150,000. In the late 1970s, the Institute expanded its Board of Directors to include many powerful women, including Elizabeth Ladu of Banque Nationale de Paris, Venetia Hands of the New York advertising firm of Ogilvy & Mather, Mary Gay Harm, who also served on the National Board of the YWCA, and Melvin Robins of Bell Telephone Labs. WWI provided crisis counseling to sexually harassed women in the New York area and across the nation. Supported by grants from the New York Foundation and the United Church of Christ, the Institute set up a model crisis counseling service in 1979, serving approximately 550 women that year. In early 1980, the Institute created a Metropolitan Sexual Harassment Project and hired a director, K.C. Wagner, who had worked with battered women before coming to the Institute. The Institute sponsored television spots in the New York area, urging victims of sexual harassment to phone the project for support and counseling. In 1980, the Institute received close to 100 letters and calls a week from women requesting help with sexual harassment. The Project offered individual and group counseling to these women and, beginning in January 1981, sponsored a Monthly Educational Series, which provided programs on issues related to sexual harassment for women who had been through the counseling service, their friends, and family members. The Project also conducted training for a broad range of local service organizations.[2] The Institute's National Information and Referral Network offered information to women and organizations across the country, providing referrals from their network of more than 500 organizations and 200 attorneys in 198 localities. The Institute conducted educational outreach at the national level, speaking to corporations, unions, educational institutions, and working women's organizations.[3] Institute representatives participated in many conferences, gave press interviews, and appeared on television and radio programs, including the *McNeil-Lehrer Report*, the *Phil Donahue Show*, and *National Public Radio*.[4]

To inform their advocacy, the Institute significantly expanded their research on sexual harassment in the late 1970s and early 1980s, led by the Institute's Research Director, Dr. Peggy Crull. In 1978, Dr. Crull published a report on the Institute's survey of state fair employment practice agencies' handling of sexual harassment complaints. In 1979, she published a study on the impact of sexual harassment on working women, based on questionnaires sent to women who sought help from the Institute, and she conducted a comprehensive program evaluation of the crisis counseling service with a grant from the United Methodist Women. Dr. Crull conducted and published many studies on sexual harassment in the 1980s and presented her research at several conferences. She focused in particular on the impact of sexual harassment on women, including the health and psychological effects, and on the causes of sexual harassment, including the motivations for different types of sexual harassment. Based on this research, Dr. Crull began to testify as an expert witness in sexual harassment cases in the 1980s. The Institute catalogued their resource collection in the spring of 1981 in an annotated list of theoretical research, policy/service research, and media studies on sexual harassment and made these resources available for purchase.[5]

In addition to direct services, education, and research, the Institute worked to shape public policy on sexual harassment by assisting lawyers litigating sexual harassment cases. In February 1980, the Institute established a National Sexual Harassment Legal Back-Up Center and hired Joan Vermeulen as Legal Director.[6] The Center had a Legal Advisory Panel composed of attorneys experienced in sexual harassment and employment discrimination litigation.[7] Financial support for the Center came primarily from the Public Interest Law Foundation, but also from the Council on Women of the United Presbyterian Church, the Boehm Foundation, and the John Hay Whitney Foundation. The Center expanded the Institute's legal brief bank, produced a pamphlet for attorneys on litigating Title VII cases, and maintained a referral network of over 200 attorneys familiar with legal issues concerning sexual harassment. The Center compiled information on institutional policies, union policies, and contract clauses on sexual harassment and maintained a Legislative Checklist, which catalogued legislative initiatives on sexual harassment throughout the country. In addition, Institute representatives participated in several state and federal hearings on sexual harassment, worked to enact and support the EEOC guidelines on sexual harassment, and filed friend-of-the-court briefs in several precedent-setting sexual harassment cases.

Over time, the Institute broadened their understanding of sexual harassment and their advocacy by working with women from different backgrounds, including blue-collar women and students. Although they initially focused on sexual advances of a male boss toward a subordinate female employee, they soon began to address co-worker harassment, nonsexual, gender-based harassment of women, and harassment of students. The Institute came to understand in their work with blue-collar women, including firefighters, coal miners, and construction workers, that sexual harassment was not only sexual

FIGURE 5.1. Women's Rights March, New York City, 1980. Courtesy of Karen Sauvigné

conduct, but also hostile conduct aimed at women to drive them out of male-dominated workplaces. One Institute volunteer in particular helped broaden the Institute's conception of sexual harassment in this way – Brenda Berkman, who sued the New York City Fire Department for refusing to hire her because she was a woman. Working with Berkman, Betty Jean Hall and Pat Baldwin of the Western Kentucky Coalmining Women's Support Team, Joyce Miller of the United Auto Workers, the Coalition of Labor Union Women, and other blue-collar women made the staff at the Institute realized that sexual conduct was "one of many tools that men use to create a hostile working environment when they want to keep women out."[8] As a national clearinghouse for information about sexual harassment, the Institute brought together the insights of the diverse array of women around the country working on sexual harassment.

Like WWI, AASC in Cambridge also expanded their activities in the late 1970s.[9] The Alliance was supported by literature sales, fees from training and consulting, and a few small grants. Lynn Wehrli and Liz Cohn-Stuntz left the organization early on, but many others joined AASC, some of whom initially came to the organization as clients.[10] By 1980, AASC had two paid staff members, Lynn Rubinett and Denise Wells, who were funded through a Comprehensive Employment Training Act grant. Lynn Rubinett had graduated from Stanford University in 1979, where she had been involved in feminist and leftist political activism. In Boston, she worked in the women's section for the socialist bookstore, Redbook. Rubinett, who identified herself as a Marxist feminist and focused on labor issues, focused on the intersections between sex and economics, which drew her to the issue of sexual harassment. Denise Wells came from a working class background and was very concerned with issues of violence against women.

In the late 1970s, to reach a larger number of women, the Alliance decided to change its focus from providing direct services to women to promoting the incorporation of sexual harassment services into existing agencies, community centers, and working women's groups.[11] The Alliance began to provide sexual harassment training and information to social service workers, community mental health workers, job counselors, union personnel, and women's groups. For example, AASC helped form the Committee Against Sexual Harassment in Columbus, Ohio, as well as sexual harassment groups in Montreal and in Connecticut, and spoke frequently to NOW chapters and at NOW conferences about sexual harassment. When K.C. Wagner was starting WWI's counseling program in 1980, she traveled to Boston to train with Freada Klein. Alliance members sought to train social service workers to recognize when women seeking their assistance were experiencing sexual harassment and to provide some guidelines on how to handle the issue. To accomplish this goal, the Alliance published a training manual in 1979 for organizations providing services to sexual harassment victims, called *Fighting Sexual Harassment: An Advocacy Handbook*. This seventy-six-page handbook defined sexual harassment, provided strategies for outreach, offered staff training suggestions, explained how to counsel victims of harassment, and described victims' legal options. In addition to working with public interest and service organizations, the Alliance provided training and consultation on sexual harassment policies and grievance procedures to employers, schools, unions, and regulatory agencies. A 1979 *Business Week* article on sexual harassment quoting Freada Klein led to AASC's first corporate client, the State Street Bank in Boston.[12] In 1980, Klein served as an advisor to the first comprehensive scientific study of sexual harassment in the workplace, conducted by the United States Merit Systems Protection Board. Klein helped develop the questionnaire and the methodology. This led to a consulting contract with General Motors. Klein also testified several times before the Massachusetts legislature on bills relating to sexual harassment.

After the EEOC issued proposed sexual harassment guidelines in April 1980, the Alliance was flooded by requests for information about sexual harassment. Whereas before the EEOC guidelines requests had come primarily from sexually harassed women, feminists activists, and social change-oriented groups, after April 1980, the Alliance began receiving numerous requests for information and training materials from employers, consulting firms who wanted to conduct training for employers, and equal employment opportunity officers in the public sector, as well as requests for information from television and radio stations, magazines, and newspapers. AASC also worked to help unionize women concerned about sexual harassment. In 1979, AASC was involved in a successful campaign to organize secretaries at Boston University. In the campaign, sexual harassment was a key organizing issue, and AASC worked with the union members to obtain a sexual harassment clause in their union contract, one of the first in the nation. AASC was also involved in a campaign to organize clerical workers at Harvard. AASC's involvement in these two university organizing campaigns indicates that women workers considered sexual harassment to be an important issue, integral to workplace equity. This involvement also reflects AASC's broad class-based orientation to the empowerment of women.[13]

In the late 1970s and early 1980s, the Alliance produced many publications on sexual harassment, focusing on both theoretical analyses of sexual harassment and practical strategies to combat harassment. In 1979, in addition to publishing their advocacy handbook, the Alliance published several articles on sexual harassment in *Aegis*, including one on myths and facts about sexual harassment, one on how widespread sexual harassment was, and one on how to combat sexual harassment. Canadian Connie Backhouse, who worked with the Alliance during 1977 and 1978 while she was studying at Harvard Law School, published one of the first books on sexual harassment with fellow Canadian Leah Cohen, *The Secret Oppression: Sexual Harassment of Working Women*, focusing on sexual harassment in Canada. Also in 1979, the Alliance published a study of why men harass. In 1980, the Alliance published an annotated bibliography on sexual harassment and a handbook on how to establish grievance procedures for sexual harassment on college campuses. In 1981, the Alliance turned to sexual harassment in secondary schools, publishing a report on sexual harassment in Massachusetts's schools written by Alliance members Freada Klein and Nancy Wilber. Also in 1981, the Alliance published two handbooks on sexual harassment, one on the law of sexual harassment written by Alliance member Laurie Dubrow, and one on strategies to combat sexual harassment, which was republished in a condensed form in the journal *Radical America* and in *Aegis*. Alliance members continued to serve on the staff of the magazine *Aegis*, which consistently published news and analysis on sexual harassment by the Alliance and others throughout 1981. The Alliance also published two brochures on sexual harassment in Spanish.

Sexual harassment activism expanded beyond WWI and AASC in the late 1970s and early 1980s, with a broad array of organizations addressing the issue in new ways and in new contexts. The most active and influential public interest law firms working on the issue at the time were the WLDF in Washington, D.C., and ERA in San Francisco. WLDF was an early leader on sexual harassment. A WLDF volunteer, Linda Singer, represented Paulette Barnes in *Barnes v. Costle*, the first successful sexual harassment case in the federal appellate courts. WLDF litigated three other sexual harassment cases in the late 1970s and filed a friend-of-the-court brief in the first successful hostile environment sexual harassment case in the federal appellate courts. Attorney Donna Lenhoff became a spokeswoman for WLDF on the issue. Lenhoff, a graduate of University of Chicago and University of Pennsylvania Law School, worked from 1976 to 1978 as the Justice Department attorney in the Antitrust Division before becoming the first WLDF staff attorney. Lenhoff testified about sexual harassment at several government hearings and before the District of Columbia Commission on Women, where she recommended that "sexual activity obtained by threats against economic interests" be made a third degree sexual assault under the D.C. Criminal Code. WLDF and NOWLDEF teamed up to submit comments on the EEOC's proposed sexual harassment guidelines on behalf of several organizations. WLDF also worked to educate the public on the issue. Lenhoff often spoke to the press, including participating in a National Public Radio program on sexual harassment, and WLDF published a handbook on sexual harassment.[14]

Equal Rights Advocates also took a leadership role on sexual harassment. In addition to representing Margaret Miller in her appeal in *Miller v. Bank of America* and filing a friend-of-the-court brief in *Tomkins v. Public Service Electric and Gas*, ERA filed friend-of-the-court briefs in *Alexander v. Yale* and in the first Supreme Court case on sexual harassment, *Meritor Savings Bank v. Vinson*. In the early 1980s, ERA submitted comments on the EEOC's 1980 sexual harassment guidelines and litigated several sexual harassment cases. ERA regularly addressed sexual harassment in their newsletter, *Equal Rights Advocate*. In early 1981, ERA established a sexual harassment project, consisting of three components: legal advice and counseling, community education and outreach, and advocacy and legal representation.[15] Other public interest law firms active in the fight against sexual harassment were the Women's Justice Center in Detroit, MI, the Center Against Sexual Harassment of the Women's Legal Clinic in Los Angeles, Women Employed Institute in Chicago, the National Organization for Women Legal Advocacy and Education Fund, ACLU's Women's Rights Project, and the National Employment Law Project, all located in New York City. In addition, many women's groups began to provide counseling and referral services to sexually harassed women and published guides about sexual harassment.[16]

Many women's political and workplace organizations worked on sexual harassment in the late 1970s. New Responses, a nonprofit public policy group in Washington, D.C., focused on violence against women and children, conducting research and training on sexual harassment. In 1978, New Responses published a fact sheet on sexual harassment and, in 1979, published a report on sexual harassment in federal employment based on a sample survey of 198 federal employees within the Department of Health, Education and Welfare, the Department of Justice, and the General Services Administration. The report revealed significant levels of harassment. New Responses' Director, Mary Ann Largen, testified about this survey in 1979 at congressional hearings on sexual harassment in the federal government. In 1980, New Responses published a guide for sexually harassed women and a counselor's guide to sexual harassment.[17] Other organizations working on sexual harassment included the National Women's Political Caucus, the Center for Women's Policy Studies, the National Council of Jewish Women, and the Cleveland-based Working Women Organizing Project, and Working Women, National Association of Office Workers, which supported the making of the popular 1980 movie addressing sexual harassment, *Nine to Five*, with Jane Fonda, Dolly Parton, and Lily Tomlin.

One of the most prominent political organizations to work on sexual harassment was NOW. At NOW's 1979 annual conference, the membership adopted a resolution stating that NOW would support litigation to establish a clear cut precedent that sexual harassment was sex discrimination under Title VII, that they would "evaluate the feasibility" of introducing legislation in Congress to explicitly prohibit sexual harassment under Title VII, and that they would develop projects for local NOW groups to publicize the issue and aid victims. This resolution supported the advocacy activities of NOW's Legal Defense and Education Fund, which filed a friend-of-the-court brief in one of the first successful co-worker hostile environment cases, *Continental Can Co. v. Minnesota*, in 1980, and litigated several other sexual harassment cases. NOWLDEF conducted a media campaign to raise awareness about sexual harassment and, in 1981, established a sexual harassment education project, headed by Anne Simon, which provided information and resources on sexual harassment.[18] At the local level, NOW chapters became active on the issue. In Reading, Pennsylvania, a local NOW chapter provided legal assistance in the sexual harassment case of Kristi Fey Napoleon, who was denied unemployment compensation after leaving her job when her boss sexually harassed her. In Fresno, California, the local NOW chapter teamed up with the Fresno City-County Commission on the Status of Women to conduct a survey of sexual harassment in city and county government. The Brooklyn Chapter of NOW submitted comments on the EEOC's proposed sexual harassment guidelines. The Big Sandy Chapter of NOW in Paintsville, Kentucky, sponsored a conference on sexual harassment, with representatives from the Kentucky Commission on Human Rights, the Coal Employment Project, and the Commission on Women.[19]

Many local groups around the country worked on sexual harassment in the late 1970s, including the Task Force on Sexual Harassment in Harrisburg, PA,[20] Action Against Sexual Harassment in Employment and Education in Madison, Wisconsin, and Women Organized for Employment in San Francisco.[21] In New York City, Women for Racial & Economic Equality (WREE) focused on sexual harassment of blue-collar women. WREE's Clearinghouse on Blue Collar Women surveyed blue-collar women about sexual harassment in 1978 and advocated for a broad understanding of affirmative action that incorporated retention and harassment.[22] In Columbus, Ohio, the Committee Against Sexual Harassment (CASH), affiliated with the Columbus YWCA, worked on sexual harassment in the workplace and in academic settings. Run by volunteers, CASH provided advice and support to victims of sexual harassment, consulted with employers and other organizations to develop policies and procedures, conducted informational seminars and workshops, and published a pamphlet on sexual harassment in 1981.[23] In New York City, Women Office Workers continued to work on sexual harassment. At a WOW conference in the spring of 1978, the sexual harassment workshop was the most popular of all the workshops.[24] In addition, several state

FIGURE 5.2. Sexual Harassment Protest, New York City, 1979. Photo by Bettye Lane

commissions on women worked on sexual harassment, including in Michigan, Washington, D.C., California, Kentucky, Illinois, and Pennsylvania. In Kentucky, the Commission on Women published a handbook on sexual harassment and the Kentucky Commission on Human Rights published a brochure and a technical assistance guide on sexual harassment for employers and women.[25]

One of the most expansive local efforts to combat sexual harassment occurred in Philadelphia. In 1977, a group of working women in the Delaware Valley formed the Interfaith Project on Working Women, later called Women's Alliance for Job Equity (WAJE), to study and improve the conditions of working women. In 1979, the Executive Director of WAJE, Robin Robinowitz, created a Sexual Harassment Prevention Program. The Program provided group and individual counseling, offered information and support to people filing

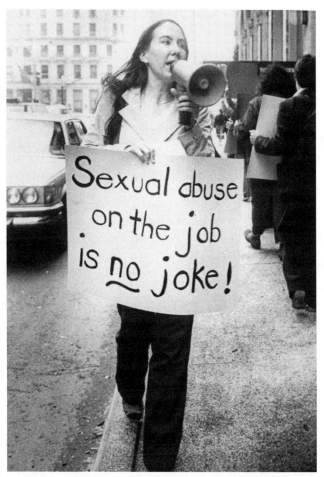

FIGURE 5.3. Sexual Harassment Protest, New York City, 1980. Photo by Bettye Lane

sexual harassment cases, conducted educational seminars on sexual harassment for workers, employers, and students, and publicized particular cases of sexual harassment. The group used humorous publicity stunts to gain media attention for their cases, like presenting an Equal Opportunity Stupidity Award – a frilly four-foot "Susie Sexpot" doll – to men who discriminated against and sexually harassed their female employees. In May of 1980, WAJE's Pamela Chilton trained the entire staff of the Philadelphia Commission on Human Relations on how to recognize sexual harassment and investigate complaints under federal law. WAJE, along with the Women's Law Project in Philadelphia, helped establish and participated on the City of Philadelphia's Task Force on Sexual Harassment, which persuaded the city to adopt the EEOC's sexual harassment guidelines for employers in the city. Then WAJE conducted a public relations campaign to educate women and businesses in the city about the new legislation. With the District Attorney's office, WAJE set up a referral system for women who were assaulted on their jobs and won a highly publicized lawsuit against a local chiropractor.[26]

In addition to the activism of organizations, several of the early plaintiffs in sexual harassment cases spoke out publicly, which gave the issue a human face and further increased the movement's visibility. These women told their stories to the print media, on television and radio, and at government hearings investigating sexual harassment. For example, Diane Williams appeared in a 1976 television documentary on sexual harassment. In 1977, one of the early sexual harassment plaintiffs, Adrienne Tomkins, testified at the *Ms.* speak-out and appeared on the *Phil Donahue Show* with Susan Meyer and Karen Sauvigné. On that show she explained, "I'm here because I think it's very important to speak out.... We do have rights. We are human beings." In 1979, *Newsweek* published a story on Adrienne Tomkins. In 1981, Tomkins and Diane Williams appeared on a *National Public Radio* program on sexual harassment. Both women also testified at congressional hearings on sexual harassment. Other sexual harassment plaintiffs also spoke out. In 1978 in Michigan, sexual harassment plaintiff Maxine Munford sparked a statewide movement against sexual harassment by speaking out about her experiences of harassment. She made appearances on Michigan radio and television talk shows and later testified at public hearings on sexual harassment. Sandra Bundy, who won the first hostile environment sexual harassment case, testified at congressional hearings on sexual harassment, spoke to the media about her case, and inspired D.C. Mayor Marion Barry to act on the issue. These early sexual harassment plaintiffs who spoke out about the issue contributed significantly toward the increased awareness of sexual harassment.[27]

Following the lead of the women at Yale, women on college campuses around the country also began to address sexual harassment. The issue aroused great controversy in 1979 on the campus of University of California at Berkeley when thirteen female students accused assistant professor of sociology Elbaki Hermassi of sexual harassment. In response to this case, students formed Women Organized Against Sexual Harassment (WOASH), which generated publicity for the case by holding public forums and press conferences and leafleting the campus to find more victims. WOASH, with the help of the Bay Area Women Against Rape hotline and legal assistance from Equal Rights Advocates provided counseling and advice to sexual harassment victims. In 1979, WOASH filed a Title IX complaint with the Department of Health, Education, and Welfare on behalf of six sexually harassed students against Professor Hermassi. In the same year, WOASH and ERA jointly filed a friend-of-the-court brief in 1979 in the appeal of *Alexander v. Yale.* WOASH also published a pamphlet on sexual harassment and developed model grievance procedures for sexual harassment at educational institutions.[28]

Antisexual harassment groups began to appear at schools around the country, including the Coalition Against Sexual Harassment at the University of Minnesota,[29] Women Against Campus Harassment at the University of

Wisconsin, Students Against Sexual Harassment at the University of Massa-chusetts, the Sexual Harassment Committee at the University of Rhode Island, Women Against Sexual Harassment at Arizona State University in Mesa, Arizona,[30] and the Sexual Harassment Task Force at California State University in Sacramento. In New York City, acting students sexually abused by Paul Mann formed Artists for Responsible Theater and held a speak-out on teacher/student violence and sexual harassment in June of 1980.[31] Surveys conducted at several universities in the late 1970s revealed high rates of sexual harassment of students and employees.[32] Other universities faced sexual harassment complaints, including San Jose State University and Harvard University.

Groups opposing sexual harassment began to work in elementary and secondary schools as well. As early as 1978, a group called Stop Sexual Abuse of Students, part of the Chicago Public Education Project of the American Friends Service Committee in Chicago, IL, focused on sexual harassment and abuse in elementary and secondary schools, gathering data on the incidence and scope of the problem and operating two 24-hour hotlines for crisis counseling and referrals. In Massachusetts, the State Department of Education commissioned AASC members Freada Klein and Nancy Wilbur to study sexual harassment in Massachusetts schools. Nan Stein developed the first curriculum on sexual harassment in schools in 1979 and also conducted the first survey in the country on peer-to-peer sexual harassment in schools in 1980.[33]

Several national educational organizations began to work on sexual harassment, putting pressure on government and institutions to address the issue. These groups conducted studies, published reports and advice books, and held seminars on sexual harassment in education. The National Advisory Council on Women's Educational Programs, a presidentially appointed body established by Congress to advise and report on attaining sex equity in education, published a paper in 1978 on university liability for sexual harassment. In 1979, the Council issued a call for information on the sexual harassment of students. The Council advertised in *National NOW Times*, requesting information from former and present victims about their experiences and from any others who may have knowledge of harassment. In August 1980, the Council published a report, which was the first attempt to examine the problem on a large scale. The report made policy recommendations for how the federal government could assist in protecting students from being sexually harassed by faculty, staff, or other employees of secondary education institutions. In the early 1980s, the Council and many other organizations urged the Department of Education's Office for Civil Rights to issue guidelines on sexual harassment, but to no avail.[34]

Another significant national organization working on sexual harassment at educational institutions was the Association of American Colleges' Project on the Status and Education of Women, directed by Bernice Resnick Sandler. In 1978, the Project published a paper defining sexual harassment, explaining the law, offering advice to educational institutions on how to deal with sexual harassment, and providing a list of organizations working on the issue. In 1980, the Project published a paper on the legal aspects of sexual harassment. The Project also regularly addressed sexual harassment in its newsletter, *On Campus with Women.* [35] Other groups working on the issue were the Office of Women for the American Council on Education, which held a series of seminars across the country on sexual harassment policy in 1979, the Modern Language Association of America's Commission on the Status of Women in the Profession, which published a guide on sexual and gender harassment in the academy, and the American Psychological Association's Division of Psychology of Women, which established a task force to investigate the problem of sexual harassment of students and to make recommendations to address the issue. In 1980, the American Association of University Professors adopted a resolution urging each local chapter to work with its institution to develop and strengthen policies prohibiting sexual harassment on campus.[36] The movement against sexual harassment was able to mobilize through existing women's movement organizations.

These efforts to combat sexual harassment in education pressured school administrators around the country to address the issue of sexual harassment. Many schools began to conduct studies of sexual harassment on their campuses, publish these studies, and adopt policies and procedures to address the problem. Rutgers University was one of the first schools to prohibit sexual harassment. On February 5, 1979, President Edward J. Bloustein issued a memorandum to all university personnel stating that the school "deplores" sexual harassment as an abuse of authority. He defined sexual harassment to be a supervisor or faculty member imposing a requirement of sexual cooperation as a condition of employment or academic advancement. In July of 1980, Rutgers issued procedures for handling sexual harassment complaints, in which the University broadened its definition of sexual harassment to include hostile environment sexual harassment. The Rutgers policy was widely circulated as an example of administrative leadership on the issue. Brown University, University of Washington, University of Louisville, Tulane University, and Stanford were also at the forefront in adopting policies against sexual harassment.[37]

FEMINIST THEORY ON SEXUAL HARASSMENT

This growing movement generated a body of theory about sexual harassment, which drew primarily upon radical feminist analysis of patriarchy and violence against women, but also on the civil rights movement's analysis of racial discrimination and harassment and a leftist analysis of exploitative labor relations of capitalism. Many feminists argued that sexual harassment was an issue of violence against women. They borrowed from antirape theory the idea that rape was a matter of power, not sex, and applied this perspective to sexual harassment, arguing that sexual harassment was primarily motivated by men's desire to control women. AASC member Mary Bularzik argued that sexual harassment was like rape and wife-beating because it was "consistent, systemic, and pervasive, not a set of random isolated acts." Bularzik described violence against women, including sexual harassment, as a "mechanism of social control" central to male oppression of women and as a social phenomenon, not an individual interaction. She argued, "the license to harass women workers, which many men feel they have, stems from notions that there is a 'woman's place,' which women in the labor force have left, thus leaving behind their personal integrity." The purpose of harassment, she argued, was to preserve male dominance and patriarchy.[38] AASC argued that sexual harassment must be understood within the broader climate of violence in American culture, especially against women, including forcible rape, wife abuse, unwanted sterilization, abusive advertising, pornography, and the institutionalization of women. They argued that harassers, rapists, and batterers were not "psychologically aberrant misfits" but were "responding 'logically' to cultural forces, which encourage their violence," like the media and male peer groups. They explained, "men are socialized to dominate women through the use and threat of violent behavior."[39] They argued that men engage in workplace harassment in order to assert power over women who are economically threatening and that they marginalized women in the workplace through the threat of violence.[40]

Feminists often analogized sexual harassment to rape, an issue that had already galvanized women around the country. In a 1975 article in *Sister Courage*, feminist activist Rochelle Leftkowitz commented that "like rape, sexual harassment is an abuse of male power … like rape, all women are its potential victims."[41] In 1977, WWUI stated, "the parallels between rape and sexual harassment are many. WWUI sees sexual harassment on the job as economic rape because it relies on economic force to extract sexual 'cooperation.'"[42] In the first government hearings on sexual harassment in 1979, several women testifying made parallels between rape and sexual harassment. Mary Largen of New Responses, Inc., argued that women who complain of sexual harassment find themselves in the same position as women who report rape: they are disbelieved and ignored, their credibility is challenged, or their complaints trivialized.[43] Catharine MacKinnon argued, "economic power is to sexual harassment as physical force is to rape."[44]

Feminists differed, however, in their analysis of the causes of sexual harassment. Some focused primarily on patriarchy and male dominance as the cause. For example, in the first book published on sexual harassment, the 1978 book *Sexual Shakedown*, Lin Farley argued that sexual harassment originated with patriarchal relations. She argued that "sexual harassment of women at work arose out of man's need to maintain his control of female labor."[45] Like Farley, Working Women's Institute publications argued that inequality between women and men in the workplace and in society was the basic cause of sexual harassment.[46] The Institute maintained that sexual harassment was rooted in the social subordination of women to men manifested by sex segregation in the labor force, unequal pay, and limited opportunities for advancement for women. In addition, they argued that men harass women because of cultural stereotypes about proper sex roles, and this led men to treat women workers as "sexual beings first and as breadwinners second."[47] Peggy Crull expanded this analysis by suggesting that men harass not only because they have the power and can but also because they do *not* have power or fear losing it. Noting high rates of sexual harassment in nontraditional jobs where women have obtained similar status to men, Crull argued that men in these jobs feel that their power at work is threatened, so they use sexual harassment as a way of "subduing women" or driving them out altogether. As opposed to an "overflow" of power, this is an "attempt to regain waning power" and "restore women to traditional roles through the use of sexual intimidation."[48]

By contrast, other early theorists offered an explicitly intersectional analysis of sexual harassment. AASC publications, in particular, criticized the "structures of power" that perpetuated sexual harassment – capitalism, sexism, racism, heterosexism, and ageism.[49] They argued that male power and class power mutually reinforced each other to create a situation in which men were socially and psychologically dominant. In the November/December 1978 issue of *Aegis* magazine, Alliance members Martha Hooven and Nancy McDonald argued that the conditions of work under capitalism, which gave women little autonomy or control, were a factor in women's vulnerability to sexual harassment. They argued that capitalism "feeds" on sexism and racism. In the May/June 1979 issue of *Aegis*, an article reprinted from *Hammer House*, the newspaper of the International Association of Machinists in Wichita, Kansas, attacked capitalism, calling on all workers to fight harassment and pointing out the class interests of employers in women's oppression. To charges that issues such as sexual harassment divide the working class, the Alliance responded that male workers did not ultimately benefit from harassing their female counterparts because sexual harassment kept female wages low, thereby creating a cheap and expendable labor force that threatened the bargaining power and strength of male workers.[50] In another early book published on sexual harassment, *The Secret Oppression: Sexual Harassment of Working Women*, AASC members Connie Backhouse and Leah Cohen located the roots of this behavior in both patriarchy and capitalism. They criticized both the sexual objectification of women and the traditional, hierarchical structure of the workplace, calling for sexual equality and "industrial democracy."[51]

These different feminist perspectives openly clashed in a 1979 exchange between Freada Klein and Lin Farley in the magazine *Aegis* when Klein criticized Farley for focusing exclusively on patriarchy as the cause of sexual harassment and ignoring class and race. According to Klein, Farley ignored the "complexities of sexual harassment" by identifying patriarchy as the "ultimate source of sexual harassment" and failing to "sort out under what conditions sex, race, or class each become the most conspicuous form of oppression."[52] Klein argued that patriarchy and capitalism reinforced each other in the phenomena of workplace harassment and that racism had a major role in the origins of working women's problems. In the next issue of *Aegis*, Farley defended her emphasis on patriarchal relations as the source of sexual harassment, noting that "the idea that capitalism itself somehow came up with the idea of sexual harassment is absurd."[53] She argued that capitalism had in fact threatened male control of women by creating a free labor market in which women competed with men. In response, male trade unions gained control of the majority of occupations by systematically denying women training and isolating them into a few occupations. Men then used sexual harassment to maintain job segregation. According to Farley, this "periodic push-pull between capitalism and the patriarchy" had frequently happened and was happening in 1978.

Feminists also differed as to their views on how most effectively to combat sexual harassment. Feminists generally looked to legal solutions to the problem. WWI, in particular, supported the development of legal avenues of relief by their attorney referral network and brief bank. AASC also advocated legal solutions, but was much more skeptical about what might be achieved through the law. The Alliance emphasized that women should not rely exclusively on grievance procedures and legal remedies developed by employers and governments but should act collectively to combat sexual harassment. As governments and employers became involved on the issue of sexual harassment in the early 1980s, the Alliance expressed skepticism about government solutions and employers' motivations. The Alliance argued that government solutions did not serve women well because they were bureaucratic and legalistic. Employer concern with sexual harassment, they suggested, stemmed not from a desire to help women but rather was an attempt to avoid lawsuits, lowered productivity, and unionization of workers.[54] The Alliance warned that government and management initiatives against sexual harassment might co-opt women's collective action to challenge the "root cause of sexual harassment – sexism."[55]

The Alliance sought not only to combat sexual harassment but also to help women take "positive steps toward gaining more control over other aspects of their lives." They emphasized the importance that women become "*active* participants" by "learning to join together and speak out against the exploitative aspects of their lives."[56] They encouraged women to take the situation into their own hands and make choices about their tactics, not give up control of the situation to an outside investigator or agency, or rely on employers to solve the problem.[57] They suggested tactics such as talking to other women in the workplace, placing leaflets in bathrooms, publicizing the name of the harasser, surveying the workplace, forming a workplace safety committee, sending a warning letter to the harasser or the employer, or conducting an educational picket in front of a workplace.[58] The Alliance also warned that employers might use sexual harassment as a tool for selective punishment of certain employees, such as members of unions or racial minorities.[59] The Alliance did not completely reject legal strategies to combat sexual harassment but argued that these strategies should "exist alongside other strategies that focus on education and organization of women to take power in their homes and their jobs."[60]

Activists often theorized about the role of race in sexual harassment. When African-American women spoke out about sexual harassment, they frequently emphasized the importance of their race to their experiences of harassment. In a May 1976 newspaper article on Diane Williams' successful sexual harassment case, Maudine Rice Cooper argued that African-American women were particularly vulnerable to sexual harassment. Citing statistics showing the economic vulnerability of African-American women, Cooper stated that sexual harassment was an issue of unique importance to African-American women: "Historically, Black women, who were slaves in their master's homes, have been slaves in their own homes and, in many instances, in their work environment as well [and they] have more often been subjected to sexual harassment than have white women dating to the time of slavery in this country." She also criticized African-American men for "turning the other cheek to the plight of Black women, or even becoming willing participants in the humiliation, degradation, and harassment of Black women," referring to the fact that the harasser in the *Williams* case was an African-American man. [61]

In the Yale case, Pamela Price emphasized the importance of both her race and gender to her experiences of harassment. In a statement issued in December 1977, she argued that "I was subjected to the assumption of my inferiority as a black person as well as the assumption of my lack of seriousness as a woman."[62] She argued that the poor grade she received after rejecting her professor's sexual advances was a "concrete expression of his racist and sexist appraisal of me as a person."[63] In a press release after the trial court ruled against her, Price expressed her belief that race was critical to the disposition of the case:

It's the same old story. Where sex is concerned, black women's accusations are considered lies and white men's denials are believed. Unfortunately, the trial, which was presided over by a [white] woman, was merely another manifestation of the racism and sexism pervasive in society and reflected in its laws. It is symbolic that I entered this case primarily because I am a woman and lost it primarily because I am a black woman. But that is all the more reason for us to continue to fight back against all forms of oppression.[64]

Price argued that her race and sex were inextricably linked and shaped the legal system's treatment of her claims.

The first scholarly treatment of race and sexual harassment was a 1981 article by EEOC attorney Judy Trent Ellis, who later became the first African-American Professor of Law at SUNY Buffalo. The article, entitled "Sexual Harassment and Race: A Legal Analysis of Discrimination," appeared in the *Journal of Legislation*. Ellis argued that racial and sexual harassment have the same underpinnings insofar as they are "both an expression of dominance and control by one group over another and a process of intimidation to maintain a certain social structure."[65] But Ellis argued for an analytical distinction between sexual harassment based on sexual exploitation and generalized sex-based harassment, which parallels racial harassment. The former involved pressure upon a woman for sexual favors with an implicit or explicit statement that noncompliance will jeopardize her employment. The latter involved ridicule, intimidation, or degradation, and often involved open hostility based on the victim's racial or sexual identity. Ellis argued that while racial harassment is easy to understand, sexually exploitative harassment lacked a ready framework for analysis and was often difficult to distinguish from flirtation. She noted that the "normalcy of male-female sexual interaction and the 'normalcy' of male aggression and dominance cloud the issue."[66] According to Ellis, this distinction was useful because some principles developed in racial harassment cases, although helpful in resolving generalized sex-based harassment complaints, may be inappropriate when applied to sexual exploitation harassment. For example, the rule that the plaintiff's case is weakened if several people do not complain of harassment should not apply to sexually exploitative harassment because this form of harassment was often directed at just one victim, as opposed to generalized harassment, which was often directed at a group. Finally, Ellis argued that African-American women were often harassed due to both race and sex, "either implicitly, so that the woman is unsure whether the harassment is racially or sexually motivated, or explicitly, where the harasser expressed his sexual interest in terms of her race," and therefore they should not be foreclosed from defining harassment in terms of race and sex discrimination.[67]

The most in-depth theoretical and legal analysis of sexual harassment was published in 1979 – Catharine MacKinnon's *Sexual Harassment of Working Women*. MacKinnon's book, drafts of which she circulated among feminists working on sexual harassment, had a significant influence on the development of legal thinking about sexual harassment. MacKinnon created terms to describe two "categories" of behavior – *quid pro quo* and condition of work sexual harassment, and suggested differing legal standards for each category. *Quid pro quo* harassment she defined as a situation where "the woman must comply sexually or forfeit an employment benefit." The second category, condition of work sexual harassment (later called hostile environment harassment), included less direct sexual behavior where the woman was "never promised or denied anything explicitly connected with her job" but which made her work environment unbearable.[68] In her analysis, MacKinnon frequently compared race and sex discrimination and analogized sexual harassment and racial harassment.

MacKinnon's primary argument was that sexual harassment was sex discrimination. She distinguished two prevailing theories of sex discrimination: the differences approach and the inequality approach. The differences approach sought to achieve equality by applying "the formula that 'similarly situated' persons should be treated the same, meaning that persons in relevantly similar circumstances should be treated relevantly similarly." The less commonly applied sex inequality theory, based on the understanding that sex discrimination was the systematic domination of women by men, asked "whether the policy or practice in question integrally contributes to the maintenance of an underclass or a deprived position because of gender status."

MacKinnon argued that sexual harassment was sex discrimination under both theories, but that the differences theory was inadequate. Under the differences approach, sexual harassment was sex discrimination because men and women were comparable with regard to sexual harassment (both sexes can be sexually harassed) but the sexes were not treated the same (women were harassed more). MacKinnon argued that this approach was inadequate because it presumed equality to measure disparity, and it ignored the fact that the sexes were in fact substantially unequal. On the other hand, under the inequality approach, sexual harassment was sex discrimination because sexual harassment expressed and reinforced women's social inequality to men.[69] MacKinnon argued that sexual harassment was not merely an individual injury but group-based discrimination that harmed all women by reinforcing women's subordinate status in the workplace. She argued that sex segregation in the workplace and male control of hiring and firing made women systematically vulnerable to sexual harassment. Like Farley, MacKinnon focused on patriarchal gender relations to explain sexual harassment, but she also discussed the significance of race and class to women's experience of harassment.[70]

In the late 1970s, activists drew upon analytical developments in the women's movement, particularly the antirape movement, black feminist thought, and socialist feminism, to frame sexual harassment as a gendered abuse of power and, in a preliminary way, to analyze how gender, race, and class intersected in women's experiences of sexual harassment.[71] Feminists then attempted to shape public discussions of this issue using this framework.

MEDIA COVERAGE OF SEXUAL HARASSMENT

In the early 1970s, when feminist organizations were some of the only sources on sexual harassment, the media regularly turned to them for help in understanding the issue, which they covered with increasing frequency. Media coverage reflected a broad range of attitudes toward sexual harassment, from trivializing the issue to treating it as a matter of serious concern. The movement's gendered framing of the issue, including the feminist understandings of sexual harassment as a form of male dominance and abuse of women, appeared in many early media reports of sexual harassment. The press even covered sexual harassment of blue-collar women. Feminists were often quoted prominently and feminist surveys cited. The movement aggressively pursued press coverage in order to spread the word and recruit new members. And indeed, press coverage raised public awareness of sexual harassment, leading more women to resist sexually harassing behavior. While Enid Nemy's August 1975 article in the *New York Times* and the January 1976 article on sexual harassment in the *Wall Street Journal* broke the ice in mainstream news reporting of sexual harassment, by the end of the 1970s, the issue had appeared in a broad array of national and local newspapers and magazines.[72] The issue appeared most often in women's magazines such as *Harper's Bazaar, Redbook, Ladies Home Journal, Ms., Essence, McCall's, Good Housekeeping,*

Mademoiselle, Working Women, and *Glamour.* But the issue also appeared frequently in news periodicals such as the *New York Times,* the *Washington Post, Business Week, Newsweek, Time Magazine,* and the *Nation.*[73] Periodical indexes reflect the growing media coverage. The *Reader's Guide* established a "Sex in Business" category beginning in 1976–1977 and created an additional category, "Sexual Harassment," in 1979–1980. Several newspaper indexes listed articles on sexual harassment under the heading of "Sexism" until they created a heading on "Sexual Harassment," which the *Washington Post Index* did in 1979, the *Chicago Tribune, Los Angeles Times,* and *New York Times* indexes did in 1980, and the *Atlanta Constitution* index did in 1982. The *Wall Street Journal* listed sexual harassment articles under "Sexuality" through the mid-1980s.[74]

Unsympathetic media outlets often characterized sexual harassment as a matter of oversensitive women or busybody bureaucrats, such as Russell Baker's editorial on *Alexander v. Yale* in the *New York Times,* the scathingly critical editorial on sexual harassment in William F. Buckley's *National Review,* or the slew of editorials criticizing Judge Richey's decision in *Williams v. Saxbe.* Sexual harassment was also often characterized as a matter of office flirtation, as in a *Time Magazine* article called "Executive Sweet: Many Office Romeos Are Really Juliets," which described a study by Barbara Gutek and Charles Nakamura finding that many men reported being victims of sexual harassment. From the cartoon showing a man being chased around a desk by a woman with hearts floating around her head, to the concluding sentence that "as more women rise to supervisory positions, it will become harder to tell who is chasing who around the desk," the article trivialized the issue of sexual harassment by ignoring power differentials based on sex and the differential impact of workplace harassment on men and women.[75] A *Washington Post* op-ed expressed sarcastic confusion as to what was sexual harassment and questioned whether sexual harassment was really sex discrimination.[76] Several magazines published articles on "office romance," with little or no discussion of the potentially coercive nature of relationships between male bosses and female subordinates.[77] Often articles on sexual harassment appeared in the family, style, or social issues sections of newspapers and magazines.[78]

Even women's magazines sometimes lacked a critical perspective on the issue of sexual harassment, such as a 1976 article in *Harper's Bazaar,* which described sexual harassers as "office Romeos" and harassment as "office sex" or a "pass." The article's suggested solutions focused on female behavior: women were encouraged to dress modestly and be more assertive, including making eye contact, using authoritative body language, speaking with conviction, and not diluting the message by smiling.[79] As late as July 1979, *Working Woman* published an article that similarly assumed that assertiveness was an adequate solution to the problem of sexual harassment and discouraged legal solutions.[80] Several articles discussed sexual relations in the workplace or educational setting without addressing the underlying power dynamics.[81] In March 1980, an article in the *Ladies Home Journal* called "Love on the Job" discussed sexual relations between male bosses and female subordinates without explicitly discussing the issue of sexual harassment.[82] Similarly, an August 1976 *Ms.* article on allegations of sexual advances toward students by the women's track coach at UCLA did not discuss the situation as sexual harassment, nor did it mention the women's movement activism on the issue.[83]

Although some articles in women's magazines lacked a critical perspective on the problem of sexual harassment, most of their coverage in the late 1970s characterized the issue as a serious one that affected women working in a broad range of occupations. In the November 1976 issue of *Redbook*, an article by Claire Safran quoted extensively from a broad cross-section of women who had answered the magazine's January 1976 survey, including a legal secretary, a factory worker, and a college professor. Safran described the problem as "pandemic," occurring "in the executive suite, in the steno pool [and] on the assembly line." She reported that changing one's behavior or dress rarely worked and that women resented the implication that they were to blame. She argued, "Both sexes arrive at work lugging the emotional baggage of a lifetime, all the childhood teachings about what's masculine and what's feminine, the cultural myths and social reflexes that make men and women behave as they do toward each other. We've just begun to unpack that baggage, to look at it and try to replace the worn-out, obsolete bits and pieces."[84] Safran then suggested ways to handle sexual harassment, including legal avenues of relief. In April 1978, *Redbook* published a follow-up report on judicial and legislative developments on sexual harassment and described WWI, providing contact information.[85]

Many women's magazines challenged traditional gender roles in the context of discussions of sexual harassment. For example, the April 1978 issue of *Redbook* published an article by anthropologist Margaret Mead called "A Proposal: We Need Taboos on Sex at Work."[86] Mead recognized the power dynamics underlying sexual harassment, noting that "so many men use sex in so many ways as a weapon to keep down the women with whom they work." Locating the roots of sexual harassment in socialization, she noted, "at home and at school we still bring up boys to respond to the presence of women in outmoded ways." Mead argued that the law is not enough to change behavior, but that we must create a taboo against sex at work, similar to incest taboos, in order to root out sexual harassment in the workplace. Other women's magazines also published articles that condemned the gendered power dynamics underlying sexual harassment. In the June 1977 issue of *Ladies Home Journal*, feminist and *Ms.* editor Letty Cottin Pogrebin wrote an article analogizing rape and sexual harassment, which she described as "a virulent form of economic coercion practiced by men who have the power to hire or fire, promote or demote, give raises or deny them." She reported on the activities of WWUI, quoting Susan Meyer and Karen Sauvigné. She also quoted several women about their experiences of harassment, and then explained legal developments on the issue, noting that often "personal solutions count for nothing."[87]

Ms., the nation's premier feminist magazine of the day, gave the issue prominent and sympathetic treatment in its November 1977 cover story. Much of the issue, in fact, was dedicated to sexual harassment. In an in-depth story, Karen Lindsey told stories of sexual harassment from women in a broad range of jobs – an executive secretary, an advertising agent, an assembly-line worker, a medical administrator, a waitress, congressional aides, and a student, often quoting these women. She argued that those hardest hit by harassment were waitresses, clerical workers, and factory workers because they were economically vulnerable. Lindsey also explained the work of AASC and WWUI, discussed surveys of sexual harassment, reviewed legal developments on the issue, described the effects of harassment, and provided suggestions for how to deal with harassment. Lindsey criticized articles suggesting that women can control sexual harassment through their behavior. She concluded with a quotation from Freada Klein saying that sexual harassment was an issue of violence against women. The same issue of *Ms.* also had three other articles on sexual harassment, one on WWUI, one on AASC, and one on sexual harassment at the United Nations. The July 1978 issue of *Ms.* published numerous letters responding to the Lindsey article, in addition to an article on the sexual harassment lawsuit against Yale University. In November 1979, an article in *Ms.* on the first National Conference of Women Coal Miners discussed the pervasive sexual harassment suffered by women coal miners. *Ms.* continued to cover the issue in the 1980s.[88] This consistent coverage solidified sexual harassment as an important issue for the women's movement and contributed toward connecting women working on the issue, thereby creating the sense of a larger community concerned about the issue.

Even women's magazines that did not specifically address the abuse of power underlying sexual harassment still addressed the issue seriously, often drawing on the expertise of WWUI. The March 1977 issue of *McCall's* ran an article discussing the work of these organizations, quoting Freada Klein and Karen Sauvigné. The April 1978 issue of *Good Housekeeping* contained an article written by a secretary who described how she successfully confronted her boss after speaking with an EEOC counselor. An article in the April 1978 issue of *Family Circle* described the WWI survey and discussed legal avenues for relief from sexual harassment. In the fall of 1979 *Mademoiselle* and *Working Women* both had articles on how to deal with sexual harassment, quoting Karen Sauvigné and an ACLU attorney and describing the work of AASC and WWI. Even *Harper's Bazaar* had come around by August 1979 to the realization of the seriousness of sexual harassment when they ran an article about how sexual harassment was the number one biggest problem of working women.[89]

Newspapers and magazines geared toward a general audience often addressed sexual harassment seriously. The *New York Times* repeatedly reported on sexual harassment, particularly on the activities of WWUI. In October of 1977, the *New York Times* covered the speak-out on sexual harassment in New York City sponsored by *Ms.* and WWUI. In 1979, the *Times* published an article about Karen Sauvigné and Susan Meyer, describing their work with WWI. In 1980, the *Times* ran an article on the opening of WWI's National

Sexual Harassment Legal Backup Center. Many other newspapers around the country began to cover sexual harassment and discuss the work of WWUI as well. In March of 1980, *USA Today* and *Newsweek* published in-depth and relatively sympathetic articles on sexual harassment, extensively quoting feminist activists. In June of 1980, the *Richmond Times-Dispatch* published a four-part series on sexual harassment. The local magazine *Pittsburgh* ran a long article on sexual harassment in May of 1978, offering several suggestions for how to deal with it, including "organize and speak out [or] form a local chapter of the Alliance Against Sexual Coercion."[90] In particular, newspapers and magazines targeted at African-American communities closely covered developments on sexual harassment, including the *New York Amsterdam News*, *Jet*, and *Essence*.[91] A 1981 article in *Essence* emphasized how black women were in the forefront of the movement against sexual harassment.[92]

Often the press coverage focused on legal developments. In June 1978, *Mother Jones* published an article on workplace sexual harassment called "Sexual Harassment: The Executive's Alternative to Rape," focusing on Diane Williams' case.[93] In April 1979, *Newsweek* reported on Adrienne Tomkins' case.[94] In 1979, the *Washington Post* had extensive coverage of legal developments related to sexual harassment, especially the events leading up to the first Congressional hearings on sexual harassment in the fall of 1979. Several newspapers and magazines ran stories on cases of sexual harassment of students at educational institutions.[95] The *New York Times* published several articles on developments in *Alexander v. Yale*, which *Time Magazine* covered as well, and the *Nation* published an in-depth article on the Yale case in January of 1978.[96]

Magazines targeting business audiences tended to focus on the legal aspects of sexual harassment, particularly on how to avoid corporate liability, but they also discussed resources for dealing with the problem, often mentioning WWI and AASC. One business periodical, *Across the Board*, provided one of the earliest in-depth discussions of the issue in April 1977. The article argued that the real issue behind sexual harassment was not sex itself, but power in which sexual abuse and coercion were means by which men socially and economically exploited women in the work force. In October 1979, *Business Week* had two articles on sexual harassment, one discussing legal cases and one discussing how to handle harassment, mentioning WWI, AASC, and several other groups that helped women troubled by sexual harassment.[97]

Sexual harassment of blue-collar women received attention not only in women's magazines but also in mainstream newspapers and magazines, especially toward the end of the decade when women were first breaking into non-traditional blue-collar occupations in significant numbers. In August 1977, the *New York Times* reported on new Labor Department regulations designed to facilitate women's entrance into the construction industry, including a requirement that contractors "ensure and maintain a working environment free of harassment, intimidation and coercion." In 1978, the *Los Angeles Times* reported on sexual harassment of women in the construction industry. An August 1979 article appearing in the magazine *Coal Age* provided the first in-depth article addressing sexual harassment of female coal miners. Soon many other newspapers were covering sexual harassment of women coal miners, including the *New York Times, Washington Post,* and *Baltimore Sun.* In 1981, the *Village Voice* ran a long article on sexual harassment of women coal miners. In 1980, the *Richmond Times* reported about sexual harassment of women in several nontraditional jobs, including mining, manufacturing, carpentry, and construction. Sexual harassment in the military also received much media attention.[98] Despite this coverage, the press tended to focus primarily on "sexual" harassment by supervisors rather than on hostile sex-based harassment by co-workers – a tendency, which neglected experiences arguably more characteristic of blue-collar women, especially those in nontraditional fields. Furthermore, there was rarely any discussion of the significance of race in the media coverage of sexual harassment, and the media illustrations generally portrayed victims to be young, attractive, white females in office settings, reflecting the race and class biases of the media.

In addition to appearing in print media, coverage of the issue of sexual harassment began to appear on radio and television programming. As early as 1976, documentaries about sexual harassment appeared on television. In the late 1970s, the *Phil Donahue Show* and *McNeil-Lehrer Report* did shows on sexual harassment. In 1979, Lin Farley and Gloria Steinem together made a film about sexual harassment. In 1980, Ed Asner teamed up with Lin Farley to create a documentary film about sexual harassment, which addressed a variety of work settings including clerical, construction, and service. Asner described sexual harassment as an abuse of power, commenting that "men have used their gender and their sexuality as symbols of their power in society" and that "women want to separate sexuality and work to improve both." The documentary won awards at both the San Francisco and New York Film Festivals. In 1981, *National Public Radio* produced a program on sexual harassment called *Beware of the Boss: Sexual Harassment on the Job* by Katherine Davis. Davis interviewed activists against sexual harassment, including WWI's Susan Meyer, WLDF's Donna Lenhoff, and NOW's Beatrice Dorne, as well as sexual harassment plaintiffs Adrienne Tomkins and Diane Williams. Davis also interviewed a broad range of sexual harassment victims, including a construction worker, a doctor, a domestic worker, a clerical worker, and an electrician. The program highlighted how men used sexual harassment as a weapon to discourage women and force them to quit. According to one woman interviewed, men use sexual harassment to keep women from "invading the boys' club."[99]

This issue of sexual harassment even appeared in movies and television sitcoms, contributing to a broader awareness of the issue and reinforcing feminist views on the issue. The 1980 hit movie *Nine to Five,* produced by Jane Fonda's IPC Films and starring Dolly Parton, Lily Tomlin, and Fonda, brought sexual harassment before a popular audience. In this zany comedy, Parton played an attractive secretary who had to fend off a lecherous boss. Her co-workers, played by Tomlin and Fonda, at first believed that Parton was using her sex appeal to get ahead but soon realized that she was tormented by her boss's advances. The three women, sharing their fantasies of revenge, conspired to kidnap the boss. In his absence, they ran the company so effectively that he was fired and the women were all promoted. The movie was inspired by Karen Nussbaum, a clerk-typist in Cleveland who was an old friend of Fonda's from the antiwar movement. Nussbaum was involved in organizing women office workers through a national network called Working Women, The National Association of Office Workers. The movie's theme song *Nine to Five*, sung by Dolly Parton, was nominated for an Academy Award for best original song and won a People's Choice Award for favorite motion picture song in 1981. The movie was nominated for several Golden Globe awards and a Writers Guild of America Screen Award. The movie was immensely popular, and even twenty-five years later is one of the all-time best grossing movies at United States box offices.[100] It was even made into a television series. In 1982, CBS produced a television movie, starring Cheryl Ladd and Ned Beatty, about a woman who was harassed and humiliated when she sought employment as a coal miner in order to support her young son and ailing father.[101] The issue of sexual harassment was also incorporated into the television situation comedy "One Day at a Time." By the early 1980s, media coverage had significantly raised public awareness of sexual harassment.

Media coverage of sexual harassment in the 1970s reflected feminist understandings of sexual harassment as a widespread and serious problem for women, with significant physical, emotional, and financial repercussions. Feminists' gendered framing of the issue influenced media coverage, which often focused on power imbalances between men and women and how sexual harassment both reflected and reinforced male dominance in the workplace and in society generally. Although some of the more radical feminist arguments never appeared in mainstream discussions of sexual harassment, such as the Alliance's analysis of the roots of sexual harassment in capitalism and racism, media coverage nevertheless raised awareness of sexual harassment and provided a powerful medium for feminists to influence public discussions of sexual harassment and recruit new participants to the movement. Through the media, feminist theory on sexual harassment was able to significantly shape popular discussions on sexual harassment and helped to propel the issue onto the public agenda.

By the end of the 1970s, the issue of sexual harassment was firmly on the mainstream feminist agenda. The movement was not only expanding, with a plethora of new and established women's organizations addressing harassment in employment and educational contexts, but the movement was maturing. Whereas in the early and mid-1970s activists were working in relative isolation, by the end of the 1970s, they became aware of each other's work and began to influence each other and in some cases work together. This was a time of information generation and dissemination, as well as a time of networking and collaboration across race, class, and institutional setting. The strength of the movement lay in the ways that activism interrelated at different levels and across different constituencies. The identity of the movement was diverse, geographically, institutionally, racially, and economically. The women who raised the issue were from all over the country, from a range of occupations, both traditional and nontraditional, white-collar, blue-collar, and pink-collar, as well as students. This diversity benefited the movement because it mobilized a wider population by providing multiple avenues of entry into the movement, as well as allowing the movement to draw on resources from a variety of existing social movements, including the civil rights movement, the women's movement, and the labor movement. Analyzing sexual harassment through a gendered framework, and characterizing the issue as one of both sex discrimination as well as violence against women, and emphasizing the economic repercussions, feminists were able to develop a shared understanding of the importance of the issue, which legitimated and motivated collective action. Activists effectively disseminated this understanding of sexual harassment through media coverage of the issue, which then brought new people and organizations to the movement. By the end of the decade, this groundswell of concern caught the attention of Congressman James Hanley, Chairman of the Subcommittee on Investigations of the House Post Office and Civil Service Committee, who called the first congressional hearings on sexual harassment in the federal workplace, hearings that would lead to several powerful government initiatives that would fundamentally shape the development of sexual harassment law in the following two decades but also change the nature of sexual harassment activism.

PART III

THE MOVEMENT'S INFLUENCE ON PUBLIC POLICY

6

Government Policy Develops

> "We've talked openly about battered wives and battered children. The next thing is battered office workers."
>
> Representative Patricia Schroeder, 1979[1]

In response to the growing movement against sexual harassment, federal, state, and local governments began to take action to combat sexual harassment. The first congressional hearings on sexual harassment in 1979 generated major press coverage and resulted in three important federal initiatives. A broad array of women's organizations, including feminist groups, labor unions, and organizations representing women of color and blue-collar women, participated in public hearings and submitted comments on policy proposals. These activists helped shaped the public discussion and the developing government policy on sexual harassment. Government officials usually took the issue seriously, expressing strong disapproval and developing remedies for victims of sexual harassment. The resulting federal guidelines on sexual harassment had a significant impact on subsequent court decisions. But perhaps most significantly, government initiatives against sexual harassment legitimized the issue and further raised public awareness of the problem.

FEDERAL POLICY

Federal initiatives to study and prevent sexual harassment in the late 1970s were inspired by publicity generated from several high-profile sexual harassment scandals in the District of Columbia government. In the spring of 1979, the Organization of Black Activist Women, which had earlier filed an amicus brief in the *Williams* case, encouraged women working for the city to speak up about sexual harassment.[2] After several city employees filed complaints, D.C. Mayor Marion Barry appointed a Sexual Harassment Task Force, which was part of the D.C. Commission on Women. The Task Force sponsored several meetings and forums to raise awareness and develop strategies to address the problem, including conducting extensive surveys to document the incidence of sexual harassment. On April 4, 1979, shortly after the Task Force was formed, a D.C. grand jury indicted George R. Harrod, director of the D.C. Office of Personnel, for allegedly assaulting a female staff aide who was seeking to end a sexual relationship with him. Three weeks later, Judge Hart issued his decision in the case of Sandra Bundy. Although he declined to offer her any legal relief, Judge Hart found that D.C. Corrections Director Delbert Jackson and three other corrections officials regularly made improper sexual advances toward Bundy. After the Bundy decision, Mayor Barry publicly announced that his administration would not tolerate the sexual harassment and abuse of employees. Around the same time, federal investigators from the DOL were probing reported allegations that employees in the District's federally funded Comprehensive Employment and Training Act (CETA) program had been sexually harassed. Based on his Task Force's recommendations, Mayor Barry issued an executive order in May 1979 prohibiting sexual harassment and establishing procedures to address the problem.[3]

The publicity surrounding these events caught the attention of Al Louis Ripskis, a mid-level official at the federal Department of Housing and Urban Development (HUD) and editor of *Impact Journal*, a "gadfly" newsletter published for workers at HUD. In the May/June issue of *Impact*, Ripskis published a sexual harassment survey, inviting readers to respond anonymously. Ripskis received 63 completed questionnaires and 103 telephone calls from women reporting widespread sexual harassment at HUD.[4] This survey, released on July 27, 1979, received extensive publicity and soon caught the attention of Congressman James M. Hanley, a Democrat from New York and Chair of the House Subcommittee on Investigations of the Post Office and Civil Service Committee. In response, Representative Hanley initiated an investigation of sexual harassment in the federal government. As part of the investigation, he asked the heads of three federal agencies to address the issue of sexual harassment. He asked Alan K. Campbell, Director of the Office of Personnel Management (OPM), to develop a model policy and procedures addressing sexual harassment to be used throughout the federal workplace and to serve as a model program for state and local governments, as well as private employers.[5] Second, he asked Eleanor Holmes Norton, Chair of the EEOC, to develop sexual harassment guidelines to facilitate the processing of complaints within the EEOC and to provide guidance to private employers covered by Title VII. Finally, he asked Ruth T. Prokop, Chair of the Merit Systems Protection Board (MSPB), to conduct a survey of sexual harassment in the federal workplace.

In addition to these initiatives, Representative Hanley held congressional hearings to investigate sexual harassment.[6] The record of these hearings provides a glimpse into early articulations of the issue of sexual harassment. Hanley's subcommittee heard testimony from representatives of eleven organizations, including women's rights advocates, union representatives, and heads of government agencies. Hanley opened the hearings on October 23, 1979, by stating that sexual harassment was a "serious issue, which cannot be ignored" and a "serious abuse of power." He described sexual harassment as "not only epidemic, it is pandemic, an everyday, everywhere occurrence," citing studies by HUD, New Responses, and *Redbook*, and noting that the subcommittee had received approximately one hundred complaints since the start of the investigation. He declared that sexual harassment would not be tolerated in the federal government, that a "boys will be boys" atmosphere would not be condoned, and that "any person guilty of sexual harassment can expect to be dealt with severely."[7] However, he defined sexual harassment very narrowly to be "sexual intimidation by a male supervisor of a subordinate female employee" who then suffered adverse employment consequences or threats of such action when she rejected the supervisor's advances.

At the hearings, feminist activists offered powerful testimony about the seriousness of sexual harassment and its effect on women. Donna Lenhoff, a staff attorney at WLDF, urged the committee to address not just supervisors pressuring subordinates for sex, but also environmental harassment by supervisors and co-workers. Lenhoff vigorously criticized the lower court decision in *Bundy v. Jackson*, emphasizing that "sexual harassment has been a historic burden on women's ability, as a class, to attain full participation in our society," especially in nontraditional jobs. Lenhoff also criticized the difficult and extended process required to pursue discrimination charges. Mary A. Largen, Director of New Responses, Inc., suggested that Congress amend Title VII specifically to include sexual harassment as a form of sex discrimination but also expressed reservations about the ability of laws to eliminate sexual harassment. Largen argued, "laws and courts alone, however, cannot eradicate sexual harassment or the imbalance of power, which fosters the behavior. It is a cultural phenomenon and will be eliminated only through resocialization and reeducation . . . a change in attitudes as well as behaviors."[8] Largen reported a great deal of management resistance to her educational programs and surveys of sexual harassment. Helen Lewis of the D.C. Commission on Women's Sexual Harassment Task Force reported that several surveys conducted by the Commission revealed high rates of sexual harassment and then called for the adoption of criminal penalties against sexual harassment. Diane Williams, the plaintiff in *Williams v. Saxbe*, described her experiences of sexual harassment and her extended and ongoing litigation against the Department of Justice, offering many suggestions of ways to improve the processing of EEO complaints. Lenhoff, Largen, and Williams all made parallels between the experiences and treatment of victims of rape and sexual harassment. In response to committee members' expressions of concern about character assassination and false accusations, the witnesses discussed women's hesitancy to reveal harassment, their shame, and their fear of being blamed and accused of lying.

In addition to oral testimony, the subcommittee received written testimony from several women's organizations. Representative Mary Rose Oakar submitted the statements of several women who had testified at an unemployment compensation hearing earlier in June of the same year. The women, including Jane Pinsky of Working Women – National Association of Office Workers, Jan Leventer of the Women's Justice Center in Detroit, and Isabelle Katz Pinzler,

Director of the ACLU's Women's Right's Project, described the severity of sexual harassment and the need to allow unemployment compensation for women who quit because of harassment. NOW submitted a copy of a policy directive on sexual harassment issued by the Department of Commerce and a table of cases that had been part of a legal brief prepared by NOW Legal Defense and Education Fund, which set forth the legal arguments for including peer harassment within the definition of sexual harassment.

The subcommittee also received oral and written testimony from several unions. Louise Smothers, Director of the Department of Women's Affairs for the American Federation of Government Employees, testified that sexual harassment was "one of the most serious occupational hazards faced by working women" around the country. She advocated for a broad definition of harassment, including co-worker and hostile environment harassment and advocated for statutory changes to facilitate complaint processing with the Merit System Protection Board. Dorothy Nelms, National President of Federally Employed Women, a union for women in federal employment, testified that, based on a survey of their membership and complaints received from members, sexual harassment was a severe problem, especially for women employed in nontraditional jobs such as construction and engineering. She emphasized the economic underpinnings of sexual harassment, namely, male economic power and female powerlessness because of economic deprivation. The subcommittee received written testimony from representatives of three other unions, all stating that sexual harassment was a severe and pervasive problem for working women: Tamara Bavar of the United Auto Workers in Michigan; Barbara Somson, Assistant General Counsel for the International Union of Electrical, Radio, and Machine Workers, also speaking for the Coalition of Labor Union Women; and Vincent R. Sombrotto, President of the National Association of Letter Carriers, AFL-CIO.

The dramatic highlight of the hearings was the subcommittee's intense questioning of William A. Medina, Assistant Secretary of Administration at the Department of Housing and Urban Development, and Joseph A. Sanchez, Director of the Equal Employment Programs of the Justice Department. Hanley had invited Medina and Sanchez to testify so they could respond to the Ripskis survey of HUD employees and Diane Williams' testimony respectively. Both Medina and Sanchez became very defensive in response to close questioning by the subcommittee. Despite Ripskis' survey showing rampant sexual harassment at HUD, Medina testified that HUD had received few formal complaints, but that he had notified employees about complaint procedures and planned to provide sexual harassment training courses for managers. Under critical questioning from the subcommittee, Medina stated that he had not spoken to Ripskis, nor had he tried to verify Ripskis' findings. Of conversations he had with HUD's Women's Caucus, he said "there were perceptions of sexual harassment that I don't think any of us in this room would really think of as being any kind of sexual harassment."[9] Then he criticized the women for failing to provide specific details about harassment. Sanchez, in his opening statement, described the Justice Department's EEO program and complaint procedures, without mentioning sexual harassment specifically. The subcommittee questioned Sanchez in detail about Williams' case, focusing, in particular, on how long the case had been pending. Sanchez stated that he had not read Williams' testimony before the committee. Surprisingly, he testified that he was unaware that the Justice Department had ever taken the position that sexual harassment was not sex discrimination. In exasperation, Representative John Cavanaugh, a Democrat from Nebraska, exclaimed that the Justice Department's testimony was "the most inadequate that I have experienced since I have been a Member of Congress," that it "reflects sadly on our Department of Justice," and that there was a "serious problem" in the Department of Justice. Hanley agreed.[10]

Finally, the committee heard from the officials that Hanley had charged with addressing the issue. EEOC Chair Norton testified that sexual harassment was "deeply rooted in male perceptions of women" and that "the Federal Government should set the tone for other employers in trying to rid the workplace of this manifestation of the culture's bias against women." Noting that "until quite recently it was thought to be unacceptable for women to engage in employment outside the home," she argued that sexual harassment was associated with the subordination of women and often intimidated women so as to circumscribe their career movements. Norton advocated preventative policies and emphasized that the burden should be on the employer, not the victim, to act "affirmatively and aggressively" to eliminate sexual harassment. Norton also testified about EEOC experience with sexual harassment claims and training.[11] Campbell testified that the Office of Personnel and Management was developing a policy, procedures, and training on sexual harassment for uniform use through the federal government, in response to Hanley's request. Prokop, the Chair of the Merit System Protection Board, testified about the survey she was developing on sexual harassment in the federal government and about avenues of relief for sexual harassment before the board.

The subcommittee's report, "Sexual Harassment in the Federal Government," issued on April 30, 1980, concluded that sexual harassment was an "extremely serious matter" and a widespread occurrence throughout the federal government that would not be tolerated. The subcommittee made twenty-one recommendations to federal agencies, state and local governments, organized labor, and the private sector, encouraging policies, training, and grievance procedures to address sexual harassment.[12] The report included an extensive bibliography on sexual harassment, including works of AASC, WWI, Lin Farley, Catharine MacKinnon, Adrienne Rich, and other feminists. This report represented a significant step toward recognition of the seriousness of this issue and in many ways vindicated years of hard work by feminists around the country. The Ranking Minority Member of the Subcommittee on Investigations, Republican Representative Gene Taylor, disapproved of the report. Criticizing the report for "jumping to conclusions" and characterizing sexual harassment as an "imagined personnel problem," Taylor stated that he did not believe that the evidence received by the committee supported a finding that sexual harassment was a widespread problem in the federal workplace. In addition, he criticized the subcommittee for failing to address the prevalence of "unfounded and frivolous complaints of sexual harassment." Finally, he expressed concern about the "right of an individual accused of sexual harassment to a presumption of innocence" and how those accused will be assured of protection of their rights under the law.[13]

Shortly before Hanley's subcommittee released its report, the EEOC proposed sweeping guidelines on sexual harassment.[14] Going beyond what any court had held at the time, the proposed guidelines made employers, public and private, liable for both coercive sexual demands made by supervisors and environmental harassment by supervisors and co-workers. No doubt Norton's background as a civil rights activist, a black feminist, and a lawyer informed her progressive approach to the problem of sexual harassment. In her early years, Norton was active with the NAACP and the Student Nonviolent Coordinating Committee and worked with Pauli Murray, Marian Wright Edelman, and Fannie Lou Hamer. Norton was a founder of the National Black Feminist Organization in the early 1970s. After graduating from Yale Law School in 1964, Norton clerked for Federal District Court Judge A. Leon Higginbotham and then worked for the American Civil Liberties Union. From 1970 until 1977, Norton chaired New York City's Commission on Human Rights, where she addressed the issue of sexual harassment in government contracts at the urging of Lin Farley. She later served on the board of WWUI. Her work on the Human Rights Commission brought her to the attention of President Jimmy Carter, who appointed her to chair the EEOC in 1977, a position she held until 1981. The year before Norton assumed leadership of the EEOC, the agency had a reputation as the "government's worst bureaucratic mess."[15] The *Washington Post* described the agency as "deeply troubled" and "demonstrably ineffective," with low morale and a "scandalous backlog" of as many as 150,000 cases. Allegations against the agency included falsification of records and "reports by female personnel of coercion by their bosses to engage in sexual games."[16] As Chair of the EEOC, Norton turned the agency around, dramatically increasing its efficiency. Within Norton's first two years, the agency cut its backlog nearly in half and increased productivity by as much as 65%, settling the average case in just seventy-two days.

The EEOC's proposed guidelines broadly prohibited sexual harassment and declared that sexual harassment was sex discrimination, in violation of Title VII of the Civil Rights Acts. The guidelines defined sexual harassment as "unwelcome sexual advances, requests for sexual favors, and other verbal or physical conduct of a sexual nature" that included both explicit sexual demands linked to job benefits and conduct that had "the purpose or effect of substantially interfering with an individual's work performance or creating an intimidating, hostile, or offensive working environment." The guidelines held employers strictly liable for the acts of their supervisory employees (liable without regard to whether the employer knew or even forbade harassment) and liable for the acts

FIGURE 6.1. Eleanor Holmes Norton, 1981. Courtesy of EEOC

of others if the employer knew or should have known of the harassment and failed to take immediate and appropriate corrective action. The guidelines also recommended that employers take preventative steps to eliminate sexual harassment from the workplace.[17]

When the EEOC issued a call for public comment on the proposed guidelines, the agency received a groundswell of responses, most of which was strongly supportive.[18] Women's organizations praised the proposed guidelines, especially the basic principle that sexual harassment was sex discrimination and the broad definition of sexual harassment. The comments discussed the prevalence and effects of sexual harassment on working women and emphasized the economic basis of sexual harassment. WWI argued that women's vulnerability to sexual harassment was based on their subordinate position in the "economic hierarchy." They described sexual harassment as the "quintessential expression of the stereotypic role expectations of both sexes."[19] Sexual harassment, they argued, denied women a role as a "contributing member of the workforce." NOW and WLDF cited many studies of sexual harassment, including the *Redbook* survey, WWI studies, and Lin Farley's book. They argued that sexual harassment was "an expression of power by men over women in the employment context."[20] Other groups, however, criticized the EEOC's exclusive focus on sexual behavior and failure to address nonsexual gender-based harassment. They also pushed for a more stringent standard of employer liability. AASC and Women in the Trades argued that the guidelines should acknowledge that sexual harassment was used by men to discriminate against women based on their race and age.

While women's organizations sought to broaden the guidelines and raise standards of liability, employers and their representatives criticized the guidelines as too expansive. They generally acknowledged that sexual harassment was a serious problem in the workplace, but they argued that liability should arise only when an employer had actual knowledge of sexual harassment and failed to act to eliminate it. Employers also strongly opposed the inclusion of "intimidating, hostile, or offensive" work atmosphere within the definition of sexual harassment, arguing that work environment did not have an adverse impact on employment. They also expressed concern that the definition of harassment was too subjective and that the guidelines would lead to many frivolous charges. The U.S. Chamber of Commerce argued against requiring employers to "police" the personal lives of supervisors and suggested that it was better to deal with these situations voluntarily.[21]

After several modifications, the EEOC adopted the final guidelines on September 23, 1980, and they were published on November 10, 1980, shortly after Ronald Reagan's landslide victory.[22] The commission changed the definition of hostile environment harassment from conduct "substantially interfering with an individual's work performance" to conduct "unreasonably interfering with an individual's work performance," a change Jan Leventer of the in Detroit criticized because of the implication that there could be "reasonable" interference with a woman's work performance. The EEOC defended this change by arguing that this was the standard used in harassment cases based on national origin, race, and religion, and that sexual harassment cases should be treated similarly. Also, the commission expressed its concern with "framing a specific definition, which does not include behavior which is perfectly acceptable social behavior."[23] The EEOC in large part maintained the proposed liability standards. In response to several written comments and a "large number of members of the public who telephoned the Commission," the revised guidelines also provided that those employees who were deprived of employment opportunities because a sexually submissive co-worker had gained an advantage through sexual compliance had a claim under Title VII. The commission noted, however, that it "does not consider this to be an issue of sexual harassment in the strict sense." Leventer criticized this change, arguing that the EEOC had codified and lent credence to the sexist stereotypes that female workers "sleep their way to the top."[24]

The debate over the guidelines was a struggle between feminist arguments that sexual harassment significantly impaired women's full participation in the workforce and employers' arguments that sexual harassment was a personal problem for which employers should not be responsible. Similar to the arguments feminist activists and employers had made before the federal appellate courts, the debate over the EEOC guidelines at its core was about power relations between men and women in the workplace. Conservatives won some concessions, namely the requirement that interference with the working environment had to be "unreasonable" and the provision of a cause of action for those disadvantaged by a sexually submissive co-worker. Feminists, on the other hand, were able to preserve the broad standards proposed, but they gained little new ground. In particular, the proposed definition of harassment was not broadened, and the guidelines did not explicitly mention nonsexual gender-based harassment. However, under Norton's leadership, the EEOC preserved the progressive liability standards it had set out in the proposed guidelines.

The EEOC's guidelines increased public awareness of the issue of sexual harassment and significantly influenced the development of the law. The media and law review commentary discussed the actions of the EEOC extensively, if often critically. For example, "Guideline-Happy at the EEOC?" in the *Wall Street Journal* described the EEOC as an "imperial bureaucracy," criticizing the EEOC for issuing "vague and sweeping guidelines that go far beyond the intent of courts and Congress." The article described the guidelines as calling for companies to "police innocent flirtation" and inviting an "avalanche of questionable charges."[25] "EEOC Gets Slapped on Sex Harassment Regs" in the *National Law Journal* quoted several employer defense attorneys saying that the EEOC's view of liability "flies in the face of basic legal principles."[26] An article in *Industry Week* quoted an attorney charging that the guidelines "confuse rather than clarify" the obligation of employers, and another saying that the guidelines "offend his sense of fairness."[27] A column in *Fortune* magazine described the guidelines as "less than satisfactory" and attributed the new attention to sexual harassment to "job possibilities for the equal opportunity bureaucracy, which had gone maybe six weeks without finding a new form of discrimination to outlaw."[28] One law review commentator described the EEOC guidelines as "enveloped in a storm of controversy" and criticized the guidelines as confusing, idealistic, unrealistic, and unfair, saying that "not all wrongs are amenable to judicial correction" and that "a balance must often be struck between what is desirable and what is possible."[29] Many other law review articles, however, responded favorably to the guidelines.[30] Media coverage of the EEOC's guidelines increased public awareness of the issue of sexual harassment. As a result, both WWI and AASC reported that they were flooded by requests for information about the problem from a wide range of individuals and organizations, including the media, management personnel, consulting firms, and EEO officers.

The EEOC guidelines have been very influential on expanding the definition of sexual harassment to include hostile environment harassment. In May 1980, a federal district court in Oklahoma cited the proposed guidelines in issuing the first federal court ruling that hostile environment sexual harassment violated Title VII in the case of *Brown v. City of Guthrie*.[31] Just two months after the EEOC adopted the final guidelines, they were explicitly approved in the case of *Bundy v. Jackson*, where the District of Columbia Circuit Court of Appeals became the first federal appellate court to hold that Title VII prohibited hostile environment sexual harassment.[32] Three progressive judges – Chief Judge J. Skelly Wright, Judges Luther Merritt Swygert and Spottswood Robinson – issued the groundbreaking decision that Title VII prohibited sexual harassment that had no tangible job consequences but affected only the psychological and emotional work environment. Noting that "'the nuances and subtleties of discriminatory employment practices are no longer confined to bread-and-butter issues,'" Judge Swygert argued that hostile environment sexual harassment "injects the most demeaning sexual stereotypes into the general work environment and always represents an intentional assault on an individual's innermost privacy."[33] Perhaps most significantly, Judge Swygert explicitly acknowledged the gendered power dynamics underlying sexual harassment when he stated, "so long as women remain inferiors in the employment hierarchy, they may have little recourse against harassment beyond the legal recourse Bundy seeks in this case." The case of *Bundy v. Jackson* set an important, influential legal precedent and became a focal point for public discussion of sexual harassment and a rallying point for feminists in the early 1980s. Bundy's case was discussed widely in law reviews and covered extensively in the press, generating sympathy for the victims of sexual harassment.[34] In addition to influencing courts, the EEOC guidelines influenced the development of sexual harassment policy at other federal agencies and in the states. For example, the Office of Federal Contract Compliance Programs modified guidelines they had proposed before the EEOC guidelines were issued to comply with the EEOC standards.[35] On the state level, the Connecticut legislature and several state human rights commissions adopting prohibitions of sexual harassment incorporated the EEOC guidelines verbatim.[36] Perhaps most importantly, the guidelines encouraged employers to adopt preventative policies and influenced the definition of sexual harassment in those policies.[37]

The EEOC continued to work on the issue of sexual harassment and, in 1980, began to keep statistics on the number of sexual harassment cases filed. The EEOC received approximately one thousand sexual harassment complaints in the first year after the guidelines were issued and quickly began to issue decisions providing additional guidance.[38] In 1981, there were six reported EEOC decisions on sexual harassment.[39] The EEOC placed sexual harassment cases into a rapid-charge processing system, whereby sexual harassment claims that were not settled were sent to headquarters in Washington, D.C. for final resolution after regional offices completed their investigations. This system ensured serious consideration and consistent rulings. To facilitate fast and fair resolution of sexual harassment cases within the federal government, the EEOC instituted a pilot program with five agencies where the commission extended its oversight at the agency level. The EEOC also continued to participate in sexual harassment litigation, gaining preliminary injunctions in several cases in the year after issuing the guidelines. In addition to adopting federal guidelines on sexual harassment, the EEOC directed all federal agencies to develop plans to educate employees about their rights, responsibilities, and remedies under the sexual harassment guidelines and to take other steps to eliminate sexual harassment. The EEOC began training its staff on sexual harassment, including regional attorneys, field managers, and supervisors, and worked with the Office of Personnel Management (OPM) to integrate the EEOC guidelines into a unified training program for all federal EEO personnel in the various agencies. Finally, EEOC Commissioners and staff made themselves available to employer and employee groups to discuss the guidelines and methods of sexual harassment prevention.[40]

The second federal initiative to emerge from the Hanley hearings was the OPM's model policy and training materials. On December 12, 1979, OPM Director Campbell issued a policy statement and definition of sexual harassment, which he sent to all heads of departments and independent agencies of the executive branch of the federal government.[41] At the time, few federal agencies had policy statements on sexual harassment, and the few that did had differing definitions, leading to confusion. OPM was the logical choice for standardizing this definition because it was the agency responsible for administering the federal merit system, including personnel policy development and employee training for the executive branch of the federal government. Campbell defined sexual harassment as "deliberate or repeated unsolicited verbal comments, gestures, or physical contact of a sexual nature which are unwelcome." The policy continued,

A supervisor who uses implicit or explicit coercive sexual behavior to control, influence, or affect the career, salary, or job of an employee is engaging in sexual harassment. Similarly, an employee of an agency who behaves in this manner in the process of conducting agency business is engaging in sexual harassment. Finally, any employee who participates in deliberate or repeated unsolicited verbal comments, gestures, or physical contact of a sexual nature, which are unwelcome and interfere in work productivity is also engaging in sexual harassment.[42]

The policy statement declared that "It is the policy of the Office of Personnel Management (OPM) that sexual harassment is unacceptable conduct in the workplace and will not be condoned. . . . At the same time it is not the intent of the OPM to regulate the social interaction or relationships freely entered into by Federal employees."[43] Campbell's model policy strongly opposed sexual harassment but was weaker than the EEOC guidelines. While clearly prohibiting coercive sexual demands by supervisors, the policy was ambiguous about whether it prohibited environmental harassment and harassment by co-workers. In addition, Campbell's policy was weak because it declined to provide penalties for sexual harassment. In testimony before the subcommittee, Campbell defended this lack of sanctions on the grounds that there was not sufficient experience with the application of specific penalties to specific actions in cases of sexual harassment. He also stated that the Merit System Protection Board was the agency responsible for deciding appropriate remedies for a particular action.[44]

An OPM survey of federal offices revealed that in response to Campbell's directive and as of September 1, 1980, sixty-two of seventy-three departments and independent agencies had issued policy statements on sexual harassment, nine were in the process of drafting statements, and two had done nothing.[45] All the policies clearly defined sexual harassment, prohibited it as a form of employment discrimination, and warned employees that disciplinary actions would be taken if the policy was violated. Most agencies informed employees that complaints of sexual harassment would be filed under EEO complaint procedures. All four defense agencies issued policy directives applicable to both civilian and military personnel. OPM also worked with state and local governments to encourage them to adopt sexual harassment policies.[46]

In addition to issuing a policy statement against sexual harassment, OPM developed a model training workshop. The objectives of the workshop were to inform employees of the federal policy and definition of sexual harassment and the course of action to be taken if sexual harassment were experienced or observed, to explain the differing perceptions of behavior that constituted sexual harassment, and to describe the impact of sexual harassment on employee morale and productivity.[47] OPM recommended training both supervisory and nonsupervisory employees. The trainer's manual contained the congressional statements of Alan Campbell, Ruth Prokop, Eleanor Holmes Norton, and James Hanley. The manual also included the OPM policy on sexual harassment, related federal personnel policies, the EEOC proposed guidelines, and procedures for processing individual complaints. Finally, the manual included a three-hour lesson plan, two handouts, notes for the trainer about the psychological effects of sexual harassment, a discussion of options open to victims of sexual harassment and the responsibilities of supervisors, and a reading list.

The training materials incorporated feminist perspectives on sexual harassment. For example, the introductory section of the trainer's manual described harassment as "evidence of the need to feel powerful, dominant, and manipulative, and sometimes the result of years of conditioning in stereotyped ways of thinking about the roles of both men and women."[48] The suggested reading list included Farley's *Sexual Shakedown*, MacKinnon's *Sexual Harassment of Working Women*, AASC's *Sexual Harassment at the Workplace*, Betty Friedan's *The Feminist Mystique*, and *Sexual Harassment: A Hidden Issue* by the Association of American Colleges' Project on the Status of Women. The suggested training program began with ten questions that attempted to get participants to think about the causes and effects of sexual harassment. One question asked, "If you consider that many people (including women) think of women as sex objects, can you name some influences that have led to this attitude? (for example, songs, commercials, advertisements, etc.)." Another question asked, "Do you think that sexual humiliation and possession are ways to shore up a threatened self-image?" Another asked participants to think about how sex segregation and women's subordinate status in the workplace related to sexual harassment on the job.[49] Following the questions, participants were asked to discuss ten quotations about sexual harassment, most of which came from feminist sources such as WWI, AASC, and the congressional testimony of Eleanor Holmes Norton. These quotations incorporated feminist ideas that sexual harassment was a serious issue that had an extremely debilitating effect on women and was rooted in cultural stereotypes of women as sex objects. One quotation from *Ms.* magazine described sexual harassment as "a symbol of superiority, dominance, and ownership."[50] The trainer's manual also included information about the effect of sexual harassment on workforce morale and productivity, quoting extensively from AASC's 1977 brochure "Sexual Harassment in the Workplace." OPM distributed the training materials to seventy agencies and to each of OPM's regions on January 7, 1980. By September 1980, most agencies were using the OPM training materials or were developing their own training materials, and many agencies had already commenced training. OPM estimated that by this time approximately 8,800 federal employees had received training on sexual harassment. OPM also began monitoring the penalties imposed on perpetrators of sexual harassment in the federal workplace.

The third federal initiative that developed out of the hearings was the Merit System Protection Board survey of sexual harassment in the federal government. Noting the lack of scientific surveys on the nature and magnitude of sexual harassment in the workplace, Hanley's subcommittee asked Ruth Prokop of the Merit System Protection Board, the grievance arbitration board for federal employees, to conduct a comprehensive survey to determine the extent of sexual harassment in the federal workplace. Several feminists, including AASC's Freada Klein, served as consultants on this survey. MSPB surveyed a random sample of 23,000 female and male federal employees, 85% of whom responded. The MSPB survey, reported in September 1980, found that 42% of the females and 15% of the males responding said they had been sexually harassed in the two years before the survey. According to the survey, victims of harassment tended to be young, unmarried, college-educated women. Most harassers were older married men acting alone. The survey revealed that most harassers were co-workers, but many were supervisors. Male victims of harassment were more likely to be members of a minority racial or ethnic group and in a trainee position or office/clerical position. Generally, employees were more likely to be harassed if they worked in a nontraditional position, such as female law enforcement or male secretaries, if they had an immediate supervisor of the opposite sex, and if they had an immediate work group composed predominantly of the opposite sex. The study also showed that black and white women in the federal government suffered sexual harassment to approximately the same degree, but that white women's harassers were white males 75% of the time and black women's harassers were white males 53% of the time. Most female respondents said they did not file a complaint because they lacked confidence in the effectiveness of the available formal procedures. Respondents also believed that the problem was no worse in the federal government than in the private sector. MSPB conservatively estimated the cost of sexual harassment to the federal government between May 1978 and May 1980 to be $189 million.[51] MSPB also began reviewing sexual harassment cases involving federal employees. In one case, the MSPB held that a male supervisory employee was properly demoted to a nonsupervisory position for making sexual advances to three female subordinates. Another case held that a male employee was properly discharged for indecent conduct toward a female co-worker, abusive language, and a threatening attitude toward another female co-worker, and repeated physical abuse of a male co-worker. A third case held that a male foreman was properly discharged for making sexually suggestive remarks to and about female employees and touching them.[52] All three cases were decided in the first half of 1980.

These three federal initiatives had a tremendous influence both on the developing law of sexual harassment and on public discussion of the issue. Most importantly, the EEOC's guidelines established an expansive and influential definition of sexual harassment and broad standards of employer liability that applied not only to the federal workplace but also to private employers. The Merit System Protection Board survey, as the first large-scale scientific study of sexual harassment, proved that sexual harassment was a serious problem in the federal workplace. By providing an objective measure of the problem, the study was influential in convincing courts that sexual harassment was a pervasive problem in the workplace. Finally, the wide distribution and adoption of OPM's policy set an example for employers seeking to establish sexual harassment policies and procedures and created a high expectation that employers should address the issue. Press coverage of the hearings and the resulting federal initiatives was extensive.[53] Business periodicals began to cover the issue of sexual harassment intensively, expressing concern about employer liability for sexual harassment. Radio and television coverage of the issue also proliferated, and several films about sexual harassment appeared.[54]

These federal initiatives inspired employers, unions, and other organizations to act. General Motors sponsored a meeting of activists to discuss how they should deal with sexual harassment in their workforce.[55] Many employers began to offer sexual harassment training in the workplace. Whereas sexual harassment training in the late 1970s was primarily offered by feminist organizations like WWI, AASC, and New Responses, by the early 1980s, management training consultants began publishing training manuals and offering programs on sexual harassment in the workplace and in educational institutions. In response to this growing interest in the issue, a broad array of activist organizations published guides on sexual harassment in the early 1980s, including women's groups, unions, and educational organizations. The Center for Women Policy Studies sponsored a meeting of researchers and public policy specialists on sexual harassment, including Freada Klein, Karen Sauvigné, Catharine MacKinnon, Barbara Gutek, and Mary Rowe at the Wingspread

Conference Center in Racine, Wisconsin. The conference participants addressed questions of how to define sexual harassment, what direction research should take, and how public policy on the issue should develop.[56] This proliferation of attention to the issue of sexual harassment was a direct result of the Hanley hearings.

Hanley's 1979 hearings were the most influential and widely publicized federal response to the issue of sexual harassment, but several other important federal investigations and initiatives were under way in the late 1970s and early 1980s in the areas of unemployment compensation, the military, the post office, and at educational institutions.[57] On December 16 and 17, 1979, the *Baltimore Sun* published several articles on allegations of widespread harassment at the military base in Fort Meade, Maryland. In response to these allegations, on February 11, 1980, the Military Personnel Subcommittee of the House Committee on Armed Services heard testimony on sexual harassment in the military, focusing on the allegations about Fort Meade. Five women serving at Fort Meade testified about their experiences of sexual harassment, and Colonel Thomas Fitzpatrick, Post Commander at Fort Meade, testified as to how he was handling the allegations.[58] One woman testified that her male superiors and peers talked "extremely dirty and nasty" and pushed her into a corner and exposed themselves to her. Others reported being sexually assaulted. In questioning Colonel Fitzpatrick about ways to address sexual harassment, Representative Patricia Schroeder suggested that he eliminate topless dancers and go-go dancers from the clubs on the base because such behavior was "an inducement to treating women a little differently, as a chattel, shall we say, and not an equal."[59]

The post office was another arena where the issue of sexual harassment arose. The Subcommittee on Postal Personnel and Modernization of the Committee on Post Office and Civil Service held two hearings in Houston, Texas, on October 27, 1980 and on July 1, 1981.[60] The hearings addressed equal employment opportunity, racial discrimination, and sexual harassment in the Texas Postal Service. The subcommittee chair, Texas Democrat Mickey Leland, explained that he was conducting the hearings because of an "inordinate" number of sexual harassment complaints from women and unions. Although the hearings focused on Texas, Leland stated that he intended to examine discrimination and sexual harassment problems in the postal service nationwide. Leland opened the July 1981 hearings with a strong statement against sexual harassment, echoing feminist rhetoric and sentiment:

There is absolutely no excuse whatsoever for women to be relegated to the role of sex objects, to be used or abused because they are considered to be culturally the weaker sex. In my opinion, this misconception is not based on fact, but rather due to cultural biases. We have, in many instances, relegated or subjugated women to lesser roles, for one reason or another, and primarily targeted them in many instances to be the object of the personal advances by supervisors, managers, and even other co-workers.[61]

Several women testified before the subcommittee about their experiences of sexual harassment in the postal service, and several male union representatives testified about sexual harassment of their female members. Although none of these hearings received the sort of media attention given the Hanley hearings, they contributed to the growing public consciousness of sexual harassment. Furthermore, the broad participation of feminist organizations, unions, and others reflected the widespread concern developing about the issue of sexual harassment at the turn of the decade.

The federal government also acted on sexual harassment in education. In August of 1981, the Office of Civil Rights of the United States Department of Education issued guidance under Title IX on sexual harassment at educational institutions. In a memorandum to regional civil rights directors, Antonio J. Califa, who was Director for Litigation, Enforcement, and Policy Service, stated that Title IX prohibited sexual harassment and provided procedures for investigating and processing sexual harassment complaints. The memorandum defined sexual harassment broadly as "verbal or physical conduct of a sexual nature, imposed on the basis of sex ... that denies, limits, provides different, or conditions the provision of aid, benefits, services, or treatment protected under Title IX."[62] Califa relied on the EEOC guidelines and Title VII case-law on sexual harassment in developing his guidance on sexual harassment at educational institutions. All of these federal initiatives reflected a new attitude that sexual harassment was a serious problem warranting government action.

STATE AND LOCAL POLICY

In the late 1970s, while federal law against sexual harassment was developing in the courts and the federal government was beginning to act on sexual harassment, state governments also turned to the issue. Wisconsin was the first state to pass a statute explicitly prohibiting sexual harassment in employment in 1978.[63] The Wisconsin legislature amended its Fair Employment Act to prohibit employers from making employment benefits contingent on consent to "sexual contact or sexual intercourse." This law, however, reached only the most severe forms of harassment because "sexual contact or sexual intercourse" was defined very narrowly by the state criminal code. Michigan, on the other hand, passed a broad prohibition of sexual harassment in 1980, inspired by publicity from the September 1977 ruling in the case of *Munford v. James T. Barnes and Co.* This case became widely known in Michigan because the plaintiff, Maxine Munford, testified at public hearings on sexual harassment and made several appearances on Michigan television and radio talk shows. In the spring of 1978, the Michigan Department of Labor's Office of Women and Work and the University of Michigan's Institute of Labor and Industrial Relations convened a meeting of representatives from labor organizations, academic institutions, state government, and women's organizations to discuss sexual harassment in the workplace and in education. This meeting led to the formation of the Michigan Taskforce on Sexual Harassment in the Workplace, a statewide group of Michigan citizens concerned with sexual harassment. Members of the task force included representatives of labor unions, which were particularly strong in Michigan, state and local government, private sector employers, educational institutions, and women's organizations, including the Michigan Women's Commission, the Coalition of Labor Union Women, Women Are Watching, Union Minorities/Women Leadership Project, the Women's Justice Center, the Michigan Nurses Association, and NOW.[64]

The goals of the task force were to increase public awareness and sensitivity to the issue of sexual harassment and to seek increased protection for Michigan workers through changes in public policy and legislation. To achieve these goals, the task force first held public hearings around the state in April and May of 1979 to collect and disseminate information on the nature and extent of sexual harassment in Michigan. The public testimony included reports from seventy-three individuals and statements from twenty-three organizations. In 1979, the task force sponsored the first statewide conference on sexual harassment. The conference objectives were to develop both individual and collective solutions to the problem of sexual harassment. The task force published educational and informational materials for labor organizations, employers, and the general public and conducted educational seminars around the state. The task force produced a brochure, *Sexual Harassment on the Job*, which they distributed to thousands of Michigan citizens.[65]

Due to the activism of the task force, the Michigan legislature passed one of the first and most progressive state laws against sexual harassment.[66] In 1979, legislators introduced a wide range of proposals to prohibit sexual harassment. The House Committee on Constitutional Revision and Women's Rights proposed amending the Michigan Civil Rights Act to include sexual harassment. The House Committee on Judiciary made two proposals: to amend the Michigan Penal Code to include sexual harassment as criminal sexual conduct and to amend the Michigan School Code to prohibit sexual harassment of school employees, teachers, or pupils. The House Committee on Labor also made two proposals: to amend the Michigan Employment Security Act to include "voluntary quits" due to sexual harassment as "good cause" for terminating employment, thus enabling victims to secure unemployment benefits, and to amend the Michigan Occupational Safety and Health Act, making it a violation for employees or employers to sexually harass other employees. The Michigan legislature decided to pass one statute with broad applicability: they amended the Michigan Civil Rights Act to prohibit sexual harassment in employment, public accommodations, public services, education, and housing.[67] The Michigan governor signed the bill into law on July 18, 1980.

The Michigan law was patterned after, but more comprehensive than, federal Title VII law and EEOC guidelines on sexual harassment. First, the Michigan law prohibited not only verbal and physical conduct of a sexual nature, but also *communication* of a sexual nature, thereby prohibiting pictures, pornography, and other forms of nonverbal sexual communication. Second, the Michigan law applied not only to employment discrimination but also to discrimination in public accommodations, public services, education, and housing. Third, unlike Title VII, which applied only to employers of fifteen or more employees, the Michigan law applied to employers with one or more employee. Finally, the Michigan Act provided for a broader range of relief than Title VII, including compensatory damages, a remedy not available under Title VII until passage of the Civil Rights Act of 1991.

Perhaps due in part to the efforts of the task force, Michigan judicial tribunals from early on heard a large number of sexual harassment complaints and often ruled in favor of plaintiffs. The Michigan Department of Civil Rights' sexual harassment caseload grew from 12 in 1977, to 35 in 1978, to 73 in 1979, and to 125 in 1980.[68] Even before the 1980 legislation prohibiting sexual harassment, the Michigan Civil Rights Commission interpreted the Michigan Civil Rights Act to prohibit sexual harassment in the case of *Tyamie Hanson v. Hasper's Sav-Mor Market*.[69] A few months later in the case of *Augustine Petro v. United Trucking Company*, the Commission ordered the defendant to pay the plaintiff $7,500 in damages along with reinstatement and back pay for sexual harassment.[70] The Michigan Employment Security Commission heard numerous early sexual harassment complaints and consistently ruled that sexual harassment was good cause to leave a job. On February 29, 1979, the Director of the Michigan Employment Security Commission published a field release to Commission personnel defining sexual harassment and directing examiners specifically to question claimants about this issue.[71] Finally, the Michigan state courts adjudicated many sexual harassment complaints based on a wide range of state law theories and Michigan federal courts heard several sexual harassment cases around this time.

Public policy on sexual harassment was advanced in Michigan and at the national level by activists from the Detroit-based Women's Justice Center, a legal aid organization founded by Jan Leventer, a white female attorney, and Connye Harper, a black female attorney. Leventer, who graduated from Barnard College and Capital University Law School, was legal director of the center from 1978 to 1980 and later became a trial attorney with the Detroit regional office of the EEOC. Harper, who graduated from University of Michigan undergraduate and law school, was a civil rights attorney and later became associate general counsel for the United Auto Workers.[72] The center litigated several sexual harassment cases in Michigan, including *Munford v. James T. Barnes and Company* on appeal and *Marentette v. Michigan Host Inc.*, in which an employer required a woman to wear a sexually revealing costume that led to harassment by customers.[73] The center also participated in the development of public policy on sexual harassment both in Michigan and at the national level. Harper helped to organize the statewide conference in 1979 and later contributed to a handbook on sexual harassment written from a union perspective published in 1980 by the Labor and Education Research Project.[74] In June 1979, Leventer testified about sexual harassment in Washington, D.C., before the National Commission on Unemployment Compensation. In 1980, the Women's Justice Center joined WWI's comments on EEOC's proposed sexual harassment guidelines. In 1981, Leventer participated in the first legal symposium on sexual harassment at Capital University Law School in Washington, D.C.[75]

Though Michigan had the most aggressive statewide campaign to combat sexual harassment, other state and local governments were also acting against harassment. In Illinois, several women's groups and other organizations concerned with the issue formed the Illinois Task Force on Sexual Harassment in the Workplace. In 1979, the task force conducted a survey of 1,495 Illinois state employees finding that more than half of the women surveyed had experienced sexual harassment.[76] The Illinois survey was one of the first scientifically conducted studies of sexual harassment.[77] On January 24, 1980, the Governor of Illinois issued an executive order prohibiting sexual harassment of state employees. The order also provided for a training program for all state EEO officers and required each state agency to disseminate information about sexual harassment, including contact information for organizations that could provide assistance.[78] In March 1980, the Illinois House Judiciary subcommittee conducted a hearing on sexual harassment, at which a member of the task force testified about their survey. However, the bill pending before the legislature never passed.

Many other state and local governments prohibited sexual harassment in the early 1980s by legislative act, executive order, and regulatory action. On October 1, 1980, the Connecticut legislature adopted a law against sexual harassment, the Act Concerning Harassment as an Unfair Employment Practice, modeled after the EEOC guidelines.[79] The state of Maryland passed a criminal law that made coercive demands for sex a fourth-degree sex offense. The law was designed to prevent landlords, employers, and others in powerful positions from abusing that power.[80] Several other states at this time considered but did not pass legislation against sexual harassment.[81] However, nine governors issued executive orders prohibiting sexual harassment in the early 1980s. The governors of Rhode Island and Utah issued executive orders in 1980 prohibiting sexual harassment in state employment, similar to the Illinois executive order. The Rhode Island order defined sexual harassment broadly to include "unsolicited, deliberate or repeated sexually explicit derogatory statements, gestures or physical contacts, which are objectionable to the recipient and which cause discomfort or humiliation." The order applied not only to male/female harassment but also to same-sex harassment and required each department head to disseminate information about sexual harassment. In 1981, the governors of Florida, Oregon, and South Dakota issued executive orders prohibiting sexual harassment. In 1982, the governors of Indiana, Kansas, and Montana issued executive orders prohibiting sexual harassment, and the governor of Massachusetts did so in 1984.[82]

Instead of prohibiting sexual harassment by legislation and executive order, some states' human rights commissions adopted rules against sexual harassment. Washington, Pennsylvania, and Kentucky human rights commissions adopted the EEOC guidelines verbatim.[83] The California Fair Employment and Housing Commission broadly prohibited sexual harassment by regulations adopted on May 1, 1980. The regulations defined sexual harassment to include verbal, physical, and visual harassment, as well as soliciting sexual favors.

Examples of visual harassment were "derogatory posters, cartoons, or draw-ings." The regulations also established stringent liability standards.[84] The Col-orado Civil Rights Commission adopted rules prohibiting sexual harassment that, while not explicitly prohibiting hostile environment harassment, were very broad in that they applied to discrimination in employment, housing, public accommodations, or advertising, just as the Michigan Act did.[85] Some states addressed the issue by distributing information kits and employer's guides on sexual harassment.[86] In Minnesota, the Equal Employment Division of the Department of Personnel published an annotated bibliography of resour-ces related to sexual harassment in the workplace.[87] The Kentucky Commis-sion on Human Rights published a brochure and a technical assistance guide on sexual harassment and held hearings on sexual harassment in 1980.[88] After the EEOC issued its proposed guidelines on sexual harassment, the Kentucky Com-mission on Human Rights held hearings around the state on sexual harassment and later adopted identical guidelines.[89]

Cities also began to address the issue. As early as 1975, in response to Lin Farley's testimony, the New York City Human Rights Commission, chaired by Eleanor Holmes Norton, drafted a standard clause for affirmative action agree-ments prohibiting "unfair abuse of sexual privacy."[90] In 1980, New York's mayor issued a mayoral directive requiring all city agencies to establish sexual harassment complaint procedures. In addition to New York City, the Provi-dence Human Relations Commission in Rhode Island passed regulations pro-hibiting sexual harassment on October 15, 1980. In Fresno, CA, the Fresno City-County Commission on the Status of Women conducted studies on sexual harassment in the public and private sectors in 1980 and 1981, respectively.[91]

Several state and local women's commissions engaged in ongoing efforts to combat sexual harassment. The D.C. Commission on Women's Sexual Harass-ment Task Force conducted extensive surveys of city employees, Andrews Air Force Base personnel, and policewomen in the city to document the incidence of sexual harassment. To remedy what they found to be a widespread problem, the Commission developed a program calling for city and private employers to offer training materials, workshops, and employee counseling. The Commis-sion criticized Mayor Barry's executive order prohibiting harassment because it was limited to city employees and did not apply to private employers. The Commission also supported sexual assault legislation that made criminal sexual conduct obtained by force or coercion, including "threats to retaliate by a per-son in authority, against a victim who believes that person in authority has the ability to execute the threat, and the threat relates to employment."[92] Finally, Commission members worked to raise public awareness of the issue by testi-fying before Congress and conducting their own hearings on sexual harassment in 1981.[93] The California Commission on Women established a special sexual harassment education program, supported by Mary Lobrato, who donated money she won in a sexual harassment lawsuit.[94] The Pennsylvania Com-mission for Women published a handbook on sexual harassment, and the Pennsylvania Task Force Against Sexual Harassment offered workshops and counseling on sexual harassment.[95] In Kentucky, the Commission on Women surveyed over two thousand women, most in state government, and found that 56% had experienced sexual harassment. The commission also conducted hearings around the state and published a handbook on sexual harassment.[96]

Government initiatives against sexual harassment legitimized the issue as a serious social problem. Over the course of just a few years, governments had significantly broadened their definitions and standards for sexual harassment, a tendency noted in the *National Law Journal*.[97] Government involvement raised public awareness in several ways: public hearings and government initiatives stimulated media coverage of the issue and generated public discussion; these initiatives included government funded training sessions that sensitized workers to sexual harassment; and EEOC guidelines pressured private employers to enact preventative measures, including policies, procedures, and training. Finally, federal involvement led to more accessible and expedient remedies for sexual harassment. The EEOC's broad definition of sexual harassment, including both supervisory sexual demands and hostile environment harassment, by both supervisors and co-workers, and its establishment of a stringent standard of employer liability fundamentally shaped the development of sexual harassment law. These guidelines influenced federal courts' interpretations of Title VII, and they served as a model for state laws, local ordinances, and employer policies.

MOVEMENT RESPONSES TO GOVERNMENT POLICY

Some feminists, however, remained skeptical of the benefits of government involvement. AASC, in particular, criticized the federal government's key role in defining the issue, arguing that the government did not share a feminist perspective and analysis of the problem but instead was primarily concerned with management and personnel solutions. The Alliance noted, for example, that the government did not provide any direct services or counseling for women being harassed and that government guidelines on harassment "failed to recognize the feelings of shame, fear, and powerlessness that inhibit women from reporting."[98] According to the Alliance, federal involvement also meant that it became harder to pose alternative ideas or solutions. Government involvement on sexual harassment took some control of the issue from the original organizations that had raised it. While in the 1970s, AASC and WWI had fundamentally shaped public discussions of sexual harassment, by the early 1980s, government officials and professionals came to dominate discussions on developing public policy.[99] In some cases, government officials, such as Norton, shared feminist concerns. Other government officials, however, such as Joseph Sanchez, Director of the Equal Employment Programs of the Justice Department, did not. But AASC members were skeptical even of Norton's guidelines, arguing that the "appearance and reassurance that adequate solutions for sexual harassment now exist" was false because the question of implementation still remained. In particular, they noted that the guidelines did not require employers to adopt policies and procedures and had no mechanism to monitor the effectiveness of procedures that did exist. They also noted that the procedures were often complicated and detailed, thus discouraging women from filing complaints.

Most importantly, AASC objected to government involvement on the grounds that government solutions were bureaucratic and legalistic, an approach that was flawed for several reasons. First, it concentrated on the individual case rather than group action, failing to address the general social behavior reinforcing sexual harassment. Second, it focused on procedural issues rather than the harassment, which often proved very frustrating for harassed women. In particular, bureaucrats were not equipped to handle the victims' intense emotions. Third, legal bureaucracies tended to treat poor people and people of color unfairly because "it takes certain kinds of skills, unconscious in people of privileged background, to manipulate the bureaucracies in our favor."[100] Also, black harassers tended to be targeted more often because "the legal system works most effectively against defendants who are the most vulnerable." Finally, the legal/bureaucratic system was economically discriminatory because a lawyer was critical to success. AASC sought to refocus attention away from the federal government and onto other groups working on sexual harassment.[101] In fact, despite increased awareness of sexual harassment and the broad EEOC guidelines, the "floodgates" never opened. Women did not file suits in large numbers because, according to Eleanor Holmes Norton, "there is so much risk in stepping forward, plus most women did not understand it to be a violation of federal law."[102]

AASC was skeptical not only of government involvement with the issue of sexual harassment but also of employers' interest in the issue. They argued that management cared about sexual harassment only because of concerns about lawsuits, lowered productivity, and the possibility that women workers would organize around the issue. AASC argued, "It is much safer, from management's perspective, to take control of sexual harassment into their own hands rather than find themselves with a strongly organized union."[103] AASC expressed dismay about the decreasing influence of feminist organizations on sexual harassment training. Whereas in the 1970s feminist organizations conducted most sexual harassment training, by the early 1980s, feminists had to compete with management consulting firms and government officials to train and sensitize people about the issue.[104]

Feminists supported the proliferation of sexual harassment training, but they were also concerned that nonfeminist professional trainers were not approaching the issue with the same fervor and sophisticated analysis of women's roles and female oppression that feminists had.[105] Whereas early government-developed training programs, like the Office of Planning and Management's model training program, had incorporated a feminist analysis of sexual harassment, management consulting firms that were beginning to develop programs on sexual harassment did not. For example, Mary Coeli Meyer and Jeanenne Oestreich, authors of the 1981 book *Sexual Harassment*, developed a training video and manual called *The Power Pinch*, which presented sexual harassment as a gender-neutral phenomenon.[106] The consulting firms that began doing sexual harassment training had neither a background in the issue nor a feminist orientation so the training did not address broader issues of sexism, power relations, and women's integration into the workplace that had been central to the training workshops of feminist activists. By contrast, AASC argued, "we have to continue to discuss sexual harassment in the context of its origins in a sexist society and a society with a rigid workplace hierarchy, and not settle for policies and procedures that aim to protect management from 'trouble.'"[107]

Feminists other than AASC criticized government policy on sexual harassment. Feminist socialist historian Linda Gordon argued against "separating sexual harassment from the larger political struggle against male supremacy" and from the "overall feminist perspective on changing the world." She warned against those who "will want to take control out of our hands, and to transform the issue into a bureaucratized, mechanistic set of procedures for disallowing certain very narrowly defined behavior." She argued that "the only reliable protection for women will be the power of the women's movement, not the threat of official punishment." She continued, "It is vital for the women's movement to retain a primary commitment to nonlegal nonbureaucratic means of struggle, means that we can control ourselves." [108] Therefore, despite the fact that government involvement legitimized the issue of sexual harassment, raising public awareness and providing new tools for combating and preventing sexual harassment, feminists were ambivalent about this involvement.[109]

This chapter demonstrates the movement's diversity as reflected in the range of activists and organizations that participated in the development of public policy on sexual harassment. The importance of grassroots activists is apparent in the influence of individuals who spoke out about their personal experiences of sexual harassment, thereby contributing to a compelling demand that resulted in federal government action on the issue. Organizations worked to generate media attention to the issue, publicizing high-profile cases involving government employees. Using survey data showing high rates of harassment among city and federal employees, activists framed sexual harassment as a widespread problem of abuse of female employees in government, which generated pressure for official action. Through the D.C. Commission on Women, activists were able to pressure the Mayor to act, which then put pressure on Congress to act. Using a range of evidence, from survey data to personal testimony, activists were able to make a compelling case for federal intervention.

The movement was then able to take advantage of political opportunities available in the waning days of the Carter administration to convince government officials to address the issue of sexual harassment. In particular, Eleanor Holmes Norton's presence at the helm of the EEOC provided an invaluable ally to movement activists.[110] Norton's background working on the issue made her knowledgeable and sympathetic to advocates, and she knew that she could receive strong support from women in the movement who cared passionately about the issue. In this manner, she was able to propose and pass sweeping guidelines prohibiting both *quid pro quo* and hostile environment sexual harassment, setting a high standard by which the issue would be framed in the coming years. In addition, the movement was able to mobilize the resources of the Merit System Protection Board and the Office of Personnel and Management to conduct the first large-scale scientific study of sexual harassment as well as develop and disseminate model sexual harassment policies and training curriculum to public and private employers around the country. Activists were also able to persuade state and local governmental bodies to act on the issue.

With the EEOC guidelines in place, the movement's framing of the issue as a civil rights violation and issue of sex discrimination solidified, but not without controversy. Within the movement against sexual harassment, there was an intramovement contest over whether to frame sexual harassment primarily as a legal violation to be addressed through lawsuits, or as a problem for women to address collectively in the workplace. AASC warned against framing the problem entirely within the legal/bureaucratic context, and they focused their efforts on empowering workers to act collectively within the workplace. WWI, on the other hand, focused on advancing women's legal rights to combat sexual harassment.[111] But the creation of the powerful new EEOC guidelines created a presumption in favor of legal action.

Although many condemned sexual harassment, commentators continued to trivialize the issue, echoing traditional views of sexual harassment as a personal moral issue. Walter Berns, a resident scholar at the American Enterprise Institute, argued in an article condemning the EEOC guidelines that "contrary to the assumption in sexual harassment literature, it is women, not men, who are ultimately responsible for what might be called the moral tone of any place where men and women are assembled, even, I think, the workplace.... In general, men will be what women want them to be." Citing Rousseau, Berns argued, "according to the order of nature, resistance belongs to them."[112] Many commentators blamed women for sexual harassment and distrusted women's accusations. In 1981, Phyllis Schlafly testified to Congress that the EEOC guidelines allowed "unscrupulous persons to file mischievous claims," that "virtuous" women were rarely victims of sexual harassment, and that "men hardly ever ask sexual favors of women from whom the certain answer is 'no.'"[113] These voices of opposition were an undercurrent that would become a full-fledged backlash in the 1980s, buoyed by the ascendancy of the conservative Reagan administration and the emerging political constraints that would challenge the movement to defend its gains.

7

Fighting the Backlash: Feminist Activism in the 1980s

> "The entire issue is a perfect example of a minor special interest group's ability to blow up an 'issue' to a level of importance which in no way relates to the reality of the world in which we live and work."
>
> -38-year old plant manager for a manufacturer of industrial goods quoted in *Harvard Business Review*[1]

By 1981, feminist activists had made significant advances in convincing the public that sexual harassment was a real and serious problem. Courts in twenty-one states and the District of Columbia had recognized that sexual harassment could give rise to a federal or state cause of action against an employer, and many states had adopted legislation, executive orders, and regulations prohibiting sexual harassment. But the newly-installed Reagan administration immediately attempted to weaken sexual harassment prohibitions and reduce the effectiveness of the EEOC. Hostile reactions arose from other quarters as well, amounting to a backlash against the anti-sexual harassment movement. While in the 1970s, most resistance to the movement came from employers defending sexual harassment suits, in the early 1980s, hostile reactions to new sexual harassment laws emerged from individuals accused of sexual harassment, conservative advocacy organizations, and even men on the left. Individuals accused of sexual harassment began to fight back more aggressively by bringing lawsuits against their accusers for defamation or their employers for wrongful termination, breach of contract, and other claims. They also filed union grievances challenging employers' disciplinary measures imposed for sexual harassment. Employers and their advocates became even more active in resisting sexual harassment prohibitions than they had been in the 1970s. Ironically, the most outspoken critic of sexual harassment prohibitions was a woman, Phyllis Schlafly, who testified before Congress on behalf of the antifeminist group Eagle Forum. The movement that had fought for sexual harassment prohibitions now worked to diffuse this backlash, drawing on the networks they had developed in the 1970s as well as new organizations addressing the issue. The changing political and legal context, however, changed the character of the movement as the 1980s progressed.

BATTLE TO PRESERVE THE EEOC GUIDELINES

Upon taking office, the Reagan administration aggressively acted to curtail affirmative action and equal employment opportunity programs. Included within this agenda was an attempt to weaken and even abolish the EEOC sexual harassment guidelines. The first attempt to overturn the EEOC guidelines came from Utah Republican Senator Orrin Hatch. Shortly after assuming leadership of the Senate Committee on Labor and Human Resources in January of 1981, Senator Hatch held a series of hearings on sex discrimination in the workplace, including a hearing on sexual harassment. The committee was considering amending Title VII to add language specifically addressing sexual harassment. The proposed bill, drafted by Senator Hatch, was weaker than the EEOC guidelines, providing that employers would be liable only when they "knowingly" condoned sexual harassment.[2] This standard would have eliminated the stringent liability standards set out by the EEOC guidelines, which made employers strictly liable for supervisory harassment.

Feminists resisted by testifying before congressional committees, writing letters, and orchestrating a national letter-writing campaign. A broad range of people testified at a hearing on the proposed amendment on April 21, 1981. The hearing focused not only on sexual harassment, but also on the Reagan administration initiatives to eliminate affirmative action and cut the budgets of the EEOC and the Office of Federal Contract Compliance Programs (OFCCP), the two federal agencies primarily responsible for enforcing antidiscrimination laws. At the start of the hearing, Senator Edward Kennedy expressed concern that Reagan administration budget cuts, especially a twenty percent budget cut for the EEOC, threatened to impede the advancement of women in the workplace, and he suggested that the sexual harassment guidelines might have in part motivated the budget cut. The Acting Chair of the EEOC, Clay Smith, then testified about the sexual harassment guidelines, EEOC decisions on sexual harassment, and EEOC involvement in sexual harassment litigation. In response to questions by Senator Edward Kennedy, Smith described sexual harassment as a serious problem and the cases filed before the EEOC as just the "tip of the iceberg."[3]

The Committee then heard testimony from Phyllis Schlafly, President of Eagle Forum, an antifeminist organization that spearheaded the movement against the ERA.[4] Schlafly argued that the EEOC guidelines were "unjust because they penalize an innocent bystander, the employer, for acts over which he has no control." Schlafly harshly criticized feminists for making "a Federal case out of the problem of bosses pinching their secretaries." She blamed women for sexual harassment, testifying that sexual harassment on the job was not a problem for "the virtuous woman except in the rarest of cases. When a woman walks across the room, she speaks with a universal body language that most men intuitively understand. Men hardly ever ask sexual favors of women from whom the certain answer is 'no.'" She continued, "virtuous women are seldom accosted by unwelcome sexual propositions or familiarities, obscene talk, or profane language."[5]

A panel of feminist women rebutted this testimony, including Eleanor Holmes Norton, Betty Jean Hall and Pat Baldwin of the Western Kentucky Coalmining Women's Support Team, and Karen Sauvigné and Joan Vermeulen of WWI.[6] These women supported the EEOC guidelines and spoke against Hatch's proposed amendment to weaken them. Norton's testimony was particularly powerful. She represented forty-eight women's organizations, with a combined membership of over 700,000 women and men, and described her testimony as "the largest and most diverse grouping of women's organizations ever to offer a single piece of congressional testimony."[7] They included all of the major women's organizations, six mining organizations, six religious organizations, eight minority women's organizations, several organizations focused on violence against women, several working women's organizations and unions, and several bar associations. Norton confronted Senator Hatch and the Republican members of the committee about their attempts to roll back affirmative action and antidiscrimination laws and programs. She criticized them for targeting budget cuts at the two primary agencies responsible for enforcing antidiscrimination laws: the EEOC and OFCCP. In particular, she noted that the committee recommended reductions in the budget of the EEOC's Office of Policy Implementation, which had produced the sexual harassment guidelines.

Betty Jean Hall and Pat Baldwin of the Western Kentucky Coalmining Women's Support Team testified that sexual harassment was a serious problem, especially for women coalminers, and that the EEOC guidelines had helped tremendously in alleviating this problem. They testified that "when employers claim that they cannot control the men, we simply send them a warning letter ... and enclose a copy of the EEOC sexual harassment guidelines. ... It is amazing how quickly the problem seems to take care of itself once the company is aware of the guidelines," thereby avoiding "lengthy and costly litigation." They opposed the proposed amendment, emphasizing the importance of affirmative action for women and urged the committee to support the EEOC and OFCCP, which they described as "the only agency that was able to respond to an industrywide pattern of blatant sex discrimination."[8]

Similarly, Karen Sauvigné and Joan Vermeulen of WWI opposed the amendment and spoke in favor of affirmative action. They described sexual harassment as an "abuse of male power and authority" and "sexual blackmail."[9] Furthermore, they explained how sexual harassment contributed to women's higher rate of unemployment and lower rate of continuous employment than men, operating to confine women to traditionally female jobs and keep them out of nontraditional jobs. They warned against a lesser degree of liability that would enable employers to hide behind the shield of individual employee action and leave women without any effective remedy for sexual harassment. The committee received written statements, studies, and articles from several groups and individuals, including Sandra Bundy and Adrienne Tomkins, who submitted testimony describing their experiences of sexual harassment and their

but also harmed businesses. One writer warned that to rescind the regulations would send a message that sexual harassment was "all right."[21] Two women wrote of their personal experiences of sexual harassment.[22] In July of 1982, Karen Sauvigné wrote another letter to Vice President Bush and to EEOC Chair Clarence Thomas, urging them to retain the EEOC guidelines as written.[23] On March 8, 1983, the EEOC voted not to review the guidelines on sexual harassment because of their public support and the deference given them by the courts.[24]

In addition to cutting the EEOC budget and attempting to abolish the EEOC sexual harassment guidelines, the Reagan administration targeted the OFCCP, the other federal agency primarily responsible for enforcing equal employment opportunity initiatives. First, the administration blocked the implementation of OFCCP sexual harassment guidelines and, more generally, relaxed regulatory control of federal contractors. Upon taking office, Reagan issued an executive order freezing the implementation of all new regulations.[25] OFCCP had previously adopted federal guidelines prohibiting sexual harassment by federal construction contractors. Reagan's regulatory freeze blocked the enactment of these guidelines before their effective date. In addition, OFCCP was forced to consider proposals by employers and their advocates to limit the effectiveness of the office's ability to combat sexual harassment. These proposals included doing away with back pay and other monetary remedies for sexual harassment, no longer requiring employers to publicize sexual harassment grievance procedures, and raising from $50,000 to $1 million the contract threshold at which employers must draw up written antiharassment programs. The administration also cut the budget of the OFCCP. In November 1981, all of the 1,181 OFCCP staffers were notified that they might be laid off as part of the Reagan cutback in government.[26] These actions by the Reagan administration slowed down efforts to combat sexual harassment. With the support of employers and their advocates, the Reagan administration was able to block new sexual harassment regulations and limit enforcement of equal employment laws, but it was not immediately able to weaken the EEOC guidelines. However, Reagan began to appoint conservative judges to the bench, which had a long-term negative impact on the development of civil rights issues, including sexual harassment jurisprudence.[27] These judges, including Clarence Thomas as a Supreme Court jurist, would later overrule the guidelines' broad liability standards.

DEFENDANTS RESIST: THE RESPONSE OF ACCUSED
MEN AND THEIR EMPLOYERS

In the early 1980s, accused men began to fight back against women alleging sexual harassment by filing civil lawsuits for defamation and slander against their accusers. For example, in 1980, a Virginia man accused of sexual harassment and assault won $95,000 in a slander suit against his accusers.[28] In the 1981 case of *Barnes v. Oody*, two male employees of the Tennessee Valley

Authority brought a defamation lawsuit against two women who accused them of sexual harassment. The women had prevailed in an internal investigation by TVA's Equal Employment Opportunity office and in arbitration of grievances filed by the men under a collective bargaining agreement. Although the court dismissed the suit, the women nonetheless spent close to a year in court defending themselves.[29]

Many of the early cases against women alleging sexual harassment arose at educational institutions. At Clark University, a sociology professor sued two professors, one graduate student, one undergraduate student, and a secretary for $23.7 million for injury to his "good name and reputation" because they had accused him of sexual harassment. At the University of Massachusetts, a program director filed a countersuit against eight students who had accused him of sexual harassment. At Carleton University School of Journalism in Ottawa, Ontario, three professors brought libel and slander suits against three students for $100,000 because the students, acting for a group of about twenty-five fellow students, staged a press conference in March of 1980 charging members of their department with sexual harassment. They did not name specific men, but three male professors felt that they were unfairly implicated.[30] These publicized lawsuits by individuals accused of sexual harassment did not succeed but probably intimidated some women from complaining of sexual harassment. Nevertheless, women continued to file charges of sexual harassment and at an increasing rate as the decade progressed.

Men accused of sexual harassment sued not only their accusers but their employers as well, alleging a wide range of tort and contract claims, as well as federal statutory and constitutional claims.[31] The professor at Clark University filed a claim before the National Labor Relations Board and threatened to file suit against the university. In 1978, a male faculty member sued New York Law School for one million dollars claiming he was forced to resign because of rumors that he made sexual advances toward his female students. He denied any misconduct and claimed that he was not allowed to be heard or confront witnesses during the school's investigation. The same year a professor accused of sexually harassing a female employee sued Texas A&M University for making him resign under duress. Professors also sued educational institutions for violating their constitutional rights to due process and equal protection.[32] These cases were usually dismissed for lack of evidence or settled out of court.

Defamation suits against employers were particularly common in the early 1980s. In one case, a man filed a suit for defamation, interference with employment contract, and violation of his first amendment rights against a fellow male employee, who he alleged imposed an unwarranted sexual harassment hearing on him. In another case, a black man sued his employer for race discrimination after he was discharged for sexual harassment. Another avenue of defense was to file grievances under collective bargaining agreements. A 1981 study found twenty-four reported sexual harassment arbitration cases between 1965 and 1981. Twenty of the twenty-four cases were disciplinary actions appealed to arbitration by a union on behalf of a male grievant who had been disciplined for engaging in some form of sexual harassment. In fourteen of nineteen cases, the arbitration boards sustained the employers' disciplinary actions against the harassers. The 1980s brought an explosion of lawsuits by male union members challenging their employers' disciplinary actions for sexual harassment. In one case, a man discharged for sexual harassment sued his employer for wrongful discharge and his union for breach of its duty of fair representation by refusing to press his grievance beyond an initial hearing.[33] Arbitrators routinely supported employers' disciplinary actions for sexual harassment.

Disciplined men also sued local, state, and federal governments and government officials. In the case of *Huff v. County of Butler*, a county employee accused of sexual harassment sued his employer under the Due Process Clause, alleging that his forced resignation was damaging to his character and reputation and that he was entitled to notice and a hearing before being compelled to resign. In the federal government, men accused of sexual harassment appealed disciplinary measures taken by the Merit System Protection Board to the federal courts. In one case, a civilian employee of the Air Force successfully sued for reinstatement after he was discharged for sexual harassment. Two high-profile cases from the early 1980s involved state politicians accused of sexual harassment. Both alleged that the investigations of those charges were politically motivated. In 1981, the Kentucky Agriculture Secretary, who was being investigated for sexual harassment, sued the governor and his administration for illegally using governmental resources to investigate civil matters, suggesting a political conspiracy against him. A member of the Florida House of Representatives, Gene Flinn, lost his 1980 bid for reelection after he was reprimanded by the State House for sexual harassment. In 1984, Flinn sued the two legislative aides who had accused him of sexual harassment, another legislative employee, Representative Elaine Gordon who had chaired the committee that investigated Flinn, and the candidate who defeated him in the 1980 election. He alleged that Gordon had abrogated her duty as chair of the House committee and that all of the defendants had conspired to release slanderous accusations of sexual misconduct by Flinn to the news media. The case was dismissed by the Eleventh Circuit for failure to state a cause of action against Gordon.[34]

Resistance to sexual harassment laws came not only from individuals accused of harassment but also from employers and their advocates. In the 1980s, employers became politically active in resisting sexual harassment laws. Many employers filed comments on the EEOC guidelines and the OFCCP guidelines on sexual harassment, suggesting narrowing these guidelines or eliminating them altogether. Employers pressured the Reagan administration to deregulate the economy and limit the reach of equal employment opportunity laws, including laws against sexual harassment. Employers' advocates filed *amicus curiae* briefs in sexual harassment cases in the 1980s, including the first Supreme Court case on sexual harassment, in which the Equal Employment Advisory Council, the United States Chamber of Commerce, and the Trustees of Boston University filed amicus briefs on behalf of the employers.

Conservative publications on sexual harassment also began to appear in the 1980s. In 1981, business management professionals Mary Coeli Meyer, Inge M. Berchtold, Jeanenne L. Oestreich, and Frederick J. Collins Published a book titled *Sexual Harassment*. Described by one reviewer as "antifeminist,"[35] this book explicitly denied the underlying gendered power dynamics of sexual harassment, characterizing the problem in individual rather than social terms. The authors argued that every individual was responsible for where they fall on the "continuum" between "authentic romantic behavior" and "harassing behavior."[36] The authors implied that women were responsible for sexual harassment because of how they dressed, behaved, and related to men. Men, on the other hand, were assumed to be innocent, merely "confused and disoriented" by women's increasing presence in the workplace. The authors also argued that sexual harassment was not a woman's issue but an employment and economic issue. They suggested that men and women experienced comparable amounts of sexual harassment in the workplace, giving examples of women harassing men as often as men harassing women. Finally, the authors explicitly contested feminist analysis of the origins of sexual harassment by saying that "the situation is considerably more complex than that of subjugation and power."[37] After providing a simplistic description of white, middle-class female and male socialization, the authors concluded that sexual harassment resulted from recent role changes, ignoring the manifestations of sexual harassment in prior times. These antifeminist arguments were only some of many that began appearing with increasing frequency as the 1980s progressed.

DEBATES ON SEXUAL HARASSMENT POLICY

Those who opposed developing antisexual harassment policies in the 1970s and early 1980s offered a range of reasons, including that sexual harassment was not really a problem, that women brought sexual harassment on themselves by their dress and behavior, that women made false charges and accusations when an affair went bad, and that it was a moral problem, not a legal problem. These themes were often advanced in opposition to laws and policies prohibiting sexual harassment as society continued to struggle with sex roles and the place of women in the workplace.

The argument that sexual harassment was not a problem appeared in many forms. Some suggested that the incidence of sexual harassment was greatly exaggerated. They questioned early studies conducted by feminists showing high rates of sexual harassment among working women, such as the WWI 1975 survey and the *Redbook* 1976 survey.[38] Others argued that sexual harassment was not serious enough to warrant legal intervention. Similar to the early courts' arguments that sexual harassment was an individual personal problem, Mary Coeli Meyer and her coauthors in their 1981 book on sexual harassment denied the significance of the problem by characterizing sexual harassment as an individual problem rather than a social problem particularly affecting women. By arguing that sexual harassment was a gender-neutral phenomenon that happened not only to women, but to men also, this book attempted to divorce sexual harassment from the feminist critique of patriarchy by ignoring the underlying power dynamics of sexual harassment. Many simply did not take the issue seriously, considering it a "frivolous concern at work compared to weighty matters of commerce, government, and education."[39]

The notion that sexual harassment was not a serious problem became less and less persuasive as studies appeared throughout the 1980s showing its widespread and serious impact particularly on women. Beginning with the Merit System Protection Board's 1980 survey of sexual harassment in the federal workplace, governments, academics, and advocacy groups conducted many studies of sexual harassment in the workplace and in educational institutions throughout the 1980s.[40] Several of these studies were large-scale scientific studies. For example, *Harvard Business Review* and *Redbook* magazine published a joint study in 1981 surveying over 1,800 business executives on their experiences and attitudes about sexual harassment, and the Merit System Protection Board conducted a follow-up survey of federal workers in 1987. These studies showed that approximately one out of every two women would be harassed at some point during her academic or working life.[41]

Another theme that pervaded the public discussion of sexual harassment in the 1980s was that women caused sexual harassment by their dress and behavior. Phyllis Schlafly's comments before the Senate Committee on Labor and Human Resources exemplified this sort of argument. In *Harper's* magazine, Walter Berns of the American Enterprise Institute argued that harassment was caused and could be controlled by women's behavior, especially their dress. He suggested that the best way to solve the problem would be dress codes for women. Similar to Schlafly, Berns held women responsible for sexual harassment.[42] The tendency to blame women was vividly manifested in an illustration accompanying an article on sexual harassment appearing in a March 1980 issue of *USA Today*. The woman in the illustration was portrayed very alluringly, wearing a revealing dress, with a short hemline and a very low neckline, and stiletto heels. Her fatherly, benign-looking boss was leaning over her with his arms wrapped around her.[43] This illustration implied that women asked for sexual harassment by their dress and behavior in the workplace. Before courts, sexual harassment victims were often treated like rape victims: defense attorneys delved into their sexual past and questioned their behavior, their dress, and their speech.

A related theme that dominated the public discussion of sexual harassment in the 1980s was the claim that women lied about sexual harassment and made false accusations when an affair went bad. Throughout the Hanley hearings, subcommittee members repeatedly questioned the witnesses about the possibility of frivolous charges. In protesting the subcommittee's report, Representative Gene Taylor, the Ranking Minority Member, criticized the report for not addressing the issue of "unfounded and frivolous complaints of sexual harassment."[44] In the 1980 congressional hearings about sexual harassment in the Texas postal service, Postmaster William Jennings testified that "allegations of sexual harassment are easily fabricated and can be as devastating to the innocent as to the guilty, if accepted at face value." He described reports of harassment he had received which were "greatly exaggerated – if not false – reports."[45] Phyllis Schlafly testified before Congress that sexual harassment laws allowed "unscrupulous persons to file mischievous claims."[46] The stereotype that women lie about sex also repeatedly appeared in Mary Coeli Meyer's book. For example, the foreword to the book was the story of Potiphar's wife found in Genesis 39 of the Bible. In this story, Potiphar's wife tried to seduce Joseph and then cried rape when he refused her advances.[47] The stereotypes that women caused sexual harassment by their dress and behavior and were likely to make false charges persisted throughout the 1980s and into the 1990s. Anita Hill, for example, was accused of lying about her charges that Clarence Thomas sexually harassed her and also accused her of being a nymphomaniac and a lesbian.[48] These stereotypes blamed women for sexual harassment, hearkening back to the nineteenth-century moral condemnation of women.

Indeed, the nineteenth-century understanding of sexual harassment as a moral issue sometimes emerged in the treatment of the issue, despite the efforts of activists in the 1970s to characterize sexual harassment as sex discrimination. For example, in *Miller v. Bank of America*, the district court ruled that the alleged conduct fell under the company's policy against "moral misconduct."[49] In another example, the Screen Actor's Guild in Los Angeles set up a "morals complaints bureau" designed to arbitrate sexual harassment charges.[50] In her 1981 testimony before Congress, Phyllis Schlafly characterized sexual harassment as a matter of morality when she argued that "virtuous women are seldom accosted by unwelcome sexual propositions or familiarities, obscene talk, or profane language."[51] Mary Coeli Meyer and her coauthors argued that "sexual harassment is basically a moral issue and therefore the overall responsibility for its elimination lies within the individual rather than the law."[52] American Enterprise Institute's Walter Berns argued, "it is women, not men, who are ultimately responsible for what might be called the moral tone of any place where men and women are assembled, even, I think, the workplace. In general, men will be what women want them to be."[53] This characterization obscured the role that gender-based abuse of power and sexual coercion played in preventing women from fully participating in the workplace.

The underlying power dynamics, in particular the issue of women's right to enter the workplace, explicitly arose in public discussions of sexual harassment. Phyllis Schlafly testified before Congress that she opposed "inducements to wives to enter the labor force or to mothers to assign care of their children to institutions," and she condemned any government action "designed to eliminate or to blur the separate identity of different sex roles for men and women."[54] Linda Gordon, on the other hand, argued that sexual harassment forced women to accept "the image of themselves as fair game in any public space" and that this maintained and reinforced "women's sense of belonging at home in the family, and hence of the most basic sexual division of labor, one of the biggest sources of sexual inequality."[55] She continued, "sexual harassment functions to keep women domestic, to reinforce the tradition that public spaces belong to men."[56] Similarly, AASC argued that women workers were not taken seriously because many people still believed that "a woman's place was in the home." They argued, "sexual harassment comes out of this lack of respect for women as workers, it's a way of saying, 'you don't belong here.'"[57] The early literature of Working Women's Institute acknowledged this issue, noting that attitudes that trivialize sexual harassment "stem from traditional societal and institutional definitions which portray women as sexual beings, not to be taken seriously as workers."[58] Sexually harassed women themselves sometimes acknowledged the relationship of sexual harassment to their participation in the workplace. In a 1981 survey of women coal miners, many of the respondents who had experienced sexual harassment reported that their male co-workers and supervisors did not want women working in the mines.[59] One of the women testifying at the 1975 speak-out in Ithaca lamented, "maybe I should've stayed home and had babies, like my mother said."[60] These comments reflected how sexual harassment was closely linked to the question of women's right to participate in the workplace.

Although feminists sought to characterize sexual harassment as an issue of power, not sex, some feminists expressed concerns about the "antisexual attitudes" and "moralism" that frequently invaded discussions of sexual harassment.[61] In a 1979 *Washington Post* article, Catharine MacKinnon emphasized, "objection to sexual harassment is not a neopuritan protest against signs of attraction, displays of affection, compliments, flirtation, or touching on the job. It is a protest against sex that is one-sided, unwelcome, or comes with strings attached . . . coming from someone with the economic power to hire or fire, help or hinder, reward or punish."[62] In 1981, MacKinnon noted, "the law against sexual harassment often seems to turn women's demand to control our own sexuality into a request for paternal protection, leaving the impression that it is more traditional morality and less women's power that is vindicated."[63] The Alliance warned against the "desexualization of the workplace," contending that "when antisex attitudes prevail then the liberation we seek is undermined by a limited vision of who we are as people and a view of sexuality, which is ultimately antiwoman." They called instead for a close examination of "sexuality, roles, and power."[64] Socialist feminist Linda Gordon, writing in the early 1980s after the Reagan administration had taken office, argued, "when a right-wing antifeminist backlash is attempting to reinstitute prudish and repressive limits on sexual freedom, it is more important than ever that feminists not project antisexual attitudes."[65] Others expressed concern that "sexual harassment might become a stalking horse for a new wave of repressive prudery."[66] These concerns were part of a larger feminist debate about sexuality, female agency, and victimization, especially in the context of pornography and prostitution. Nevertheless, while these latter issues created deep divisions among feminists, sexual harassment did not, perhaps because the EEOC guidelines had defined sexual harassment as unwelcome and economically coercive. Whereas pornography had no clear broad-based economic effect on women, workplace sexual harassment clearly did.

BACKLASH FROM LEFTISTS: THE CASE OF XIMENA BUNSTER

Resistance to sexual harassment prohibitions came not only from the right but sometimes also from people identified with the left. Many unions, in particular, were slow to act on claims of sexual harassment made against union members out of concern that the issue might divide the working class or be used by management against union leaders.[67] Division within the left on the issue manifested itself most clearly in a high-profile case that arose at Clark University in Worcester, Massachusetts.[68] In June 1980, Ximena Bunster, a visiting associate professor of Anthropology and Women's Studies at Clark University, filed a formal sexual harassment complaint with the university against Sidney M. Peck, Chair of the Sociology/Anthropology Department. Bunster made this formal complaint after unsuccessfully trying informal channels to address the problem, including talking to tenured men in the department, a dean, and the Provost. Bunster was a forty-eight-year-old Chilean political exile and noted scholar who came to the United States in 1975 under the sponsorship of Margaret Mead. Peck was a well-connected leftist activist. In a ten-page, single-spaced, typewritten complaint, Bunster alleged that Peck had tried to kiss her, had made repeated demeaning sexual innuendoes and characterizations, frequently in the presence of students and department colleagues, and had told her he would help her stay at the university only if she acceded to his sexual demands. According to the complaint, when Bunster told Peck that his behavior was inappropriate and unwanted, Peck used his power as department chair to interfere with her teaching and research activities.

Within three weeks after Peck received notice of Bunster's complaint, supporters of Peck formed the "Committee to Support Sid Peck," which defended Peck by attempting to discredit Bunster and by accusing the university administration of targeting him because of his political activism. Peck, with over twenty years of labor and antiwar organizing, was able to form an extensive network of support across the country and raise significant financial support to defend himself. The committee established fundraising branches in San Francisco, Chicago, Los Angeles, New York, Washington, D.C., Milwaukee, and Cleveland. Peck's supporters argued that the dispute was motivated by "administrative enmity at Clark" toward Peck. In particular, Peck had chaired a committee on faculty compensation that had resulted in one million dollars in salary increases for faculty over a four-year period. Peck had also founded an affirmative action committee at the university and had fought to reverse a negative tenure decision against a radical colleague in the sociology department.

The Committee to Support Sid Peck deluged the area with their material. In August of 1980, Peck's supporters sent out a fundraising letter focusing on Peck's long-term activism in "movements for peace and justice," "his unwavering commitment to principle," and "his acute political and sociological insight." The letter implied Bunster was a puppet of the administration. The letter characterized the complaint as part of a "national pattern of assault upon progressive academics," which "can only have a chilling effect upon everyone's right to engage in advocacy and social activism." Peck's supporters called for a resolution of the dispute outside of the university, within "our own community."[69]

Peck's supporters also attacked Bunster's character and motivations. At the 1980 meeting of the American Sociological Association and the Society for the Study of Social Problems in New York, at least one of Peck's supporters characterized Bunster as "crazy, childless, lonely, and unstable." Feminists at the meeting were so outraged that they convinced the Steering Committee of Sociologists for Women in Society to pass a unanimous resolution condemning the practice of attacking women who have charged sexual harassment by attacking their moral, political, or personal character and by using "psychiatric vocabularies of motives to discredit her."[70] Bunster supporters characterized the attack on Bunster as racist and antiimmigrant because Peck supporters implied that "she did not understand American culture, that her 'Latin style' invited sexual overtures, that her rights and motives were inferior because she was not a permanent resident; she was just a 'visitor' or, as one of Peck's supporters' leaflets said, 'an ordinary foreign worker.'"[71]

Peck's efforts to vindicate himself and discredit Bunster continued into the 1980 fall semester. Peck and his wife, Louise, hosted several wine-and-cheese parties for students and faculty to present his side of the story. Peck also gave interviews to the Clark student newspaper and to *Worcester Magazine*. Finally, he circulated a 104-page document denying that he had attempted to coerce her into sleeping with him or that he had attempted any reprisals. He questioned the credibility of Bunster and several students he thought might testify against him in hearings on the charges. Peck's supporters argued that Bunster was trying to help the university get rid of Peck in exchange for extension of her contract. His support committee continued to send out fundraising letters, including to students taking courses in his department at the time. Peck received support not only from the left, but also from feminists. On October 15, 1980, thirty-five women circulated a letter in the Boston/Cambridge feminist community, stating that they were "deeply troubled" by the allegations against Peck and that they had questioned Peck and decided that he was innocent. They apparently did not talk to Bunster before coming to this conclusion.

Support also formed for Bunster and grew steadily with time. In October of 1980, Clark Professor Cynthia Enloe organized a group of supporters, who formed the Committee for Fairness to Ximena Bunster, known as the Fairness Committee. The committee included Gilda Bruckman, Estelle Disch, and Rita Arditti. Arditti, who was co-owner of New Words bookstore in Boston, was from Argentina, and was particularly offended by Peck's supporters' use of racist stereotypes in their campaign against Bunster.[72] Bunster's supporters raised funds through a film benefit in May 1981 and, in October 1981, Adrienne Rich and Andrea Dworkin did a benefit reading in Boston to an audience of over 500. In addition, Persephone Press donated several cartons of books to be sold on behalf of the women, and hundreds of individuals sent contributions and notes of support. Finally, Members of Sociologists for Women in Society supported Bunster by raising funds for her early on, and two feminist lawyers worked for Bunster for reduced fees.

The Fairness Committee circulated a letter in November of 1980 testifying to Bunster's high standards as a scholar, to the unacceptability of racist characterizations of her, and to the necessity of taking sexual harassment seriously as an issue. The committee explained feminists' opposition to Bunster as often based on inaccurate information, but in some cases as growing from a "profound uneasiness about sexual harassment as an issue." According to the Fairness Committee, some women feared that making sexual harassment an issue could be equated with an antisex attitude. They feared that "sexual harassment might become a stalking horse for a new wave of repressive prudery."[73] The committee attacked Peck's argument that a conservative administration was using naïve women to rid the campus of "radical" professors, noting that "the bumbling way in which the administration proceeded testifies not to political vengeance against Peck but bureaucratic indifference to sexual harassment."[74] The committee also criticized the concern expressed by Peck's supporters of "splitting the left" because of the assumption that "the complaints of the women took second place to the alleged necessity of maintaining a solid front in the current political climate." They explained, "some leftist men [have] been sheltered from accusations of sexual harassment by virtue of their status as worthy political allies."[75]

After receiving Bunster's formal complaint, the university handed the matter over to the Committee on Personnel, consisting of six faculty members, four men and two women. The committee conducted a preliminary investigation, including a confidential hearing with witnesses for both Bunster and Peck. Several women testified that Peck had made unwanted sexual advances to them, including Professor Betsy Stanko, an untenured sociologist and the only other full-time female member of the Sociology/Anthropology Department, a graduate student, an undergraduate student, and a department secretary. On November 10, 1980, the Personnel Committee concluded that there was substantial evidence to support some of the charges. On November 19, 1980, Bunster and Stanko filed discrimination charges against Clark University with the EEOC, protesting both the sexual harassment and the university's failure to address the charges appropriately and to prevent retaliation against them for complaining. They asked the EEOC to force Clark to "seriously, thoroughly, and promptly address these complaints of sexual harassment." On December 8, 1980, the President of Clark issued formal charges against Peck for "lack of fitness as a faculty member," naming several women who had testified during the preliminary investigation. On January 5, 1981, the university proposed a format for a hearing on the charges, which according to the Fairness Committee "would have violated the civil rights of all involved."[76] The university also filed a motion with the EEOC to dismiss the complaints against it filed by Bunster and Stanko.

In January 1981, Peck filed a complaint against Clark with the National Labor Relations Board, claiming that Clark was investigating him not because of its concern for women, but because of his leftist political activity. Peck and the school then entered into a process of negotiation to settle the dispute. On March 23, 1981, the lawyer representing Bunster and Stanko told the university that they would not participate in another proceeding scheduled by the institution to consider the charges against Peck because the institution was not fairly addressing the issues of sex discrimination and sexual harassment. In particular, they objected to the fact that Bunster and Stanko could not call witnesses on their own behalf, that they had no right to receive a copy of the decision, and that they were not allowed to comment on the composition of the hearing board. The next day, March 24, 1981, the university and Peck signed an agreement dropping the charges. Under the agreement, the university agreed that no further action would be taken on the charges drawn up against Peck, and Peck agreed to drop his NLRB claim against the university and his plans to sue the university. The agreement also prohibited Peck from serving as chair of any department at Clark in the future and prohibited him from participating in any employment decisions concerning Bunster or Stanko. Finally, the agreement provided that, because of "tensions within the university as a result of the matters in dispute which need time to abate," Peck would take a leave of absence to begin March 31 and in September begin a half-year sabbatical at full pay, during which he would not be present on the campus.

Supporters of Bunster wrote to the president, protesting the settlement and the university's failure to address the sexual harassment charges. They argued that, "the consequences of this false resolution are disturbing and far-reaching," and that those who testified before the Committee on Personnel "participated in good faith in the university's grievance procedure and are now being penalized because the university truncated this procedure in return for a settlement that provides legal protection for some parties but not for others."[77] The day after signing the settlement with the university, Peck sued Bunster, Stanko, and the other women who accused him of sexual harassment for $23.7 million in state court for defamation and injury to his "good name and reputation." The women learned of the suit when Peck supporters distributed a broadsheet across Clark campus including articles titled, "Mutual Charges Dropped," "Peck to Lead Peace Drive," stating that Peck had requested a leave of absence to do peace work, and "Peck Files Suit." Peck lost much of his support after filing this suit. By April 1981, a variety of organizations and individuals had written private and public letters to Peck asking him to drop the suit, including the editorial staffs of *Radical America* and *Socialist Review*; George Wald, a Harvard University biologist and Nobel Prize winner; Howard Zinn, a political scientist at Boston University and a longtime political activist, and AASC. At Clark, petitions were circulated among students, faculty, and staff calling on the university administration to take action to protect the women from this further intimidation. Local Worcester feminists picketed Clark's graduation ceremony and feminist Adrienne Rich refused to accept an honorary degree from Clark, saying she did not want "to be used as a token feminist, and as a screen for the realities of women's status within the university." All five women had to hire attorneys to respond to Peck's suit. In spring of 1982, Peck dropped the defamation suit against the women who accused him of sexual harassment. Peck signed a public statement admitting that his suit was an act of intimidation and advising other men that such suits were not effective techniques when used against women who filed sexual harassment complaints against them.

On October 13, 1981, Bunster and Shanko filed suit against Clark and its administrators, alleging that they had violated both federal and Massachusetts civil rights law because they had no procedures for protecting women from sexual harassment.[78] The case was settled in May 1982, on commencement day. The Clark University Board of Trustees agreed to award Bunster and Stanko $95,000 in attorney's fees and damages and agreed to establish effective grievance procedures, including employing a full-time sexual harassment grievance officer. After her initial two-year appointment in sociology from 1978 to 1980, Bunster received a one-year appointment from 1980 to 1981 as visiting associate professor of women's studies but was not rehired after that.

This controversy at Clark University grew out of the political landscape of the 1980s. Men in the left had often resisted feminist concerns. But in the atmosphere of conservative backlash of the 1980s, some became concerned about the possibility that the issue of sexual harassment could become a conservative tool to repress progressives, men of color, and immigrant men. Peck was not alone, in the early 1980s, in claiming that conservative university administrations targeted leftists with sexual harassment charges. In a high-profile case at the University of California at Berkeley, sociology professor Elbaki Hermassi, who was suspended without pay for one quarter for sexual harassment of students, contended, "These people are looking for a cause, and I got in the way. I am not an American citizen, and because of my origins they regard me as easy to victimize."[79] A 1980 article in the *Chronicle for Higher Education* characterized sexual harassment charges as "mean little cases" that threatened academic freedom.[80]

Progressives' fears of the issue were sometimes fueled by sexist assumptions and an ignorance of the significant deleterious impact that sexual harassment might have on the lives of women. But in some cases, feminists committed to the eradication of sexual harassment expressed ambivalence about the issue. AASC, for example, expressed concerns about employers using sexual harassment as a "union-busting technique." They acknowledged that employers might use sexual harassment as a tool for selective punishment of certain employees, such as members of unions or racial minorities.[81] At a public forum on sexual harassment in Boston in February 1981, feminist socialist historian Linda Gordon warned of the "civil liberties dangers" of sexual harassment investigations. She argued that "the government and institutions are more likely to act against accused men who are themselves members of vulnerable social groups – racial minorities, or leftists, for example."[82] According to Gordon, sexual harassment procedures could also be used against lesbians and gays as part of a homophobic campaign, or against heterosexual women, with women of color, or other oppressed groups, again most vulnerable.

Some of these tensions played themselves out in even more complex forms in the 1990s in the sexual harassment scandals involving Supreme Court nominee Clarence Thomas in 1991 and President Bill Clinton in the late 1990s. Thomas was able to recharacterize Anita Hill's sexual harassment charges against him as racist political harassment by calling the investigation a "high-tech lynching for uppity blacks." Clinton was also able to dodge the issue, with feminists' blessings, by characterizing Paula Jones' sexual harassment charges as a partisan attack.[83] Repeatedly, those accused of sexual harassment have been able to eclipse these charges by focusing on the perceived political motivations of those investigating and enforcing the laws against sexual harassment. Whereas sexual harassment policy could be used for political purposes, especially against members of disempowered groups, such claims certainly have been used to escape responsibility for discriminatory conduct. This politicization of sexual harassment charges has often deflected attention away from the underlying charges.

THE EVOLUTION OF THE ANTISEXUAL HARASSMENT MOVEMENT

Over the course of the 1980s, opposition to sexual harassment became increasingly professionalized. The grassroots feminist activism of AASC found much less support in the conservative climate of the early 1980s. Tensions developed within AASC about whether to change the organization to adapt to this new climate. Whereas some sought to make the organization more professionally oriented, others expressed ambivalence about working in the mainstream. In the end, AASC did not change its structure. In 1981, Freada Klein left AASC to go back to graduate school in social policy and research at the Heller School for Advanced Studies in Social Welfare at Brandeis University. In 1982, AASC moved their offices from downtown Boston to the basement of a church in Cambridge. They finally shut their doors in 1984 due to lack of funds.[84]

Several AASC members, however, continued to work on sexual harassment. Klein wrote her dissertation on sexual harassment in employment, focusing on factors affecting its incidence, severity, duration, and relationship to productivity. After graduating, she became the Director of Organizational Development at Lotus Development Corporation and later founded a management consulting firm focused on workplace bias, harassment, and discrimination. Klein has served extensively as an expert witness on sexual harassment and was a television commentator during the Anita Hill/Clarence Thomas hearings. Lynn Rubinett also continued to work on sexual harassment. After graduating from Northeastern Law School, Rubinett became a labor lawyer in Texas and conducted sexual harassment training with unions. In 1986, she published a law review article on sexual harassment. Later, she worked for the Texas Commission on Human Rights, where she continued to conduct workplace training on discrimination.[85]

WWI survived a few years longer than AASC but also eventually closed its doors. The conservative backlash of the early 1980s led to decreased foundational support to WWI, which suffered large budget cuts and had to reduce staff.[86] The Institute shifted to reliance on smaller individual and corporate donations, as well as self-generated income from fees for speaking engagements, training, consulting, counseling services, and distribution of materials. In early 1982, Bell Telephone Laboratories hired the Institute to conduct employee training on sexual harassment. In the summer and fall of 1982, the Institute conducted nearly one hundred training workshops for management and staff. The Institute also raised funds by launching a membership campaign in August of 1982. Julie Goldscheid became membership director for the Institute. As part of their membership drive, the Institute held a monthly forum series and published a newsletter, *On the Job*, which appeared twice, in the summer of 1982 and in early 1983. In addition to encouraging readers to join and volunteer for the Institute, the newsletter contained stories about the activities of the Institute and narratives from sexually harassed women. The Institute raised over $7,500 in membership dues. The Institute also held several fundraising events and social gatherings. In the summer of 1982, Eleanor Holmes Norton wrote a fundraising letter for the Institute. As a result, by late 1982, the Institute staff found themselves sandwiched between the demands of corporate workshops, which required them to be out of the office, and increased demands from membership, clients, and the public. In 1982, Susan Meyer stepped down as Executive Director of the Institute, and Karen Sauvigné took over.

In 1983, the Institute conducted many corporate training seminars and began offering workshops to educational institutions, including University of Massachusetts, Yale, Fairleigh-Dickenson, and Columbia. Sauvigné, Goldscheid, Wagner, and Crull conducted these trainings. They raised money from expert testimony, membership, and fundraising events. Despite these efforts, the Institute consistently ran at a budget deficit. In June of 1983, the board decided to begin winding down operations. The board members felt that the Institute had accomplished its mission of raising public awareness of sexual harassment, noting that there were now many places for sexually harassed women to turn for help. The Institute stopped recruiting new members and no longer published its newsletter. To spin off its counseling project, the Institute trained the Barnard Women's Counseling Project and New York Women Against Rape on the counseling and legal aspects of sexual harassment and began to refer women to these organizations. The Institute donated its brief bank to Rutgers University *Women's Rights Law Reporter*, which published an annotated and indexed list of the contents of the brief bank and made these materials available to the public.[87] Karen Sauvigné stepped down as Executive Director of the Institute in February of 1984 to become the Development Director at CUNY Law School, but she continued to serve on the board.

Despite these developments, four staff members, including Peggy Crull and K. C. Wagner, remained at WWI on a part-time basis to wind down the Institute's activities. Although the Institute did not do policy work or provide direct services to sexually harassed women as they had in earlier years, the organization continued to conduct educational programs on sexual harassment through the mid-1980s. In 1983, the Institute published four pamphlets entitled "Know Your Rights," which explained how to file sexual harassment claims at the federal, state, and local levels.[88] The Institute also surveyed unions on sexual harassment.[89] In 1984, the Institute staff members conducted corporate workshops, including a survey and training program for the Federal Aviation Administration, and trained more local groups to take on the Institute's counseling functions, targeting minority communities, including the Chinatown Planning Council, the Medgar Evers Women Center, and the Center for Immigration Rights. In addition, the Institute staff developed a self-help packet to send out to callers. K. C. Wagner promoted the Institute's "Know Your Rights" pamphlets on a radio outreach program, and several pamphlets were translated into Spanish. Finally, the Institute staff members served as expert witnesses in sexual harassment cases.

In 1985, the Institute staff continued to conduct sexual harassment training for corporations and educational institutions and continued to testify as expert witnesses. However, training opportunities had waned by the end of 1985, when Peggy Crull left the Institute and K.C. Wagner became Executive Director. Wagner closed WWI's Park Avenue office in 1985 and moved the Institute to the Cornell School of Industrial and Labor Relations on 26th Street, which provided free office space. In 1986, the Institute participated in filing a friend-of-the-court brief in the first Supreme Court case on sexual harassment in 1986, *Meritor Savings Bank v. Vinson*. The Institute officially folded in 1987.

Despite the demise of the first two organizations formed to work on sexual harassment, their work of raising awareness of the issue contributed to the birth of many new organizations around the country that addressed the issue. For example, in 1982, Dr. Mary Lebrato launched the Sexual Harassment in Employment Project in Sacramento, California, with money from an out-of-court settlement of a sexual harassment and sex discrimination case brought by Dr. Lebrato against the state. In cooperation with the California Commission on the Status of Women, Dr. Lebrato researched current laws, procedures, and strategies for dealing with sexual harassment and created a statewide information network to assist sexually harassed women.[90] Similarly, in 1988, Cheryl Gomez-Preston founded the Association for the Sexually Harassed in Philadelphia after she successfully sued the Detroit police department for sexual harassment, winning $675,000. The Association presented seminars, offered support groups, advised businesses on sexual harassment policies, and conducted statistical research.[91] The feminist effort to influence legal developments on sexual harassment manifested itself most clearly in a highly coordinated and extensive campaign to support Mechelle Vinson in *Meritor Savings Bank v. Vinson*. Several women's rights groups organized moot courts for Vinson's attorney, Patricia Barry, to practice her oral argument. Catharine MacKinnon wrote the appellate brief in the case.

As women in a broad variety of occupations increasingly protested sexual harassment, this resistance more often centered on legal challenges to the behavior. For example, law came to dominate the discussions of sexual harassment among coal mining women. In 1980, the sexual harassment work-shop at the National Conference of Women Coal Miners was very much like a speak-out, with women telling their stories of sexual harassment and abuse. The workshop produced nine resolutions that focused on understanding sexual harassment, educating miners about the issue, generating discussion about it, and organizing against it in the workplace and in unions.[92] The 1981 work-shop, in contrast, had a markedly more legal focus.[93] By 1989, the sexual ha-rassment workshop was almost entirely legally focused: the panel of speakers consisted of two lawyers, one male and one female, and a male union admin-istrator, and the discussion primarily addressed legal remedies under Title VII sex discrimination law. When one workshop participant suggested that sexual harassment was a safety issue and that women might approach union safety committees about the issue, the female attorney said, "I've never thought of it that way. But then that wouldn't be the lawyer doing the case." The male attorney on the panel, who seemed equally surprised by the suggestion, was hesitant and discouraging, saying, "You can do what you can do. You can do anything you can get away with. If your objective is to stop the harassment, that's a clever way of doing it. But that's a *bold* way of doing it. I bet not too many people would have the wherewithal to get that done. I think that's a major step. And I tip my hat to that person. I'm not going to say it can't be done."[94] Outside of this interchange, there was little discussion of nonlegal solutions to sexual harassment.

In the early 1980s, women miners filed more and more sexual harassment cases against coal companies. After the settlement of the 1978 lawsuit against CONSOL, the female miners at Shoemaker mine continued to experience ha-rassment. In 1981, they sued for invasion of privacy and sexual harassment, alleging that CONSOL permitted the operation of a peephole into the women's shower at Shoemaker for thirteen months. During the trial of the case, the par-ties settled for an undisclosed amount. This case inspired other women miners to bring sexual harassment cases. In 1983, women in Sabine, West Virginia, sued Ranger Fuel Corporation, a subsidiary of the Pittston Company, alleging that women were given the hardest, dirtiest jobs in the mines because of their sex or because they refused to have sex with management personnel. In another case, women miners sued Standard Oil of Ohio and its subsidiary Old Ben Coal Company for sexual harassment, seeking $26.4 million. Women miners in Loveridge, West Virginia, sued Consolidation Coal Corporation, alleging that they were subject to verbal and physical harassment and that their job assign-ments were threatened. As a direct result of these suits, one major coal company began to conduct employee training on women in mines.[95]

There was extensive media coverage of sexual harassment of women coal miners. In August and September of 1982, local newspapers in the coal mining states, especially West Virginia and Kentucky, widely covered a sexual harass-ment case brought by women coal miners against Consolidation Coal Com-pany. One editorial was scathingly critical of the women miners, arguing that "this foolishness doesn't belong in a federal court" and asking, "have our people lost the ability to enforce common standards of decency without help from federal judges?" The editorial commended a female miner who testified in defense of the coal company that the male coal miners were "ornery and contrary, but men are basically like that." The editorial noted another defense witness who testified that the plaintiffs "brought it on themselves."[96] Sexual harassment of women miners appeared in the feminist press and on national television, including on 60 *Minutes* in October of 1982.[97]

Women challenged sex discrimination and harassment in other nontraditional occupations as well, including public utilities, law enforcement, road construction, air traffic control, and the military. In 1983, female utility workers filed a class-action sex discrimination complaint with the city's Human Rights Department against Seattle's public power utility, City Light, alleging discrimination and harassment. One plaintiff, Karen Meadows, found human feces covering the shower floor in the women's locker room, and another, Jody Olivera, received obscene pamphlets. Much of the harassment was violent and dangerous. Olivera said she was "set up" to receive electric shocks and was hit with a hammer and chain saw. Dorris Harris reported she was "constantly being called names and constantly told how terrible the black race is." Nina Firey employed by City Light sued the city of Seattle and her co-workers in state court after she quit a lineman's apprenticeship program three months before completion because of "humiliating and demeaning sexual harassment." She also alleged that co-workers endangered her life on at least two occasions. Heidi Durham fell twenty-five feet from a utility pole and broke her back, which she attributed to "intense pressure, harassment, and discrimination in the field."[98]

In 1985, a nine-year veteran police officer Louette Columbano, represented by Equal Rights Advocates, sued the city and county of San Francisco for sexual harassment. After enduring years of harassment from her co-workers, Columbano finally reached her limit when officers at a department party hired a prostitute to perform sexual acts on a new recruit before the assembled police officers. Columbano informed police department officials and the media of what had happened and was then subjected to severe, life-threatening harassment, driving her from her job. Around the same time, police officer Janie Stewart sued the Sonoma County Sheriff's Department after she left her job because fellow officers humiliated and degraded her, threatened not to assist her in the field, and ostracized her within the department.[99] In the late 1980s, an Ohio road worker, Tracy Burnett, sued the state Department of Transportation for sexual harassment. NOW, which had their annual meeting in Ohio in the spring of 1987, sponsored a campaign, "Declaring War on Sexual Harassment," along with the Columbus, Ohio, Committee Against Sexual Harassment to support Burnett.[100]

In the area of education, many organizations were working on sexual harassment. The Project on the Status and Education of Women continued to publish papers on the issue and cover the issue in its newsletter, *On Campus With Women*. NOW's Legal Defense and Education Fund established a Sexual Harassment in Education Project in the early 1980s, headed by Anne Simon, the attorney who worked on *Yale v. Alexander*. The project produced a resource packet on sexual harassment, which was sent to anyone who inquired about the issue. In 1982, the project published an annotated bibliography on sexual harassment in education. In 1983, the National Association for Women Deans, Administrators, & Counselors dedicated an entire issue of their journal to sexual harassment in education, as did the Center for Sex Equity in Schools based in Ann Arbor, MI, focusing on sexual harassment in high schools. In the same year, the American Association of University Professors issued a paper suggesting policies and procedures for handling complaints of sexual harassment. University of New Hampshire established a Sexual Harassment and Rape Prevention Program, which created support services for victims and offered training on sexual harassment and rape. The Program distributed a flyer on sexual harassment to faculty and students and hung posters on sexual harassment, assault, and rape around campus. In 1984, Billie Wright Dzeich and Linda Weiner published *The Lecherous Professor, Sexual Harassment on Campus*, the first book on sexual harassment in education. The Center for Women Policy Studies published a guide on sexual harassment for students in 1986.[101]

Students continued to resist sexual harassment in the 1980s. In the spring of 1980, three female graduate students at Cornell University charged government Professor Werner J. Dannhauser with sexual harassment. This led Cornell President Frank H. T. Rhodes to issue an official memorandum on June 20, 1980, to deans, directors, and department heads that said Cornell would not tolerate sexual harassment, which he described as a threat to the "basic integrity" of the university. In response to this statement, two members of the New York Civil Liberties Union Cornell chapter surveyed students about sexual harassment. In late 1981, the *Cornell Daily Sun* published a series of articles taking an in-depth look at sexual harassment at Cornell, examining the views of students, administrators, and faculty regarding the extent of the problem and attitudes toward proposed solutions.[102] Within a decade's time, sexual harassment activism had expanded far beyond the fledgling women's organizations that had first identified the phenomenon of sexual abuse on the job. But the type of activism on the issue had evolved too to focus on largely legal solutions.

BUILDING AN UNDERSTANDING OF SEXUAL HARASSMENT

Theory and research on sexual harassment flourished in the 1980s, and academics and lawyers, rather than feminist activists, came to dominate the discussion, which appeared most often in academic and legal contexts. This literature, which peaked after the Supreme Court decision in *Meritor Savings Bank v. Vinson* in 1986, was decidedly more legally focused, more academic, and incorporated a broader range of perspectives than literature on sexual harassment in the 1970s. Although a few of these publications advocated legislative action on sexual harassment, most were content to work within the Title VII framework, urging courts to expand the notion of discrimination to include sexual harassment. Representatives of employers began to publish on sexual harassment as well, focusing on legal standards under Title VII and how employers could avoid liability.[103]

In the early 1980s, three different journals dedicated entire issues to sexual harassment. *Capital University Law Review* published the proceedings of the first legal symposium on sexual harassment held in Washington, D.C. in 1981. Participants included Catharine MacKinnon, EEOC Acting Chair Clay Smith, Joan Vermeulen of WWI, Jan Leventer of the EEOC, who was the former Legal Director of the Women's Justice Center in Detroit Michigan, and Jill Laurie Goodman of the Department of Education's Office of Civil Rights. The symposium addressed the history of sexual harassment, the EEOC guidelines, and caselaw on the issue. In the winter of 1982, the *Journal of Social Issues* published an entire issue on sexual harassment, containing articles on sexual harassment in the workplace and at educational institutions. It reported on studies, including one looking at heterosexual and lesbian women, and discussed explanations for sexual harassment. In the winter of 1983, the *Journal of the National Association for Women Deans, Administrators, and Counselors* published an issue on sexual harassment that was pragmatically oriented, focusing on defining the problem, discussing solutions, and sharing experiences. The articles discussed studies of sexual harassment, coping strategies, administrative responses to the issue, and training programs.[104]

As theory on sexual harassment appeared mainly in professional and academic legal publications, research on sexual harassment appeared primarily in professional and academic social science publications. In the 1970s, feminist activists had conducted most of the surveys on sexual harassment, but in the 1980s, social scientists and academics began to research the issue, although studies were still conducted primarily by women. Researchers studied sexual harassment in a variety of contexts, including the public sector, the private sector, and at educational institutions. Social scientific research in the 1980s focused on two areas: the prevalence of sexual harassment and people's perceptions and attitudes toward sexual harassment. The studies on the prevalence of sexual harassment found high rates of harassment in the workplace.[105] Two social scientists reviewing the literature concluded that conservative estimates suggested that one out of every two women would be harassed at some point during her academic or working life, from which they concluded that "sexual harassment is the most widespread of all forms of sexual victimization studied to date."[106] Studies of perceptions and attitudes about sexual harassment showed a perceptual gender gap. Women were far more likely than men to view such behavior as offensive. Furthermore, men were significantly more likely to distrust the motivations of those claiming sexual harassment and hold "victim-blaming" attitudes. For example, men were more likely to believe that reports of harassment were generally just attempts to cause trouble, that people who were harassed had usually "asked for it" in some way, and that the issue of sexual harassment had been greatly exaggerated. Men were also more likely to believe that sexual harassment was simply normal sexual interaction between men and women.[107]

Social scientist Barbara Gutek was a leading researcher on sexual harassment. In 1979, sponsored by the NIMH, Gutek conducted a study of sexual harassment of working men and women in Los Angeles county. She later expanded on that study and published a book in 1985, called *Sex and the Workplace*, in which she reported that 53% of the women in her study had been harassed at least once. Gutek also found that men and women perceived sexual harassment differently, in that women were more likely to call sexual conduct in the workplace harassment than men. Gutek concluded that there was a great deal of ambiguity surrounding sexuality in the workplace. In another study, Gutek and Inger Jensen found that those who had traditional versus feminist sex-role beliefs were more likely to hold women responsible for sexual harassment incidents. The authors concluded that "only by changing people's general sex-role beliefs can one effect a change in the attitudes toward victims of harassment."[108]

In addition to Gutek's work, several other important studies showed high rates of sexual harassment and perceptual and attitudinal differences toward sexual harassment between men and women. In 1980, *Redbook* and *Harvard Business Review* surveyed over 7,000 *Harvard Business Review* subscribers on their perceptions of the seriousness of sexual harassment. Most respondents agreed on what harassment was, but female respondents believed that sexual harassment occurred much more frequently than male respondents. In 1987, the U.S. Merit System Protection Board conducted a second study of sexual harassment in the federal workplace, which found rates of harassment similar to the 1981 study. In 1988, a large study of sexual harassment in the military showed extensive harassment. Several studies focused on women in blue-collar and nontraditional occupations. There was little research on sexual harassment of ethnic, racial, or sexual minorities, but one study in 1982 found that lesbians were more likely than heterosexual women to identify sexual behavior in the workplace as sexual harassment.[109]

Toward the end of the decade, social scientists began to point out the limitations and gaps in sexual harassment research. Some criticized sexual harassment research for a lack of conceptual clarity and specificity and substantial differences in research methodology, including sample size, survey response rate, sample diversity, harassment frame of reference, number of harassment categories, and types of words or phrases used to elicit responses. Others called for research into new areas, such as the effectiveness of training interventions and organizational response patterns to sexual harassment. By the end of the decade, researchers had moved beyond documenting the existence and perceptions of sexual harassment to address other issues, including victim response, coping behavior, and the impact and consequences of harassment for the victim, as well as organizational factors leading to sexual harassment such as gender ratio, workplace norms, and organizational climate.[110] Advocates and policymakers used these studies to justify laws and policies against sexual harassment. For example, studies showing that men and women perceived sexual behavior in the workplace differently were used at the decade's end to justify the creation of a legal standard for evaluating harassing behavior that incorporated women's perspectives.

The federal government under Carter had established an aggressive antisexual harassment policy, which had quickly pervaded the federal executive agencies through OPM and EEOC actions. However, with the ascendancy of the Reagan administration, which was strongly supported by business and employers, many state actors sought to roll back civil rights protections and enforcement, including the EEOC sexual harassment guidelines, in the spirit of deregulation. The changing political climate of the early 1980s generated an episode of "contentious politics" with multiple combatants, including both institutionalized political groups as well as previously unorganized nonpolitical actors, who framed the issue in new ways.[111] Opposing the new antisexual harassment policy were the Reagan administration, employers and probusiness advocacy groups, the socially conservative Eagle Forum, and men accused of sexual harassment. These actors articulated a range of arguments against sexual harassment policy – arguments for government deregulation to arguments that sexual harassment was not a problem or was something women bring on themselves by inappropriate behavior. Supporting progressive sexual harassment policy were not only a range of established women's organizations, such as WWI and CEP, but also previously unorganized or nonpolitical challengers, including individual women who had been plaintiffs or experienced sexual harassment, like Sandra Bundy and Adrienne Tomkins. These advocates made the familiar arguments that sexual harassment was widespread and posed a barrier to equal employment opportunity, but they made new arguments to appeal to the increasingly conservative probusiness environment: they argued that sexual harassment was bad for business, resulting in low morale, absenteeism, and high turnover, all of which lead to lower productivity. Contention also arose within the left and the feminist movement, with concerns that conservative elites would use sexual harassment charges to punish male leftists or that the issue played into traditional ideas about women as victims or antisexual attitudes.

In the early 1980s, the antisexual harassment movement faced an increasingly conservative environment that decreased political opportunities and increased political constraints. Ronald Reagan replaced Eleanor Holmes Norton with Clarence Thomas as chair of the EEOC and his vice president, George H.W. Bush, began a campaign to rescind the EEOC guidelines. In addition, resistance to sexual harassment prohibitions by the accused, employers, and their advocates further contributed toward a hostile climate for sexual harassment claimants. These developments threatened the movement's achievements, causing participants to shift to more defensive strategies. Many of the organizations that worked on sexual harassment in the late 1970s continued their efforts in the 1980s, but in the face of decreasing political opportunities and a dwindling resource base, as a result of the conservative climate of the decade, activists focused more narrowly on legal solutions to the problem and strategically framed sexual harassment in terms of sex discrimination.

Professionals – lawyers, training consultants, and academics – began to dominate public discussions of the issue, and feminist theory on sexual harassment appeared primarily in academic journals and law reviews. In the 1980s, the character of the movement shifted, becoming increasingly professionalized and focused on legal solutions to the problem of sexual harassment. The movement remained diverse and active and, despite the political climate, was able to maintain the significant legal gains they had won. Successful lawsuits had the effect of encouraging others to employ the same tactics, giving the courts ample opportunity to wrestle with the legal issues relating to sexual harassment. By 1986, sexual harassment jurisprudence had gained so much momentum that even a Rehnquist Supreme Court could not deny that sexual harassment, including hostile environment harassment, was sex discrimination in violation of Title VII.

8

Legal Victory: The Supreme Court and Beyond

Throughout the 1980s, feminist activists were integrally involved in the development of sexual harassment jurisprudence, participating in all of the precedent-setting sexual harassment cases. The powerful collaboration of diverse constituencies working against sexual harassment peaked at two points in the 1980s – in efforts to preserve the EEOC guidelines in 1981 and in broad support for the plaintiff Mechelle Vinson in the first Supreme Court sexual harassment case. In 1986, the Supreme Court finally spoke on the issue of sexual harassment in the case of *Meritor Savings Bank v. Vinson*. To feminists' delight, the Court ruled that Title VII prohibited sexual harassment, including both *quid pro quo* and hostile environment harassment. The Court, however, erected several obstacles to obtaining relief, most notably rejecting the lower court's ruling that employers were strictly liable for sexual harassment by supervisors. As sexual harassment came to dominate headlines more and more in the 1990s, the courts continued to struggle with an array of legal questions left open by this decision.

THE SUPREME COURT CASE

Mechelle Vinson began working at Meritor Savings Bank in 1974 under the supervision of Sidney Taylor, a vice-president of the bank and branch manager of the bank. Both Vinson and Taylor were African-American. According to Vinson, Taylor repeatedly forced her to engage in sexual relations, usually at the bank, both during and after business hours. Vinson estimated that over the next two years she had sexual intercourse with Taylor forty to fifty times and that on one occasion in May 1976 he so brutally raped her that it led to serious vaginal bleeding for which she was required to seek a doctor's care. Vinson also alleged that Taylor fondled her breasts and buttocks on the job, sometimes in the presence of co-workers, followed her into the ladies' room when she was there alone, and exposed himself to her several times.

According to Vinson, sexual intercourse between them ceased in 1977, when she started regularly dating another man. She testified that when she refused to continue having sex with him, Taylor retaliated by tampering with her personnel records, lodging false complaints about her work performance with management, denigrating and abusing her in front of other employees, entrapping her into work errors, and threatening her life when she threatened to report him. Once she heard him tell another employee that he was trying "to get rid of her."[1] In addition to sexually harassing her, Vinson alleged that Taylor fondled other female employees at the bank and made suggestive remarks in their presence. Vinson testified that she had never reported the harassment to any of Taylor's supervisors and never attempted to use the bank's complaint procedure because Taylor had threatened to kill her or rape her if she did.

Taylor denied any sexual relations with Vinson but testified that Vinson made sexual advances to him, which he declined. He contended that Vinson was accusing him of sexual harassment in retaliation for a business-related dispute. The bank defended itself by arguing that any sexual harassment by Taylor was unknown and unauthorized by the bank. Over Vinson's objections, the defendants introduced evidence that she wore revealing clothes and discussed her sexual fantasies with co-workers. In particular, one witness testified that Vinson told her of a dream in which her deceased grandfather appeared to her as a young man and they had sexual relations. Vinson vehemently denied this testimony.

Patricia Barry, a young trial lawyer in Washington, D.C., who specialized in employment discrimination cases, represented Vinson. Barry was a feminist who had adopted her maternal grandmother's maiden name when she became a lawyer.[2] After an eleven-day bench trial in January 1980, Judge John Garrett Penn, a 1979 Carter appointee, ruled that the bank was not liable for Taylor's conduct because it had no notice of the harassment and that the sexual relationship was voluntary and had nothing to do with Vinson's continued employment or her advancement or promotions. In her appeal to the District of Columbia Circuit Court of Appeals,[3] Vinson was again represented by Barry and supported by Equal Rights Advocates, WWI, and Women Employed in Chicago, which filed a friend-of-the-court brief on her behalf.

Among other things, Patricia Barry argued that Judge Penn allowed "inflammatory and sensational testimony" in order to establish that Vinson was "lewd, lascivious, given to open discussions of unusual sexual fantasies for a woman, [and] bent on seducing her boss by throwing her exposed body at him." Had she not known that the testimony occurred in a twentieth-century courtroom, Barry said, she would have thought it was from a "medieval tract on women and the evils they pose for men." She then quoted extensively from Barbara Tuchman's *A Distant Mirror: The Calamitous 14th Century*, describing the depictions of women in *Speculum*, a medieval treatise by the Dominican Vincent de Beauvais. She argued that Judge Penn's courtroom was not a "rational, orderly attempt to get at the truth of what happened to Mechelle Vinson, but rather a ritualistic psychodrama based on enduring but extremely hostile, and even possibly subconscious, notions of who a woman is."[4]

The District of Columbia Court of Appeals reversed the dismissal on January 25, 1985. Two veterans of sexual harassment cases were on the appellate panel: Judges Spottswood Robinson and J. Skelly Wright. The third judge was Judge Edward Skottowe Northrop, appointed to the federal district court in Maryland by President John F. Kennedy in 1961 and sitting temporarily on the appellate court for the case. In an opinion written by Judge Robinson, this panel of judges reversed Judge Penn's dismissal for its failure to make a determination as to whether Vinson had proven a claim of hostile environment harassment. Judge Robinson described the two types of sexual harassment that violated Title VII—"abolition of the job of a female employee because she spurned her male superior's sexual advances" prohibited in *Barnes v. Costle* and "pervasive on-the-job sexual harassment by ... superiors" prohibited in *Bundy v. Jackson*.[5] Noting that Judge Penn had issued his decision before *Bundy v. Jackson*, he pointed out that Judge Penn had not undertaken a determination of whether a violation of this type had occurred, but had in fact supported the dismissal in part on a finding that Vinson had not suffered any tangible employment consequences. Therefore, Judge Robinson directed the district court to determine whether Vinson had been subjected to "sexually stereotyped insults" or "demeaning propositions" that illegally poisoned her "psychological and emotional work environment."[6] Judge Robinson also ruled that employers were strictly liable for sexual harassment by supervisors, a ruling consistent with the EEOC guidelines.

After the court delivered its opinion, Meritor Savings Bank filed a petition for a rehearing by the entire court, which was denied.[7] Three federal judges filed a vigorous dissent to the denial of a rehearing: Judges Robert Heron Bork, Antonin Scalia, and Kenneth Winston Starr, all very conservative Reagan appointees. Reagan later nominated Judge Bork to the Supreme Court in 1987, but the Senate rejected the nomination because of Bork's extremely conservative views. President Reagan successfully nominated Judge Scalia to the Supreme Court in 1986, and he has proved to be one of the most conservative jurists on that court. Judge Starr resigned from the Court of Appeals in 1989 and later became the independent counsel in charge of the Whitewater investigation that led to impeachment proceedings against democratic President William J. Clinton. The judges' dissent strenuously objected to the idea that Title VII should prohibit hostile environment sexual harassment.

THE BANK APPEALS

The bank appealed the circuit court's decision to the Supreme Court. Robert Troll, Charles Fleischer, and Randall Smith of the Washington law firm of Ross, Marsh, & Foster represented the bank. Four *amicus curiae* briefs were filed in support of the bank, submitted by the EEOC, the United States Chamber of Commerce, the Trustees of Boston University, and the Equal Employment Advisory Council, the group that filed a brief on behalf of the defendant in *Miller v. Bank of America*. The EEOC, which had once been an ally to sexual harassment victims, had changed significantly after six years under the Reagan administration. Conservative Clarence Thomas, later accused of sexual harassment by Professor Anita Hill when he was nominated to the Supreme Court, was chair of the EEOC at the time the commission entered the case on the side of the bank.[8]

The bank's arguments echoed those made in earlier sexual harassment cases – that Taylor's behavior was a matter of private morality, that it was natural and harmless, and that women were likely to lie or act vindictively. The bank emphasized that sexual harassment was different from racial or religious harassment because "racially or religiously derogatory workplace activity cannot reasonably be conceived as occupationally neutral or desirable," whereas sexual activity in the workplace may be "socially acceptable and wholly unrelated to the job."[9] The United States and the EEOC argued that hostile environment sexual harassment was "special" and "distinct" because of "the naturalness, the pervasiveness, and what might be called the legal neutrality of sexual attraction (as contrasted to racial prejudice)." They explained, "[w]hereas racial slurs are intrinsically offensive and presumptively unwelcome, sexual advances and innuendo are ambiguous."[10] Several of the bank's supporters made the related argument that sexual harassment was unique because of the "personal" nature of the disputed conduct, echoing the defense tactic used in early sexual harassment cases. The U.S. Chamber of Commerce described the sexual harassment at issue as "individualized," "private," "purely personal," and as "individual sexual activity which is essentially unconnected with the employment."[11] They argued that Title VII was not intended to govern "the sexual mores of employees" or make the federal courts "arbiters of good taste in the workplace."[12]

The bank's supporters also argued that employers should not be held strictly liable for hostile environment by supervisors and that the court should allow evidence of Vinson's dress and conversations in the workplace to determine the voluntariness of her sexual interactions with Taylor. The defendants' arguments were reminiscent of arguments made by defendants in the early sexual harassment cases that assumed women alleging harassment were likely to be dishonest. For example, Clarence Thomas' EEOC brief expressed concern that "sexual harassment charges do not become a tool by which one party to a consensual sexual relationship may punish the other."[13] Finally, taking a cue from Judge Bork's dissent in the lower court, the bank also argued that Title VII did not prohibit hostile environment sexual harassment because Congress did not intend to regulate "purely psychological aspects" of the workplace environment under Title VII.

The tone of the briefs filed in support of the bank varied considerably. The Trustees of Boston University condemned sexual harassment but opposed strict liability because it would not encourage victims to report harassment or employers to adopt policies and procedures to prevent harassment. The Equal Employment Advisory Council, on the other hand, was alarmist, repeatedly quoting Judge Bork's dissent to the denial of a rehearing in the Circuit Court and arguing that strict liability would subject employers to onerous punitive damage awards under other laws prohibiting sexual harassment. Similarly, the U.S. Chamber of Commerce quoted heavily from Judge Bork's dissent, trivializing the effects of sexual harassment on women. The EEOC arguments implied that women often lie about sexual harassment, and it selectively read the record to attack Vinson's credibility. All of the bank's supporters expressed concern about protecting the rights of workers to make sexual advances in the workplace and to engage in sexual conduct in the workplace.

SUPPORT FOR MECHELLE VINSON

The far-flung strands of the movement against sexual harassment came together in support of Mechelle Vinson case before the Supreme Court. Patricia Barry and Catharine MacKinnon wrote Vinson's appellate brief, and Barry presented the oral argument. Over forty organizations, eight states, and twenty-nine members of Congress filed seven *amicus curiae* briefs. Vinson's supporters represented a diverse range of people, including women of color, homemakers, unions, coal miners, feminists, lawyers, educators, and mothers.[14] Several organizations that had been active on the issue since the late 1970s participated, including WWI, ERA, WLDF, Women Employed in Chicago, NOW Legal Defense and Education Fund, and Women's Alliance for Job Equity of Philadelphia. But many more organizations joined the fight. Seven organizations representing women of color participated in the lawsuit, including the Organization of Pan Asian American Women, the National Institute for Women of Color, the Mexican American Women's National Association, the National Conference of Black Lawyers, the Asian Pacific American Bar Association of the Greater Washington, D.C. Area, the Sisterhood of Black Single Mothers, and the Women's Rights Project of the Instituto Puertorriqueno de Derechos Civiles. Several organizations representing blue-collar women participated, including the CEP, the Coalition of Labor Union Women, Wider Opportunities for Women, and Non-Traditional Employment for Women.

Many other organizations joined as well, representing a broad spectrum of interests. They included the National Board of the YWCA of the USA, the American Association of University Women, NOW, the Connecticut Women's Educational and Legal Fund, the New York State Committee on Pay Equity, Women on the Job of Port Washington, New York, Women in Self-Help of the New York State Displaced Homemaker Program, New York Women Against Rape, the Women's Counseling Project, the Committee Against Sexual Harassment in Sacramento, California, and the Women's Law Project. Women's bar associations from around the country participated as well, including from the Massachusetts, Minnesota, Michigan, Colorado, New York, and D.C. Several general civil rights organizations participated, including the Employment Law Center of the Legal Aid Society in San Francisco, National Emergency Civil Liberties Committee, the Center for Constitutional Rights, the Workers Defense League, and the American Federation of Labor and Congress of Industrial Organizations. Governments who participated were the states of New Jersey,

California, Connecticut, Illinois, Minnesota, New Mexico, New York, Vermont, and the Pennsylvania Human Relations Commission as well as twenty-nine members of Congress, twenty-seven Democrats and two New York Republicans, who filed a brief in support of Vinson (no members of Congress supported the petitioner). The broad participation in the *Meritor* case illustrates how diverse and broad-based the movement against sexual harassment had become by the mid-1980s.

ARGUMENTS FOR VINSON

Supporters of Mechelle Vinson made four major arguments on the merits of the case. First, they argued that the bank used the phrase "sexual activity" to refer to welcome and forced sex alike, conflating "unwanted forcible sexual initiation with welcome friendly suggestions ... as if the two are properly indistinguishable for legal purposes."[15] Barry and MacKinnon argued "sexual *abuse* is no more wanted than racial abuse, and friendly discussions of race are no more inherently offensive than friendly discussions of sex."[16] The WWI brief argued that "behavior which is intimidating, degrading, and offensive to women should not be immunized from the purview of Title VII simply because some men find it socially acceptable any more than derogatory epithets used about blacks should be immunized because some whites find them 'socially acceptable.'"[17] The WLDF brief, written in part by veteran sexual harassment litigators Linda Singer, Anne Simon, and Nadine Taub, noted, "[t]he appropriate comparison is not between sexual 'activity,' which would include both consensual and coerced sex, and racially or religiously 'derogatory workplace activity.'" The proper comparison, they argued, was between "two forms of unwelcome harassment: sexually derogatory workplace activity, and racially or religiously derogatory workplace activity."[18]

The second major argument made by supporters of Vinson was that Title VII prohibited hostile environment sexual harassment. The WWI brief relied on sociological research to show that sexual harassment was a pervasive practice that circumscribed women's employment opportunities and impaired their health. They cited numerous studies, including WWI studies and surveys, the Merit System Protection Board Study, and the 1981 *Harvard Business Review* and *Redbook* study. They argued that women were especially vulnerable to sexual harassment due to their lower status in the workforce hierarchy, particularly in predominately male occupations, citing studies of women in the construction trades and the auto industry. They noted that black women were even more vulnerable than women generally because of their inferior economic position and their unique place in American history, including the "legacy of slavery," which led to the "stereotype of black women as sexually available, sexually promiscuous, and unprotected by black men."[19] Reminiscent of plaintiff's arguments in the early sexual harassment cases, WWI argued that women were also vulnerable to sexual harassment because of socialization: "men are usually the initiators of purely social interaction and women the recipients."[20]

They argued that sexual harassment led to women's higher job turnover, which substantially contributed to the wage gap between men and women.

Similar to WWI, women's bar associations from Massachusetts, Minnesota, Michigan, and Colorado submitted a brief relying extensively on empirical studies to argue sexual harassment had a profound and deleterious impact on many working women. They argued that, based on the empirical studies, sexual harassment was not social or courting behavior, but "an assertion of power by the harasser over the victim," which they called the "power dominance theory."[21] WLDF argued that Title VII prohibited *quid pro quo* and environmental sexual harassment, citing the 1980 report from Hanley Congressional hearings, the EEOC guidelines, and case law involving sexual, racial, and religious harassment, including *EEOC v. Rogers*. They argued that "sexual harassment of working women expresses stereotypic role expectations because it emanates from the view that women employees are sexual objects."[22]

Other arguments made by Vinson's supporters were that employers should be strictly liable for hostile environment sexual harassment by supervisory employees and that the evidence of Vinson's dress and reports of fantasies was properly excluded on remand. On the latter, they argued that the evidence was not relevant to whether the advances were welcome because "women simply do not volunteer to be sexually harassed by their clothing or the purported content of their voluntary conversations."[23] The WLDF brief argued that evidence of a victim's dress and personal fantasies was irrelevant because "voluntary conversations with co-workers are very different from required acquiescence in unwelcome assaultive and intrusive behavior by supervisors." They explained, "a woman's choice of clothing and her private fantasy life are no more relevant to her claim of sexual harassment than a fraud victim's generosity or extravagance." They argued that the bank was resurrecting "the discredited myth that only women who ask for trouble get it" and that a "sexually active woman would never find sexual advances unwelcome." They argued that the evidence was an inflammatory attempt to impugn her character, did not impeach her credibility, could not establish a habit, was an unwarranted invasion of privacy, and that the prejudice produced by such evidence outweighed its probative value.

They also argued that the unwelcomeness standard should be applied to distinguish consensual sexual activity in the workplace from sexual harassment. They argued that sexual advances by a male supervisor against a female subordinate is "inherently coercive" because the employee risks retaliation if she rejects the advances. Therefore, the focus of the court's inquiry should be on whether the advances were unwelcome, not on whether the employee voluntarily acquiesced. Similarly, the women's bar associations argued that unwelcomeness distinguished "innocent forms of social-sexual conduct which naturally occur in the workplace" from sexual harassment and that conduct should be evaluated from the perspective of the reasonable victim.[24]

Surprisingly, little discussion of race occurred in the legal discourse. None of the judicial opinions ever mentioned the race of Vinson or Taylor. At one point,

Barry and MacKinnon suggested how Vinson's race may have affected her claim: "all too often, it is Black women like Ms. Vinson who have been specifically victimized by the invidious stereotype of being scandalous and lewd women, perhaps targeting them to would-be perpetrators ... minority race aggravates one's vulnerability as a woman by reducing one's options and undermining one's credibility and social worth."[25] WWI also mentioned how the history of slavery shaped stereotypes of black women, which made them more vulnerable to harassment.[26]

THE COURT'S DECISION

Justice William Rehnquist, appointed to the Supreme Court by President Richard Nixon in 1971, delivered the opinion of the court, joined by Justices Burger, White, Powell, Stevens, and O'Conner. Justice Marshall filed an opinion concurring in the judgment, in which Justices Brennan, Blackmun, and Stevens joined. The decision of the Supreme Court in the *Meritor* case was a remarkable victory for feminists in that the Court held that sexual harassment was sex discrimination and that Title VII prohibited both *quid pro quo* sexual harassment and hostile environment sexual harassment. The Court cited the language of Title VII, prohibiting discrimination in the "terms, conditions, or privileges of employment," as well as the EEOC guidelines on sexual harassment and several racial harassment cases, including *EEOC v. Rogers*.[27] Even in cases where there was no direct economic injury, the Court held that women could pursue a claim for sexual harassment under Title VII. The Court confirmed many of the principles that had been developing in the lower courts for the previous ten years.

The *Meritor* decision, however, was not a complete victory. The Court placed several limitations on the ability of plaintiffs to gain relief for sexual harassment under Title VII. First, the Court created a threshold for actionable sexual harassment, holding that sexual harassment must be "sufficiently severe or pervasive 'to alter the conditions of the victim's employment and create an abusive working environment,'" citing the language of *EEOC v. Rogers*.[28] Second, on the issue of voluntariness, the Court held that the fact that a complainant was not forced to participate against her will was not a defense to sexual harassment suit under Title VII. The heart of a sexual harassment claim was whether the alleged advances were "unwelcome." However, the Court held that a plaintiff's sexually provocative speech or dress was "obviously relevant" to the issue of whether the plaintiff found the alleged sexual advances unwelcome. Third, the Court declined to rule definitively on the issue of employer liability because of the "rather abstract quality" of the debate "given the state of the record" in the case. Departing from the EEOC guidelines, the Court held that the lower court had erred in holding employers automatically liable for hostile environment harassment, but also held that the mere existence of a grievance procedure and a policy against discrimination, coupled with the plaintiff's failure to invoke that procedure, did not insulate an employer from liability.

On remand, the case stretched out for another five years. Finally, on August 22, 1991, the parties settled the case for an undisclosed amount.[29] After she left the bank, Vinson experienced severe financial troubles. After being "black-balled" in the banking industry, she filed for bankruptcy. In 1982, she returned to live with her parents in Washington, D.C. She later enrolled in nursing school with the help of a student loan but had to drop out because of finances.[30] Patricia Barry also experienced financial problems, eventually ceasing her employment discrimination practice because she could not make ends meet. Barry, who was originally from California and graduated from UCLA law school in 1973, returned there in September of 1982. In 1987, Barry filed for bankruptcy and moved back to her parents' home. In 1988, after thirteen years as a civil attorney and having an impressive track record, winning or settling more than half of the seventy cases she took, she decided she could no longer afford to take civil rights cases.

THE IMPACT OF LEGAL DEVELOPMENTS ON SEXUAL HARASSMENT

The development of sexual harassment law in the 1980s had a significant influence on employers' attitudes toward sexual harassment. By the end of the 1980s, businesses began to take sexual harassment more seriously. In 1988, *Working Woman* magazine surveyed Fortune 500 companies on whether they had sexual harassment policies. Of the 160 companies responding, 76% had written policies banning sexual harassment and an additional 16% had a general policy against discrimination that included sexual harassment.[31] In response to this concern, feminist groups and management consulting firms began to produce training materials and videos for employers on sexual harassment.[32] Educational institutions also addressed the issue more seriously. University communities discussed the issue, and many schools conducted studies of sexual harassment at their institutions and adopted policies prohibiting the conduct. The studies and policies covered a broader range of conduct. For example, in 1983, Massachusetts Institute of Technology conducted a survey on sexual harassment between students. In November of the same year, University of California adopted a ban on sex between teachers and their students, stating that even "consenting" relationships can inflict "irreparable" damage to the educational environment. Hampshire College in Massachusetts adopted a policy discouraging relationships between faculty and students, pointing out the "unequal power relationship" between students and teachers. At the same time, educational institutions began to investigate and censure faculty and staff members for sexual harassment. Employees at several universities sued for sexual harassment in the early 1980s. Beginning in the early 1980s, Lloyds of London began offering insurance policies to colleges and universities to cover the legal costs of harassment cases.[33]

The expanding law encouraged women to file more sexual harassment claims in a wider variety of contexts. In 1981, the EEOC received 3,661 sexual harassment complaints. In 1990, they received 5,557 sexual harassment charges. Some of the top awards in sexual harassment cases in the late 1980s, all filed under state law, included a $3.1 million settlement in a 1986 Ohio case, a $2 million settlement in a 1990 case in Los Angeles, a $1.4 million settlement in a 1988 case in Oregon, a $1.1 million settlement in a case involving an apprentice asbestos worker in Illinois, and a $900,000 settlement in a 1987 case involving a police officer in Michigan.[34] Sexual harassment plaintiffs in the 1980s also began to file class action suits and bring sexual harassment claims in new areas. In 1980, the National Labor Relations Board ruled that firing an employee who helped a co-worker file a harassment complaint violated the National Labor Relations Act.[35] In 1981, a federal district court in Illinois held that sexual harassment by a supervisor of the same sex was actionable under Title VII, but another court in the same district rejected a similar case in 1988.[36] In 1984, the Eighth Circuit allowed the first class action sexual harassment suit.[37] In a 1985 Ohio case, *Shellhammer v. Lewallen*, the Sixth Circuit upheld a charge of sexual harassment under the Fair Housing Act against a landlord who evicted a tenant for refusing to pose nude and have sexual intercourse.[38] Feminists continued to be integrally involved in the development of this law.

The victory in *Meritor Savings Bank v. Vinson* was the crowning achievement of the early movement against sexual harassment. Whereas at the beginning of the 1980s only a few lower courts had ruled in women's favor on cases involving the most extreme factual scenarios, by the end of the 1980s, federal law had developed significantly, and employers and educational institutions took the issue very seriously. Courts expanded the definition of sexual harassment to include hostile environment harassment and held employers liable for tolerating co-worker harassment. Some courts even recognized the gendered power dynamics underlying sexual harassment. By the end of the 1980s, women had significantly more legal protection against sexual harassment than they had had at the beginning of the 1980s and the movement had achieved victory before the highest court in the land, but there were many unanswered questions with regard to legal standards.

Sexual Harassment after *Meritor*

Shaped by the activism and legal developments of the 1970s and 1980s, the issue of sexual harassment finally landed squarely in the center of the mainstream public agenda when law professor Anita Hill stepped forward in the fall of 1991 to describe her experiences of sexual harassment by Supreme Court nominee Clarence Thomas when she had worked for him at the EEOC a decade earlier. Hill's story echoed the stories of Paulette Barnes and Diane Williams – a black woman harassed by her black male supervisor in an agency that had the purpose of fighting discrimination. The televised Senate hearings riveted the nation. Anita Hill was one of many powerful women who stepped forward in the 1990s to tell their stories of sexual harassment. Female navy pilot Lieutenant Paula Coughlin exposed widespread and severe sexual harassment in the Navy's Tailhook Association. Stanford neurosurgeon and professor,

FIGURE 8.1. Anita Hill, 1991. AP/Wide World

Dr. Frances Conley resigned her position after 25 years to protest sexual harassment by her male colleagues, including her department head. Boston
Herald sportswriter Linda Olson sued the New England Patriots football team
because members made obscene comments and gestures to her when she was
interviewing a player in the team's locker room.

As the 1990s progressed, women repeatedly accused federal government officials of sexual harassment. Several members of Congress faced such
accusations, including Senator Brock Adams (D-WA), who terminated a bid
for reelection as a result, Senator Daniel K. Inouye (D-HI), Senator Dave
Durenberger (R-MN), and Senator Bob Packwood (R-OR), who eventually
resigned in September of 1995. President Bill Clinton was impeached based

on charges related to allegations of sexual harassment. In the late 1990s, two high-profile sexual harassment scandals involving the military surfaced, one involving extensive sexual harassment at the Aberdeen Proving Ground in Aberdeen, Maryland, and the other involving the Sergeant Major of the Army, Gene McKinney, the Army's highest-ranking enlisted man. Throughout the decade, Congress held hearings and investigations into sexual harassment in a variety of contexts, including the federal workplace, the Veteran's Administration, and educational institutions.

As a result of these many high-profile sexual harassment scandals involving all three branches of the federal government, the military, and the private sector, media coverage of sexual harassment skyrocketed. Whereas the *New York Times* had 85 stories on sexual harassment in 1990, it had 406 in 1991, 372 in 1992, 313 in 1993, and 419 in 1994.[39] Hollywood put a twist on the issue with the 1994 movie *Disclosure,* in which Demi Moore played a corporate executive who sexually harassed a male subordinate, played by Michael Douglas. Even a board game called *Harassment* was released to favorable reviews in 1992, the same year *Oleanna* premiered off-Broadway, a play about a university student accusing her professor of sexual harassment. Reflecting this increased awareness of sexual harassment, charges filed with the EEOC and state Fair Employment Practice Agencies surged in the 1990s, growing from about 5,500 complaints in 1990 to over 15,500 complaints in 1995. The number of complaints stayed over 15,000 through year 2000, after which it decreased to 12,679 in 2005.[40]

Courts significantly advanced sexual harassment law in the 1990s. The U.S. Supreme Court issued seven decisions on sexual harassment, four on sexual harassment in the workplace under Title VII, and three on sexual harassment of students under Title IX. The cases on harassment in employment involved standards for assessing harassing behavior, same-sex harassment, and employer liability. In 1993, the Court ruled in *Harris v. Forklift Systems* that a sexual harassment plaintiff does not have to prove that she suffered serious psychological damage in order to recover under Title VII but need only show that the harassment was sufficiently severe or pervasive to create an objectively hostile or abusive working environment – one that a reasonable person would find hostile or abusive – and that the plaintiff subjectively perceived the environment to be abusive. In this decision, the Court rejected a gendered "reasonable woman" standard advocated by the plaintiffs in the case. In 1998, the Court ruled in *Oncale v. Sundowner Offshore Services* that same-sex sexual harassment violates Title VII. The latter two rulings reflected how far the law had come from the early feminist framing of sexual harassment as a distinctively women's experience.[41] The issue had become conceptually degendered, no longer necessarily linked to women's subordination as it had in the early feminist theory on sexual harassment.

In two other cases in 1998, *Faragher v. City of Boca Raton* and *Burlington Industries v. Ellerth,* the Court ruled that employers are strictly liable for harassment that results in tangible employment action by a supervisor; liable for harassment by co-workers and nonemployees only if the employer knew or should have known of the conduct and did not take immediate and appropriate corrective action; and, when no tangible employment action is taken, liable for harassment by supervisors unless the employer exercised reasonable care to prevent and correct promptly any sexually harassing behavior, and the plaintiff unreasonably failed to take advantage of any preventative or corrective opportunities provided by the employer or to avoid harm otherwise.[42] In 2004 and 2006 respectively, the Supreme Court again addressed issues related to sexual harassment: constructive discharge in *Pennsylvania State Politice v. Suders* and retaliation in *Burlington Northern v. White*.[43] The Supreme Court cases on sexual harassment of students allowed private individuals to recover monetary damages under Title IX for sexual harassment, established that a school board must demonstrate deliberate indifference to a report of sexual harassment in order to be liable, and allowed peer harassment cases.[44]

Lower courts established important precedents as well, often expanding sexual harassment jurisprudence. For example, in *Robinson v. Jacksonville Shipyards*, a district court in Florida allowed a sexual harassment claim based on obscenity in the workplace. The Ninth Circuit in *Ellison v. Brady* ruled that courts should evaluate harassment from the perspective of a reasonable woman, although other circuits have disagreed. Feminists advocated for the "reasonable woman standard" based on social scientific research showing that men and women perceive sexual behavior in the workplace differently. The Eighth Circuit in *Jenson v. Eveleth Taconite* allowed a class action sexual harassment suit, and the Seventh Circuit in *DiCenso v. Cisneros* allowed a claim for tenant harassment.[45] The *Jenson* case was later turned into a Hollywood movie titled *North Country*.[46] The EEOC and the Office of Civil Rights of the Department of Education repeatedly issued policy and enforcement guidance on sexual harassment during the decade. Finally, in 1994, Congress amended the Federal Rules of Evidence to make evidence of a plaintiff's "other sexual behavior" or "sexual predisposition" presumptively inadmissible in sexual harassment lawsuits. At the state level, legislatures passed prohibitions against sexual harassment in a variety of contexts. For example, in 1994, California passed an expansive law prohibiting sexual harassment in any "business, service, or professional relationship," including in relationships between a physician and a patient, an attorney and a client, a landlord and a tenant, and in schools.[47] The 1990s also saw several large monetary awards in sexual harassment cases, including a jury award of $7.1 million against the law firm of Baker & McKenzie in California and a $34 million settlement in a case against Mitsubishi in 1998.[48]

Feminist activists continued to be involved in precedent-setting sexual harassment lawsuits and public policy debates after *Meritor*. Feminist organizations participated in many significant court cases on sexual harassment and in government hearings on the issue. Hundreds of organizations across the country provided direct services to victims of sexual harassment. Advocacy groups, including unions, published guides and handbooks on sexual harassment and also produce films and workshop materials on sexual harassment. Feminist legal theory on sexual harassment expanded significantly and became increasingly complex and fragmented. Outside of feminist circles, discussions of sexual harassment flourished. Many books appeared on sexual harassment, especially on harassment of students. Discussions and activism expanded to include sexual harassment in new contexts, such as street harassment, harassment in housing, harassment on the Internet, and harassment of young girls.[49] Finally, research on sexual harassment expanded significantly, including many surveys showing continued high rates of harassment.

While feminist activism expanded, so did criticism of sexual harassment policies. Some of the critics echoed those of the 1980s by claiming that women provoke harassment, exaggerate, or lie about it. Women alleging sexual harassment were often criticized and the issue trivialized. Critics of feminism, such as Katie Roiphe, Camille Paglia, and Christina Hoff Summers, attacked the feminist focus on sexual harassment as an example of "victim feminism" or "puritan feminism," which they argued portrayed women consistently as passionless victims. Similarly, University of Massachusetts English Professor Daphne Patai accused the "sexual harassment industry" of blurring the distinction between gross offensiveness and a "word or gesture heard by a bystander as 'uncomfortable.'"[50] In *Feminist Accused of Sexual Harassment*, Jane Gallop, who was accused of sexual harassment by two graduate students, argued that sexual harassment policies threatened civil liberties as well as ordinary social behavior in the workplace and in colleges.[51] In legal commentary, objections to sexual harassment policy developed based on First Amendment free speech challenges, due process challenges, and privacy challenges. Some of these objections succeeded in the courts. In 1993, English professor J. Donald Silva sued the University of New Hampshire for violating his First Amendment rights because the university suspended him for sexual harassment. A New Hampshire district court ordered the university to reinstate Silva until the court could resolve the case. In 1994, the case settled out of court, making Silva's reinstatement permanent, removing the charge from his record, and granting him $60,000 in back pay and $170,000 in legal fees.[52] In 2001, the Third Circuit invalidated a school district's antiharassment policy on free speech grounds in the case of *Saxe v. State College Area School District*, an opinion authored by Circuit Judge Samual Alito, who was elevated to the Supreme Court by President George W. Bush in 2006.[53]

The Supreme Court's decision in *Meritor Savings Bank v. Vinson* paved the way for sexual harassment to become the high-profile issue that repeatedly brandished newspaper headlines in the 1990s. The decision was a turning point for the movement against sexual harassment. With a Supreme Court stamp of approval, the movement shifted from localized struggles in a variety of arenas to a more specialized, legalized, national effort with new women's organizations and actors joining the movement. Sexual harassment advocacy became a mainstay of the women's movement, nested into the leading feminist organizations as one of the core issues, and fully integrated into the equal employment opportunity agencies and offices of federal and state governments, as well as private employers. The legal framework was a powerful advocacy tool in late twentieth-century American society, but it depends on receptive judges. The movement took advantage of the political opportunities created by a diverse group of circuit court judges who had been influenced by the civil rights movement and the Vietnam era. Women have come a long way in winning the legal right to enter the workplace without being subjected to sexual harassment. However, women continue to experience high rates of sexual harassment, and the legal processes associated with winning relief are often slow and costly, emotionally and financially. In addition, conservative judicial appointments of the Reagan and both Bush administrations may stymie the effectiveness of legal remedies in the future.

Conclusion: Entering the Mainstream

Despite continuing struggles, the history of the movement against sexual harassment is in many ways an incredible success story. The movement against sexual harassment emerged at the intersection of multiple social movements percolating in American society in the 1970s – the women's movements, the civil rights movement, the labor movement, the gay and lesbian rights movement, and the sexual revolution. The sexual revolution brought about changes in sexual morality and behavior, ushering in more open and positive attitudes toward sex. But as the sexual revolution articulated the right to engage in sex, the antirape movement asserted women's right to say no to sex and, along with the battered women's movement, asserted women's right to be free from physical violence. The women's health movement, including the reproductive rights movement, articulated women's right to control their bodies – for women to understand their health and be able to make decisions regarding medical care, including childbearing decisions. The women's movement protested the sexual objectification and exploitation of women and the lesbian rights movement supported women's sexual autonomy by asserting the right of women to choose other women as sexual and life partners. More generally, the women's and civil rights movements promised equal employment opportunity, without regard to sex or race. These movements offered women hopes of economic independence and sexual autonomy.

But the reality of sexual coercion in the workplace cut to the heart of these hopes. Sexual harassment denied women sexual autonomy, threatened their physical safety and integrity, deprived them of employment opportunities and, for women of color, was often a form of racism. At a time when women heavily populated the lower rungs of the workforce, but many aspired to work their way up, sexual harassment was a particularly personal and insulting form of discrimination. Not only were women not taken seriously as workers, but they were treated as sexual objects. The issue of sexual coercion in the workplace was first raised by lesbian feminists and African-American women working in the civil rights movement, but quickly spread to women in a range of contexts, including nontraditional occupations and educational institutions. The strength of the movement was how this diverse group of women was able to work in coalition across differences to achieve major social change in American society. With roots in the civil rights movement, the women's movements, and the labor movement, activists against sexual harassment drew upon the ideologies, strategies, and constituencies of these movements in varied ways to articulate their experiences of sexual harassment and combat this behavior in a broad range of contexts. This diverse and committed group of grassroots activists succeeded in raising awareness of sexual harassment and shaping laws that addressed sexual harassment not only in the office, but in coal mines, on construction sites, in factories, and at educational institutions.

The movement against sexual harassment was shaped by the political opportunities, mobilizing structures, and framing processes employed by movement participants. The movement took advantage of the growing institutional structure created by governments in response to the civil rights and women's movements, particularly the agencies developed to enforce the equal opportunity laws. As a result of the civil rights and women's movements, the nation had an expanding system of federal and state equal employment opportunity offices, civil rights agencies, human rights commissions, and commissions on the status of women. These agencies and commissions were committed to advancing civil rights, equality, and employment opportunity in the United States. Activists against sexual harassment used this new institutional structure to articulate their grievances about sexual harassment. Women also took advantage of elite allies in government – the progressive judicial and executive agency appointments of presidents Johnson, Kennedy, and Carter. Judges Richey and Robinson, Commissioner Norton, and other importantly positioned government officials advanced the movement's agenda. Despite these political opportunities, the movement was constrained by its limited ability to achieve legislative change because of its lack of lobbying capacity and influence on political parties.

The movement also took advantage of the "expanding cultural opportunities" that increased the likelihood of movement activity.[1] The movement emerged out of the glaring contradiction between a "highly salient cultural value" – equal employment opportunity – and conventional social practices – sexual coercion and harassment of women in the workplace. In a relatively short period of time, women across the country were raising grievances about sexual harassment and these "suddenly imposed grievances" were confirmed as a widespread phenomena through surveys and studies, which dramatized the vulnerability or even illegitimacy of the system by calling into question the meritocracy of the workplace and the court's enforcement of equal employment opportunity in the American workplace. The movement created an innovative "master frame" for sexual harassment – the Title VII sexual harassment claim – within which subsequent challengers could map their own grievances and demands.

The movement was also shaped by the mobilizing structures through which activists sought to organize. Mobilizing structures are "the collective vehicles, informal as well as formal, through which people mobilize and engage in collective action."² The movement drew upon the resources of other social movements of the day. The civil rights movement, the women's movements, and the labor movement provided key mobilizing structures and resources through which activists organized the movement against sexual harassment. Through formal organizational structures and informal networks of these broader movements, sexual harassment activists were able to generate collective action. Multiple locations, including the workplace, employment associations, unions, and schools were grassroots settings from which the movement facilitated collective action. They created their own organizations – WWI and AASC – but also used existing organizations at the national, state, and local levels to further their cause, such as NOW or the WLDF. They worked through organizations of the women's movement, but also organizations of other social movements of the day, such as the Mexican American Legal Defense Fund and unions. They also applied for grants from organizations such as the Ford Foundation, Ms. Foundation, and federal granting agencies for research grants. Using this wide range of resources, they were able to mobilize women from diverse constituencies to work together within the movement against sexual harassment.

The third important factor that shaped the movement against sexual harassment was the framing processes – "the collective processes of interpretation, attribution, and social construction that mediate between opportunity and action."³ Frames help define a problem and suggest actions to remedy the problem. For a social movement to arise, people must feel "both aggrieved about some aspect of their lives and optimistic that, acting collectively, they can redress the problem."⁴ As chapter five demonstrates, the movement against sexual harassment drew heavily upon ideas of the women's and civil rights movements to frame the issue of sexual harassment as a gendered phenomenon that violated women's civil rights. By highlighting the contradiction between the principle of sex equality and women's experience of sexual coercion in the workplace, activists were able to challenge prevailing understandings of sexual coercion in the workplace as a private problem and recast this behavior as a barrier to equal opportunity for women.⁵ Drawing on the rhetoric of the civil rights and women's movements, activists invoked the powerful ideology of human equality and equal opportunity as well as sexual autonomy and bodily integrity to argue that sexual harassment was a basic violation of women's economic and physical well-being. By coining the term "sexual harassment" and characterizing it as a violation of equal employment opportunity, the movement offered "cognitive liberation"⁶ from the indignities women suffered in the workplace as well as an avenue for action to address these violations. Movement participants fashioned a shared understanding that sexual coercion in the workplace was a violation of Title VII, thereby legitimating and motivating collective action. Activists framed the issue of sexual harassment dramatically as "economic rape" and as a manifestation of male domination in the workplace and society at large. Activists invoked radical feminist theory to argue that sexual harassment was a manifestation of male domination, anti-racist theory to analyze the racist manifestations and causes of sexual harassment, and socialist analysis to understand the class-based implications of the behavior. Activists effectively used the media to communicate their understanding of the issue and bring more people into the movement.

The strength of the movement against sexual harassment stemmed from its racial and economic diversity. Women of color were critical contributors to the movement against sexual harassment, acting both individually and collectively to combat sexual coercion on the job and at educational institutions. African-American women brought most of the early precedent-setting sexual harassment cases, including the first successful Title VII cases in the federal district court (Diane Williams), the federal courts of appeals (Paulette Barnes), and the Supreme Court (Mechelle Vinson), and the first successful cases involving a student (Pamela Price), co-worker harassment (Willie Ruth Hawkins), and hostile environment harassment at the federal appellate level (Sandra Bundy). Plaintiffs in three of the first six published sexual harassment cases were young African-American women (Diane Williams, Paulette Barnes, and Margaret Miller). The case of another African-American woman (Maxine Munford) inspired one of the early statewide campaigns to address the issue of sexual harassment, leading to the passage in 1980 of one of the first and most progressive state laws against sexual harassment. The significance of these cases was that they established the movement's framework by successfully articulating sexual harassment as discrimination based on sex and as a violation of women's civil rights under Titles VII and IX. This framework focused liability on employers rather than harassers – a more systemic approach that had a wider impact by encouraging institutions to take preventative action against sexual harassment.

African-American women's identities and backgrounds were significant in how they experienced sexual harassment, how they articulated the issue, and the methods they used to seek relief. Several of the women had experience with race discrimination or had experience in the civil rights movement, and hence had some knowledge of the mechanisms for relief from discrimination. Two of the plaintiffs in early precedent-setting sexual harassment cases – Diane Williams and Paulette Barnes – were African-American women who worked in government agencies established to combat race discrimination, so they had an understanding of civil rights concepts and processes. They felt a great sense of indignation at being sexually harassed by people who were supposed to be fighting discrimination. Both Williams and Barnes obtained counsel through LCCRUL, a private organization in Washington, D.C. that provided free counsel in civil rights cases and made referrals to cooperating attorneys who handled cases on a *pro bono* or contingency basis. The white male attorneys who represented Williams and Barnes – Warwick Furr and Michael Hausfeld – both had backgrounds in civil rights law. Sandra Bundy, who brought the first successful hostile environment sexual harassment case in the federal appellate courts, had a long history of participation in the civil rights movement in the

1960s. She had attended marches and demonstrations and had helped to organize a union that worked to end racial segregation in the workplace. Both Williams and Bundy spoke out about the issue in the media and testified at federal hearings on sexual harassment. Finally, Chilean exile Ximena Bunster's case at Clark University spurred the growing trend of educational institutions to adopt sexual harassment policies. Anita Hill brought the issue to the attention of the mainstream public when she testified against Clarence Thomas before Congress.

In addition to individual resistance to sexual harassment, women of color acted collectively to combat sexual harassment. Several organizations representing women of color were active in the development of public policy on sexual harassment. The D.C.-based OBAW filed a friend-of-the-court brief in support of Diane Williams in the 1976 case of *Williams v. Saxbe*. African-American attorneys Maudine Rice Cooper and Benjamin L. Evans, both of whom had backgrounds in the civil rights movement, wrote the brief. A couple of years later, in response to the case of Sandra Bundy case, OBAW urged female D.C. city employees to speak up about sexual harassment, leading to Mayor Barry's executive order prohibiting sexual harassment. They also sponsored a forum on sexual harassment to kick off a major survey of sexual harassment sponsored by the D.C. Commission on Women. The Mexican-American Legal Defense Fund was the most active friend-of-the-court participant in early sexual harassment cases, filing briefs in *Miller v. Bank of America* and *Tomkins v. Public Service Electric and Gas*. Pamela Price, who brought the first successful sexual harassment case against an educational institution, was supported by the Afro-American Cultural Center at Yale and the Council of Third World Women at Yale. When the case reached the United States Court of Appeals for the Second Circuit, Price and the other plaintiffs received the support of the National Conference of Black Lawyers and Black Women Organized for Political Action, both of which signed onto an amicus brief.

In the 1980s, organizations representing women of color continued to participate in shaping public policy on sexual harassment. At 1981 congressional hearings on sexual harassment, Eleanor Holmes Norton testified on behalf of many organizations including the Black Women's Organizing Collective, the Mexican American Women's National Association, the National Association of Black Women Attorneys, the National Conference of Puerto Rican Women, the National Council of Negro Women, the National Hookup of Black Women, Women for Racial and Economic Equality, and the Women's Division of the National Conference of Black Lawyers. Several groups representing women of color participated as *amici* in *Meritor Savings Bank v. Vinson*, including the Sisterhood of Black Single Mothers, the National Conference of Black Lawyers, the National Institute for Women of Color, the Women's Rights Project of the Instituto Puertorriqueno de Derechos Civiles, the Mexican American Women's National Association, the Asian Pacific American Bar Association of the Greater Washington, D.C. Area, and the Organization of Pan Asian American Women, Inc.

In addition to the efforts of these activists, two of the most important government officials to shape sexual harassment law were Eleanor Holmes Norton and Judge Spottswood Robinson, both African-Americans with backgrounds in the civil rights movement. Norton chaired the EEOC when that agency issued guidelines on sexual harassment in 1980. These guidelines were the single most important policy development involving sexual harassment and were extremely influential on the development of sexual harassment law. Norton also testified at congressional hearings on sexual harassment in 1979 and 1981 and was a powerful voice for aggressive laws against sexual harassment. The single most influential federal judge in the development of sexual harassment law was Judge Spottswood Robinson, III. Judge Robinson issued groundbreaking rulings on sexual harassment in favor of Paulette Barnes, Sandra Bundy, and Mechelle Vinson, and upheld the legal ruling in favor of Diane Williams. Judge Robinson had been a long-time civil rights attorney and activist; he had been one of the attorneys who argued the case of *Brown v. Board of Education* on behalf of the NAACP before the Supreme Court.

Public policy on sexual harassment was shaped not only by people with backgrounds in the civil rights movement but also by the legal legacy of that movement. Feminist litigators attempting to establish precedent favorable to sexual harassment victims relied upon race discrimination cases. For example, the racial harassment case of *Rogers v. Equal Employment Opportunity Commission* was cited in several early briefs filed by sexual harassment plaintiffs and in several early decisions on sexual harassment. Catharine MacKinnon, in her influential 1979 book *The Sexual Harassment of Working Women*, argued that sexual harassment was as serious as racial harassment and discussed race discrimination cases in detail. WWI's comments on the 1980 EEOC sexual harassment guidelines relied on race discrimination cases. In the first Supreme Court case on sexual harassment, the primary focus of the parties' arguments before the court was whether the same legal standards should apply to sexual harassment as applied to racial harassment.

Many have commented on the prominent role African-American women have played in the development of sexual harassment law. About the prevalence of African-American women among early sexual harassment plaintiffs, Eleanor Holmes Norton has said, "With black women's historic understanding of slavery and rape, it is not surprising to me."[7] Judy Trent Ellis, the first African-American professor of law at SUNY Buffalo, has argued that African-American women's activism in protecting themselves against sexual harassment was probably due both to the greater or more severe harassment visited upon them and their long familiarity with discrimination and willingness to seek redress through the courts. Ellis has argued that African-American women were extremely vulnerable to sexual harassment because of their unique position in American history and mythology. First, the history of slavery still marked African-American women as sexually available, sexually promiscuous, and unprotected by African-American men. Second, African-American women's history of slavery and oppression created conditions of extreme economic vulnerability for them.[8]

Similarly, law professor Kimberlé Crenshaw has argued that the dispropor-
tionate representation of African-American women plaintiffs in early cases was
perhaps due to the "racialization of sexual harassment"—"a merging of racist
myths with their vulnerability as women." Crenshaw argued, "Racism may
well provide the clarity to see that sexual harassment is neither a flattering
gesture nor a misguided social overture but an act of intentional discrimination
that is insulting, threatening, and debilitating."[9] Others have argued that
African-American women were less likely than white women to view sexual
harassment as a personal problem "because sexual exploitation had been integral to racial oppression in this country."[10] The author of a 1981 article in
Essence magazine, Yla Eason, argued that African-American women were
"sensitized to discriminatory acts on the job and thus more aware of and less
conditioned to abiding by them."[11]

Indeed the harassment experienced by several of the early plaintiffs had
racial overtones. Margaret Miller's supervisor appeared uninvited at Miller's
residence, with a bottle of wine in hand, and stated to Miller, "I've never felt this
way about a black chick before" and indicated that he would get her "off the
machines" if she would cooperate with him sexually. He fired her when she
refused.[12] Maxine Munford's supervisor asked her the first day of work "if she
would make love to a white man and if she would slap his face if he made a pass
at her." He later fired her for refusing to comply.[13] In the case of *Continental
Can v. Minnesota*, a co-worker of Willie Ruth Hawkins said that he "wished
slavery days would return so that he could sexually train her and she would be
his bitch," making reference to the movie *Mandingo*.[14] All three of these cases
involved white men harassing African-American women. The racial overtones
of sexual harassment surely contributed to a heightened consciousness among
African-American women about the discriminatory nature of sexual harassment. And when African-American women spoke out about sexual harassment,
they often emphasized the importance of race to their experiences of harassment.

Yet, most of the precedent-setting sexual harassment cases involved intraracial harassment – allegations by Africa-American women that they were
harassed by men of the same race. Diane Williams, Paulette Barnes, Sandra
Bundy, Michelle Vinson, and Anita Hill all alleged that their black male supervisors sexually harassed them. Speaking out against intraracial sexual harassment has opened African-American women to criticism, such as Harvard
sociologist Orlando Patterson's attack on Anita Hill for oversensitivity to
Thomas' "down-home style of courting." Kimberlé Crenshaw has responded
that Patterson's "cultural defense" fails to distinguish between sexual practices
that occur privately and those that occur within the work environment, and
fails to account for the sexual dynamics that shape those sexual practices in the
first place.[15] Despite the political intersectionality that leads to criticism of
African-American women for raising claims of sexual harassment, especially
against African-American men, Africa-American women have been willing to
speak up, and their success before the courts has perhaps been due to the same
stereotypes that underlie Patterson's "cultural defense" argument. Nevertheless,

the intersectional nature of sexual harassment has surely contributed to the prevalence of cases brought by African-American women, who have been economically marginal and sexually stereotyped because of racism and sexism.

In addition to the civil rights movement, opposition against sexual harassment had roots in the women's movement. The founders of WWU and AASC were white middle-class women who had been active in the women's movement. They often worked with women in pink-collar occupations and working-class white-collar occupations – clerical workers like Carmita Wood, waitresses, and flight attendants. These women used a feminist analytic framework to understand sexual coercion, and they drew upon the strategies, tools, and resources of the women's movement to raise public awareness of sexual harassment. Lin Farley, Karen Sauvigné, and Susan Meyer all had experience working in radical feminist organizations, such as the Furies collective, New York Radical Feminists, and Lesbian Feminist Liberation, where they developed their understanding of feminist theory, including feminist theory on rape and domestic violence. Farley and Meyer had experience working with the media – Farley as an associated press reporter and Meyer as a member of the Rat Collective, an underground feminist newspaper. Sauvigné had worked at the ACLU's Women's Rights Project and for the LSCRRC, where she gained an understanding of civil rights law as well as fundraising experience and contacts in the legal community. All three used the theory, strategies, skills, and resources developed in their experience in the women's movement.

The founders of AASC were also active in the women's movement, gaining experience that they used in their work on sexual harassment. Freada Klein, Lynn Wehrli, and Elizabeth Cohn-Stuntz had all worked extensively in the rape crisis movement – Klein with Bay Area Women Against Rape and Prisoners Against Rape, Klein and Wehrli with Feminist Alliance Against Rape, and all three with the D.C. Rape Crisis Center. Cohn-Stuntz had written her senior thesis at Smith on women's emotional reactions to rape, and Klein had worked on the rape chapter of *Our Bodies, Ourselves* in the mid-1970s and had helped produce a documentary film called *Rape Culture* produced by Cambridge Documentary Films. Through this work, Klein, Wehrli, and Cohn-Stuntz gained an understanding of feminist theory on violence against women, as well as tools and strategies for feminist organizing.

The founders of WWI and AASC used their backgrounds in the women's movement to understand sexual harassment and organize against it. They applied feminist theory on rape to understand sexual harassment as a form of sexual coercion. They applied socialist feminist understandings of the interaction of capitalism, racism, and patriarchy to understand women's vulnerability to sexual harassment. They applied feminist legal theory to develop remedies for sexual harassment. In addition to feminist theory, they used strategies and techniques from the women's movements, such as holding speak-outs, writing press releases, publishing newsletters, and developing myth/fact sheets. They used their education to articulate the experience of sexual harassment and promote public awareness of the issue through the media. They had all attended college, and several had attended graduate school. With this educational background, they were able to conduct surveys, develop a theoretical analysis of sexual harassment, and write and publish articles on the issue. Wehrli wrote her master's thesis at MIT on sexual harassment, Farley wrote a book on the issue, and Meyer and Sauvigné applied for grants to conduct studies on sexual harassment. Later members of these organizations, such as Constance Backhouse, Leah Cohn, and Peggy Crull, continued this important work.

In addition to the founders and members of WWI and AASC, feminist attorneys with backgrounds in the women's movement played a critical role in the fight against sexual harassment. Heather Sigworth was a founding member of NOW in Tucson, and Nadine Taub directed Rutgers Law School's Women's Rights Litigation Clinic. Both had published articles on feminist issues. Linda Singer had worked with the WLDF, and Mary Dunlap was co-founder of ERA. These feminist attorneys were part of the growing trend within the women's movement in the 1970s to use the courts to expand women's rights. By the mid-1970s, feminists had succeeded in gaining rights for women to birth control and abortion as well as enhancing constitutional guarantees of equality. Similarly, feminists attempted to use federal statutory law – Title VII and Title IX – to protect women from sexual harassment in the workplace and at educational institutions. As the movement against sexual harassment matured, feminist attorneys played an increasingly central role in the development of public policy on sexual harassment.

By the early 1980s, a wide range of feminist organizations were working on sexual harassment, including public interest law firms, women's political organizations, and employee associations, and women in pink-collar and working-class white collar occupations participated actively in these organizations. Large feminist organizations such as NOW, the National Women's Political Caucus, and the National Association of Office Workers worked on the issue, as well as smaller feminist organizations such as New Responses in Washington, D.C., the Women's Justice Center in Detroit, Working Women Organizing Project in Cleveland, Women Employed Institute in Chicago, and the Women's Alliance for Job Equity in Philadelphia. Representatives of these feminist organizations contributed to the movement against sexual harassment in many ways, including testifying at government hearings, submitting comments on the EEOC guidelines, conducting research and training on sexual harassment, publishing pamphlets and guides on sexual harassment, advising and supporting victims of harassment, and speaking out to the media on the issue.

The third leg of the movement against sexual harassment was the activism of women working in male-dominated fields. As women began to break into nontraditional blue-collar occupations in the late 1970s, many experienced tremendous hostility from men who resented women's encroachment upon traditionally masculine spheres of activity. Blue-collar women experienced harassment not only from supervisors but also from co-workers, in forms sometimes sexual, but also often misogynist and violent, including physical assault and work sabotage. Drawing upon the resources of unions and working women's organizations, blue-collar women organized against sexual harassment. They contributed to the movement by broadening the public understandings of sexual harassment to include not just *quid pro quo* harassment but also hostile environment harassment.

Blue-collar women brought several of the early precedent-setting sexual harassment cases. Phyllis Brown, a civilian police dispatcher, won the first successful hostile environment claim under Title VII in May of 1980. Factory worker Willie Ruth Hawkins won the first successful co-worker harassment case in July of 1980. Barbara Henson, also a police dispatcher, brought the precedent-setting hostile environment sexual harassment case, *Henson v. City of Dundee*, decided by the Eleventh Circuit in 1982. In the late 1970s and early 1980s, women working in a broad range of blue-collar occupations filed claims for sexual harassment, including janitors, security guards, police officers, and assembly-line workers. In addition, women in traditionally male occupations, such as construction and coal mining, brought sex discrimination lawsuits including allegations of sexual harassment. In response to a 1976 lawsuit brought by female construction workers, the DOL issued the first federal regulations on harassment in the workplace in 1978. Several organizations representing female construction workers participated in the lawsuit and in the process leading to the adoption of the federal regulations, including Advocates for Women in San Francisco, Women in Trades in Seattle, United Trade Workers Association in Tacoma, Washington, Wider Opportunities for Women and Women Working in Construction, both based in Washington, D.C., and the Coalition of Labor Union Women. In 1978, women coal miners brought a suit against Consolidated Coal Company of Pittsburgh, the largest coal company in the United States, leading to a federal investigation of the entire coal mining industry and resulting in an out-of-court settlement that called for hiring quotas, back pay, and affirmative programs to protect female miners from discrimination and harassment underground.

Blue-collar women and organizations representing them not only brought lawsuits to protest sexual harassment but also were extensively involved in raising awareness about sexual harassment. Jean McPheeters, a letter carrier, served as chair of Working Women United, which included many blue-collar women. In New York City, the Clearinghouse on Blue Collar Women of Women for Racial and Economic Equality surveyed blue-collar women about sexual harassment in 1978, and the CEP later surveyed female coal miners about their experiences of harassment. Blue-collar women won attention to the issue of sexual harassment through media coverage of their cases, which often involved extreme violence and clear discriminatory intent. For example, sexual harassment of female coal miners was covered extensively in the press in the early 1980s. This coverage provided a very sympathetic case to convince people that men used sexual harassment to keep women out of the workplace.

Female union members also worked on the issue of sexual harassment. In Michigan, the Coalition of Labor Union Women and the Union Minorities/

Women Leadership Project were members of the Michigan Taskforce on Sexual Harassment in the Workplace, formed in 1978. In Detroit, the Labor Education and Research Project published a booklet on sexual harassment in 1980 written by four white union women and an African-American female attorney. Women and men in unions around the country supported victims of sexual harassment and worked to raise awareness of the issue by surveying union members, publishing and distributing information on harassment, providing educational programs, and fighting for clauses against sexual harassment in union contracts. Women's activism within the United Mine Workers of America led in 1979 to President Arnold Miller making a public commitment to eradicating sexual harassment in the mines.

Blue-collar women's organizations shaped public policy by presenting testimony at government hearings on sexual harassment and participating in filing friend-of-the-court briefs in significant sexual harassment lawsuits. In 1981, representatives of blue-collar women testified at congressional hearings on sexual harassment, including Betty Jean Hall of the CEP and Pat Baldwin of the Western Kentucky Coalmining Women's Support Team. Other blue-collar women's groups supported the testimony of Eleanor Holmes Norton, including the Association of Illinois Women Coal Miners, the Coalition of Labor Union Women, the East Tennessee Coalmining Women's Support Team, the Lady Miners of Utah, Wider Opportunities for Women, and Women Miners of Wyoming. Several other blue-collar women's groups submitted statements to the congressional committee, including the Phoenix Institute in Salt Lake City, Utah, a community-based employment and training contractor focused on placing low-income women in blue-collar jobs. Pat Baldwin of the Western Kentucky Coalmining Support Team testified at hearings on sexual harassment held by the Kentucky Commission on Civil Rights. The Coal Employment Project later participated in filing a friend-of-the-court brief in *Meritor Saving Bank v. Vinson*. Several other organizations representing working-class women participated as amici in that case as well, including Non-Traditional Employment for Women, Wider Opportunities for Women, the Workers Defense League, the American Federation of Labor and Congress of Industrial Organizations, and the Coalition of Labor Union Women.

In addition to the diversity of women involved in the movement against sexual harassment, several men made significant contributions to the movement. Warwick Furr and Michael Hausfeld represented early sexual harassment plaintiffs, Judge Charles Richey had the courage to issue his precedent-setting decision in *Williams v. Saxbe*, Judges Spottswood Robinson and Skelly Wright repeatedly ruled in favor of sexually harassed women, Al Ripskis pushed the issue of sexual harassment in Washington, D.C., leading James Hanley to call the first congressional hearings on sexual harassment in 1979, which had a tremendous impact on the development of a strong public policy against sexual harassment. The U.S. government, both the courts and the Congress, as well as state and local governments at the time were very male-gendered institutions, which were confronted by a very female-gendered social movement about an issue of male sexual coercion of females in the very institutions of that government as well as the broader society. Whether motivated by paternalism or conservative sexual morality, feminism, social justice concerns, or political expediency, these male-dominated institutions responded to feminist demands.

The grassroots diversity of the movement against sexual harassment led to strong, broad-based public policy against sexual harassment. The movement's diffuse participants – individuals, organizations, and informal groups – arose from multiple locations, but intersected at critical junctures, before Congress and the Supreme Court. With the perspectives of differing constituencies represented in the political discourse around sexual harassment, public policy developed in such a way as to incorporate the experiences of a diverse array of women working in a wide range of contexts, including white- and blue-collar work settings and educational institutions. This activism came together in the sexual harassment lawsuits filed around the country in the 1970s and early 1980s.

Reflecting the separate spheres ideology that had historically shaped the law's treatment of women, courts initially denied relief, portraying sexual harassment as natural, personal, sexually-motivated but gender-neutral conduct that was not related to the plaintiffs' employment. In describing the facts of the cases, these courts focused on the sexual advances but not on the employment ramifications. By emphasizing the sexual aspects of the case, they were able to personalize the conduct and excuse the employer for tolerating it. In so doing, the judges in the early cases denying relief obscured the underlying power dynamics of the behavior – the abuse of authority and the economic coercion involved. But the women appealed their cases. Feminist attorneys represented the plaintiffs, and feminist organizations filed friend-of-the-court briefs supporting them. Drawing upon studies and stories, history and sociological data, and feminist and legal theories, feminists argued that sexual harassment was not trivial personal conduct, but was a widespread, serious problem that deprived women of equal employment opportunities. They also relied on early racial harassment cases, making parallels between sexual harassment and racial harassment. The plaintiffs prevailed on appeal before judges who were significantly more liberal than the judges in the lower courts. Whereas the lower court judges had largely been older, white, male, Nixon-appointees, the appellate court judges were the more liberal and diverse appointees of Kennedy and Johnson.

By the late 1970s, as women were beginning to break into nontraditional occupations, they spoke up about a broader range of harassing conduct. Women filed suits seeking relief for hostile environment harassment, again relying on racial harassment cases. In the early 1980s, courts began to rule that Title VII prohibited hostile environment harassment as well *quid pro quo* sexual harassment. Government initiatives against sexual harassment, including Eleanor Holmes Norton's EEOC guidelines, legitimized the issue of sexual harassment and increased public awareness of the problem. In 1986, the U. S. Supreme Court agreed that Title VII prohibited *quid pro quo* and hostile environment sexual harassment in an opinion written by conservative jurist Justice Rehnquist. This ruling fundamentally undermined traditional sex roles that required women to stay in the private sphere, but also reinforced traditional notions of male sexual aggression and female passivity, perhaps the key to why the Court was willing to adopt this revolutionary jurisprudence. Furthermore, this outcome was consistent with conservative views of sexual morality, creating an alignment similar to that between some feminists and social conservatives against pornography. The fact that the plaintiffs in most of the early precedent-setting cases were African-Americans may also have contributed to courts' willingness to set aside the idea that women belonged in the private sphere because so many African-American women had always been in the workplace.

Prohibitions on sexual harassment led to sexual harassment training in workplaces across the country, raising the issue with thousands people in a broad range of occupations. These training workshops provided a forum to discuss women's status in the workplace, gender roles, and sexual stereotypes. In this training, women's right to participate in the workplace on an equal footing with men was assumed, challenging traditional and persisting notions that women were not serious participants in the workplace. By the 1990s, most employers had policies against harassment, and many offered training to sensitize workers. Women were challenging sexual harassment across the country in a broad range of occupations and sometimes even winning large verdicts in sexual harassment cases. Through these successes, the movement had come a long way in achieving their goal of claiming the right of women to enter the public sphere, both political spaces as well as workplaces and schools. The movement achieved social change not only by achieving legal changes through court houses and legislatures, but also by achieving cultural changes in workplaces and educational institutions. The movement raised consciousness about women's right to enter the workplace and function there free from sexual coercion and molestation. Women are no longer outsiders or interlopers, but have a central place in these institutions, a shift for which the movement against sexual harassment deserves significant credit.

This success, however, is tempered by the continuing high rates of sexual harassment and the persisting stereotypes used against women who resist harassment. Rates of sexual harassment are similar to what they were twenty-five years ago when reliable studies of the phenomenon first appeared.[16] The public/private sphere ideology that historically justified and reinforced male dominance and that undergirded courts' early denials of sexual harassment claims continues to shape public discussion of sexual harassment.[17] The issue is often still seen as a matter of private sexual conduct, not abuse of power. Longstanding stereotypes blaming women for sexual harassment or accusing them of lying about it, existing from the earliest days of this country's history, still plague women who bring accusations of sexual harassment. According to political science professor Gwendolyn Mink, women complaining of sexual harassment face a "regime of disbelief."[18] Powerful biases against women continue to shape public opinion and court opinions on sexual harassment.

Furthermore, the conceptualization of sexual harassment primarily as a legal claim, in particular a claim of sex discrimination, placed the issue squarely within a highly contentious adversarial framework that has often not led to satisfactory solutions to the problem, especially for women who do not have the resources to use the legal system. The bureaucratic and legalistic procedures for addressing sexual harassment are often slow, costly, and contentious, and women have often felt victimized again by these processes. Although employers are providing training on sexual harassment, many are motivated more out of concerns for liability rather than integration of women into the workplace. Workers often resent the threat of lawsuits and the close oversight of employers seeking to avoid liability. The framing of the issue as a legal question narrowed the strategic options available to women resisting sexual coercion in the workplace, leaving many women without recourse.

Early feminist activists did not achieve their larger goal of undermining the system of dominance that produced sexual harassment. The founders of WWI and AASC had viewed sexual harassment as part of a larger struggle against sexism, classism, and racism and they understood sexual harassment to be symptomatic of a deeply flawed patriarchal, capitalist, racist system. They hoped to use the issue to inspire collective action to fight the root causes of injustice and transform society. In arguing that sexual harassment was sex discrimination, they conceptualized sexual harassment as a group harm. They argued that sexual harassment harmed not just individual women but women as a class by reinforcing sex segregation and subordination of women in the workforce. By focusing on employer liability for sexual harassment, feminists attempted to address this harm to women. Despite this approach, individualized solutions to sexual harassment came to dominate the movement's agenda. As has been true in other areas, the legal remedies were a valuable tool for individuals seeking relief from sexual harassment, but they undermined collective efforts that might have led to deeper societal transformation and reached the root causes of sexual harassment in society.[19] Despite feminist hopes to challenge broader injustices in America, liberal legal gains eclipsed these radical hopes in the 1980s. The movement against sexual harassment shifted away from collective protest and toward individual legal solutions to sexual harassment. Although legal solutions have offered much, and the recent possibility of class action suits is promising, they have left in place the basic societal structure that allows sexual harassment to continue. As Joan Hoff has argued, the Supreme Court's 1986 decision in *Meritor Savings Bank v. Vinson* was a "bright legal light on the gender horizon" but that this decision "did not have any redistributive or fundamentally unsettling economic or moral impact on American society."[20]

Nevertheless, the movement was a powerful step toward claiming the right of women to enter the public sphere, both political spaces as well as workplaces. Women have growing economic power – some have risen from the lowest rungs of the American workplace – but they rarely achieve the highest rungs, the workplace is still highly segregated, the wage gap persists, and women still experience high rates of sexual harassment. And although sexual harassment law has provided some protection for women in the workplace, the sexual objectification of women in the broader culture has increased significantly and is being increasingly internalized by girls and women.[21] The issue of sexual harassment is often de-gendered and, in practice, is often disconnected from the feminist analysis of systems of privilege, domination, and oppression so that the underlying power relationships remain obscured.[22] The challenge is to reanalyze sexual harassment in the context of interlocking systems of oppression, to regender the issue by analyzing the ways American culture still embraces hegemonic discourses of male sexual dominance, and to challenge that discourse collectively both inside and outside the workplace. Remembering the origins of the movement against sexual harassment and understanding the theories and tactics of the movement's founders will help us to meet this challenge today.

Appendix A: Time Lines of Significant Events

July 2, 1964	Civil Rights Act of 1964 (Title VII) enacted
December 20, 1971	Paulette Barnes files race discrimination complaint with EPA's Equal Opportunity Office in Washington, D.C.
June 23, 1972	Education Amendments of 1972 (Title IX) enacted
September 13, 1972	Diane Williams files sex discrimination complaint with Justice Department's Equal Opportunity Office in Washington, D.C.
October 12, 1973	Jane Corne and Geneva DeVane file sex discrimination complaint with the EEOC against Bausch & Lomb in Pima County, AZ
August 9, 1974	Barnes v. Train, District of Columbia: district court dismisses case
August 19, 1974	Adrienne Tomkins files sex discrimination complaint with EEOC against Public Service Electric & Gas, Inc. in Newark, NJ
December 2, 1974	Carmita Wood files unemployment compensation claim in Ithaca, NY after she left her job because of sexual harassment
January 8, 1975	Darla Jeanne Garber files sex discrimination complaint with EEOC in Fairfax, VA
January 17, 1975	EEOC files friend-of-the-court brief in *Corne v. Bausch & Lomb*
March 14, 1975	*Corne v. Bausch and Lomb, Inc.*, Tucson, AZ: district court dismisses case
March 1975	Feminists coin term "sexual harassment"
April 21, 1975	Lin Farley testifies about sexual harassment before the New York City Human Rights Commission, chaired by Eleanor Holmes Norton

May 4, 1975	Speak-out on Sexual Harassment and founding of Working Women United, Ithaca, NY
August 1975	Working Women United Institute founded, Ithaca, NY
August 19, 1975	*New York Times* publishes Enid Nemy's article on sexual harassment
December 16, 1975	Margaret Miller files race and sex discrimination complaint with EEOC in San Francisco, CA
January 19, 1976	*Wall Street Journal* publishes article on sexual harassment
January 1976	*Redbook* survey published (results published in November 1976)
March 18, 1976	*Garber v. Saxon Industries*, Fairfax, VA: district court dismisses case
April 1976	*New York Review Law Review* publishes first law journal article on sexual harassment
April 24, 1976	*Williams v. Saxbe*, District of Columbia: Judge Richey rules in favor of Williams; first successful Title IX sexual harassment case
June 1976	Alliance Against Sexual Coercion founded, Cambridge, MA.
August 19, 1976	*Miller v. Bank of America*, San Francisco, CA: district court dismisses case
November 22, 1976	Tomkins v. Public Service Electric and Gas, Inc., Newark, NJ: district court dismisses case
December 1976	Lynn Wehrli completes master's thesis at MIT: *Sexual Harassment at the Workplace: A Feminist Analysis and Strategy for Social Change*
February 14, 1977	*Garber v. Saxon Industries*, Fairfax, VA: Fourth Circuit reverses district court dismissal, becoming first federal appellate court to rule that sexual harassment violates Title VII
June 1977	Working Women United Institute moved to New York City
July 7, 1977	*Alexander v. Yale* filed in New Haven, CT: first case to allege sexual harassment in violation of Title IX,
July 27, 1977	*Barnes v. Costle*, District of Columbia: D.C. Circuit reverses district court dismissal, ruling in a full written opinion that sexual harassment violates Title VII
July 28, 1977	*Corne v. Bausch and Lomb, Inc.*, Tucson, AZ: Ninth Circuit vacates district court dismissal and remands the case

August 16, 1977	In response to a lawsuit by female construction workers, the Department of Labor proposes regulations that require federal construction contractors to provide a workplace free of "harassment, intimidation, and coercion"
September 1, 1977	Equal Rights Advocates and the Mexican American Legal Defense and Education Fund file a friend-of-the-court brief in *Tomkins*
October 22, 1977	Speak-out sponsored by *Ms.* magazine and Working Women United Institute in New York City
November 1977	*Ms.* cover story on sexual harassment
November 23, 1977	*Tomkins v. Public Service Electric and Gas, Inc.*, Newark, NJ: Third Circuit reverses district court dismissal, ruling that sexual harassment violates Title VII
December 21, 1977	*Alexander v. Yale*, New Haven, CT: Magistrate judge rules that Title IX prohibits sexual harassment in education; allows claim of Pamela Price
March 30–April 20, 1978	*Munford v. James T. Barnes and Co.*: First federal jury trial in case alleging sexual harassment; plaintiff loses.
April 7, 1978	The Department of Labor adopts regulations that require federal construction contractors to provide a workplace free of "harassment, intimidation, and coercion," which are the first federal regulations against sexual harassment
Spring 1978	Michigan Task Force on Sexual Harassment formed
May 9, 1978	Wisconsin passes first state law prohibiting prohibit employers from making employment benefits contingent on consent to "sexual contact or sexual intercourse"
September 19, 1978	*Williams v. Saxbe*, District of Columbia: D.C. Circuit affirms that sexual harassment violates Title VII but remands case for new trial
October 1, 1978	Lin Farley publishes *Sexual Shakedown*
April 7, 1979	Constance Backhouse and Leah Cohen release *The Secret Oppression: Sexual Harassment of Working Women* (copyright 1978)
May 24, 1979	D.C. Mayor Marion Barry issues executive order prohibiting sexual harassment

June 28, 1979	*Miller v. Bank of America*, San Francisco, California: Ninth Circuit reverses lower court dismissal, ruling that Title VII prohibits sexual harassment
July 2, 1979	*Alexander v. Yale*, New Haven, Connecticut: After a bench trial, district court rules against the plaintiff Pamela Price
September 10, 1979	Catharine MacKinnon publishes *Sexual Harassment of Working Women*
October 23, November 1, & November 13, 1979	Representative James Hanley conducts hearings on sexual harassment before the House Subcommittee on Investigations of the Post Office and Civil Service Committee
December 12, 1979	Office of Personnel Management adopts model policies and training materials on sexual harassment
April 11, 1980	EEOC Chair Eleanor Holmes Norton proposes guidelines against sexual harassment
July 3, 1980	*Continental Can Company Co., Inc. v. Minnesota*: Minnesota Supreme Court rules that co-worker harassment violates Minnesota Human Rights Act
July 18, 1980	Michigan passes law prohibiting sexual harassment in employment, public accommodations, public services, education, and housing
September 23, 1980	EEOC adopts final guidelines on sexual harassment
January 12, 1981	*Bundy v. Jackson*, District of Columbia: D.C. Circuit rules that hostile environment harassment violates Title VII
March 1981	Merit Systems Protection Board issues report showing high levels of sexual harassment in the federal government workplace
June 19, 1986	*Meritor Savings Bank v. Vinson*: Supreme Court rules that quid pro quo and hostile environment sexual harassment violate Title VII

Appendix B: Glossary of Select Cases

Alexander v. Yale University, 459 F. Supp. 1 (D. Conn. 1977), affirmed 631 F.2d 178 (2nd Cir. 1980): Several students and a faculty member alleged that a male faculty member sexually pressured female students and that Yale did not respond adequately to student complaints. On December 21, 1977, the lower court dismissed most of the claims but allowed the claim of Pamela Price, who alleged that a male professor had given her a C because she refused his sexual advances. On July 2, 1979, the trial court ruled against Price. On September 22, 1980, the Second Circuit affirmed. Attorneys of record for the plaintiffs were Anne Simon of the New Haven Law Collective, Margaret Kohn of the National Women's Law Center, and on appeal, Nadine Taub, law professor and the Director of the Women's Rights Litigation Clinic at Rutgers Law School. Catharine MacKinnon also assisted with the case. Multiple friend-of-the-court briefs were filed on behalf of the plaintiffs. This case was the first case to rule that sexual harassment of a student by a teacher was sex discrimination in violation of Title IX of the Education Amendments of 1972.

Barnes v. Train, 13 Fed. Empl. Prac. Cas. 123 (D.D.C. 1974), reversed under the name of Barnes v. Costle, 561 F. 2d 983 (D.C. Cir. 1977): Paulette Barnes alleged that her employment was terminated after rejecting the sexual advances of her supervisor, who was the Director of the Office of Equal Opportunity of the Environmental Protection Agency in Washington, D.C. On August 9, 1974, a federal district court ruled that sexual harassment did not violate Title VII of the Civil Rights Act of 1964. On July 27, 1977, the Circuit Court of Appeals for the District of Columbia reversed in an opinion written by Judge Spottswood Robinson, becoming the first federal appellate court to issue a full written opinion ruling that Title VII prohibited sexual harassment. Warwick Furr represented Barnes before the district court, and Linda Singer represented her on appeal. No friend-of-the court briefs were filed in the case, but Catharine MacKinnon provided to the court a brief on sexual harassment.

Bundy v. Jackson, 19 FEP 828 (D.D.C. 1978), reversed, 641 F.2d 934 (D.C. Cir. 1981): Sandra Bundy alleged that her co-workers and supervisors at the Department of Corrections in Washington, D.C. subjected her to hostile environment sexual harassment. On April 25, 1979, the federal district court ruled that this behavior was not sex discrimination under Title VII. On January 12, 1981, the D.C. Circuit ruled that hostile environment sexual harassment violates Title VII, becoming the first federal circuit court to do so. Barry Gottfried represented the plaintiff. The Women's Legal Defense Fund and the Equal Employment Opportunity Commission filed friend-of-the-court briefs on Bundy's behalf.

Continental Can Co., Inc. v. Minnesota, 297 N.W. 2d 241 (Minn. 1980): Factory worker Willie Ruth Hawkins alleged that three white male co-workers created a hostile environment by sexually harassing her. On July 3, 1980, the Supreme Court of Minnesota ruled that an employer's toleration of co-worker sexual harassment was sex discrimination in violation of the Minnesota Human Rights Act. The plaintiff was represented by the state of Minnesota. The National Organization for Women and Working Women's Institute filed a friend-of-the-court brief. This case was one of the first successful co-worker hostile environment cases.

Corne v. Bausch and Lomb, 390 F. Supp. 161 (D. Ariz. 1975), vacated and remanded, 562 F.2d 55 (9th Cir. 1977), cert. denied, 434 U.S. 956 (1977): Jane Corne and Geneva DeVane alleged that they lost their jobs after rejecting the sexual advances of their supervisor at Bausch & Lomb in Pima County, AZ. On March 14, 1975, a federal district court ruled that Title VII did not prohibit sexual harassment. On July 28, 1977, the Circuit Court of Appeals for the Ninth Circuit reversed, ruling that Title VII prohibited sexual harassment. Corne and DeVane's attorneys were Heather Sigworth and Mary-Lynne Fisher from the Center for Law in the Public Interest in Los Angeles. The Equal Employment Opportunity Commission filed its first friend-of-the-court brief on sexual harassment in this case.

Garber v. Saxon Industries, Inc., 14 Empl. Prac. Deci. ¶7586 (E.D. Va. 1976), reversed and remanded, 552 F.2d 1032 (4th Cir. 1977): Darla Jeanne Garber alleged that her employment was terminated after she rejected the sexual advances of her supervisor, the Branch Manager of Saxon Business Products, Inc. in Fairfax, VA. On March 18, 1976, a federal district court ruled that Title VII did not prohibit sexual harassment. On February 14, 1977, the Circuit Court of Appeals for the Ninth Circuit reversed in a brief written opinion, ruling that Title VII prohibited sexual harassment. Garber's attorney was Elaine Majors. This case was the first federal court case to rule that sexual harassment violated Title VII.

Kyriazi v. Western Electric Company, 461 F. Supp. 894 (D.N.J. 1978): A female engineer, Kyriaki Cleo Kyriazi, was ridiculed and harassed by male co-workers, who speculated about her virginity and circulated an obscene cartoon of her at Western Electric's Kearny, NJ, plant. After Kyriazi complained to her supervisor, she was fired. On October 30, 1978, a federal district court ruled that the employer and co-workers had conspired to deprive Kyriazi of her civil rights in violation of § 1985 of the 1871 Civil Rights Act. Judith Vladeck of Elias, Vladeck, and Lewis represented Kyriazi. This case was one of the first successful co-worker hostile environment cases.

Meritor Savings Bank v. Vinson, 477 U.S. 57 (1986): Mechelle Vinson alleged that her supervisor created a hostile environment by pressuring her to engage in sexual contact. After an eleven-day bench trial in January 1980, the federal district court ruled in favor of the bank and dismissed the case on the grounds that the plaintiff had not proved *quid pro quo* harassment. On January 25, 1985, the D.C. Circuit Court reversed in an opinion written by Judge Spottswood Robinson, ruling that the plaintiff had alleged hostile environment sexual harassment prohibited by Title VII. On June 19, 1986, the Supreme Court ruled that Title VII prohibits *quid pro quo* and hostile environment sexual harassment. The plaintiff was represented by Patricia Barry and Catharine MacKinnon. Multiple friend-of-the-court briefs were filed on behalf of the plaintiff. This case was the first Supreme Court ruling on sexual harassment under Title VII.

Miller v. Bank of America, 418 F. Supp. 233 (N.D. Cal. 1976), reversed, 600 F.2d 211 (9th Cir. 1979): Margaret Miller alleged race and sex discrimination on the grounds that her employment as a proofing machine operator was terminated after she rejected the sexual advances of her supervisor at the Bank of America in San Francisco. On August 19, 1976, a federal district court ruled that Title VII did not prohibit sexual harassment. On June 28, 1979, the Circuit Court of Appeals for the Ninth Circuit reversed, ruling that Title VII prohibited sexual harassment. Miller's attorney was Stuart Wein. Equal Rights Advocates and the Mexican Legal Defense and Education Fund filed a friend-of-the-court brief before the appellate court.

Munford v. James T. Barnes and Co., 441 F. Supp. 459 (E.D. Mich. 1977): On October 27, 1976, Maxine Munford filed a complaint alleging sex and race discrimination after she was terminated for rejecting the sexual advances of her supervisor. On September 9, 1977, a federal district court ruled that Title VII prohibited *quid pro quo* sexual harassment, allowing Munford's case to go to trial but dismissed her race discrimination claim. After a jury trial from March 30 to April 20, 1978, the district court judge entered judgment against Munford. This was the first federal jury trial in a case involving sexual harassment. On appeal, the Sixth Circuit affirmed. Thomas Oehmke represented Munford at trial, and Jan Leventer of the Women's Justice Center represented Munford on appeal. Two amicus curiae briefs were filed by the Metropolitan Detroit Branch of the American Civil Liberties Union and the Women Lawyers Association of Michigan. Munford helped to start a statewide campaign in Michigan against sexual harassment.

Tomkins v. Public Service Electric and Gas Company, 422 F. Supp. 553 (D.N.J. 1976), reversed, 568 F.2d 1044 (3rd Cir. 1977): Adrienne Tomkins alleged that her employment as a stenographer was terminated after she rejected the sexual advances of her supervisor at Public Service Electric & Gas Company in Newark, NJ. On November 22, 1976, a federal district court ruled that Title VII did not prohibit sexual harassment. On November 23, 1977, the Circuit Court of Appeals for the Ninth Circuit reversed, ruling that Title VII prohibited sexual harassment. Tomkins' attorney was Nadine Taub, a law professor and the Director of the Women's Rights Litigation Clinic at Rutgers Law School in Newark, New Jersey. Equal Rights Advocates and the Mexican Legal Defense and Education Fund filed a friend-of-the-court brief before the appellate court, as did the EEOC. This case was the first federal case to use the term "sexual harassment."

Williams v. Saxbe, 413 F. Supp. 654 (D.D.C. 1976), reversed in part and vacated in part, 190 F.2d 343 (D.C. Cir. 1978): Diane Williams alleged that her employment was terminated after she rejected the sexual advances of her supervisor at the Justice Department's Community Relations Service. On April 20, 1976, Judge Richey of the D.C. District Court ruled that Title VII prohibited sexual harassment – the first federal court to do so. The Organization of Black Activist Women submitted a friend of the court brief before the district court. On appeal, the Circuit Court for the District of Columbia affirmed this ruling on September 19, 1978 in an opinion written by Judge Spottswood Robinson. Michael Hausfield represented Williams.

Notes

Introduction: Enter at Your Own Risk

1. Stephen J. Morewitz, *Sexual Harassment & Social Change in American Society* (Bethesda: Austin & Winfield, 1996), 23–29, 49; Kerry Segrave, *The Sexual Harassment of Women in the Workplace, 1600 to 1993* (Jefferson, NC: McFarland & Company, Inc., 1994); Ruth Milkman, *Women, Work and Protest—A Century of U.S. Women's Labor History* (Boston: Routledge & Kegan Paul, 1985); Philip S. Foner, *Women and the American Labor Movement—From Colonial Times to the Eve of World War I* (New York: Free Press, 1979), 357, 421–22, 462; Mary Bularzik, "Sexual Harassment at the Workplace: Historical Notes," *Radical America* 12 (June 1978): 25–43.
2. Harriet Jacobs, *Incidents in the Life of a Slave Girl*, ed. by Jean Fagan Yellin (Cambridge: Harvard University Press, 1987), 27.
3. Louisa May Alcott, "How I Went Out to Service," *The Independent*, June 4, 1874, 1.
4. John D'Emilio and Estelle B. Freedman, *Intimate Matters: A History of Sexuality in America* (New York: Harper & Row,1988), 12–13; *see also* Julia Cherry Spruill, *Women's Life and Work in the Southern Colonies* (New York: Norton, 1972), 321–22 (describing statutes prohibiting masters from benefiting from impregnating their indentured servants).
5. Spruill, *Women's Life and Work*, 322.
6. Segrave, *The Sexual Harassment of Women*, 20–21; Herbert G. Gutman, *The Black Family in Slavery and Freedom, 1750–1925* (New York: Pantheon Books, 1976), 393, 399.
7. *Martin v. Jansen*, 193 P. 674 (Wash. 1920).
8. Bularzik, "Sexual Harassment at the Workplace," 36.
9. Ibid.
10. *Life and Labor*, vol. 4, no. 8, August 1914, 242 (publication of the National Women's Trade Union League).
11. Maud Nathan, *The Story of an Epoch-Making Movement* (New York: Doubleday, 1926), 15–16.
12. "Striking Flint: Genora Dollinger Remembers the 1937 Sitdown" (oral history interview by Susan Rosenthal in February 1995), in Sol Dollinger and Genora Johnson Dollinger, *Not Automatic: Women and the Left in the Forging of the Auto Workers' Union* (New York: Monthly Review Press, 2000), 124.

13. Glenna Matthews, *The Rise of Public Woman: Woman's Power and Woman's Place in the United States, 1630–1970* (New York: Oxford University Press, 1992), 5.

14. Mary Conyington, "Relations Between Occupation and Criminality of Women," in U.S. Congress. Senate, *Report on Conditions of Women and Child Wage-Earners in the United States,* 61ˢᵗ Cong., 2d sess., Document #645 (Washington, D.C.: Government Printing Office, 1911), vol. 15, 53, 65, 81-114; Helen Campbell, *Women Wage-Earners, Their Trades and Their Lives* (Boston: Roberts Brothers, 1887).

15. Judith Baer, *The Chains of Protection: The Judicial Response to Women's Labor Legislation* (Westport, CT: Greenwood Press, 1978); Susan Lehrer, *Origins of Protective Labor Legislation for Women, 1905–1925* (Albany: State University of New York, 1987).

16. Doug McAdam, John D. McCarthy, and Mayer N. Zald, *Comparative Perspectives on Social Movements* (New York: Cambridge University Press, 1996).

17. Nancy Whittier, "Meaning and Structure in Social Movements," in *Social Movements: Identity, Culture, and the State,* eds. David S. Meyer, Nancy Whittier, and Belinda Robnett (New York: Oxford University Press, 2002), 292.

18. Ibid., 291.

19. Winifred Breines, *The Trouble Between Us: An Uneasy History of White and Black Women in the Feminist Movement* (New York: Oxford University Press, 2006); Nancy MacLean, *Freedom is Not Enough: The Opening of the American Workplace* (Cambridge: Harvard University Press, 2006), 117–54; Kimberly Springer, *Living for the Revolution: Black Feminist Organizations, 1968–1980* (Durham, NC: Duke University Press, 2005); Benita Roth, *Separate Roads to Feminism: Black, Chicana, and White Feminist Movements in America's Second Wave* (New York: Cambridge University Press, 2004); Premilla Nadasen, "Expanding the Boundaries of the Women's Movement: Black Feminism and the Struggle for Welfare Rights," *Feminist Studies* 28 (2002): 271–301; Maria Bevacqua, "Anti-Rape Coalitions: Radical, Liberal, Black, and White Feminists Challenging Boundaries," in *Forcing Radical Alliances Across Difference: Coalition Politics for the New Millennium,* ed. by Jill Bystydzienski & Steven P. Schacht (New York: Rowman & Littlefield, 2001), 163–76; Dennis A. Deslippe, *"Rights, Not Roses": Unions and the Rise of Working-Class Feminism, 1945–1980* (Urbana: University of Illinois Press, 2000); see also Rosalyn Baxandall and Linda Gordon, eds., *Dear Sisters: Dispatches from the Women's Liberation Movement* (New York: Basic Books, 2000); Kimberlé Williams Crenshaw, "Mapping the Margins: Intersectionality, Identity Politics, and Violence Against Women of Color," in *The Public Nature of Private Violence,* eds. Martha Albertson Fineman and Fixanne Mykitiuk (New York: Routledge, 1994), 93–118.

20. Lee Ann Banaszak, "Women's Movements and Women in Movements: Influencing American Democracy from the 'Outside'?" Presented at the annual meeting of the Midwest Political Science Association, Chicago, IL, 20–23 April 2006, (noting scholarship by Nancy Whittier, Mary Bernstein, and Jo Reger that show how diversity of identity can benefit movement groups).

21. Cynthia Harrison, "Creating a National Feminist Agenda: The Women's Action Alliance and Feminist Coalition Building in the 1970s," in *Feminist Coalitions: Historical Perspectives on Second-Wave Feminism in the United States,* ed. Stephanie Gilmore (Urbana: University of Illinois Press, 2007); Springer, *Living for the Revolution;* Wendy Kline, "'Please Include This in Your Book': Readers Respond to *Our Bodies, Ourselves,*" *Bulletin of the History of Medicine,* 79 (2005): 81–110;

Roth, *Separate Roads to Feminism*; Anne Enke, "Smuggling Sex Through the Gates: Race, Sexuality, and the Politics of Space in Second Wave Feminism," *American Quarterly* 55.4 (2003): 634–67; Gilmore, "The Dynamics of the Second-Wave Feminist Activism in Memphis"; Nadasen, "Expanding the Boundaries of the Women's Movement"; Judith Ezekiel, *Feminism in the Heartland* (Columbus: Ohio State University Press, 2002); Kathy Davis, "Feminist Body/Politics as World Traveller: Translating *Our Bodies, Ourselves*," *The European Journal of Women's Studies* 9(3): 223–47; Bevacqua, "Anti-Rape Coalitions"; Valk, "'Mother Power'"; Naples, *Grassroots Warriors*; Amy Farrell, "'Like a Tarantula on a Banana Boat': *Ms.* Magazine, 1972–1989," in *Feminist Organizations: Harvest of the New Women's Movement*, eds. Myra Marx Ferree and Patricia Yancey Martin (Philadelphia: Temple University Press, 1995), 53–68.

22. Sara M. Evans, "Beyond Declension: Feminist Radicalism in the 1970s and 1980s," in *The World the 60s Made: Politics and Culture in Recent America*, eds. Van Gosse and Richard Moser (Philadelphia: Temple University Press, 2003), 52–66; Sara M. Evans, "Re-Viewing the Second Wave," *Feminist Studies* 28:2 (Summer 2002): 264.

Chapter 1. Articulating the Wrong: Resistance to Sexual Harassment in the Early 1970s

1. Nancy Cott, *Public Vows: A History of Marriage and the Nation* (Cambridge: Harvard University Press, 2000), 11–12, 160; Linda Gordon, *Heroes of Their Own Lives: The Politics and History of Family Violence* (New York: Penguin Books, 1988), 255; Jean Bethke Elshtain, *Public Man, Private Woman* (Princeton: Princeton University Press, 1981).

2. Nancy Cott, *The Bonds of Womanhood: 'Woman's Sphere' in New England, 1780–1835* (New Haven: Yale University Press, 1977), 64–67.

3. Patricia Hill Collins, *Black Feminist Thought: Knowledge, Consciousness, and the Politics of Empowerment* (New York: Routledge, Chapman, and Hall, 1991); Kimberlé Crenshaw, "Whose Story Is It Anyway? Feminist and Antiracist Appropriations of Anita Hill," in *Race-ing Justice, En-Gendering Power*, ed. Toni Morrison (New York: Pantheon Books, 1992), 411.

4. *Bradwell v. Illinois*, 83 U.S. (16 Wall) 130 (1873); *Muller v. Oregon*, 208 U.S. 412 (1908); *Goesaert v. Cleary*, 335 U.S. 464 (1948); Nadine Taub and Elizabeth M. Schneider, "Women's Subordination and the Role of Law," in *Feminist Legal Theory: Foundations*, ed. D. Kelly Weisbert (Philadelphia: Temple University Press, 1993), 9–21.

5. D'Emilio and Freedman, *Intimate Matters*.

6. Alice Kessler-Harris, *In Pursuit of Equity: Women, Men, and the Quest for Economic Citizenship in 20th-Century America* (New York: Oxford, 2001).

7. Sara M. Evans, *Born for Liberty: A History of Women in America* (New York: Free Press, 1989), 302.

8. Teresa Amott and Julie Matthaei, *Race, Gender, and Work: A Multicultural Economic History of Women in the United States* (Boston: South End Press, 1991).

9. Charles E. Marske, Steven Vago, and Arlene Taich, "Combatting Sexual Harassment: A New Awareness," *USA Today*, March 1980, p. 47.

10. Aileen C. Hernandez, "The Women's Movement: 1965–1975," p. 9 (paper presented at the Symposium on the Tenth Anniversary of the United States Equal

Employment Opportunity Commission, Rutgers University Law School, 28–29 November 1975), University of California Library, Santa Barbara, CA.

11. MacLean, *Freedom Is Not Enough*, 129; Dorothy Sue Cobble, *The Other Women's Movement: Workplace Justice and Social Rights in Modern America* (Princeton: Princeton University Press, 2004), 209–11; Drew Whitelegg, "Cabin Pressure: The Dialectics of Emotional Labour in the Airline Industry," *Journal of Transport History* 23(2002): 73–86; Flora Davis, *Moving the Mountain: The Women's Movement in America Since 1960* (Chicago: University of Illinois Press, 1999), 16–25; "Fly Me," *Time Magazine*, 15 November 1971.

12. Roth, *Separate Roads to Feminism*.

13. *Reed v. Reed*, 404 U.S. 71 (1971); *Frontiero v. Richardson*, 411 U.S. 677 (1973); *Craig v. Boren*, 429 U.S. 190 (1976).

14. Joan Hoff, *Law, Gender, and Injustice: A Legal History of U.S. Women* (New York: New York University Press, 1991), 249.

15. *Rogers v. Equal Employment Opportunity Commission*, 454 F.2d 234 (5th Cir. 1971), *cert. denied*, 406 U.S. 957 (1972).

16. Charles and Barbara Whalen, *The Longest Debate: A Legislative History of the 1964 Civil Rights Act* (Washington, D.C.: Seven Locks Press, 1985): 115–18.

17. Jeffrey Toobin, "The Trouble With Sex," *The New Yorker*, 9 February 1998, 48–55; see also Whalen, *The Longest Debate*, 69, 115–16.

18. Whalen, *The Longest Debate*, 49.

19. A bipartisan coalition of five Congresswomen spoke in support of the amendment – Frances P. Bolton (R-Ohio), Martha W. Griffiths (D-Mich.), Catherine May (R-Wash.), Edna F. Kelly (D-N.Y.), and Katherine St. George (R-N.Y.).

20. 110 Cong. Rec. 2584 (1964).

21. Doug McAdam has argued that the post World War II American government responded to the civil rights movement at least in part because the movement framed "American-style racism as a profound threat to the realization of foreign policy aims." Institutionalized racism compromised America's view of itself as the leader of the free and democratic world. Doug McAdam, *Political Process and the Development of Black Insurgency, 1930–1970*, 2nd ed. (Chicago: University of Chicago Press, 1999), xxiii–xxiv.

22. *Barnes v. Train*, 13 Fed. Empl. Prac. Cas. 123 (D.D.C. 1974), *rev'd sub nom, Barnes v. Costle*, 561 F.2d 983 (D.C. Cir. 1977); *Corne v. Bausch and Lomb*, 390 F. Supp. 161 (D. Ariz. 1975), *vacated and remanded*, 562 F.2d 55 (9th Cir. 1977), *cert. denied*, 434 U.S. 956 (1977); *Garber v. Saxon Business Products*, 14 Empl. Prac. Deci. 7586 (E.D. Va. 1976), *rev'd and remanded*, 552 F.2d 1032 (4th Cir. 1977); *Williams v. Saxbe*, 413 F. Supp. 654 (D.D.C. 1976), *rev'd in part and vacated in part*, sub nom. *Williams v. Bell*, 587 F.2d 1240 (D.C. Cir. 1978); *Miller v. Bank of America*, 418 F. Supp. 233 (N.D. Cal. 1976), *rev'd*, 600 F.2d 211 (9th Cir. 1979); *Tompkins v. Public Service Electric and Gas Company*, 422 F. Supp. 553 (D.N.J. 1976), *rev'd*, 568 F.2d 1044 (3rd Cir. 1977).

23. Affidavit of Diane Rennay Williams (Exhibit 3), Administrative Record, Joint Appendix at 36, *Williams v. Bell*, 587 F.2d 1240.

24. Brief for Appellant, *Miller v. Bank of America*, 600 F. 2d 211.

25. Complaint, Filed 29 September 1975, *Tomkins*, 422 F. Supp 533, *rev'd*, 568 F.2d 1044.

26. Anna-Marie Marshall, "Closing the Gaps: Plaintiffs in Pivotal Sexual Harassment Cases," *Law and Social Inquiry* 23 (Fall 1998): 785–86.

27. Defendant Russell E. Train's Motion for Summary Judgment, *Barnes v. Train*, 13 FEP 123 at 6–9.
28. Plaintiff's Memorandum of Points and Authorities in Opposition to Defendant's Motion for Summary Judgment, *Barnes v. Train*, 13 FEP 123 at 9-13 (quoting *Sprogis v. United Airlines, Inc.*, 444 F.2d 1194 [7th Cir. 1971]).
29. Defendants' Brief in Support of the Motion to Dismiss, *Williams v. Saxbe*, 413 F. Supp. 654 at 5–6.
30. Plaintiff's Motion for Judgment, *Williams v. Saxbe*, 413 F. Supp. 654 at 8.
31. Thomas H. Watkins, "Briefs from the Publisher's Desk: About Black Women . . ." *N.Y. Recorder*, 8 May 1976; Maudine Rice Cooper, interview with author, tape recording, Washington, D.C., 24 February 2000; Ann Schneider, "Sexual Harassment Brief Bank and Bibliography," *Women's Rights Law Reporter* 8 (Fall 1985): 294.
32. Thomas H. Watkins, "Briefs from the Publisher's Desk: About Black Women . . ." *N.Y. Recorder*, 8 May 1976.
33. Brief of the Equal Employment Opportunity Commission as Amicus Curiae in Opposition to Defendants' Motions to Dismiss, Dated 17 January 1975, *Corne v. Bausch and Lomb*, 390 F. Supp. 161.
34. Brief in Support of Motion to Dismiss the Sex Discrimination Allegations of the Plaintiff's Complaint as to Defendant, Public Service Electric and Gas Company, *Tompkins*, 422 F. Supp. 553 at 5.
35. Ibid., 6.
36. Ibid.
37. Memorandum in Opposition to Defendant Company's Motion to Dismiss Plaintiff's Title VII Claim, *Tompkins*, 422 F. Supp. 553, cited in Catharine MacKinnon, *Sexual Harassment of Working Women* (New Haven: Yale University Press, 1979), 70.
38. Right before oral arguments in the case, Taub solicited support from the EEOC. An EEOC attorney from Washington joined Taub at oral arguments. Taub also had several of her clinical students in court during oral arguments. Nadine Taub, telephone interview by author, tape recording, Newark, NJ, 21 March 2001; *Tomkins*, 422 F. Supp. at 557 (referring to EEOC's participation at oral arguments).
39. *Barnes*, 13 FEP at 124.
40. *Corne*, 390 F. Supp. at 163.
41. *Miller*, 418 F. Supp. at 235, 236.
42. *Tomkins*, 422 F. Supp. at 557.
43. Ibid., 556.
44. *Barnes*, 13 FEP at 124.
45. *Corne*, 390 F. Supp. at 163.
46. Ibid., 164.
47. *Miller*, 418 F. Supp. at 236.
48. Ibid., 557.
49. As early as August 5, 1974, Judge Richey ruled that Williams had produced evidence of discrimination and that therefore the government had the burden of affirmatively establishing the absence of discrimination by the clear weight of the evidence.
50. *Williams*, 413 F. Supp. at 655–56.
51. Ibid., 657.
52. Ibid., 660.

53. Ibid. at 659 n. 6.
54. Judge Charles R. Richey Papers: news articles, 1971 March 3–1996 May 13, Index, at 262–267, Ohio Wesleyan University Manuscript Collection #2.
55. Ibid., 268–75.
56. See, for example, Art Buchwald, "Those Are Stunning Socks You're Wearing, Callihan," *Washington Post*, 27 April 1976, § B, 1.
57. See also Ralph de Toledano, Editorial, *Naugatuck Daily News*, 18 May 1976.
58. "Sex Rears Its Mixed-Up Head," *Los Angeles Times*, 26 April 1976.
59. "The Law and Threats to Virtue," *Wall Street Journal*, 27 April 1976, 22; Judge Charles R. Richey Papers: news articles, 1971 March 3–1996 May 13, Index at 273, 275, Ohio Wesleyan University Manuscript Collection #2.
60. Dick Hitt, "One More Rule to Remember," *Dallas Times Herald*, 22 April 1976.
61. Jim Wright, "Now, Guidelines for That, Too," *Dallas Morning News*, 4 May 1976, § D, 1.
62. See, for example, *Everywoman: Sexual Harassment on the Job* (Washington, D.C.: WDVM-TV, 1976) (highlighting the case of *Williams v. Saxbe*).
63. Stanley Sporkin, "In Memoriam: Charles R. Richey," *George Washington Law Review* 66 (April 1998): 744.
64. Testimony of Dianne Williams, *Sexual Harassment in the Federal Government: Hearings before the Subcommittee on Investigations of the Committee on Post Office and Civil Service*, U.S. House of Representatives, 96th Congress, First Session, October 23, November 1, 13, 1979, 69–88 (hereafter cited as *1979 Hanley Hearings on Sexual Harassment*).
65. The judges ruling in these early sexual harassment cases were generally older conservative white males. President Richard Nixon appointed the judges who presided in *Corne, Williams, Miller,* and *Tomkins*. Judge William C. Frey, appointed in 1970, was 56 when he ruled in *Corne*. Judge Charles Richey, appointed in 1971, was 53 when he ruled in *Williams*. Judge Spencer Williams, appointed in 1971, was 54 when he ruled in *Miller*. Judge Herbert Jay Stern, appointed in 1973, was only 39 when he ruled in *Tomkins*. Judge Stern had a law and order reputation, earned for gaining convictions in political corruption cases while serving in the office of the United States Attorney in Newark. Alfonso A. Narvaez, "Judge's Years with U.S.: From Malcolm X to Berlin," *New York Times*, 9 November 1986, §1, part 2, p. 56. The judge in *Barnes*, Judge John Lewis Smith, Jr., was a Republican appointed to the federal bench in 1966 by President Lyndon B. Johnson and was 61 at the time of the decision. The judge in *Garber*, Judge Oren Ritter Lewis, was appointed to the federal bench in 1960 by President Dwight D. Eisenhower and was 74 at the time of the decision.

Chapter 2. Speaking Out: Collective Action against Sexual Harassment in the Mid-1970s

1. McAdam, *Political Process*, xxi.
2. This account comes from the following sources: Transcript of Hearing, February 18, 1975, *In re Carmita Wood*, Case No. 75-92437, New York State Department of Labor, Unemployment Insurance Referee Section, Decision and Notice of Decision, 7 March 1975, 15 (hereafter *Hearing Transcript In re Carmita Wood*); Brief for Claimant-Appellant and Affidavit of Carmita Wood, *In re Carmita Wood*, Appeal

No. 207.958, New York State Department of Labor, Unemployment Insurance Appeal Board (6 October 1975) (hereafter *Wood's Appellate Brief and Affidavit of Carmita Wood*).

3. *Hearing Transcript In re Carmita Wood.*
4. *Wood's Appellate Brief; Affidavit of Carmita Wood* at 3.
5. *Affidavit of Carmita Wood* at 15–21, 27, 30.
6. Ibid., 34; *Wood's Appellate Brief.*
7. *Hearing Transcript In re Carmita Wood.*
8. Susan Meyer, telephone interview by author, tape recording, New York, New York, 17 February 2001; Susan Brownmiller, *In Our Time: Memoir of a Revolution* (New York: Dial Press, 1999), 279–80.
9. *Rat* was a leftist newspaper that radical feminist women took over because it was sexist. Meyer, telephone interview, 17 February 2001.
10. Meyer, telephone interview, 17 February 2001; Brownmiller, *In Our Time*, 279–80; Lawrence Stessin, "Two Against Harassment," *New York Times*, 23 December 1979, § 3, 7.
11. Karen Sauvigné, telephone interview by author, tape recording, Brooklyn, New York, 4 February 2001; Brownmiller, *In Our Time*, 279–80; Lawrence Stessin, "Two Against Harassment," *New York Times*, 23 December 1979, § 3, 7. Meyer and Sauvigné were lesbian partners. Their relationship ended in 1982. Sauvigné does not believe that her sexual identity was significant to her activism on the issue of sexual harassment and that it did not play much of a role in her recognition of sexual harassment as a form of exploitation.
12. Lin Farley, *Sexual Shakedown: The Sexual Harassment of Women on the Job* (New York: McGraw-Hill Book Company, 1978), 11–12.
13. Brownmiller, *In Our Time*, 281.
14. Karen Sauvigné, telephone interview by author, tape recording, 4 February 2001, Brooklyn, NY.
15. Ibid.; Meyer, telephone interview, 17 February 2001.
16. Letter to "Mauri," Dated 28 March 1975, (from Karen Sauvigné), *Working Women's Institute Collection* (hereafter *Mauri Letter*). This account of the formation of Working Women United is based on the following sources: the archives of Working Women's Institute, located at the Barnard Center for Research on Women in New York City (hereafter *Working Women's Institute Collection*); Papers of Karen Sauvigné, Brooklyn, NY (hereafter *Karen Sauvigné 's Private Papers*); Karen Sauvigné, telephone interviews by author, tape recording, Brooklyn, NY, 4, 12 February 2001 and 25, 26 June 2001; Meyer, telephone interview, 17 February 2001; Peggy Crull, telephone interview by author, tape recording, New York, NY, 27 February 2001; Brownmiller, *In Our Time*, and media accounts as cited.
17. Susan Brownmiller quotes Sauvigné describing the meeting as follows: "Eight of us were sitting in an office of Human Affairs brainstorming about what we were going to write on posters for our speak-out. We were referring to it as 'sexual intimidation,' 'sexual coercion,' 'sexual exploitation on the job.' None of those names seemed quite right. We wanted something that embraced a whole range of subtle and unsubtle persistent behaviors. Somebody came up with 'harassment.' *Sexual harassment* ! Instantly we agreed. That's what it was." Brownmiller, *In Our Time*, 281. The earliest written use of the term "sexual harassment" in the Working Women's Institute archives appears in a March 28, 1975 letter from Karen Sauvigné to Mauri Heins, *Mauri Letter.*

18. Barbara Geehan, "Women Fight 'Intimidation,'" *Ithaca Journal*, 5 April 1975, 4; L. Scott, "Protest Sexploitation," *Ithaca New Times*, 13 April 1975; Brenda Jacobs, "Working Women Form Campaign to Expose Sexual Harassment," *Cornell Daily Sun*, 18 April 1975, 15.

19. Carmita Wood, "Opinion Editorial: Reach Out and Touch Them," *Ithaca Journal*, 24 April 1975; Publicity Letter from Carmita Wood, *Working Women's Institute Collection*.

20. L. Scott, "Protest Sexploitation," *Ithaca New Times*, 13 April 1975 (WSKG-TV, Binghamton, 15 April 1975; WCIC-TV, 22 April 1975; "The Time is Now," WNYS-TV, Syracuse).

21. "NOW President Lauds Speak-out," *Ithaca Journal*, 1 May 1975, 6.

22. Testimony of Lin Farley, Commission on Human Rights of the City of New York, Hearings on Women in Blue-Collar, Service, and Clerical Occupations, "Special Disadvantages of Women in Male-Dominated Work Settings," 21 April 1975; Barbara Geehan, "Ithacan Testifies on Job Sexual Harassment," *Ithaca Journal*, 22 April 1975, 6; "Women's Organized Labor Pains," *New York Post*, 22 April 1975; Enid Nemy, "Women Begin to Speak-out Against Sexual Harassment at Work," *New York Times*, 19 August 1975, 38.

23. Brownmiller, *In Our Time*, 282; Farley, *Sexual Shakedown* (discussing the speak-out testimony).

24. Sauvigné, telephone interview, 4 February 2001.

25. WWU later distributed the questionnaire to female food service workers who were members of the Civil Service Employee Association in Binghamton, New York.

26. Working Women's Institute, "Sexual Harassment on the Job: Results of Preliminary Survey," Research Series, Report No. 1, Fall 1975.

27. "Our First Issue" and "Why Working Women United," *Labor Pains* 1, no. 1 (August 1975): 2–3.

28. "Issue Draws National Support," *Labor Pains* 1, no. 1 (August 1975): 10.

29. Enid Nemy, "Women Begin to Speak-out Against Sexual Harassment at Work," *New York Times*, 19 August 1975, 38.

30. Susan Brownmiller and Dolores Alexander, "How We Got Here: From Carmita Wood to Anita Hill," *Ms.*, January/February 1992, 70–71.

31. "Sexual Harassment: Now a National Issue," *Labor Pains* 1, no. 2 (November 1975): 7.

32. Mary Bralove, "A Cold Shoulder, Career Women Decry Sexual Harassment by Bosses and Clients," *Wall Street Journal*, 19 January 1976, 1.

33. "A Redbook Questionnaire: How Do You Handle Sex on the Job?" *Redbook* 146 (January 1976): 74–75.

34. Rhoda Koenig, "The Persons in the Office: An Ardent Plea for Sexual Harassment," *Harper's Magazine*, February 1976, 87–88, 90.

35. Working Women United Institute Board of Director's Meeting, May 11, 1976, *Working Women's Institute Collection*. According to these minutes, Sauvigné and Meyer had moved the Institute's files out of the HAP office to their own house "because of the mistrust in HAP."

36. According to Susan Brownmiller's 1999 book, *In Our Time*, another point of contention was over who had come up with the phrase "sexual harassment." Farley contended that she had coined the term "sexual harassment," but Sauvigné and Meyer believed that "if eight people were tossing around words in one room, the eureka moment belonged to the group." Brownmiller, *In Our Time*, 285. Credit for

the term has been attributed to many people over time. A 1979 *Washington Post* article reported that Catharine MacKinnon claimed she coined the term "sexual harassment." Carol Krucoff, "Careers: Sexual Harassment on the Job," *Washington Post*, 25 July 1979, § B, 5. A 1979 *New York Times* article reported that Meyer and Sauvigné had coined the term. Lawrence Stessin, "Two Against Harassment," *New York Times*, 23 December 1979, § 3, 7. In a 1980 documentary film on sexual harassment with Lin Farley, host Ed Asner stated that Farley had coined the term. *The Workplace Hustle: A Film About Sexual Harassment of Working Women* (San Francisco: Clark Communications, Inc., 1980), videocassette.

37. In her publications, Farley repeatedly gave credit for the speak-out survey to the women's section of HAP, referring to the survey as the "Cornell poll," never mentioning Working Women United. *See, e.g.*, Lin Farley, "Sexual Harassment," *New York Sunday News*, 15 August 1976, 10.

38. Sauvigné, telephone interview, 4 February 2001.

39. Ann Crittenden, "Women Tell of Sexual Harassment at Work," *New York Times*, 25 October 1977, 35; Letter Protesting Comments of Stanley Siegel on WABC-TV, Dated 27 October 1977, *Working Women's Institute Collection*; "N.Y. Speakout: Women Describe Indignities They Face at Work," *Women's Agenda*, December 1977, 9 (published by the Women's Action Alliance); "Sex on the Job: Where We Are Now," *Redbook*, April 1978, 38; Merrill Rogers Skrocki, "Sexual Pressure on the Job," *McCall's*, March 1978, 43; Letty Cottin Pogrebin, "The Working Woman: Sex Harassment," *Ladies Home Journal* 94, June 1977, 24; Janet Harris, "Dealing With Bosses," *Family Circle*, 24 April 1978, 191; Susan Hobart, "Awareness Helps Women Overcome Sexual Indignities," *The Oregonian*, 23 January 1978, § B, 1; Dorothy Austin, "Institute Fights Sex Harassment," *Milwaukee Sentinel*, 2 June 1978, 10; Patsy Miller, "Fighting Harassment a Job," *Fort Worth Star-Telegram*, 7 June 1978; Jane See White, "Sexual Harassment: New Groups Fighting Problem," *Pueblo (Colorado) Star-Journal and Sunday Chieftain*, 20 August 1978. Meyer and Sauvigné appeared on the David Hartmann morning news show in New York. Meyer, telephone interview, 17 February 2001.

40. 1979 Annual Program Report and Audited Financial Statement, p. 1, Papers of Karen Sauvigné, Brooklyn, New York (hereafter *1979 Annual Report*); "Sexual Harassment on the Job," *Phil Donahue Show* (Princeton: Films for the Humanities and Sciences, 1988) (1977 Phil Donahue show with Susan Meyer and Karen Sauvigné); Meyer, telephone interview, 17 February 2001.

41. Letter to Karin Lippert of *Ms. Magazine* from Karen Sauvigné, Dated 17 August 1978, *Working Women's Institute Collection*.

42. Crull, telephone interview, 27 February 2001; *Responses to Fair Employment Practices Agencies to Sexual Harassment Complaints: A Report and Recommendations*, Research Series, Report No. 2 (New York: Working Women's Institute, 1978); Peggy Crull, *The Impact of Sexual Harassment on the Job: A Profile of the Experiences of 92 Women*, Research Series, Report No. 3 (New York: Working Women's Institute, 1979).

43. Sauvigné, telephone interview, 4 February 2001.

44. The first office of AASC was at 575 Massachusetts Avenue in Cambridge. They later moved to 120 Boylston Street in Boston, on the Boston Commons. This account about the formation of Alliance Against Sexual Coercion is based on the following sources: Freada Klein, interview by author, tape recording, 26 March 2001, 1, 13 April 2001 (San Francisco, CA), 25 June 2001 (New York City); Alliance Against

Sexual Coercion Ephemeral Materials, 1976–77, Wilcox Collection of Contemporary Political Movements, Schlesinger Library, Radcliffe College, Cambridge (hereafter *AASC Materials at Schlesinger*); Lynn Wehrli, "Sexual Harassment at the Workplace: A Feminist Analysis and Strategy for Social Change," (Master's Thesis, Massachusetts Institute of Technology, 1976) (hereafter *Wehrli Master's Thesis*); "Working Women Unite!" *FAAR News*, September/October 1976, 7; Freada Klein and Lynn Wehrli, "Sexual Coercion on the Job?" *Sister Courage*, October 1976, 6; "Interview with the Alliance Against Sexual Coercion," *Sister Courage*, June 1977; "Dear Sir: That's Not Part of My Job," *FAAR News*, May/June 1977, 13; Jane Albert, "Tyranny of Sex In the Office," *Equal Times*, 7 August 1977, 7; Alliance Against Sexual Coercion, *Sexual Harassment at the Workplace* (Cambridge: Alliance Against Sexual Coercion, 1977); Rochelle Lefkowitz, "Help for the Sexually Harassed: A Grass-Roots Model," *Ms.*, November 1977, 49; "All About the Alliance Against Sexual Coercion," *Aegis*, July/August 1978, 27–28; "Sexual Harassment and Coercion: Violence Against Women," *Aegis*, July/August 1978, 28–29; Martha Hooven and Freada Klein, "Is Sexual Harassment Legal?" *Aegis*, September/October 1978, 27–30; Martha Hooven and Nancy McDonald, "The Role of Capitalism: Understanding Sexual Harassment," *Aegis*, November/December 1978, 31–33; Freada Klein, "Book Review, *Sexual Shakedown: The Sexual Harassment of Women on the Job* by Lin Farley," *Aegis*, November/December 1978, 33–35; Constance Backhouse and Leah Cohen, *The Secret Oppression: Sexual Harassment of Working Women* (Toronto: Macmillan, 1978); Alliance Against Sexual Coercion, *University Grievance Procedures, Title IX and Sexual Harassment on Campus* (Cambridge: Alliance Against Sexual Coercion, 1980); Laurie Dubrow, *Sexual Harassment and the Law* (Cambridge: Alliance Against Sexual Coercion, 1980); Alliance Against Sexual Coercion, *Fighting Sexual Harassment: An Advocacy Handbook* (Boston: Alyson Publications, Inc. and Alliance Against Sexual Coercion, 1981); Alliance Against Sexual Coercion, "Organizing Against Sexual Harassment," *Radical America* 15 (July/August 1981): 17–34.

45. According to Klein, the protocol of rape crisis centers was advocacy with the police, the hospital, the district attorney, and the court, none of which was relevant in the employment context.

46. Freada Klein and Lynn Wehrli, "Sexual Coercion on the Job?" *Sister Courage*, October 1976, 6.

47. *Wehrli Master's Thesis* at 55–79; Catharine MacKinnon cited Wehrli's thesis in her 1979 book, *Sexual Harassment of Working Women*, in which MacKinnon develops a dominance theory of sexual harassment. MacKinnon, *Sexual Harassment of Working Women*, 48, 281 n. 39, 264 n. 152.

48. AASC chose to make contact with women workers independently through a telephone hotline rather than by working through unions or other workplace organizations because only eleven percent of women workers were unionized at the time and unions were not initially interested in addressing sexual harassment. Alliance Against Sexual Coercion, "Organizing Against Sexual Harassment," 26, 29.

49. Karen Lindsey, "Sexual Harassment on the Job," *Ms.*, November 1977, 78.

50. Rochelle Lefkowitz, "Help for the Sexually Harassed: A Grass-Roots Model," *Ms.*, November 1977, 49. Freada Klein and some other AASC members attended the October 1977 speak-out in New York City. Klein, telephone interview, 26 March 2001.

51. Portions of this brochure and later publications by AASC were often reproduced in corporate training manuals and other sexual harassment publications. Klein, telephone interview, 13 April 2001.
52. Alliance Against Sexual Coercion, *Sexual Harassment at the Workplace*, 4–5.
53. Ibid., 11.
54. Bularzik, "Sexual Harassment at the Workplace," 25; Mary Bularzik, "An Historical Analysis of Sexual Harassment in the U.S.," *Aegis*, January/February 1979, 26–30. Freada Klein participated in monthly meetings of leaders and founders of groups opposing violence against women. Klein, telephone interview, 13 April 2001.
55. Alliance Against Sexual Coercion, *Sexual Harassment at the Workplace*, 2.
56. Freada Klein, "Book Review, *Sexual Shakedown: The Sexual Harassment of Women on the Job* by Lin Farley," *Aegis*, November/December 1978, 33.
57. Martha Hooven and Nancy McDonald, "The Role of Capitalism: Understanding Sexual Harassment," *Aegis*, November/December 1978, 31–33.
58. Martha Hooven and Freada Klein, "Is Sexual Harassment Legal?" *Aegis*, September/October 1978, 28.
59. Ibid.
60. Ibid.
61. Ibid.
62. Karen Lindsey, "A National Resource," *Ms.*, November 1977, 49; Rochelle Lefkowitz, "Help for the Sexually Harassed: A Grass-Roots Model," *Ms.*, November 1977, 49; Sauvigné, telephone interview, 4 February 2001.
63. Minutes of Meeting with AASC and WWUI, 1 April 1978, *Working Women's Institute Collection*; Letter from Karen to AASC Sisters, Dated 13 April 1978, *Working Women's Institute Collection*.
64. There was an ownership dispute over the film between Margaret Lazarus and AASC. Klein, telephone interview, 4 April 2001.
65. Nadine Brozen, "A Demand To Be More Than Just 'Office Girls,'" *New York Times*, 17 October 1975, 45; "Office Workers to Hold Hearings," *Majority Report*, V, no. 11 (4–18 October 1975): 10; "WOW Speaks," *Majority Report*, 5, no. 13 (1–15 Nov. 1975): 5; "One Third of Office Workers Report Sexual Harassment on the Job," *Womanpower Newsletter*, vol. 6, no. 2, February 1976, 1–2; Paula Bernstein, "Sexual Harassment on the Job," *Harper's Bazaar*, August 1976, 12.
66. Mimi Kelber, "Sexual Harassment . . . The UN's Dirty Little Secret," *Ms.*, November 1977, 51; *see also*, "Handling Sex in the Office," *Personal Report for the Professional Secretary*, 28 October 1976, 1–4 (published by the Research Institute of America, New York, NY, reporting on letters received in response to questions about sexual harassment posed to readers).
67. The naming of sexual harassment illustrates discourse theory's claim that "discourses operate at the level of meaning, shaping what is thinkable, possible, comprehensible." Whittier, "Meaning and Structure in Social Movements," 303.

Chapter 3. A Winning Strategy: Early Legal Victories against Sexual Harassment

1. After the district court had dismissed Barnes' case, her attorney, Warwick Furr, asked the Lawyers' Committee for Civil Rights Under Law to find another lawyer to handle the appeal. LCCRUL found Linda Singer through the WLDF. Marshall, "Closing the Gaps," 786 (based on interviews with Linda Singer and Warwick Furr).

2. Marshall, "Closing the Gaps," 786; Heather Sigworth, "Abortion Laws in the Federal Courts: The Supreme Court as Supreme Platonic Guardian," *Indiana Law Review* 5 (1971): 130; Heather Sigworth, "The Legal Status of Antinepotism Regulations," *AAUP Bulletin* (Spring 1972): 31–34; *Laks v. Laks,* 540 P.2d 1277 (Ariz. Ct. App. 1975). Before *Corne* was decided, Sigworth was appointed Deputy Attorney General for the State of Arizona, so Mary-Lynne Fisher from the Center for Law in the Public Interest in Los Angeles took over the case. Notice of Appearance, Filed June 27, 1977, *Corne v. Bausch and Lomb, Inc.,* 562 F.2d 55.

3. Notes from Conversation with Heather Sigworth, Dated 28 April 1975, *Working Women's Institute Collection;* Taub, telephone interview, 21 March 2001; Marshall, "Closing the Gaps," 786 (based on interviews with Simon, Taub, Dunlap, and Singer); Klein, telephone interview, 13 April 2001; Reply Brief of Appellant at 16, *Miller v. Bank of America,* 600 F.2d 211 (filed 9 March 1977); Plaintiff-Appellant's Appeal Brief at 16, *Tomkins v. Public Service Electric and Gas Co.,* 568 F.2d 1044; Brief on Behalf of Plaintiffs-Appellants at 19–21, 27, *Alexander v. Yale,* 631 F.2d 178 (2nd Cir. 1980).

4. Brief for Appellant at 13, *Barnes v. Costle,* 561 F.2d 983.

5. Appellants' Reply Brief at 7–8, *Corne,* 562 F.2d 55.

6. Plaintiff-Appellant's Appeal Brief at 16, *Tomkins,* 568 F.2d 1044.

7. Plaintiff-Appellant's Appeal Brief at 14–18, *Tomkins,* 568 F.2d 1044.

8. Brownmiller, *In Our Time,* 286.

9. Plaintiff-Appellant's Appeal Brief at 20–21, *Tomkins* 568 F.2d 1044 (citations omitted).

10. Plaintiff-Appellant's Appeal Brief at 22, *Tomkins,* 568 F.2d 1044.

11. Ibid., 23.

12. Brief of Equal Rights Advocates, Inc. and Mexican-American Legal Defense and Education Fund, as Amici Curiae at 18–21, *Tomkins,* 568 F.2d 1044.

13. Ibid.

14. In *Garber,* all three judges were appointed by Johnson. In *Barnes,* Judge Spottswood was appointed by Johnson, Judge Bazelon by Truman, and Judge MacKinnon by Nixon. In *Tomkins,* Judge Aldisert was appointed by Johnson and Judges Rosenn and Garth were appointed by Nixon. In *Miller,* Judge Duniway was appointed by Kennedy, Judge Kilkenny was appointed by Eisenhower, and Judge McGovern was appointed by Nixon.

15. In a 1990 *New Yorker Magazine* interview, MacKinnon reported that she gave a copy of a paper she had written for an independent study course at Yale to a law clerk assigned to the *Barnes* case. According to MacKinnon, this paper became the basis for MacKinnon's 1979 book, *The Sexual Harassment of Working Women.* Jeffrey Toobin, "The Trouble With Sex," *New Yorker,* 9 February 1998, 50. No amicus curiae briefs were recorded on the docket in the *Barnes* case.

16. *Barnes v. Costle,* 561 F.2d 983, 990.

17. According to *Shepard's Federal Citations, Barnes v. Costle* has been cited, discussed, or mentioned in over 450 cases, articles, and books.

18. "Sex and Judicial Progress," *National Review,* 3 March 1978, 299.

19. Farley, *Sexual Shakedown,* 176–77; Shelby White, "The Office Pass (Continued)," *Across the Board,* March 1978, 51.

20. Taub, telephone interview, 21 March 2001; Adrienne Tomkins, "Sex Discrimination: Adrienne Tomkins, Stenographer," *Civil Liberties Review* (September/October 1978): 22. According to *Shepherd's Federal Citations, Tomkins* has been discussed,

cited, or mentioned in over eighty cases and in hundreds of secondary sources. *See,* for example, Marie Nardino, "Note: Discrimination: Sex—Title VII—Cause of Action Under Title VII Arises When Supervisor, With Employer's Knowledge and Acquiescence, Makes Sexual Advances Toward Subordinate Employee and Conditions Employee's Job Status on Favorable Response—*Tomkins v. Public Service Electric and Gas Co.,* 568 F.2d 1044 (3d Cir. 1977)," *Seton Hall Law Review* 9 (1978); Diane K. Shah, "A Steno Who Said 'No!'" *Newsweek,* 30 April 1979, 72.

21. Civil Docket, *Williams v. Civiletti,* Case No. 74-186, United States District Court for the District of Columbia, at supp. 14–15; Cooper, personal interview, 24 February 2000.

22. *Munford v. James T. Barnes and Co.,* 441 F. Supp. 459, 466 (E.D. Mich. 1977).

23. Munford's trial was the first jury trial in a sexual harassment case in federal court. The jury ruled against Munford on the state law claims and sat as an advisory jury on Munford's Title VII claim, finding five-to-one against her. The judge concluded that Munford had not proved that she was sexually harassed. *Munford,* 441 F. Supp. 459.

24. Gedaliahu H. Harel and Karen Cottledge, "Combatting Sexual Harassment: The Michigan Experience," *Human Resource Management* 21 (Spring 1982): 2.

25. *Ludington v. Sambo's Restaurants, Inc.,* 474 F. Supp. 480, 483 (E.D. Wisc. 1979).

26. *Neely v. American Fidelity Assurance Company,* 17 Fair Employment Prac. Cas. 482 (W.D. Okla 1978).

27. 19 Fair Empl. Prac. Cas. (BNA) 828 (D.D.C. 1979). *See also Cordes v. County of Yavapai,* 17 Fed. Empl. Prac. Cas. 1224 (D. Ariz. 1978) and *Shanks v. Harrington,* 21 Fed. Empl. Prac. Cas. 590 (N.D. Iowa 1979) (both denying relief).

28. EEOC Decision No. 77-36, 1974–83 CCH EEOC DECISIONS 6588 at 4456 (1977).

29. *Alexander v. Yale,* 459 F. Supp. 1 (D. Conn. 1977).

30. Letter from Phyllis Crocker, Dated March 1978, in *Alexander v. Yale: Collected Documents from the Yale Undergraduate Women's Caucus and Grievance Committee* (New Haven: Yale University, 1978) (ERIC No.: ED180385): 18–19 (hereafter *Alexander v. Yale: Collected Documents*); Billie Wright Dziech and Linda Weiner, *The Lecherous Professor: Sexual Harassment on Campus* (Boston: Beacon Press, 1984), 163 (noting that the case "startled campus communities across the country into realizing that they needed to deal with the sexual harassment issue").

31. *Alexander v. Yale: Collected Documents,* 27; Anne Simon, telephone interview by author, tape recording, 25 April 2001, Oakland, CA.

32. *Alexander v. Yale: Collected Documents,* 1–27; Simon, telephone interview, 25 April 2001.

33. *Alexander v. Yale,* 459 F. Supp. 1. Magistrate Latimer later denied Price's motion for class certification because her claim would not likely become moot and any equitable relief would benefit others. The Second Circuit subsequently denied the plaintiffs' appeal based in part on mootness.

34. Memorandum of Decision, Civil. No. N-77-277, 2 July 1979 (Judge Ellen Bree Burns).

35. Two amicus curiae briefs were filed by the American Civil Liberties Union, the Women's Equity Action League Educational and Legal Defense Fund, Working Women's Institute, the National Conference of Black Lawyers, Black Women Organized for Political Action, Equal Rights Advocates, Inc. and Women Organized Against Sexual Harassment, a student group at the University of California at Berkeley.

36. *Alexander v. Yale,* 631 F.2d 178.

37. *See*, for example, "2 Yale Faculty Accused of Sex Harassment," *Washington Post*, 19 July 1977, § A, 5; Diane Henry, "Yale Faculty Members Charged With Sexual Harassment," *New York Times*, 22 August 1977, 30; Diane Henry, "Yale Student Withdraws from Lawsuit," *New York Times*, 10 September 1977, 52; "Yale and Woman Senior Reach an Accord on Suit," *New York Times*, 15 January 1978, 40; "Ex-Student Wins Right to Sue Yale on Sex Charge," *New York Times*, 1 December 1978, § C, 26; "A College Woman Loses Test on Sexual Harassment," *New York Times*, 12 July 1979, § B, 6.

38. Russell Baker, "The Courts of First Resort," *New York Times*, 26 July 1977, § A, 29.

39. Diane Henry, "Yale Faculty Members Charged With Sexual Harassment," *New York Times*, 22 August 1977, 30.

40. "Bod and Man at Yale," *Time*, 8 August 1977, 52–53. Jose Cabranes was later appointed to the United States District Court for the District of Connecticut by President Jimmy Carter and to the U.S. Court of Appeals for the Second Circuit by President William Clinton.

41. Anne Nelson, "Sexual Harassment at Yale," *Nation*, 14 January 1978, 7–10.

42. Alice Dembner, "A Case of Sex Discrimination," *Yale Graduate Professional*, 8 March 1978, 1.

43. *See*, for example, "Sexual Harassment in Education," *National NOW Times*, February 1978, 14–15; Marcia Rockwood, "The Yale Suit: On To Round Two," *Ms.*, July 1978, 85; "Sexual Harassment Challenged," *Off Our Backs*, December 1979, 8; "Court to Hear Argument In Sexual Harassment Appeal," *National NOW Times*, June 1980, 14.

44. Simon, telephone interview, 25 April 2001.

45. Press Release Issued by the Yale Undergraduate Women's Caucus Grievance Committee, Not Dated, *Alexander v. Yale: Collected Documents*, 13–14.

46. Statement Issued by Pamela Price, December 21, 1977, *Alexander v. Yale: Collected Documents*, 16–17.

47. Ronni Alexander, Pamela Price, and Linda Hoaglund, "*Alexander v. Yale*," *Alexander v. Yale: Collected Documents*, 4.

48. *Alexander v. Yale: Collected Documents*, 21–22.

49. Letter from Phyllis L. Crocker for the Grievance Committee of the Yale Undergraduate Women's Caucus, March 1978, *Alexander v. Yale: Collected Documents*, 18.

50. Simon, telephone interview, 25 April 2001.

51. *Franklin v. Gwinnett County Public Schools*, 523 U.S. 60 (1992).

52. *See*, for example, *WOASH v. University of California, Berkeley*, Office of Civil Rights Case No. 09-79-2048 (San Francisco Region, Department of Education, 1980); Elizabeth Markson, "Sexual Harassment: Self-Reports by Women Members of the Eastern Sociological Society," *New England Sociologist* 1 (Fall 1978): 45–57; Kenneth S. Pope, Hanna Levenson, and Leslie R. Schover, "Sexual Intimacy in Psychology Training: Results and Implications of a National Survey," *American Psychologist* 34 (August 1979): 682–89; Jo Ann Livingston, "Sexual Harassment of Working Women," Master's Thesis, University of Vermont, 1979.

53. Senate Report No. 91-1137, 91st Congress, 2nd Session 15 (1970); Farley, *Sexual Shakedown*, 75–76, citing to Susan C. Ross, *The Rights of Women, An American Civil Liberties Handbook* (New York: Avon Books, 1973), 33–38.

54. Whittier, "Meaning and Structure in Social Movements," 310.

55. Ibid., 303.

Chapter 4. Blue-Collar Workers and Hostile Environment Sexual Harassment

1. Molly Martin, ed., *Hard-Hatted Women: Life on the Job* (Seattle: Seal Press, 1997), 195.
2. Clara Bingham and Laura Leedy Gansler, *Class Action: The Story of Lois Jenson and the Landmark Case that Changed Sexual Harassment Law* (New York: Doubleday, 2002), chapter 3.
3. Martin, *Hard-Hatted Women*, 33–34, 51, 257; *see also* Jean Reith Schroedel, *Alone in the Crowd: Women in the Trades Tell Their Studies* (Philadelphia, PA: Temple University Press, 1986); Susan Eisenberg, *We'll Call You If We Need You: Experiences of Women Working Construction* (Ithaca, NY: Cornell University Press, 1999).
4. Construction Contractors, Affirmative Action Requirements, 42 *Federal Register* 41381 (1977) (codified at 41 C.F.R. Ch. 60) (proposed on 16 August 1977).
5. This account is based on the following resources: Joan Graff, telephone interview by author, tape recording, San Francisco, CA, 14 February 2001; Trudy Levy, telephone interview by author, tape recording, Washington, D.C., 14 February 2001; Katherine Mazzaferri, telephone interview by author, tape recording, Bethesda, MD, 10 February 2001; Trudy Levy Papers, Falls Church, VA (private collection); Katherine Mazzaferri Papers, Bethesda, MD (private collection); Georgia Dullea, "Women Win Fight for More Construction Jobs, Less Harassment," *Washington Post*, 23 August 1977, 30.
6. Katherine Mazzaferri, telephone interview by author, tape recording, Bethesda, MD, 10 February 2001.
7. *Advocates for Women et al. v. Usery et al.*, Civil Action No. 76-0862, U.S. District Court for the District of Columbia (filed 14 May 1976) (later known as *Advocates for Women v. Marshall*).
8. *Women Working in Construction et al. v. Usery et al.*, Civil Action No. 76–527, U.S. District Court for the District of Columbia (filed 13 April 1976) (later *Women Working in Construction v. Marshall*).
9. Plaintiffs' Memorandum of Points and Authorities in Opposition to Defendants' Motion for Summary Judgment, 25–27, *Advocates for Women v. Marshall*, (with attached affidavits).
10. These organizations included Skilled Jobs for Women in Madison, WI, the Tucson Women's Commission, the Chicana Service Action Center in Los Angeles, Women in Apprenticeship Program in San Francisco, and the Chicana Rights Project of the Mexican American Legal Defense and Education Fund in San Antonio, TX.
11. Women in Construction, 43 *Federal Register* 14891 (1978) (DOL's summary of comments submitted by women's groups on the proposed guidelines).
12. Women in Construction, 43 *Federal Register* 14888 (7 April 1978), codified at 41 C.F.R. § 60-4 (1978); Equal Opportunity in Apprenticeship, 43 *Federal Register* 20760 (12 May 1978), codified at 29 C.F.R. § 30 (1978).
13. 41 C.F.R. § 60-4.3 (7a) (1978) (effective 8 May 1978).
14. Raymond M. Lane, "A Man's World: An Update on Sexual Harassment," *Village Voice*, 16–22 December 1981, 22; Order, *Advocates for Women v. Marshall*, and *Women Working in Construction v. Marshall* (5 December 1978).
15. Wider Opportunities for Women, *A Territorial Issue: A Study of Women in the Construction Trades* (Washington, D.C.: Wider Opportunities for Women and the Center for National Policy Review, 1982), 16. The Carter Administration

debarred eighteen contractors from future business with the federal government for noncompliance, while all other administrations had debarred only twelve companies. Peter Behr and Joanne Omang, "Impact of Regulation Freeze is Unclear; Targets Not Yet Identified," *New York Times*, 30 January 1981, § A, 4.

16. WOW, *A Territorial Issue*, 74.

17. Graff, telephone interview, 14 February 2001.

18. 44 *Federal Register* 77006 (29 December 1979).

19. Department of Labor, Office of Federal Contract Compliance Programs, Final Rule, 45 *Federal Register* 86216 (30 December 1980).

20. Department of Labor, Office of Federal Contract Compliance Programs, Final Rule, 46 *Federal Register* 42968 (1981); Peter Behr and Joanne Omang, "Impact of Regulation Freeze is Unclear; Targets Not Yet Identified," *New York Times*, 30 January 1981, § A, 4.

21. This account is based on documents in the Coal Employment Project Records. Archives of Appalachia, Sherrod Library, East Tennessee State University, Johnson City, TN. (hereafter *Coal Employment Project Collection*).

22. Maggie Prieto, "Women Coal Miners Fight Sexual Harassment," *Off Our Backs*, August/September 1983, 2.

23. "Women Coal Miners Fight Sexual Harassment," *Off Our Backs*, August/September 1983, 3. The conference was in Beckley, WV.

24. Ibid.; Sexual Harassment in the Mines Workshop, Second National Conference of Women Coal Miners, Beckley, West Virginia, May 1980 (videocassette), *Coal Employment Project Collection* (Accession 355, Tape 59).

25. The ten states were Alabama, Illinois, Indiana, Kentucky, Ohio, Pennsylvania, Tennessee, Virginia, West Virginia, and Wyoming.

26. Connie White, Barbara Angle, and Marat Moore, *Sexual Harassment in the Coal Industry: A Survey of Women Miners* (Oak Ridge, TN: Coal Employment Project, 1981).

27. Marat Moore and Connie White, *Sexual Harassment in the Mines—Legal Rights, Legal Remedies* (Oak Ridge, TN: Coal Employment Project, 1981); Coal Employment Project, *Sexual Harassment in the Mines—Bringing the Issue to Light* (Oak Ridge, TN: Coal Employment Project, 1981).

28. "Combat Sexual Harassment on the Job," *Aegis*, May/June 1979, 24.

29. Marcia L. Greenbaum and Bruce Fraser, "Sexual Harassment in the Workplace," *Arbitration Journal*, 36, no. 4 (December 1981): 30–41.

30. Elaine Weeks, et al., "The Transformation of Sexual Harassment from a Private Trouble into a Public Issue," *Sociological Inquiry* 56 (1986): 437 n.2; American Federation of State, County and Municipal Employees, *On the Job Sexual Harassment: What the Union Can Do* (Washington, D.C.: American Federation of State, County and Municipal Employees, 1981), 25–26; *see also* In the Matter of: Department of Personnel and Department of Administrative Services, Charging Parties, and American Federation of State, County and Municipal Employees, Council 31, Respondent, Case No. ULP-129-OCB, State of Illinois, Office of Collective Bargaining, 28 March 1980 (discussing distribution of pamphlet on sexual harassment by AFSCM member).

31. Alliance Against Sexual Coercion, "Organizing Against Sexual Harassment," 28–29.

32. *See*, for example, "Combat Sexual Harassment on the Job," *Hammer House: Voice of the International Association of Machinists Rank and File—Local 774*,

November/December 1978 (Cessna Aircraft Plant, Wichita, Kansas); Sarah Slaughter, "Sexual Favors to Foreman: It's Not My Job!" *Local 1010 Steelworker*, February 1980; Karl Mantyla, "The Hazards of Sexual Harassment," *Solidarity*, March 1981, 12 (UAW newsletter); Marcia Hams, "Electrical Workers Wildcat Over Sexual Assault on Union Member," *Labor Notes*, 25 June 1981, 7; Elissa Clarke, et al., *Stopping Sexual Harassment: A Handbook* (Detroit: Labor and Education Research Project, 1980), 26 (discussing using union newspapers to combat sexual harassment); "Sexual Harassment on the Job: How to Fight Back Within the Law," *Women in the Trades News*, Winter 1983, 4.

33. Statement of William C. Marshall, Michigan State AFL-CIO, 25 April 1979, *Coal Employment ProjectCollection* (Accession 355, Box 73, Folder 19); Alliance Against Sexual Coercion, "Organizing Against Sexual Harassment," 28; Clarke, et al., *Stopping Sexual Harassment*, 24–25; UAW-Chrysler, *Agreement Between Chrysler Corporation and the UAW*, 1979; Douglas A. Fraser, President, International Union, UAW, "Policy on the Elimination of Sexual Harassment at the Workplace," *UAW Administrative Letter*, 15 January 1981, 1; Karl Mantyla, "The Hazards of Sexual Harassment," *Solidarity*, February 1981, 12; Michele Noah, "Sexual Harassment on the Job," *Sister Courage*, May 1978, 9.

34. Clarke, et al., *Stopping Sexual Harassment*.

35. Alliance Against Sexual Coercion, "Organizing Against Sexual Harassment," 28; Clarke, et al., *Stopping Sexual Harassment*, 25.

36. Alliance Against Sexual Coercion, *Fighting Sexual Harassment*, 80, 84; Clarke, et al., *Stopping Sexual Harassment*, 22–24; Peggy Crull, "Sexual Harassment and Women's Health," in *Double Exposure: Women's Health Hazards on the Job and in the Home*, ed. Wendy Chavkin (New York: Monthly Review Press, 1984), 114–15.

37. EEOC Decision No. 70-401, Case No. YAT9-211, 1968-73 CCH EEOC DECISIONS ¶6100 (1970); EEOC Decision No. 71-2725, 1968-73 CCH EEOC DECISIONS ¶6290 (1971); EEOC Decision No. 72-0679, 4 Fair. Empl. Prac. Cases (BNA) 441, 442 (1971); EEOC Decision No. 76-72, 1974-83 CCH EEOC DECISIONS ¶6652 (1975).

38. *Macey v. World Airways*, 14 Fair Empl. Prac. Cas. (BNA) 1426 (N.D. Cal. 1977).

39. Judith Vladeck of Elias, Vladeck, and Lewis in New York City represented the plaintiff. *Kyriazi v. Western Electric Company*, 461 F. Supp. 894 (D.N.J. 1978). *Ms.* magazine reported on this case. Eric Matusewitch, "*Kyriazi v. Western Electric*: Court Fines Five Bosses for Sexual Harassment," *Ms.*, April 1980, 27.

40. *Continental Can Company v. Minnesota*, 297 N.W.2d 241, 246 (Minn. 1980).

41. Brief of Amici Curiae of the National Organization for Women and Working Women's Institute at 16 n. 6, *Continental Can Co.*, 297 N.W.2d 241.

42. *Pantchenko v. C. B. Dolge Co.*, 18 Fair Empl. Prac. Cas. 686 (D. Conn. 1977), *aff'd in relevant part*, 594 F.2d 852 (2d Cir. 1978).

43. *Smith v. Rust Engineering Co.*, 20 Fair Empl. Prac. Cas. 1172 (N.D. Ala. 1978).

44. Marshall, "Closing the Gaps," 781.

45. *Bundy v. Jackson*, 19 FEP 828 at 12.

46. Ibid.

47. Susan M. Hartmann, *The Other Feminists: Activists in the Liberal Establishment* (New Haven: Yale University Press, 2000): 46–52.

Chapter 5. Expansion of the Movement against Sexual Harassment in the Late 1970s

1. The account of Working Women's Institute is based on the following sources: *Working Women's Institute Collection*; *Karen Sauvigné's Private Papers*; Sauvigné, telephone interviews, 4, 12 February 2001 and 25, 26 June 2001; Meyer, telephone interview, 17 February 2001; Crull, telephone interview, 27 February 2001; K. C. Wagner, interview with author, tape recording, New York, NY, 28 February 2000, 25 June 2001; Brownmiller, *In Our Time*; Working Women's Institute reports and publications most of which are contained in the Barnard collection; and contemporaneous media accounts.

2. Some of the organizations that received training were Jobs for Youth, National Council of Negro Women, United Tradeswomen, Displaced Homemakers Program, the National Congress of Neighborhood Women, Hunter College School of Social Work, the New York City Commission on Human Rights, and the Long Island Center for Women's Rights. "Sexual Harassment Lands Companies in Court," *Business Week*, 1 October 1979, 120; Nancy Josephson, "Sexual Harassment on the Job: Why More and More Women Are Fighting Back," *Glamour*, May 1980, 288–89, 338–41.

3. Working Women's Institute staff members conducted educational programs for Princeton University, New York University, California Polytechnic University, the American Federation of Government Employees, the Business and Professional Women's Association, Office Workers of New Haven, Hoffman-LaRouch, Bell Labs, the Professional Secretaries International Convention, Ramsey County Affirmative Action Council in St. Paul, MN, Loyola University Law School, Chrysalis, A Center for Women in Minneapolis, MN, and the National Association of Accountants.

4. Karen Sauvigné spoke on sexual harassment at the Women and Law Conference almost every year from about 1976 to 1985. At the start and the end of her presentations, Sauvigné would ask the audience how many had ever experienced sexual harassment and invariably more people would raise their hands at the end of her presentation once they had reflected on the range of harassing behavior. Susan Meyer appeared on the *Phil Donahue Show* in 1977 and 1979 and on *National Public Radio* in 1981. Katherine Davis, *Beware of the Boss: Sexual Harassment on the Job* (New York: National Public Radio, 1981), audiocassette.

5. Peggy Crull, "Responses to Fair Employment Practices Agencies to Sexual Harassment Complaints: A Report and Recommendations," Research Series, Report No. 2 (New York: Working Women's Institute, 1978); Crull, *The Impact of Sexual Harassment on the Job*; WWI, *Sexual Harassment on the Job and in Education: A Comprehensive Bibliography* (New York: Working Women's Institute, Fall 1979); and the following articles from the *Working Women's Institute Collection*: "Research Clearinghouse" (New York: Working Women's Institute, 1981); "General Resource Materials" (New York: Working Women's Institute, 1982); "Sexual Harassment Resource Materials" (New York: Working Women's Institute, n.d.); "Sexual Harassment on the Job and in Education: Resource Materials: Addendum" (New York: Working Women's Institute, n.d.). Two of the pamphlets were produced in Spanish.

6. "Sex Harassment Legal Back-Up Center Opens," *Spokeswoman*, April 1980, 13. Vermeulen had graduated from Rutgers Law School in 1975, where she had been a student of Nadine Taub's. Vermeulen brought in several law students as legal interns to assist in the legal work of the Institute. After leaving Working Women's

Institute, she became the Acting Director of Rutgers Women's Rights Litigation Clinic in 1981.

7. Letter from Joan Vermeulen to "Dear Friends," Dated 1 March 1980 (on new National Sexual Harassment Legal Back-Up Center), NOW Collection, Schlesinger Library, Radcliffe Institute, Harvard University, Cambridge, MA (hereafter *NOW Collection*). The panel members included Mauri Heins (Carmita Wood's attorney), Jill Laurie Goodman, Jan Leventer (Maxine Munford's attorney), Catharine MacKinnon, Linda Singer (Paulette Barnes' attorney), Nadine Taub, and Stuart Wein (Margaret Miller's attorney). Program Opening Celebration for the National Sexual Harassment Legal Backup Center, 21 February 1980, *Karen Sauvigné, Private Papers*.

8. Sauvigné, telephone interview, 12 February 2001.

9. This account about the formation of Alliance Against Sexual Coercion is based on the following sources: Klein, telephone interviews, 26 March 2001, 1, 13 April 2001, 25 June 2001; Lynn Rubinett, telephone interview by author, tape recording, 23 June 2001, Austin, TX; *AASC Materials at Schlesinger*; Constance Backhouse, et al., *Fighting Sexual Harassment: An Advocacy Handbook* (Cambridge: Alyson Publications, Inc. and Alliance Against Sexual Coercion, 1981); Alliance Against Sexual Coercion, *Fighting Sexual Harassment: An Advocacy Handbook* (Cambridge: Alliance Against Sexual Coercion, 1979) (this earlier edition was written and coordinated by Connie Backhouse, Rags Brophy, Alice Friedman, Beth Johnson, Freada Klein, Margaret Lazarus, Anne Lopes, Martha Hooven, Denise Wells, and Kate Swann), and contemporaneous media accounts.

10. AASC did not pursue grants because they wanted to shape their programs independent of control by grantors.

11. In 1979, AASC responded to about ten calls a week, which was double the number they had received the year before. "Sexual Harassment Lands Companies in Court," *Business Week*, 1 October 1979, 120.

12. "Sexual Harassment Lands Companies in Court," *Business Week*, 1 October 1979, 120 (appearing in the social issues section); "How to Tame the Office Wolf – Without Getting Bitten," *Business Week*, 1 October 1979, 107–8 (in the personal business section).

13. AASC also organized a women's picket against sexual harassment at the Actor's Workshop in Kenmore Square. "Actor's Workshop Accused of Sexual Harassment," *Equal Time*, 10 June 1979.

14. Statement of Donna Lenhoff, *1979 Hanley Hearings on Sexual Harassment*, 3–9; *Hearings on Pressures in Today's Workplace*, 152–169; Arkie Byrd and Donna Lenhoff, *Testimony of the Women's Legal Defense Fund Before the D.C. Commission for Women: Public Hearing on Sexual Harassment*, Washington, D.C., 31 January 1981 (describing the law of sexual harassment); Donna Lenhoff, "Sexual Harassment: No More Business as Usual," *Trial* 17 (July 1981): 42; Women's Legal Defense Fund, *Legal Remedies for Sexual Harassment* (Washington, D.C.: Women's Legal Defense Fund, 1983).

15. "Sexual Harassment Project," *Equal Rights Advocate* (March 1981): 2.

16. Women's groups that provided referrals were 9-to-5 in Boston, Cambridge Women's Center and Vocations for Social Change in Cambridge, MA, and Cleveland Women Working. Examples of organizations publishing guides were the Women in the Work Force Committee of the American Friends Service Committee, the Federation of Organizations for Professional Women, and the Women's Labor Project in San Francisco.

17. *Sexual Harassment on the Job: A Fact Sheet* (Arlington, VA: New Responses, Inc., 1978); Mary Ann Largen, *Report on Sexual Harassment in Federal Employment, November 1978-July 1979* (Arlington, VA: New Responses, Inc., 1979); 2; Mary Ann Largen, *What to Do If You're Sexually Harassed* (Arlington, VA: New Responses, Inc., 1980); Mary Ann Largen and Alyce McAdam, *The Sexually Harassed Woman: A Counselor's Guide* (Arlington, VA: New Responses, Inc., 1980).

18. Simon, telephone interview, 25 April 2001.

19. Information in this paragraph is based on documents in the *NOW Collection*.

20. "Sexual Harassment Challenged," *Off Our Backs*, December 1979, 8.

21. Jerrold K. Footlick, "Legal Battle of the Sexes," *Newsweek*, 30 April 1979, 75; Jeannette Orlando, *Sexual Harassment in the Workplace: A Practical Guide to What It Is and What to Do About It* (Los Angeles: Women's Legal Clinic, Center Against Sexual Harassment, 1981), 51–52.

22. "Harassment of Women on the Job: Survey," *The WREE-View*, November-December 1978, 5; "Blue Collar Women: Harassed, Forced Out: WREE Clearing House to Collect Data and Push for Protection," *The WREE-View*, September-October 1978.

23. Columbus Committee Against Sexual Harassment, *Combating Sexual Harassment* (Columbus, OH: Committee Against Sexual Harassment, 1981).

24. Janet Harris, "Dealing With Bosses," *Family Circle*, 24 April 1978, 191.

25. Kimberly K. Greene and Susan B. Tatnall, *Sexual Harassment of Working Women in Kentucky: "She Gave at the Office": A Handbook* (Louisville: Kentucky Commission on Women, no date); Kentucky Commission on Human Rights, *Sexual Harassment on the Job Is Against the Law* (Louisville: Kentucky Commission on Human Rights, June 1980); Kentucky Commission on Human Rights, *Stop Sexual Harassment on the Job* (Louisville: Kentucky Commission on Human Rights, no date).

26. Alisa Fuller, "City Is Fighting Sex Harassment," *Center City Welcomat*, 19 November 1980, 6; Letter from Robin Robinowitz, Director, WAJE, to Karen Sauvigné, Dated 7 April 1981 (with attached draft of a funding proposal), *Working Women's Institute Collection*.

27. *Everywoman: Sexual Harassment on the Job* (Washington, D.C.: WDVM-TV, 1976); "Sexual Harassment on the Job," *Phil Donahue Show* (Princeton: Films for the Humanities and Sciences, 1988) (including appearance by Adrienne Tomkins); Diane K. Shah, "A Steno Who Said 'No!'" *Newsweek*, 30 April 1979, 72 (Adrienne Tomkins); Katherine Davis, *Beware of the Boss: Sexual Harassment on the Job* (Washington, D.C.: National Public Radio, 1981) audiocassette (interviewing Diane Williams and Adrienne Tomkins); *1979 Hanley Hearings on Sexual Harassment*, 87–88; Harel and Cottledge, "Combatting Sexual Harassment," 2; *1981 Hatch Hearings on Sex Discrimination*, 590–95, 682–84; Laura A. Kiernan, "Barry Says District Will Not Tolerate Sex Harassment, Abuse of Employees," *Washington Post*, 27 April 1979, §B, 1.

28. *See* Dziech and Weiner, *The Lecherous Professor*, 27–28; Donna J. Benson and Gregg E. Thomson, "Sexual Harassment on a University Campus: The Confluence of Authority Relations, Sexual Interest, and Gender Stratification," *Social Problems* 29 (February 1982): 236–51; Working Women's Institute Survey of Women Organized Against Sexual Harassment, May 1979, *Working Women's Institute Collection*; "Women Devise Ways to Combat Sexual Harassment," *On Campus With Women* (Summer/Fall 1979): 12; Women Organized Against Sexual

Harassment, *Sexual Harassment: What Is It, What To Do About It* (Berkeley, CA: Women Organized Against Sexual Harassment, 1979); Women Organized Against Sexual Harassment, *Conditions for a Title IX Grievance Procedure* (Berkeley, CA: Women Organized Against Sexual Harassment, 1980).

29. Coalition Against Sexual Harassment, *Checklist and Position Paper* (Minneapolis: Coalition Against Sexual Harassment, 1981). Professionals from social service agencies throughout the Minneapolis/St. Paul area came together in December 1978 to form CASH, which served not only students but also women in the community experiencing sexual harassment in employment and other contexts. CASH engaged in public education, consultation about grievance procedures, advocacy for adult victims of harassment, gathering data, and sharing information. "Women Devise Ways to Combat Sexual Harassment," *On Campus With Women* (Summer/Fall 1979): 12; James C. Renick, "Sexual Harassment at Work: Why It Happens, What to Do About It," *Personnel Journal*, August 1980, 662.

30. Joint Committee to Study Sexual Harassment, *Final Report* (Tempe: Arizona State University, 1980); WASH moved off campus after several male professors objected to the organization's practice of maintaining confidential files describing harassment incidents, which the professors called, "another form of McCarthyism." "Students Organize to Battle Sexual Harassment," *On Campus With Women* (Spring 1980): 12.

31. "Equity Forum on Teacher/Student Violence and Sexual Harassment," Artists for Responsible Theater, 23 June 1980, *Working Women's Institute Collection*; "Committee Re: Women Holds Forum on Sexual Harassment and Violence," *Equity News*, August 1980, 9.

32. *See*, for example, Donna Benson, "The Sexualization of Student-Teacher Relationships," unpublished paper, University of California, Berkeley, 1977 (reporting on a survey of students at the University of California at Berkeley); Markson, "Sexual Harassment," 45–57; Pope, Levenson, and Schover, "Sexual Intimacy in Psychology Training," 682–89; Livingston, "Sexual Harassment of Working Women" (surveying women employed in a New England university); Judy Charla Oshinsky, "Sexual Harassment of Women Students in Higher Education" (Ph.D. diss., University of Florida, 1980) (surveying 1,111 women students at the three largest state universities in Florida).

33. Jodi L. Short, "Creating Peer Sexual Harassment: Mobilizing Schools to Throw the Book at Themselves," *Law and Policy* 28 (January 2006): 31–59; Project on the Status and Education of Women, *Sexual Harassment: A Hidden Issue* (Washington, D.C.: Project on the Status and Education of Women, 1978), 6; Freada Klein and Nancy Wilber, *Who's Hurt and Who's Liable: Sexual Harassment in Massachusetts Schools. A Curriculum and Guide for School Personnel* (Boston: Massachusetts State Dept. of Education, 1981).

34. Alexandra Buek, *Sexual Harassment: A Fact of Life or Violation of Law? University Liability Under Title IX* (Washington, D.C.: National Advisory Council on Women's Educational Programs, 1 July1978); "Extension of Call for Information on Sexual Harassment of Students," *National NOW Times*, May 1980, 13; Frank Till, *Sexual Harassment: A Report on Sexual Harassment of Students* (Washington, D.C.: National Advisory Council on Women's Educational Programs, August 1980); Dziech and Weiner, *The Lecherous Professor*, 19–20.

35. Project on the Status and Education of Women, *Sexual Harassment: A Hidden Issue*; Susan Howard, *Title VII Sexual Harassment Guidelines and Educational*

Employment (Washington, D.C.: Association of American Colleges Project on Status and Education of Women, August 1980).

36. Dziech and Weiner, *The Lecherous Professor*, 163, 173, 198–99; Phyllis Franklin, Helene Moglen, Phyllis Zatlin-Boring, and Ruth Angress, *Sexual and Gender Harassment in the Academy: A Guide for Faculty, Students, and Administrators* (New York: Modern Language Association of America, 1981); "Women Devise Ways to Combat Sexual Harassment," *On Campus With Women* (Summer/Fall 1979): 12.

37. Sara Terry, "U.S. Colleges Respond to Sexual Harassment Problem," *Christian Scientist Monitor*, 24 March 1980, 10 (reporting on how MIT, University of Washington, and other universities were dealing with sexual harassment); Dziech and Weiner, *The Lecherous Professor*, 13–14, 163–64; Bloustein, Edward J., President, Rutgers University, "Memo Regarding Issue of Sexual Harassment," Dated 5 February 1979; John R. Martin, Vice President for University Personnel, Rutgers University, "Memo Regarding Sexual Harassment: Procedures for the Handling of Complaints," Dated 28 June 1980 (Rutgers University, Newark, NJ); "Women Devise Ways to Combat Sexual Harassment," *On Campus With Women* (Summer/Fall 1979): 12 (discussing procedure at Brown University); Kenneth S. Pope, Hanna Levenson and Leslie R. Schover, "Sexual Behavior Between Clinical Supervisors and Trainees: Implications for Professional Standards," *Professional Psychological* 11 (February 1980): 157–62 (discussing how in 1979, Stanford University formed a committee to handle sexual harassment complaints).

38. Bularzik, "Sexual Harassment at the Workplace," 26.

39. AASC, *Sexual Harassment at the Workplace*, 4–5; *see also* AASC, "Sexual Harassment: A Form of Violence Against Women," *FAAR and NCN Newsletter*, July/August 1978, 28–29 (precursor to *Aegis*).

40. AASC, "Three Male Views on Harassment," *Aegis*, Winter/Spring 1980, 52; AASC, "Sexual Harassment and Coercion: Violence Against Women," *Aegis*, Winter/Spring 1981, 18; AASC, "Organizing Against Sexual Harassment," 18.

41. Rochelle Lefkowitz, "Sexual Harassment at Work," *Sister Courage*, October 1975, 9.

42. "Referrals Wanted," *FAAR News*, November/December 1977, 7.

43. Statement of Mary Largen, *1979 Hanley Hearings on Sexual Harassment*, 47, 51. Largen had previously worked on the Prince Georges County rape task force. Ibid.

44. MacKinnon, *Sexual Harassment of Working Women*, 217–18.

45. Ibid., 261.

46. Crull, "Sexual Harassment and Women's Health," 116.

47. Peggy Crull, "Sexual Harassment and Male Control of Women's Work," Research Series, Report No. 5, Fall 1982 (New York: Working Women's Institute, 1981), *Working Women's Institute Collection*, published in *Women: A Journal of Liberation* 8 (1982): 4–5 (quoting 1981 publication); Suzanne C. Carothers and Peggy Crull, "Understanding Sexual Harassment: A Way For Women to Gain Control of the Conditions of Their Work," (New York: Working Women's Institute, 1982): 5–7, *Working Women's Institute Collection*; Peggy Crull, Karen Sauvigné, and Marilyn Cohen, "Combatting Sexual Harassment on the Job: The Social and Legal Basis for the U.S. Movement," 27 (unpublished paper), *Working Women's Institute Collection*.

48. Crull, "Sexual Harassment and Male Control of Women's Work," 6.

49. See, for example, AASC, "Sexual Harassment and Coercion: Violence Against Women," *Aegis*, Winter/Spring 1981; AASC, "Organizing Against Sexual Harassment," 24; AASC, *University Grievance Procedures*, 28.
50. Martha Hooven and Nancy McDonald, "The Role of Capitalism: Understanding Sexual Harassment," *Aegis*, November/December 1978, 31–33; Hammer House, "Combat Sexual Harassment on the Job," *Aegis*, May/June 1979, 24–28; AASC, *Fighting Sexual Harassment*, 1981 ed., 90.
51. Backhouse and Cohen, *The Secret Oppression*.
52. Freada Klein, "Book Review of *Sexual Shakedown: The Sexual Harassment of Women on the Job* by Lin Farley," *Aegis*, November/December 1978, 34.
53. Lin Farley, "Response to Sexual Shakedown Review," *Aegis*, January/February 1979, 25.
54. AASC, *Fighting Sexual Harassment*, 85–87; Dubrow, *Sexual Harassment and the Law*, 25 (arguing that employer anti-sexual harassment policies are "primarily to protect the companies from liability, rather than out of genuine concern about women"); AASC, *University Grievance Procedures*, 8 (arguing that educational institutions adopted grievance procedures primarily to protect themselves from liability).
55. AASC, *Fighting Sexual Harassment*, 91.
56. Ibid. However, AASC also acknowledged that a "strategy that most expediently stops the harassment of an individual woman is not necessarily the same tactic that challenges the power structures and ideologies that allow and create harassment." Nevertheless, AASC remained "committed to a woman's right to decide what action to take in a given situation." Ibid., 26.
57. Dubrow, *Sexual Harassment and the Law*, 25; AASC, "Organizing Against Sexual Harassment," 33.
58. AASC, "Organizing Against Sexual Harassment," 31, 32.
59. Ibid., 28, 33 (arguing that employers had used sexual harassment as a "union-busting technique").
60. Ibid. AASC's handbook on the law of sexual harassment also emphasized that feminists should not rely on the law or employers and that they should not abandon direct action. The handbook provided a section on extra-legal tactics for relief from sexual harassment. Dubrow, *Sexual Harassment and the Law*, 2, 25, 47–49.
61. Thomas Watkins, "Briefs From the Publisher's Desk: About Black Women . . ." *N.Y. Recorder*, 8 May 1976.
62. Statement Issued by Pamela Price, 21 December 1977, *Alexander v. Yale: Collected Documents*, 16.
63. Ibid., 17.
64. July 1978 Statement, *Alexander v. Yale: Collected Documents*, 2–3.
65. Judy Trent Ellis, "Sexual Harassment and Race: A Legal Analysis of Discrimination," *Journal of Legislation* 8 (1981): 32.
66. Ibid., 35.
67. Ibid., 42.
68. MacKinnon, *Sexual Harassment of Working Women*, 32, 40.
69. This latter argument was very similar to the dominance theory of sexual harassment developed by Lynn Wehrli in her 1976 Master's Thesis at MIT. *Wehrli Master's Thesis*. This argument was later developed more fully by MacKinnon in *Feminism Unmodified: Discourses on Life and Law* (Cambridge: Harvard University Press, 1987) and *Toward a Feminist Theory of the State* (Cambridge: Harvard University Press, 1989).

70. MacKinnon, *Sexual Harassment of Working Women*, 156–58, 174–92. MacKinnon's later works explored the role of capitalism in the subjugation of women. *See* MacKinnon, *Toward a Feminist Theory of the State*.

71. Farley, *Sexual Shakedown*, 60–63 (white women), 63–68 (African-American women); MacKinnon, *Sexual Harassment of Working Women*, 30–31, 53–54, 176–77 (race), 29, 175 (class); Backhouse and Cohen, *The Secret Oppression*, 13–17, 48, 61, 63–68; Dierdre Silverman, "Sexual Harassment: Working Women's Dilemma," *Quest: A Feminist Quarterly* 3, no. 3 (1976–77): 15–24; Goodman, "Sexual Demands on the Job," 56 (describing experiences of women at a shipyard); Michele Noah, "Sexual Harassment on the Job," *Sister Courage*, May 1978, 9 (auto plan workers); "Sexual Harassment Challenged," *Off Our Backs*, December 1979, 9 (discussing harassment of women coal miners and workers at a plywood plant).

72. Weeks, et al., "The Transformation of Sexual Harassment," 440. This paper provides a graph of the number of articles on sexual harassment in selected newspapers, magazines, and journals from 1970 to 1982. Articles began appearing in the mid-1970s, increased dramatically in 1980 when the EEOC issued guidelines on sexual harassment, peaked in 1981, and dropped off in 1982. A Lexis-Nexis search of *New York Times* articles mentioning sexual harassment revealed a similar pattern: 1975–2; 1976–1; 1977–8, 1978–2, 1979–7; 1980–34; 1981–50; 1982–27. Lexis-Nexis search of the *New York Times* by the author, 27 December 2006.

73. As early as 1971, the *New York Times* had an article about street harassment of female New York City government workers. "Women Are Tired of Being Harassed," *New York Times*, 7 September 1971, 44.

74. Weeks, et al., "The Transformation of Sexual Harassment," 444.

75. "Executive Sweet: Many Office Romeos Are Really Juliets," *Time*, 8 October 1979, 76.

76. William Raspberry, "Just What Is Sexual Harassment?" *Washington Post*, 22 September 1980, § A, 15.

77. Madeline Rogers, "Is The Office Affair Worth It?" *MBA*, February 1978, 65; Marylin Bender, "Changing Rules of Office Romances," *Esquire*, 24 April 1979, 46; Robert E. Quinn and Noreen A. Judge, "Office Romance: No Bliss for the Boss," *Management Review*, July 1978, 43–49; Beatryce Nivens, "The Office Romance: Should You or Shouldn't You?" *Essence*, February 1978, 16; Robert Quinn, "Coping with Cupid: The Formation, Impact, and Management of Romantic Relationships in Organizations," *Administrative Scientific Quarterly* (March 1977): 40–45.

78. *See*, for example, Enid Nemy, "Women Begin to Speak-out Against Sexual Harassment," *New York Times*, 19 August 1975, 38 (family/style section); Carol Krucoff, "Careers: Sexual Harassment on the Job," *Washington Post*, 25 July 1979, § B, 5 (style section); "Sexual Harassment Lands Companies in Court," *Business Week*, 1 October 1979, 120 (social issues section); Jill Bettner, "How to Tame the Office Wolf—Without Getting Bitten," *Business Week*, 1 October 1979, 107.

79. Paula Bernstein, "Sexual Harassment on the Job," *Harper's Bazaar*, August 1976, 12; *see also* Shirley J. Longshore, "Job Frustrations: How To Solve Them Quickly, Diplomatically, Out of Court," *Glamour*, October 1977, 218 (also focusing on women's behavior).

80. Joyce Dudley Fleming, "Shop Talk About Sex," *Working Woman*, July 1979, 31–34; *see also* Margaret Hennig and Anne Jardim, "Survival Strategy in the Mostly Male Office," *Working Woman*, March 1977, 40–41 (focusing on individual solutions to sexual advances in the workplace, ignoring male/female, boss/subordinate power relations) but *see* Susan Jacoby, "The Awful Truth About Office Affairs," *Working Woman*, May 1977, 28–31 (arguing that office affairs tend to backfire on women because women are economically vulnerable if affairs do not work out).

81. Rosemary Kent, "Should You Sleep With Your Boss?" *Harper's Bazaar*, November 1975, 147 (one of the first magazine articles on sexual harassment); Sally Platkin Koslow, "Are You Crazy-in-Love or Simply Crazy To Be Involved in an Office Romance," *Glamour*, September 1979, 250; Jane Adams, "The Sexual Triangle: Women, Success, and Men," *Glamour*, October 1979, 60.

82. Letty Cottin Pogrebin, "Love on the Job," *Ladies Home Journal*, March 1980, 10, 14; Letty Cottin Pogrebin, "The Working Woman: Sex Harassment," *Ladies Home Journal* 94, June 1977, 24; *see also* Letty Cottin Pogrebin, "8 Hours a Day, 5 Days a Week, 50 Weeks a Year: The Intimate Politics of Working with Men," *Ms.*, October 1975, 48 (quoting women from a variety of professions about working with men).

83. Cheryl Bentsen, "Women Men Coach Women—Do They Have To Score?" *Ms.*, August 1976, 24–31; see also Peggy Magner Holter, "The College Couch," *Playgirl*, October 1977, 35–37 (instructing readers how to seduce their college professors); Adrienne Munich, "Seduction in Academe," *Psychology Today*, February 1978, 82.

84. Claire Safran, "What Men Do To Women on the Job: A Shocking Look at Sexual Harassment," *Redbook*, November 1976, 220.

85. "Sex on the Job: Where We Are Now," *Redbook*, April 1978, 38.

86. Margaret Mead, "A Proposal: We Need Taboos on Sex at Work," *Redbook*, April 1978, 31, 33, 38.

87. Letty Cottin Pogrebin, "The Working Woman: Sex Harassment," *Ladies Home Journal* 94, June 1977, 24.

88. Karen Lindsey, "Sexual Harassment on the Job and How to Stop It," *Ms.*, November 1977, 47; Karen Lindsey, "A National Resource," *Ms.*, November 1977, 49; Rochelle Lefkowitz, "Help for the Sexually Harassed: A Grass-Roots Model," *Ms.*, November 1977, 49; Mimi Kelber, "Sexual Harassment . . . The UN's Dirty Little Secret," *Ms.*, November 1977, 51; "Update: Sexual Harassment on the Job," *Ms.*, July 1978, 85–88; Marcia Greenwood, "The Yale Suit: On to Round Two," *Ms.*, July 1978, 85; Jacqueline Bernard, "A Meeting of the [Women] Miners," *Ms.*, November 1979, 33; Eric Matusewitch, "*Kyriazi v. Western Electric*: Court Fines Five Bosses for Sexual Harassment," *Ms.*, April 1980, 27.

89. Merrill Rogers Skrocki, "Sexual Pressure on the Job," *McCall's*, March 1978, 43; "My Problem and How I Solved It: My Boss Wanted More Than a Secretary," *Good Housekeeping*, April 1978, 28; Janet Harris, "Dealing With Bosses," *Family Circle*, 24 April 1978, 191; Marilyn Achiron, "Solving Your Problem: Sexual Harassment on the Job," *Mademoiselle*, October 1979, 116; Jane Williamson, "I'm Being Sexually Harassed. What Can I Do?" *Working Woman*, November 1979, 30; Joan Faier, "The Working Woman's 7 Biggest Problems and How to Solve Them," *Harper's Bazaar*, August 1979, 90; *see also* Karen Levett Andes, "On Campus: Sexual Harassment," *Mademoiselle*, February 1979, 174

(discussing sexual harassment in educational institutions); "Sexual Discrimination and Harassment," *Today's Secretary*, February 1979, 9–10 (quoting Karen Sauvigné).

90. Ann Crittenden, "Women Tell of Sexual Harassment at Work," *New York Times*, 25 October 1977, 35; Lawrence Stessin, "Two Against Harassment," *New York Times*, 23 December 1979, § 3, 7; Enid Nemy, "Center Helps Fight Sexual Harassment," *New York Times*, 2 March 1980, § D, 7; *see also* "Most Women in Survey in Illinois Report Sex Harassment at Work," *New York Times*, 9 March 1980, 42, (discussing survey and proposed legislation to combat sexual harassment); Susan Hobart, "Awareness Helps Women Overcome Sexual Indignities," *The Oregonian*, 23 January 1978, § B, 1; Dorothy Austin, "Institute Fights Sex Harassment," *Milwaukee Sentinel*, 2 June 1978, 10; Patsy Miller, "Fighting Harassment a Job," *Fort Worth Star-Telegram*, 7 June 1978; Jane See White, "Sexual Harassment: New Groups Fighting Problem," *Pueblo (Colo.) Star-Journal and Sunday Chieftain*, 20 August 1978; Mike Winerip, "C'mon Guys, Cut Out the Sexist Jibes," *Miami Herald*, 22 October 1978, 6G; Charles E. Marske, et al., "Combatting Sexual Harassment: A New Awareness," *USA Today*, March 1980, 45–48 (quoting Lin Farley and Karen DeCrow) (despite the sympathetic text, the illustration was not sympathetic); Aric Press, "Abusing Sex at the Office," *Newsweek*, 10 March 1980, 81–82 (quoting San Francisco lawyer Judith Kurtz, Eleanor Holmes Norton, Karen Sauvigné, Susan Blumenthal of NOWLDEF, Nadine Taub of Rutgers School of Law, Erin Sneed of Women for Change, Inc. of Dallas, and Catharine MacKinnon); "Sexual Harassment: No Longer a Hidden Issue," *Richmond Times-Dispatch*, 1–4 June 1980; Eileen Colianni, "Sex at Work," *Pittsburgh*, May 1978, 43.

91. *See*, for example, Thomas Watkins, "Briefs from the Publisher's Desk: About Black Women" *N.Y. Recorder*, 8 May 1976; Wista Johnson, "On the Job: Women Seek Advances in Work, Not Sex," *New York Amsterdam News*, 9 June 1979; "Sexual Harassment on Job Now Illegal: EEOC's Norton," *Jet*, 1 May 1980, 55; "Sex Harassment Ruled in Firing of D.C. Woman," *Jet*, 29 May 1980, 49; "Woman Wins $15G on Sexual Advances," *New York Amsterdam News*, 15 January 1983, 1.

92. Yla Eason, "When Your Boss Wants Sex," *Essence*, March 1981, 82.

93. Caryl Rivers, "Sexual Harassment: The Executive's Alternative to Rape," *Mother Jones*, June 1978, 21–25.

94. Diane K. Shah, "A Steno Who Said 'No!'" *Newsweek*, 30 April 1979, 72; *see also* Jerrold Footlick, "Legal Battle of the Sexes," *Newsweek*, 30 April 1979, 68–75.

95. *See*, for example, "Professor Says Sex Charges Forced Him to Resign," *Chronicle of Higher Education*, 23 January 1978, 2 (reporting that former professor was suing New York Law School for forcing him to resign because of rumors he made sexual advances toward students); Erika Munk, "A Case of Sexual Abuse," *Village Voice*, 22 October 1979, 1; "Fighting Lechery on Campus," *Time*, 4 February 1980, 84; Sara Terry, "U.S. Colleges Respond to Sexual Harassment Problem," *Christian Science Monitor*, 24 March 1980, 10; Maria Riccardo, "Harassment on Campus," *Boston Globe*, 21 December 1980, §D, 1; Noel Epstein, "When Professors Swap Good Grades for Sex," *Washington Post*, 6 September 1981, §C, 1.

96. Diane Henry, "Yale Faculty Members Charged With Sexual Harassment," *New York Times*, 22 August 1977, 30; Diane Henry, "Yale Student Withdraws from Lawsuit," *New York Times*, 10 September 1977, 52; "Yale and Woman Senior

Reach an Accord on Suit," *New York Times*, 15 January 1978, 40; "Ex-Student Wins Right to Sue Yale on Sex Charge," *New York Times*, 1 December 1978, § C, 26; "A College Woman Loses Test on Sexual Harassment," *New York Times*, 12 July 1979, § B, 6; *see also*, Deborah Markow, "Obnoxious Professors" (Letter to the Editor), *New York Times*, 27 August 1977, 20; "Bod and Man at Yale," *Time*, 8 August 1977, 52; Anne Nelson, "Sexual Harassment at Yale," *Nation*, 14 January 1978, 7–10.

97. Mary D. Faucher and Kenneth J. McCulloch, "Sexual Harassment in the Workplace: What Should the Employer Do?" *EEO Today* (Spring 1978): 38–44; "Is Sexual Harassment Sex Discrimination?" *EEO Review*, September 1978, 6–8; Patricia A. Somers and Judith Clementson-Mohr, "Sexual Extortion in the Workplace," *Personnel Administrator*, April 1979, 23–28 (providing contact information for WWI, AASC, Cleveland Working Women, 9-to-5 in Boston, and Vocations for Social Change in Cambridge); "Sexual Harassment on the Job," *Personnel Management – Policies and Practices Report Bulletin*, 10 July 1979, 437–38 (quoting Karen Sauvigné); James C. Renick, "Sexual Harassment at Work: Why It Happens, What to Do About It," *Personnel Journal*, August 1980, 660; Shelby White, "The Office Pass," *Across the Board*, April 1977, 17; *see also* Shelby White, "The Office Pass (Continued)," *Across the Board*, March 1978, 48–51 (reporting on *Barnes v. Costle*); Jill Bettner, "How to Tame the Office Wolf—Without Getting Bitten," *Business Week*, 1 October 1979, 107; "Sexual Harassment Lands Companies in Court," *Business Week*, 1 October 1979, 120–21.

98. Georgia Dullea, "Women Win Fight for More Construction Jobs, Less Harassment," *Washington Post*, 23 August 1977, 30; William J. Easton, "Hard Hat Women Make a Dent in Jobs," *Los Angeles Times*, 20 May 1978, 1; Allanna M. Sullivan, "Women Say No to Sexual Harassment," *Coal Age*, August 1979, 74–78; Ben Franklin, "Women Work in Mines Assail Harassment and Unsafe Conditions," *New York Times*, 11 November 1979; "Women Miners Reassured," *Washington Post*, 13 November 1979, § A, 4; "Women Fight Sex Bias, Superstition in Mines," *Baltimore Sun*, 17 July 1980, § K, 12; Jerry W. Williamson, "A Deep Vein of Hostility," *In These Times*, 27 August to 2 September 1980, 24; Bob Dvorchak, "Women Miners: It's a Long Haul," *Pittsburgh Press*, 8 August 1982, § C, 2; Kipp Dawson, "Women Miners Meet," *Bentworth Times*, 3 August 1982, 1; Raymond M. Lane, "A Man's World: An Update on Sexual Harassment," *Village Voice*, 16–22 December 1981, 1; Estelle Jackson, "Mother Had Same Problem," *Richmond Times*, 3 June 1980, 1; "Jeers, Threats and Assaults Reported to Occur Regularly," *Baltimore Sun*, 16 December 1979, 1; "Army Recruits Most Open to Abuse," *Baltimore Sun*, 17 December 1979, 1; "Harassment at Fort Meade Makes Base 'Hell' for Women Soldiers and Civilians," *Baltimore Sun*, 17 December 1979, 1; "First Lesson in the Army: Don't Report Harassment," *Baltimore Sun*, 17 December 1979, 1; "Women Soldiers Angry Over Sex Discrimination and Sexual Harassment," *Enlisted Times*, April 1979, 5; "Army Survey Finds Sexual Harassment of Military Women Overseas," *Baltimore Sun*, 26 March 1980, 7; "Woman Soldier is Jailed: Convicted of Sexual Harassment," *Washington Post*, 23 April 1980, § A, 5.

99. *Everywoman: Sexual Harassment on the Job*, prod. Shirley Robson, Washington, D.C.: WDVM-TV, 1976, videocassette (focusing on case of *Williams v. Saxbe*); *Sexual Harassment on the Job*, prod. Phil Donahue (Princeton: Films for the Humanities and Sciences, 1988), videocassette (aired in 1977 including appearance by Adrienne Tomkins); *Sexual Harassment: No Place in the Workplace*,

Michigan Media, 1979, videocassette; *The Workplace Hustle: A Film About Sexual Harassment of Working Women* (San Francisco: Clark Communications, Inc., 1980); Katherine Davis, *Beware of the Boss: Sexual Harassment on the Job* (Washington, D.C.: National Public Radio, 1981), audiocassette.

100. Internet Movie Database Ltd., The Top Grossing Movies of All Time at the USA Box Office, as of March 13, 2001, available from *http://us.imdb.com/boxoffice/alltimegross*, accessed 20 July 2005.

101. *Women in the Mines* (New York: CBS-TV, 1982), videocassette.

Chapter 6. Government Policy Develops

1. "Sexual Harassment Lands Companies in Court," *Business Week*, 1 October 1979, 120–21.

2. Laura A. Kiernan, "Barry Says District Will Not Tolerate Sex Harassment, Abuse of Employees," *Washington Post*, 27 April 1979, § B, 1; D.C. Commission for Women, "Commission for Women Tests Survey Questionnaire on Sexual Harassment," Press Release, 4 June 1979, *Working Women's Institute Collection*; Organization of Black Activist Women, "Sexual Harassment in Employment," Flyer, June 6, 1979, *Working Women's Institute Collection*.

3. Laura A. Kiernan, "Barry Says District Will Not Tolerate Sex Harassment, Abuse of Employees," *Washington Post*, 27 April 1979, §B, 1; Helen Lewis, "Initial Survey Results Point to Evidence of Sexual Harassment," *City Hall New Times*, 25 June 1979, 1; Milton Coleman, "Barry Acts to Bar Sex Harassment in District Jobs," *Washington Post*, 25 May 1979, § B, 1. The task force members included Judith Rogers, Acting Corporation Counsel; Anita Shelton, Acting Director of the Office of Human Rights; Burtell Jefferson, Chief of Police; Jose Gutierrez, Acting Director of Personnel; and E. Veronica Pace, Chairperson of the Women's Coordinator Program. *1979 Hanley Hearings on Sexual Harassment*, 55–64 (containing the final report from the Mayor's Task Force on Sexual Harassment, Dated 18 May 1979, and Mayor Barry's Executive Order 79–89, Dated 24 May 1979).

4. Mike Causey, "Sex and the GS-3: Favors, Favoritism," *Washington Post*, 31 July 1979, § C, 2; *see also* Nancy Josephson, "Sexual Harassment on the Job: Why More and More Women are Fighting Back," *Glamour*, May 1980, 341; Al Louis Ripskis, "Sexual Harassment at HUD," *Impact* 7 (May/June 1979): 1; Al Louis Ripskis, "Sexual Harassment Rampant at HUD," *Impact Journal* 7 (July/August 1979): 1.

5. *Sexual Harassment in the Federal Government (Part II), A Hearing before the Subcommittee on Investigations of the Committee on Post Office and Civil Service*, U.S. House of Representatives, 96th Congress, Second Session, September 25, 1980, 39 (statement of Representative James Hanley) (hereafter *Hanley Hearings on Sexual Harassment [Part II]*).

6. James M. Hanley, Chairman, Subcommittee on Investigations of the Committee on Post Office and Civil Service, U.S. House of Representatives, Letter to Alan K. Campbell, Director, U.S. Office of Personnel Management, October 9, 1979, 1; Statement of Representative Hanley, *1979 Hanley Hearings on Sexual Harassment* (explaining how Ripskis' survey led to hearings); Mike Causey, "Hill Panel Probes Sexual Harassment," *Washington Post*, 8 August 1979, at § B, 2.

7. *1979 Hanley Hearings on Sexual Harassment*, 1–3.

8. Ibid., 41.

9. Ibid., 130–38.

10. Ibid., 138–53.
11. Ibid., 91, 93.
12. *Sexual Harassment in the Federal Government, A Report from the Subcommittee on Investigations of the Committee on Post Office and Civil Service*, U.S. House of Representatives, 96th Congress, Second Session, 30 April 1980 (hereafter *Sexual Harassment Report*).
13. Letter from Gene Taylor to James Hanley, Dated 18 April 1980, ibid., 31–32 (published at the end of the subcommittee's report).
14. At the time the EEOC adopted the guidelines, the commission members were Chair Eleanor Holmes Norton, Vice Chair Daniel E. Leach, Ethel Bent Walsh, Armando M. Rodriguez, and J. Clay Smith.
15. James C. Miller, III, Introduction to *A Conversation with Commissioner Eleanor Holmes Norton* (Washington, D.C.: American Enterprise Institute, 1979), 1.
16. "The Mess at EEOC," *Washington Post*, 28 April 1987, § A, 12.
17. 45 *Federal Register* 25024–25025 (11 April 1980).
18. The EEOC received 168 letters commenting on the guidelines, plus commentary from other federal agencies. J. Clay Smith, Jr., "Prologue to the EEOC Guidelines on Sexual Harassment," *Capital University Law Review* 10 (1981): 472. Joan Vermuelen of Working Women's Institute (WWI) submitted comments on behalf of Working Women, National Association of Office Workers, the National Employment Law Project, the Women's Justice Center, the Women's Litigation Clinic of Rutgers School of Law, and the National Emergency Civil Liberties Committee. Susan Blumenthal of NOW Legal Defense and Education Fund (NOWLDEF) and Donna Lenhoff of Women's Legal Defense Fund (WLDF) submitted comments on behalf of those organizations and the National Organization for Women, the National Women's Political Caucus, the New York City Commission on the Status of Women, the Center for National Policy Review, the Women Employed Institute, and the Women's Equity Action League Educational and Legal Defense Fund. Comments were also submitted by Alliance Against Sexual Coercion, Equal Rights Advocates, Inc., Brooklyn Chapter of the National Organization for Women, National Council of Jewish Women, National Advisory Council on Women's Educational Programs, Rhode Island Rape Crisis Center, and Women in the Trades in New York City.
19. Joan Vermuelen, Working Women's Institute, "Comments on the Equal Employment Opportunity Commission's Proposed Amendment Adding Section 1604.11, Sexual Harassment, to Its Guidelines on Sexual Discrimination," *Women's Rights Law Reporter* 6 (Summer 1980): 286 (hereafter *WWI Comments*).
20. NOW Legal Defense and Education Fund, Women's Legal Defense Fund, et al., *Comments on the Equal Employment Opportunity Commission's Interim Guidelines on Sexual Harassment*, 10 June 1980, 6, *Working Women's Institute Collection* (hereafter *NOW/WLDF Comments*).
21. 45 *Federal Register* 74676 (10 November 1980); 104 Labor Relations Reporter (BNA) 148, 23 June 1980.
22. 45 *Federal Register* 74676 (10 November 1980), codified in 29 C.F.R. §1604.11.
23. Smith, "Prologue to the EEOC Guidelines on Sexual Harassment," 473, 477; *1981 Hatch Hearings on Sex Discrimination*, 338; Jan C. Leventer, "Sexual Harassment and Title VII: EEOC Guidelines, Conditions Litigation, and the United States Supreme Court," *Capital University Law Review* 10 (1981): 484–85.
24. 45 *Federal Register* 74677 (10 November 1981).

25. Joann Lublin, "Guidelines-Happy at the EEOC?" *Wall Street Journal*, 28 August 1980, 18.
26. Ruth Marcus, "EEOC Gets Slapped on Sex Harassment Regs," *National Law Journal*, 7 July 1980, 4.
27. Bruce Jacobs, "Fixing the Blame for Sexual Harassment," *Industry Week*, 27 October 1980, 29.
28. David Seligman, "Sex in the Office," *Fortune*, 7 April 1980, 42.
29. Ronald Groeber, "A Survey of Sexual Harassment: A Wrong Redressable Under Title VII Only When Discrimination is Shown," *Northern Kentucky Law Review* 8 (1981): 409.
30. *See*, for example, Nancy Fisher Chudacoff, "New EEOC Guidelines on Discrimination Because of Sex: Employer Liability for Sexual Harassment Under Title VII," *Boston University Law Review* 61 (1981): 535; Leventer, "Sexual Harassment and Title VII," 481–97; Robert Martin, "EEOC's New Sexual Harassment Guidelines: Civility in the Workplace," *Nova Law Journal* 5 (Spring 1981): 405–19; Marta-Ann Schnabel, "Sexual Harassment in the Workplace: New Guidelines from the EEOC," *Loyola Law Review* 27 (1981): 512–31; Lynne Stanley-Elliott, "Sexual Harassment in the Workplace: Title VII's Imperfect Relief," *Journal of Corporation Law* 6 (Spring 1981): 625–56.
31. 22 Fair Empl. Prac. Cas. (BNA) 1627 (W.D. Okla. 1980).
32. *Bundy*, 641 F.2d 934.
33. *Bundy*, 641 F.2d at 944, *citing EEOC v. Rogers*, 454 F.2d 234, 238, *cert. denied*, 406 U.S. 957 (1972).
34. *See*, e.g., Merrick T. Rossein, "Sex Discrimination and the Sexually Charged Work Environment," *NYU Review of Law and Social Change* 9 (1979–1980): 271; Judy Mann, "The 'Delicate Situation' Now Has Another Name," *Washington Post*, 27 April 1979, § B, 1; Laura A. Kiernan, "Ruling Widens Protections in Sex Bias Cases," *Washington Post*, 13 January 1981, § A, 1.
35. Department of Labor, Office of Federal Contract Compliance Programs, Final Rule, 45 Fed. Reg. 86216 (1980); Department of Labor, Office of Federal Contract Compliance Programs, Proposed Rule, 46 Fed. Reg. 42968 (1981).
36. *See*, for example, Conn. Gen. Stat. § 46a-60(8); *Policy Statement on Sexual Harassment*, Washington State Human Rights Commission, 23 December 1980; *Guidelines on Sexual Harassment*, Pennsylvania Human Relations Commission, 31 January 1981; *Kentucky Administrative Regulations Service*, Title 104, Ch. 1, effective 1 April 1981.
37. *See*, for example, Martin, "Memorandum to Members of the University Community," 28 June 1980 (using the definition of sexual harassment in EEOC's interim guidelines).
38. EEOC Case Nos. 81-16 (26 January 1981), 81-17 (6 February 1981), and 81-18 (3 April 1981) (all unpublished). By April of 1981, EEOC had 130 sexual harassment cases awaiting action, 118 of which had corroborating evidence. Smith, "Prologue to the EEOC Guidelines on Sexual Harassment," 474, 477; *Hanley Hearings on Sexual Harassment (Part II)*, 43 (statement of Eleanor Holmes Norton).
39. CCH EEOC DECISIONS (1983) ¶¶ 6756, 6756, 6757, 6827, 6829, 6830 (decided in 1981); CCH EEOC DECISIONS (1983) ¶¶ 6818, 6842, 6834 (decided in 1982).
40. *1981 Hatch Hearings on Sex Discrimination*, 345, 341; *Hanley Hearings on Sexual Harassment (Part II)*, 43–44, 46–47 (statement of Eleanor Holmes Norton); *Sexual Harassment Report*, 16.

41. Alan K. Campbell, Director, U.S. Office of Personnel Management to Heads of Departments and Independent Agencies, Re: Policy Statement and Definition of Sexual Harassment, 12 December 1979.
42. Ibid.
43. Ibid.
44. *1979 Hanley Hearings on Sexual Harassment*, 159.
45. *Hanley Hearings on Sexual Harassment (Part II)*, 31–39.
46. *1979 Hanley Hearings on Sexual Harassment*, 32 (statement of Julie M. Sugarman, Deputy Director, Office of Personnel Management).
47. United States Office of Personnel Management, *Workshop on Sexual Harassment: Trainer's Manual*. Washington, D.C.: Government Printing Office, 1980, 2 (including participant materials).
48. Ibid., 3.
49. Ibid., 47 (Handout #1).
50. Ibid., 53 (Handout #2).
51. Merit Systems Protection Board, *Sexual Harassment in the Federal Workplace: Is It A Problem?: A Report of the U.S. Merit Systems Protection Board, Office of Merit Systems Review and Studies* (Washington, D.C.: Government Printing Office, 1981).
52. MSPB Doc. PH075209077, 25 January 1980; MSPB Doc. DA075209096, 13 February 1980; MSPB Doc. AT075209026, 30 May 1980.
53. Statement by Representative Cavanaugh, *1979 Hanley Hearings on Sexual Harassment*, 125 (stating that "the public consciousness heightening that these hearings have initiated is overwhelming").
54. *The Power Pinch: Sexual Harassment in the Workplace* (Northbrook, IL: MTI Teleprograms, Inc., 1981), videocassette; *Preventing Sexual Harassment* (Rockville, MD: BNA Communications, Inc., 1980), videocassette; *No Laughing Matter: High School Students and Sexual Harassment* (Boston: Boston Women's Teachers Collective and Media Works, Inc., 1982), videocassette; Katherine Davis, *Beware of the Boss: Sexual Harassment on the Job* (Washington, D.C.: National Public Radio, 1981); *Workplace Hustle* (San Francisco: Clark Communications, Inc., 1980), videocassette.
55. Klein, telephone interview, 13 April 2001.
56. Klein, telephone interview, 13 April 2001. The conference was titled Discrimination and Harassment of Women in Employment. Correspondence to author from Grazyna T. Elwell, The Johnson Foundation, Racine, WI, Dated 18 April 2001.
57. National Commission on Unemployment Compensation, *Consideration of the Issue of Sexual Harassment and Disqualification: Hearings*, 28 June 1979 (hereafter *Unemployment Compensation Hearings*); *Pressures in Today's Workplace (Vol. II)*, Oversight Hearings before the Subcommittee on Labor-Management Relations of the Committee on Education and Labor, U.S. House of Representatives, 96th Congress, First Session, December 4 and 6, 1979, 152–169.
58. *Women in the Military, Hearings before the Military Personnel Subcommittee of the Committee on Armed Services*, U.S. House of Representatives, 96th Congress, First and Second Sessions, 13–16 November 1979 and 11 February 1980, 22–25, 298–350.
59. Ibid., 324.
60. *Racial Discrimination and Sexual Harassment in the U.S. Postal Service: Hearings before the Subcommittee on Postal Personnel and Modernization of the Committee on Post Office and Civil Service*, U.S. House of Representatives, 97th

Congress, First Session, 1 July 1981 (hereafter *Racial Discrimination and Sexual Harassment in the U.S. Postal Service Hearings*); *Equal Employment Opportunity and Sexual Harassment in the Postal Service, Hearings before the Committee on Post Office and Civil Service*, U.S. House of Representatives, 96th Congress, Second Session, 27 October 1980.

61. *Racial Discrimination and Sexual Harassment in the U.S. Postal Service Hearings*, 1.

62. Antonio J. Califa, Memorandum to Regional Civil Rights Directors, Regions I–X, Office for Civil Rights, United States Department of Education, Re: Title IX and Sexual Harassment Complaints, 31 August 1981.

63. Wis. Stat. Ann. §108.04(7)(i) (1979) (West) (sexual harassment is "good cause" under unemployment compensation law); Wis. Stat. §111.32(5)(g)(4)(1979) (prohibiting sexual harassment in employment).

64. Harel and Cottledge, "Combatting Sexual Harassment," 2; Michigan Task Force on Sexual Harassment in the Workplace, *Conference Report: Sexual Harassment at the Workplace* (Ann Arbor: Program on Women and Work, 1979), 1 (reporting on the 1978 meeting).

65. S. Gomez, R. Brown and L. Martin, "Public Hearings on Sexual Harassment in the Workplace: Analysis of Testimony," Office of Women and Work, Michigan Department of Labor, November 1979; "Sexual Harassment: Hazard in the Workplace," *Solidarity*, 2 July 1979, 15 (describing the testimony of two sexually harassed women who testified at the hearings); Testimony of Louise Smothers, *1979 Hanley Hearings on Sexual Harassment*, 110 (testifying that the Michigan Task Force on Sexual Harassment sponsored a seminar on sexual harassment the previous Saturday with over 600 people attending); "Sexual Harassment on the Job: How to Recognize It, How to Stop It, Who To Go to For Help," (Lansing: Michigan Task Force on Sexual Harassment in the Workplace and WJBK-TV2, Detroit, no date), *Coal Employment Project Collection* (Accession 355, Box 73, Folder 23); Harel and Cottledge, "Combatting Sexual Harassment," 3.

66. Amendment to the Elliott-Larson Civil Rights Act, Mich. Comp. Laws Ann. §37.2103, as amended by Pub. Act No. 202, §1, 1980 Mich. Legis. Serv. 626 (West); Act Concerning Harassment as an Unfair Employment Practice, Pub. Act No. 80-285, 1980 Conn. Legis. Serv. 634 (West) (codified as Conn. Gen. Stat. Ann. §1-126(a)(8)).

67. Harel and Cottledge, "Combatting Sexual Harassment," 5.

68. Ibid. at 8, Figure 1.

69. Michigan Civil Rights Commission, *Annual Report, 1979–1980* (1 October 1979–20 September 1980), 7.

70. *Petro v. United Trucking Company*, No. 31422-S7F (State of Michigan Civil Rights Commission, February 1980).

71. Testimony of Jan Leventer, Women's Justice Center, Detroit, MI, *1979 Hanley Hearings on Sexual Harassment*, 29.

72. Leventer, "Sexual Harassment and Title VII," 481; *Martindale-Hubbell Law Directory* (Reed Elsevier, Inc., 2001).

73. *Marentette v. Michigan Host Inc.*, 506 F. Supp. 909 (E.D. Mich. 1980).

74. Michigan Task Force, *Conference Report*; Clarke, et al., *Stopping Sexual Harassment*.

75. Testimony of Jan Leventer, Women's Justice Project, submitted to *1979 Hanley Hearings on Sexual Harassment*, 27–29; Leventer, "Sexual Harassment and Title VII," 481–97.

76. The organizations were Rape Information Counseling Center, Center for Policy Studies and Program Evaluation of Sangamon State University, Women's Studies Committee of Sangamon State University, AFSCME Illinois Council 31, Fair Employment Practices Commission, and Labor Union Women Committee of the Illinois Commission on the Status of Women. *See* Press Release Dated 4 March 1980 of the Illinois Task Force on Sexual Harassment in the Workplace, *Working Women's Institute Collection*; "Most Women in Survey in Illinois Report Sex Harassment at Work," *New York Times*, 9 March 1980, 42.

77. Testimony of Barbara Hayler, Member of Illinois Task Force on Sexual Harassment in the Workplace and Assistant Professor, Sangamon State University, before the Illinois House Judiciary II Committee (March 4, 1980). Of the 4,859 women surveyed, approximately fifteen percent of the women employed by the State of Illinois, 1,495 completed questionnaires, a response rate of 31 percent.

78. *Sexual Harassment*, Illinois Executive Order 80-1, 24 January 1980.

79. Pub. Act No. 80-285, 80-422, Conn. Gen. Stat. Ann. § 31-126(a)(8) (1980), later recodified at Conn. Gen. Stat. § 46a-60(8) (1999).

80. Elizabeth Sullivan, "Survey Shows Few States Have Systems to Resolve Sexual Harassment Complaints," *Intergovernmental Personnel Notes*, November/December 1979, 3. The Maryland Commission on Women conducted a study of sexual harassment in 1980.

81. *See* Backhouse and Cohen, *The Secret Oppression*, 144 (mentioning that bills were pending in Virginia, Florida, and Minnesota). In 1979, Assemblywoman Mary Newburger, a women's rights activist, introduced a bill to allow unemployment compensation for an employee who quits because of sexual harassment. *See* A.7236 N.Y. State Legislature, 1979–80 Sess. Senators Winikow, Berman, Bernstein, Conner, Gold, Mendez, and Ohrenstein introduced similar legislation before the Senate in the 1979–80 session. A.5011 N.Y. State Legislature, 1979–80 Sess. Working Women United Institute helped to develop and supported a similar bill in 1977. *See* Working Women's United Institute Letter to Legislators dated 27 April 1979, *Working Women's Institute Collection*. Representatives in New Jersey and Ohio also introduced sexual harassment legislation. Working Women's Institute, "Discussion of Legislation, Executive Order, Policies and Procedures Regarding Sexual Harassment in Employment," August 1981, *Working Women's Institute Collection*.

82. Utah Executive Order on Sexual Harassment, 29 December 1980; Executive Order No. 80-9, issued by the Governor of Rhode Island on 24 March 1980, CCH Emp. Prac. Guide (CCH) §27,680 (1980); Florida Executive Order 81-69 (1981); Oregon Executive Order 81-7 (1981); South Dakota Executive Order 81-08 (1981); Indiana Executive Order 6-82 (1982); Kansas Executive Order 82-55 (1982); Montana Executive Order No. 7-82 (1982); Massachusetts Executive Order No. 240 (1984).

83. *Policy Statement on Sexual Harassment*, Washington State Human Rights Commission, 23 December 1980; *Guidelines on Sexual Harassment*, Pennsylvania Human Relations Commission, 31 January 1981; *Kentucky Administrative Regulations Service*, Title 104, Ch. 1, effective 1 April 1981.

84. California Fair Employment and Housing Commission Rules § 7287.6, Cal. Admin. Code. tit. 2, div. 4 (West 1980), effective 1 May 1980.

85. Rule 80.11, Sex Discrimination Rules, Colorado Civil Rights Commission, 31 October 1980.

86. New Hampshire Advisory Committee, Agenda and Notice of Open Meeting, 45 Fed. Reg. 64226 (1980); New Hampshire Advisory Committee, Agenda and Notice of Open Meeting, 45 Fed. Reg. 21797 (1981); Maine Advisory Committee, Agenda and Open Meeting, 46 Fed. Reg. 8632 (1981); Vermont Advisory Committee, Agenda and Notice of Open Meeting, 46 Fed. Reg. 37299 (1981); Massachusetts Advisory Committee, Agenda and Notice of Public Meeting, 48 Fed. Reg. 22768 (1983); Massachusetts Advisory Committee, Agenda and Public Meeting, 48 Fed. Reg. 32616 (1983). In New Hampshire and Massachusetts, the State Advisory Commissions to the U.S. Commission on Civil Rights published sexual harassment guides for employers. "Sexual Harassment on the Job," *On Campus With Women* (Spring 1985) (describing Massachusetts guide); "Employee Harassment," *On Campus With Women* (Summer 1983) (describing New Hampshire guide).

87. "States Enlist to Battle Sexual Harassment," *On Campus With Women* (Summer 1980): 14.

88. Kentucky Commission on Human Rights, *Sexual Harassment on the Job Is Against the Law*; Kentucky Commission on Human Rights, *Stop Sexual Harassment on the Job*.

89. Public Hearings on Sexual Harassment before the Kentucky Commission on Human Rights, 10 July 1980, Frankfort, KY (videocassette), *Coal Employment Project Collection* (Accession 355, Tape 193).

90. Barbara Geehan, "Ithacan Testifies on Job Sexual Harassment," *Ithaca Journal*, 22 April 1975, 6; Enid Nemy, "Women Begin To Speak-out Against Sexual Harassment," *New York Times*, 19 August 1975, 38.

91. Letter from Donna McKittrick, Chair of the Fresno City-County Commission on the Status of Women, Dated 1 June 1981, with *Survey of Sexual Harassment in the Private Sector Within Fresno County* by Marilyn Watts, *NOW Collection*.

92. D.C. Commission on Women, "Commission for Women Tests Survey Questionnaire on Sexual Harassment," 4 June 1979 (press release), *Working Women's Institute Collection*.

93. *1979 Hanley Hearings on Sexual Harassment*, 66–67; D.C. Commission on Women, *Public Hearing on Sexual Harassment*, 30 January 1981; District of Columbia Commission for Women, "Projects and Outreach," in *Annual Report, 12th, April 1980* (Washington, D.C.: District of Columbia Commission for Women, 1980): 51–61.

94. Crull, Sauvigné, and Cohen, "Combatting Sexual Harassment on the Job," unpublished paper, 15, *Working Women's Institute Collection*.

95. Clarke, et al., *Stopping Sexual Harassment*, 48.

96. Greene and Tatnall, *Sexual Harassment of Working Women in Kentucky*. The commission based their questionnaire on *Redbook*'s 1976 survey on sexual harassment. Ibid., 6.

97. James T. Prendergast, "Sexual Harassment Bills: Definitions Keep Changing," *National Law Journal*, 21 April 1980, 6.

98. AASC, *Fighting Sexual Harassment*, 81.

99. *See* Weeks, et al., "The Transformation of Sexual Harassment," 446.

100. AASC, *Fighting Sexual Harassment*, 87.

101. Ibid., 84, 81–88.

102. Brownmiller, *In Our Time*, 288 (quoting Eleanor Holmes Norton).

103. Ibid., 86.

104. Klein, telephone interview, 26 March 2001. According to Peggy Crull, "once the issue becomes something that the popular culture has taken up and that people accept as a real issue, then the organizations that are more connected with businesses are the ones who get the jobs." Crull, telephone interview, 27 February 2001.

105. Sauvigné, telephone interview, 12 February 2001.

106. Mary Coeli Meyer and Jeanenne Oestreich, *The Power Pinch: Sexual Harassment at the Workplace, Film, Leader's Guide for Conducting a Sexual Harassment Workshop and Manager's Handbook for Handling Sexual Harassment in the Workplace* (Northbrook, IL: MTI Teleprograms, Inc., 1981).

107. Ibid., 86.

108. Linda Gordon, "The Politics of Sexual Harassment," *Radical America* (July/August 1981): 10, 13, 14.

109. For a discussion of how legal remedies can co-opt collective change-oriented approaches to social problems, *see* Thomas Geoghegan, *Which Side Are You On? Trying To Be For Labor When It's Flat On Its Back* (New York: Farrar, Straus, Giroux, 1991).

110. The EEOC, and Norton's leadership in this agency, is an example of what Nancy Whittier describes as the "interpenetration of institutional and extra-institutional agents of social change. Whittier, "Meaning and Structure in Social Movements," 294.

111. The differences between WWI and AASC illustrate how the beliefs and identities of groups influence their organizational structure and strategies for social change. Ibid., 296.

112. Walter Berns, "Terms of Endearment: Legislating Love," *Harper's* 261 (October 1980): 18, 20.

113. *1981 Hatch Hearings on Sex Discrimination*, 396–427.

Chapter 7. Fighting the Backlash: Feminist Activism in the 1980s

1. Eliza G. C. Collins and Timothy B. Blodgett, "Sexual Harassment . . . Some See It . . . Some Won't," *Harvard Business Review* (March/April 1981): 76 (quotation from survey conducted by *Harvard Business Review* and *Redbook* magazine).

2. *1981 Hatch Hearings on Sex Discrimination*, 333–706. The bill defined sexual harassment as "the unsolicited, non-reciprocal, offensive sexual behavior that exploits an employee's or prospective employee's sex role such that his/her performance and/or potential as a worker is impaired." The bill provided that "an employer who knowingly, by an act of omission or commission, encourages, fails to prevent, or redress the practice or incident of sexual harassment shall be liable for violations." Orrin Hatch, "Sexual Harassment Awareness and Prevention Act" (draft), United States Senate, 96th Congress, 2nd Session, *Working Women's Institute Collection*. This bill was never introduced.

3. *1981 Hatch Hearings on Sex Discrimination*, 369.

4. Ibid.

5. Ibid., 400.

6. Karen Sauvigné remembers being very impressed because Betty Jean Hall, who testified on behalf of women coal miners, "completely broke any of their stereotyped images" by wearing a pink pastel suit. Sauvigné, telephone interview, 4 February 2001.

7. *1981 Hatch Hearings on Sex Discrimination*, 465.
8. Ibid., 501–11.
9. Ibid., 513.
10. Testimony was also submitted by the Center for Women's Policy Studies, New Responses, Inc., Federally Employed Women, the American Federation of State, County and Municipal Employees, the American Federation of Government Employees, the Project on the Status and Education of Women of the Association of American Colleges.
11. *1981 Hatch Hearings on Sex Discrimination*, 701.
12. Ibid., 678.
13. Ibid., 73.
14. "Sexual Harassment," *Congressional Quarterly Researcher*, 9 August 1991, 548.
15. EEOC Decision 82-13, 29 Fair Empl. Prac. Cas. 1855 (1982).
16. Brief for the United States and the Equal Employment Opportunity Commission as Amici Curiae at 20, *Meritor Savings Bank v. Vinson*, 477 U.S. 57 (1986).
17. Executive Order 12291, 17 February 1981, 46 *Fed. Reg.* 13193 (1981); *see also* Martha Derthick and Paul J. Quirk, *The Politics of Deregulation* (Washington, D.C.: The Brookings Institute, 1985), 31–32.
18. Howell Raines, "U.S. Begins Deregulation Review on Rights and Ecology Guidelines," *New York Times*, 12 August 1981, § A, 1.
19. Letter from Karen Sauvigné, Working Women's Institute, to David Stockman, Office of Management and the Budget, Dated 21 August 1981, *Working Women's Institute Collection*.
20. Letter from Susan Meyer, Executive Director, Working Women's Institute, to Friends of Working Women's Institute (Donors), Dated 21 August 1981, *Working Women's Institute Collection*; Letter from K. C. Wagner, Counseling Director, Working Women's Institute, to Friends (former clients), Dated 21 August 1981 (to clients), *Working Women's Institute Collection*; Letter from Karen Sauvigné to Friends (advocacy organizations), Dated 21 August 1981, *Working Women's Institute Collection*.
21. Letter from Jean D. Linehan to Vice President George Bush, Dated 26 November 1981, *Working Women's Institute Collection*.
22. Letter from Addy Zeni to Vice President George Bush, Dated 14 September 1981, *Working Women's Institute Collection*; Letter from Cynthia Butler to Vice President George Bush, Boyden Gray, David Stockman, Jim Miller, Edwin Harper, and Nathanial Scurry, Dated 30 September 1981, *Working Women's Institute Collection*.
23. Letter from Karen Sauvigné to Vice President Bush, Dated 30 July 1982, *Working Women's Institute Collection*; Letter from Karen Sauvigné to Clarence Thomas, Dated 30 July 1982, *Working Women's Institute Collection*.
24. Letter from Phyllis Berry, Acting Director of the EEOC, to Honorable Bill Bradley, not dated, *Working Women's Institute Collection*; Equal Employment Opportunity Commission, Meeting Notice, 48 Fed. Reg. 9417 (1983).
25. Peter Behr and Joanne Omang, "Impact of Regulation Freeze is Unclear; Targets Not Yet Identified," *New York Times*, 30 January 1981, § A, 4.
26. Raymond M. Lane, "A Man's World: An Update on Sexual Harassment," *Village Voice*, 16–22 December 1981, 22.
27. Lani Guinier, *The Tyranny of the Majority: Fundamental Fairness in Representative Democracy* (New York: The Free Press, 1994), 23–24 (noting Reagan

appointed 366 predominately white male judges to the bench, filling over half the federal judiciary, and that his advisors tested prospective judicial nominees by using ideological litmus tests on civil rights issues such as school desegregation, affirmative action, and other race-conscious remedies).

28. Philip Tyson, "Cassidy Wins," *Potomac News*, 22 September 1980, § A, 1.

29. *Barnes v. Oody*, 514 F. Supp. 23 (E.D. Tenn. 1981).

30. Cheryl M. Fields, "Accused of Sexual Harassment, Male Professor Sues Female Complainants for $23.7-Million," *Chronicle of Higher Education*," 4 May 1981, 1; Anne Field, "Harassment on Campus: Sex in a Tenured Position?" *Ms.*, September 1981, 68; Elizabeth Gray, "Heading Them Off at the Passes," *MacLeans* 94 (1981): 26.

31. *See* Barbara Lindemann and David D. Kadue, *Sexual Harassment in Employment Law* (Washington, D.C.: Bureau of National Affairs, Inc., 1992), 520–34.

32. "In Brief: Professor Says Sex Charges Forced Him To Resign," *Chronicle of Higher Education*, 23 January 1978, 5; *Van Arsdel v. Texas A&M University et al.*, 628 F.2d 344 (5ᵗʰ Cir. 1980) (male professor accused of sexual harassment by female employee); *Korf v. Ball State University et al.*, 726 F.2d 1222 (7ᵗʰ Cir. 1984) (male professor accused of sexual harassment by male students sued for violation of his due process and equal protection rights); *Levitt v. University of Texas at El Paso*, 759 F.2d 1224 (5ᵗʰ Cir. 1985) (male professor accused of sexual harassment by female students sued for violation of his due process rights).

33. *Wiggins v. Whirlpool*, Civil Action No. 85-2200-S (D. Kan. 1985); *Axelrad v. Byoir & Associates, Inc. et al.*, No. 84 Civ. 8936-CSH (S.D.N.Y. 1985); *Spisak v. McDole*, 472 N.E.2d 347 (Ohio 1984); *Equal Employment Opportunity Commission v. Levi Strauss & Co.*, 515 F. Supp. 640 (N.D. Ill. 1981); *Arenas v. Ladish Co.*, 619 F. Supp. 1304 (E.D. Wisc. 1985); *Walker v. Gibson*, 604 F. Supp. 916 (N.D. Ill. 1985) (dismissing the first amendment claim but allowing the other claims); *Arnold v. Burger King Corp. et al.*, 719 F.2d 63 (4ᵗʰ Cir. 1983); Greenbaum and Fraser, "Sexual Harassment in the Workplace," 30–41; Michael Marmo, "Arbitrating Sex Harassment Cases," *Arbitration Journal* 35, no. 1 (March 1980): 35–40;
Lindemann and Kadue, *Sexual Harassment in Employment Law*, 391–401; *McNaughton v. Dillingham Corp. et al.*, 707 F.2d 1042 (9ᵗʰ Cir. 1983).

34. Lindemann and Kadue, *Sexual Harassment in Employment Law*, 530–32; *Huff v. County of Butler*, 524 F. Supp. 751 (W.D. Pa. 1981); *Vanelli v. Reynolds School Dist.*, 667 F.2d 773 (9ᵗʰ Cir. 1982); *Downes v. Federal Aviation Administration*, 775 F.2d 288; *Jackson v. Veterans Administration*, 768 F.2d 1325 (Fed. Cir. 1985); *Snipes v. U.S. Postal Service*, 677 F.2d 375 (4ᵗʰ Cir. 1982); *Barkley v. State Personnel Board*, Civ. No. 81-Ci-0690 (Franklin County, Ky. Cir. Ct., April 30, 1981); *Flinn v. Gorden et al.*, 775 F.2d 1551 (11ᵗʰ Cir. 1985).

35. Verta A. Taylor, "How To Avoid Taking Sexual Harassment Seriously: A New Book That Perpetuates Old Myths: A Review of *Sexual Harassment*—by Mary Coeli Meyer, Inge M. Berchtold, Jeanenne L. Oestreich, and Frederick J. Collins," *Capital University Law Review* 10 (1981): 678.

36. Mary Coeli Meyer, Inge M. Berchtold, Jeannenne L. Oestreich, and Frederick J. Collins, *Sexual Harassment* (New York: Petrocelli Books, Inc. 1981), 109.

37. Ibid., 49.

38. *See*, for example, Letter from Gene Taylor to James Hanley, Dated 18 April 1980, *Sexual Harassment Report*, 31–32 (questioning whether sexual harassment was

really a problem and implying that feminists testifying as to the scope of the problem were unreliable because they "represented a particular point of view").

39. Barbara Gutek, *Sex and the Workplace: The Impact of Sexual Behavior and Harassment on Women, Men, and Organizations* (San Francisco: Jossey-Bass Publishers, 1985), 5.

40. M. Dawn McCaghy, *Sexual Harassment: A Guide to Resources* (Boston: G. K. Hall & Co., 1985), 28–43 (workplace), 75–86 (educational institutions).

41. Collins and Blodgett, "Sexual Harassment," 76; Merit System Protection Board, *Sexual Harassment in the Federal Government: An Update,* (Washington, D.C.: Government Printing Office, 1987); Louise F. Fitzgerald and Sandra L. Shullman, "Sexual Harassment: A Research Analysis and Agenda for the 1990s," *Journal of Vocational Behavior* 42 (1993): 8.

42. Walter Berns, "Terms of Endearment: Legislating Love," *Harper's*, October 1980, 14–16, 18, 20.

43. Charles E. Marske, Steven Vago, and Ariene Taich, "Combatting Sexual Harassment: A New Awareness," *USA Today*, March 1980, 45.

44. *Sexual Harassment Report*, 31.

45. *Equal Employment Opportunity and Sexual Harassment in the Postal Service, Hearings before the Committee on Post Office and Civil Service*, U.S. House of Representatives, 96th Congress, Second Session, 27 October 1980, 12.

46. *1981 Hatch Hearings on Sex Discrimination*, 397.

47. Meyer, et al., *Sexual Harassment*, xi.

48. Anita Hill, *Speaking Truth to Power* (New York: Doubleday, 1997).

49. *Miller*, 418 F. Supp. at 236.

50. Mary Bralove, "A Cold Shoulder, Career Women Decry Sexual Harassment by Bosses and Clients," *Wall Street Journal*, 19 January 1976, 1.

51. *1981 Hatch Hearings on Sex Discrimination*, 400.

52. Meyer, et al., *Sexual Harassment*, 79.

53. Walter Berns, "Terms of Endearment: Legislating Love," *Harper's*, October 1980, 18.

54. Ibid., 396–99.

55. Ibid., 9.

56. Ibid., 13.

57. AASC, *Fighting Sexual Harassment*, 89.

58. "Statement of Purpose," Working Women's Institute, 1977, *Karen Sauvigné, Private Papers*.

59. White, Angle, and Moore, *Sexual Harassment in the Coal Industry*.

60. Speak-out on Sexual Harassment of Women at Work, May 4, 1975, Ithaca, NY, (transcript), 12, *Karen Sauvigné, Private Papers*.

61. Gordon, "The Politics of Sexual Harassment," 12.

62. Carol Krucoff, "Careers: Sexual Harassment on the Job," *Washington Post*, 25 July 1979, § B, 5.

63. Catharine MacKinnon, "Introduction," *Capital University Law Review* 10 (1981): ii.

64. AASC, "Organizing Against Sexual Harassment," 21–22, 33.

65. Gordon, "The Politics of Sexual Harassment," 12.

66. Fairness Committee, "The Politics of Sexual Harassment," *Aegis*, Summer 1982, 11.

67. "Combat Sexual Harassment on the Job," *Aegis*, May/June 1979, 24; *Gates v. Brockway Glass Co., Inc.*, 93 L.R.R.M. 2367 (C.D. Cal. 1976). *See* discussion of union responses to the issue in chapter 5.

68. The following description of this case is based on several articles, including Fairness Committee, "The Politics of Sexual Harassment," *Aegis*, Summer 1982, 5; Anne Field, "Harassment on Campus: Sex in a Tenured Position?" *Ms.* September 1981, 68; Cheryl M. Fields, "Accused of Sexual Harassment, Male Professor Sues Female Complainants for $23.7-Million," *Chronicle of Higher Education*, 4 May 1981, 1.

69. Fairness Committee, "The Politics of Sexual Harassment," *Aegis*, Summer 1982, 10.

70. Ibid., 8–9.

71. Ibid., 6.

72. Rita Arditti, interview by author, Orlando, FL, 10 June 2005; Estelle Disch, interview by author, Orlando, FL, 10 June 2005.

73. Fairness Committee, "The Politics of Sexual Harassment," *Aegis*, Summer 1982, 11.

74. Ibid., 10.

75. Ibid., 11.

76. Ibid., 8.

77. Cheryl M. Fields, "Accused of Sexual Harassment, Male Professor Sues Female Complainants for $23.7-Million," *Chronicle of Higher Education*, 4 May 1981, 4.

78. *Stanko and Bunster v. Clark University*, No. 81-5088, Mass. Super. Ct., Middlesex Cty. (filed 13 October 1981).

79. Dziech and Weiner, *The Lecherous Professor*, 28.

80. Lorenzo Middleton, "'Mean Little Cases' Give New Dimension to Controversies over Academic Freedom," *Chronicle of Higher Education*, 28 April 1980, 1. A subsequent letter to the editor protested this characterization. Letter to the Editor by Donna Moore and Betty Schmitz of Montana State University, *Chronicle of Higher Education*, 28 May 1980.

81. AASC, "Organizing Against Sexual Harassment," 28, 33.

82. Gordon, "The Politics of Sexual Harassment," 11.

83. *See* Gwendolyn Mink, *Hostile Environment: The Political Betrayal of Sexually Harassed Women* (Ithaca: Cornell University Press, 2000), 114–40.

84. Weeks, et al., "The Transformation of Sexual Harassment," 449 (based on an interview with Maura T. Zlody).

85. Klein, telephone interview, 26 March 2001; Rubinett, telephone interview, 23 June 2001; Lynn Rubinett, "Sex and Economics: The Tie That Binds. Judicial Approaches to Sexual Harassment as a Title VII Violation," *Journal of Law and Inequality* 4 (July 1986): 245–93.

86. According to Sauvigné, big foundations redirected their money to address the urgent need to provide the social safety net that Reagan Republicans were dismantling. Sauvigné, telephone interview, 12 February 2001. K. C. Wagner attributed this loss of foundation support to the "conservative backlash against priorities, programs, and services to women." K. C. Wagner, "A Socialist Feminist Perspective," in *Not for Women Only: Social Work Practice for a Feminist Future*, eds. Mary Bricker-Jenkins and Nancy R. Hooyman (Silver Springs, MD: National Association of Social Workers, 1986), 66; *see also WWI 1982 Report*, 2. *Working Women's Institute Collection*.

87. "Sexual Harassment Brief Bank and Bibliography," *Women's Rights Law Reporter* 8 (Fall 1985): 267–98.

88. WWI, *Equal Employment Opportunity Commission: How to File a Job-Related Sexual Harassment Complaint* (New York: Working Women's Institute, 1983);

WWI, *National Labor Relations Board: How to File an Unfair Labor Practice Charge for Job-Related Sexual Harassment* (New York: Working Women's Institute, 1983); WWI, *New York City Commission on Human Rights and New York State Division of Human Rights: How To File a Job-Related Sexual Harassment Complaint* (New York: Working Women's Institute, 1983); WWI, *Tort and Contract Law: How to File a Job-Related Sexual Harassment Complaint* (New York: Working Women's Institute, 1983).

89. Working Women's Institute Union Survey on Sexual Harassment, *Working Women's Institute Collection*.

90. Fact Sheet: Joint Project on Sexual Harassment/Sex Discrimination in Employment, *Working Women's Institute Collection*.

91. "Sexual Harassment," *Congressional Quarterly Research*, 9 August 1991, 545.

92. "Sexual Harassment in the Mines Workshop," Second National Conference of Women Coal Miners, Beckley, WV, May 1980 (videocasette), *Coal Employment Project Collection* (Accession 355, Tape 59).

93. "Sexual Harassment Workshop," Third National Conference of Women Coal Miners, 1981 (videocasette), *Coal Employment Project Collection* (Accession 355, Tape 66).

94. "Sexual Harassment/Discrimination and CEP Legal Referral Network," Eleventh National Conference of Women Coal Miners, June 1989, IL, *Coal Employment Project Collection* (Accession 355, Tape 14, Series XII A).

95. Letter from Joyce Dukes to Jerry King, Dated 4 August 1980, with attached Coal Employment Project Proposal, *Coal Employment Project Collection* (Accession 355, Box 2, Folder 14); Jan Hoffman, "Digging in Hell: The Story of Women Coal Miners," *Mademoiselle*, May 1983, 166; Raymond M. Lane, "A Man's World: An Update on Sexual Harassment," *Village Voice*, 15–22 December 1981, 1; "Sexual Harassment Cases Against Coal Companies Increase," *Coal Age*, November 1984, 19.

96. "No Gentleman," *Mail* (Charleston, WV), 30 September 1982.

97. Diane Nelson, "Ending Sexual Harassment," *Dominion Post* (Morgantown, WV), May 1983; "What Are the Men Doing Down There?" *News* (Welch, WV), May 1983; Jan Hoffman, "Digging in Hell: The Story of Women Coal Miners," *Mademoiselle*, May 1983, 166; Maggie Prieto, "Women Coal Miners Fight Sexual Harassment," *Off Our Backs*, August/September 1983, 2 ; "Goes With the Job," *60 Minutes*, 3 October 1982, *Coal Employment Project Collection* (Accession 355, Tapes 153–154); "Woman to Woman," KTLA, Los Angeles, CA, 8 November 1983, *Coal Employment Project Collection* (Accession 355, Tapes 156); "Burns Sexual Harassment Suit," Newswatch 4, WOAY-TV 4, Thomas Broadcasting Company, Oak Hill, WV, undated, *Coal Employment Project Collection* (Accession 355, Tapes 163, 167).

98. Molly Martin, "City Light: Women Workers File Suit," *Seattle Post Intelligencer*, in *Coal Employment Project Collection* (Accession 355, Box 73, Folder 23); *see also* Martin, *Hard-Hatted Women*.

99. "Sexual Harassment of Women in Law Enforcement," *Equal Rights Advocate* (Winter 1985): 1.

100. "Declaring War on Sexual Harassment," Annual Meeting of the National Organization for Women, 1987, Ohio (audiocassette), *NOW Collection*.

101. Bernice R. Sandler, *Writing a Letter to the Sexual Harasser: Another Way of Dealing With the Problem* (Washington, D.C.: Project on the Status and Education

of Women, 1983); Project on the Status and Education of Women, *Sexual Harassment on Campus* (Washington, D.C.: Association of American Colleges, 1985) (articles on sexual harassment reprinted from *On Campus With Women,* Summer 1982 to Spring 1985); Simon, telephone interview, 25 April 2001; Phyllis L. Crocker, "Annotated Bibliography on Sexual Harassment in Education," *Women's Rights Law Reporter* 7 (Winter 1982): 91–106; *Journal of the National Association for Women Deans, Administrators, & Counselors* (Winter 1983); *Title IX Line* (Fall 1983); "AAUP Condemns Sexual Harassment and Offers Procedure for Complaints," *On Campus With Women* (Fall 1983); "University Allocates $7,500 to Prevent Sexual Harassment and Rape," and "How to Distinguish Sexual Harassment from Flirtation," *On Campus With Women* (Fall 1983); Dzeich and Weiner, *The Lecherous Professor;* Jean Hughes and Bernice Sandler, *In Case of Sexual Harassment—A Guide for Women Students* (Washington, D.C.: Center for Women Policy Studies, 1986).

102. Wendy Cole, "Students Reveal Instances of Sex Harassment at C.U.," *Cornell Daily Sun,* 5 November 1981, 14; Wendy Cole, "Officials Discuss Grievance Channels," *Cornell Daily Sun,* 6 November 1981, 1; Wendy Cole, "Professors Discuss Sexual Harassment," *Cornell Daily Sun,* 9 November 1981, 1.

103. Martha Chamallas, "Writing About Sexual Harassment: A Guide to the Literature," *UCLA Women's Law Journal* 4 (1993): 39; Rossein, "Sex Discrimination," 271–305; Nadine Taub, "Keeping Women in Their Place: Stereotyping *Per Se* as a Form of Employment Discrimination," *Boston College Law Review* 21 (January 1980): 345–418; Gary R. Siniscalco, "Sexual Harassment and Employer Liability: The Flirtation that Could Cost a Fortune," *Employee Relations Law Journal* 6 (1980–1981): 277.

104. "Sexual Harassment Symposium," *Capital University Law Review* (Spring 1981): 445–606; "Beyond Nine to Five: Sexual Harassment on the Job," *Journal of Social Issues* (Winter 1982): 1–148; "Sexual Harassment on Campus," *Journal of the National Association for Women Deans, Administrators, & Counselors* (Winter 1983): 1–50.

105. The rate of sexual harassment in the studies reviewed in the Gruber article ranged from 28% to 75%. From this, Gruber estimated that 44% of women have been sexually harassed. James E. Gruber, "Methodological Problems and Policy Implications in Sexual Harassment Research," *Population Research and Policy Review* 9 (1990): 238, 248.

106. Fitzgerald and Shullman, "Sexual Harassment," 8.

107. Gruber, "Methodological Problems," 235–54; McCaghy, *Sexual Harassment,* 28–43, 75–85 (listing surveys); Kenneth R. Wilson and Linda A. Kraus, "Sexual Harassment in the University," *Journal of College Student Personnel* (May 1983) (finding that one in three female students reported experiencing sexual harassment by one or more male teachers); Barbara Gutek, Bruce Morasch, and Aaron G. Cohen, "Interpreting Social-Sexual Behavior in a Work Setting," *Journal of Vocational Behavior* 22 (1983): 30–48; Fitzgerald and Shullman, "Sexual Harassment," 12–13 (listing subsequent studies replicating this finding).

108. Inger W. Jensen and Barbara A. Gutek, "Attributions and Assignment of Responsibility in Sexual Harassment," *Journal of Social Issues* (Winter 1982): 121–36; *see also* Barbara Gutek, et al., "Sexuality and the Workplace," *Basic and Applied Social Psychology* (September 1980): 255–65; Barbara A. Gutek, *Experiences of Sexual Harassment: Results from a Representative Survey* (Bethesda, MD: National

Institute of Mental Health, 1981); Barbara Gutek and Bruce Morasch, "Sex Roles, Sex-Role Spillover, and Sexual Harassment of Women at Work," *Journal of Social Issues* (Winter 1982): 30–48; Barbara Gutek and C. Nakamura, "Gender Roles and Sexuality in the World of Work," in *Changing Boundaries*, ed. Elizabeth Allgeier and Naomi McCormick (Palo Alto, CA: Mayfield Publishing Company, 1983); Gutek, *Sex and the Workplace*.

109. Collins and Blodgett, "Sexual Harassment," 76–95; Merit System Protection Board, *Sexual Harassment in the Federal Government: An Update*; M. Martindale, *Sexual Harassment in the Military: 1988* (Arlington, VA: Defense Manpower Data Center, 1988); Donald E. Maypole and Rosemarie Skaine, "Sexual Harassment of Blue Collar Workers," *Journal of Sociology and Social Welfare* 9 (1982): 682–95; James E. Gruber and Lars Bjorn, "Blue-Collar Blues: The Sexual Harassment of Women Autoworkers," *Work and Occupations* 9 (August 1982): 271–98 (finding that black women were more likely to be severely harassed); Muriet Faltz Lembright and Jeffrey W. Riemer, "Women Truckers' Problems and the Impact of Sponsorship," *Work and Occupations* 9 (November 1982): 457–74; Edward LaFontaine and Leslie Tredeau, "The Frequency, Sources and Correlates of Sexual Harassment Among Women in Traditional Male Occupations," *Sex Roles* 15 (1986): 423–32; Beth E. Schneider, "Consciousness About Sexual Harassment Among Heterosexual and Lesbian Women Workers," *Journal of Social Issues* (Winter 1982): 75–98.

110. Dair L. Gillespie and Ann Leffler, "The Politics of Research Methodology in Claims-Making Activities: Social Science and Sexual Harassment," *Social Problems* 34 (1987): 490–508; Gruber, "Methodological Problems," 237; Fitzgerald and Shullman, "Sexual Harassment," 13–16, 19.

111. McAdam, *Political Process*, xxvi.

Chapter 8. Legal Victory: The Supreme Court and Beyond

1. Testimony of M. Vinson, Tr. Jan. 23, 1980, Vol. III at 50–59, 69, 81. *Meritor Savings Bank v. Vinson*, 477 U.S. 57 (1986).
2. Judith Ludvic, an attorney who had represented Vinson in a divorce proceeding, referred Vinson to another attorney, John Meisburg, Jr., who initially represented her in the district court. Meisburg withdrew in June of 1979, before the trial of the case. Barry then represented Vinson in the district court, on appeal, before the Supreme Court, and on remand. Brief for Mechelle Vinson at 4 & 32, *Vinson v. Taylor*, 753 F.2d 141 (D.C. Cir. 1985) (hereafter *Vinson's Brief*); *see also* Marshall, "Closing the Gaps," 784; Lynn Simross, "An Endangered Species: Discrimination Law a Losing Proposition, Says Attorney Pat Barry," *Los Angeles Times*, 6 April 1988, § 5, 1.
3. Vinson applied to appeal *in forma pauperis*, which would have waived the appeal costs based on allegations of poverty, and she sought to have the United States pay the cost of her trial transcript for use on appeal, but Judge Penn denied both requests. *Vinson v. Taylor*, 27 Fair Empl. Prac. Cas. (BNA) 948 (1980).
4. Vinson's Reply Brief at 4–5, *Vinson v. Taylor*, 753 F.2d 141.
5. *Vinson v. Taylor*, 753 F.2d at 141, 144–45. Judge Robinson cited Catharine MacKinnon's *Sexual Harassment of Working Women* at 146 n. 37.
6. Ibid., 145.
7. Per Curiam Order Denying Appellees' Suggestion for Rehearing En Banc, 14 May 1985. *Vinson v. Taylor*, 753 F.2d.

8. The sole female commissioner briefed the commission on the issue and suggested the position later taken in the amicus brief, in contradiction to the recommendations of the commission's Acting General Counsel. Memorandum from Commissioner R. Gaull Silberman to Chairman Clarence Thomas, Commissioner Tony Gallegos, Commissioner William Webb, and Commissioner Fred Alvarez, Dated 28 October 1985, Subject: Commission Participation as Amicus Curiae in *PSFS Savings Bank, FSB v. Vinson,* No. 84–1979 (S. Ct.), reprinted in *Daily Labor Report* 210 (30 October 1985): E-1; Memorandum from Johnny J. Butler, General Counsel (Acting), to Chairman Clarence Thomas, Commissioner Tony Gallegos, Commissioner William Webb, Commissioner Fred Alvarez, and Commissioner R. Gaull Silberman, Dated 24 October 1984, Subject: *PSFS Savings, FSB v. Mechelle Vinson, et al. (Vinson v. Taylor,* 753 F.2d 141), reprinted in *Daily Labor Report* 210 (30 October 1985): E-2.
9. Brief of Petitioner at 10, *Meritor,* 477 U.S. 57.
10. Brief for the United States and the Equal Employment Opportunity Commission as Amici Curiae at Part A, *Meritor,* 477 U.S. 57 (hereafter *United States and the EEOC Brief*).
11. U.S. Chamber of Commerce Brief, *Meritor,* 477 U.S. 57 at 2, 4, 7, 9, 11, 15, 16.
12. Ibid., 5.
13. *United States and the EEOC Brief* at Part A.3.
14. Working Women's Institute wrote a brief joined by the Committee Against Sexual Harassment in Sacramento, CA, the Connecticut Women's Educational and Legal Fund, the Women's Rights Committee of the New York County Lawyers' Association, New York State Committee on Pay Equity, Women on the Job of Port Washington, NY, Women's Alliance for Job Equity of Philadelphia, Women in Self-Help of the New York State Displaced Homemaker Program, New York Women Against Rape, the Women's Counseling Project, Non-Traditional Employment for Women, the Sisterhood of Black Single Mothers, the Women's Rights Project of the Instituto Puertorriqueno de Derechos Civiles, and the Workers Defense League. Brief of Working Women's Institute, et al. as Amici Curiae at 8–37, *Meritor,* 477 U.S. 57, 65–66 (hereafter *Working Women's Institute Brief*). The Women's Legal Defense Fund wrote a brief supported by the American Association of University Women, the Asian Pacific American Bar Association of the Greater Washington, D.C. Area, the Center for Constitutional Rights, the Employment Law Center of the Legal Aid Society in San Francisco, Equal Rights Advocates, the Mexican American Women's National Association, the National Conference of Black Lawyers, the National Emergency Civil Liberties Committee, the National Institute for Women of Color, the National Organization for Women, NOW Legal Defense and Education Fund, the Organization of Pan Asian American Women, Inc., Wider Opportunities for Women, the Women's Bar Association of D.C., Women Employed in Chicago, Women's Law Project, and the National Board of the YWCA of the USA. Brief Amicus Curiae of the Women's Legal Defense Fund, et al., *Meritor,* 477 U.S. 57, 65–66 (hereafter *Women's Legal Defense Fund Brief*). Other amici included Equal Rights Advocates and Women Employed; women's bar associations from Massachusetts, Minnesota, Michigan, Colorado, and New York; The American Federation of Labor and Congress of Industrial Organizations (AFL-CIO), the Coal Employment Project, the Coalition of Labor Union Women, and the National Education Association; the states of New Jersey, California, Connecticut, Illinois, Minnesota, New Mexico, New York, Vermont, and the Pennsylvania Human Relations Commission; and twenty-nine members of Congress.

15. *Respondent's Brief, Meritor,* 477 U.S. 57 at 17–18.
16. Ibid., 18.
17. *Working Women's Institute Brief,* 55–58.
18. *Women's Legal Defense Fund Brief,* Part I.
19. *Working Women's Institute Brief,* 24–26.
20. Ibid., 26–27.
21. Women's Bar Associations Brief at 11, *Meritor,* 477 U.S. 57.
22. *Women's Legal Defense Fund Brief,* Part I.
23. *Vinson's Brief,* 43.
24. Women's Bar Associations Brief at 9, 11, *Meritor,* 477 U.S. 57.
25. *Vinson's Brief,* 45–46.
26. *Working Women's Institute Brief,* 24–26.
27. *Meritor,* 477 U.S. 57, 65–66.
28. *Meritor,* 477 U.S. 57, 67 (italics added). This standard, however, was more favorable to plaintiffs than the one set out in *Henson,* which required that the alleged conduct must be "sufficiently severe and persistent to affect seriously the psychological well-being of employees." 682 F.2d at 904.
29. "Vinson Vindicated," *Legal Times,* 14 October 1991, 3 (reporting that Vinson received some money in the settlement and that one of her attorneys said she was "very pleased" with the settlement).
30. Lynn Simross, "An Endangered Species: Discrimination Law a Losing Proposition, Says Attorney Pat Barry," *Los Angeles Times,* 6 April 1988, § 5, 1.
31. Ronni Sandroff, "Sexual Harassment in the Fortune 500," *Working Woman,* December 1988, 69, 71.
32. *Sexual Harassment: Walking the Corporate Fine Line,* New York: NOW Legal Defense and Education Fund, 1987, videocassette; *Sexual Harassment: No Laughing Matter,* Advantage Media Inc., 1984, videocassette; *Sexual Harassment Awareness Programs,* Philips Office Associates, 1983, videocassette.
33. "Harvard Women Subject to Harassment," *On Campus With Women* (Spring 1985); "Sexual Harassment at Penn State," *On Campus With Women* (Summer 1984); "Punishable at Princeton: University Adopts New Rules on Harassment," and "Sexual Harassment Study at Iowa State University," *On Campus With Women* (Fall 1982); "Harvard Releases Sexual Harassment Report," *On Campus With Women* (Winter 1984); "Distinguishing Between Sexual Attraction and Sexual Harassment: MIT," *On Campus With Women* (Spring 1983); "Sexual Harassment and Professional Fitness," *On Campus With Women* (Fall 1983); "Professor Suspended Without Pay for Harassing Student," *On Campus With Women* (Summer 1984); "Professor Violates Terms of Suspension for Sexual Harassment Charge," *On Campus With Women* (Spring 1984) (University of Minnesota); "Michigan, Minnesota, and Idaho: Resignations Due to Harassment Charges," *On Campus With Women* (Winter 1984); "Sexual Harassment Charges Cause Censure and Suspension," *On Campus With Women* (Spring 1983) (president of Hillsborough Community College in Florida received a ninety-day suspension for sexual harassment of female employees and a student); "Minnesota Law School Settles Sexual Harassment Suit for $300,000," *On Campus With Women* (Spring 1985); "Minnesota Law School Charged in $3 Million Harassment Suit," and "Showing Pornographic Film Leads to $4 Million Lawsuit," *On Campus With Women* (Summer 1984) (St. Louis University); "$230,000 Settlement in New Jersey Harassment Suit," *On Campus With Women* (Spring 1984) (Ramapo College in New Jersey);

"A New Sort of Policy: Sexual Harassment Defense Insurance," *On Campus With Women* (Spring 1983).

34. "Top Awards to Victims," *Congressional Quarterly Researcher*, 9 August 1991, 542.
35. "Firing Employee Who Helped Co-Worker File Harassment Complaint Violates Law," *On Campus With Women* (Summer 1980): 14 (*Jordan v. Blaw Knox Foundry and Machinery in Wheeling, WV*).
36. *Wright v. Methodist Youth Services*, 511 F. Supp. 307 (N.D. Ill. 1981) (black male was terminated from defendant social services agency because of his resistance to homosexual advances from his supervisor); *Goluszek v. H.P. Smith*, 697 F. Supp. 1452 (N.D. Ill. 1988).
37. *Craik v. University of Minnesota*, 731 F.2d 465 (8th Cir. 1984).
38. *Shellhammer v. Lewallen*, 770 F.2d 167 (6th Cir. 1985); "Housing Law Used in Sex Harassment Case," *New York Times*, 11 December 1983, 20.
39. Lexis-Nexis search of the *New York Times* by the author, 27 December 2006. The following years were: 1995–280, 1996–238, 1997–379, 1998–640, 1999–236, 2000–138, 2001–140, 2002–115, 2003–124, 2004–155, and 2005–99.
40. Equal Employment Opportunity Commission, Sexual Harassment Charges, EEOC & FEPAs Combined: FY 1992–FY 2005, at *htto://www.eeoc.gov/stats/harass.html* (accessed 27 December 2006). The percentage of men filing cases has steadily risen and in 2005 represented 14.3% of all cases filed.
41. *Harris v. Forklift Systems, Inc.*, 510 U.S. 17 (1993); *Oncale v. Sundowner Offshore Services*, 523 U.S. 75 (1998);
42. *Faragher v. City of Boca Raton*, 524 U.S. 775 (1998); *Burlington Industries v. Ellerth*, 524 U.S. 742 (1998).
43. *Pennsylvania State Police v. Suders*, 542 U.S. 129 (2004); *Burlington North v. White*, 126 S. Ct. 2405 (2006) (case involving a white male supervisor harassing a black female plaintiff).
44. *Franklin v. Gwinnett County Public Schools*, 523 U.S. 60 (1992); *Gebster v. Lago Vista Independent School District*, 523 U.S. 274 (1998); *Davis v. Monroe County Board of Education*, 526 S. Ct. 629 (1999).
45. *Robinson v. Jacksonville Shipyards*, 760 F. Supp. 1486 (M.D. Fl. 1991); *Ellison v. Brady*, 924 F. 2d 872 (9th Cir. 1991); *DiCenso v. Cisneros*, 96 F.2d 1004 (7th Cir. 1996); *Jenson v. Eveleth Taconite*, 842 F. Supp. 847 (1993), 130 F.3d 1287 (8th Cir. 1997).
46. *North Country*, Warner Brothers Entertainment Corp., 2005. The movie was based on a book by Clara Bingham and Laura Leedy Gansler entitled *Class Action: The Story of Lois Jenson and the Landmark Case that Changed Sexual Harassment Law.*
47. Unruh Civil Rights Act, California Civil Code, § 51.9 (1995); California General Education Code, § 212.5, 48900.2 (1995).
48. Harriet Chiang, "Judge Halves $7.1 Million Award in Harassment Case But Bay Area Woman Will Still Get Record Sum," *San Francisco Chronicle*, 29 November 1994, §A, 14; EEOC, *EEOC Responds to Final Report of Mitsubishi Consent Decree Monitors*, 23 (Washington, D.C.: EEOC, May 2001) (EEOC press release).
49. The Street Harassment Project in New York City and Hollabac NYC are two example of local collective action. The Street Harassment Project at *http://www.streetharassmentproject.org/*; HollabanNYC at *http://www.hollabacknyc.blogspot.com/*; see also Maggie Hadleigh-West's film War Zone (Media Educaiton Foundation, 1998).

50. Daphne Patai, *Heterophobia: Sexual Harassment and the Future of Feminism* (Lanham, MD: Rowman & Littlefield Publishers, 1998).
51. Jane Gallop, *Feminist Accused of Sexual Harassment* (Durham, NC: Duke University Press, 1997). *See also* Elizabeth Fox-Genovese, "Rethinking Sexual Harassment," *Partisan Review* (1996): 366–74. Fox-Genovese was also accused of sexual harassment by an employee who was a former graduate student.
52. National Council for Research on Women, *Sexual Harassment: Research and Resources*, 3rd ed. (New York: National Council for Research on Women, 1995), 50.
53. 240 F.3d 200 (3rd Cir. 2001).

Conclusion: Entering the Mainstream

1. McAdam, McCarthy, and Zald, *Comparative Perspectives*, 25.
2. Ibid.
3. Ibid. at 2.
4. Ibid. at 5.
5. Lacking the information and perspective that others afford, isolated individuals would seem especially likely to explain their troubles on the basis of personal rather than system attributions. The movement provided "system attributions" that afforded the necessary rationale for resistance. Ibid. at 9.
6. Ibid.
7. Susan Brownmiller and Delores Alexander, "How We Got From Here: From Carmita Wood to Anita Hill," *Ms.*, January/February 1992, 71.
8. Ellis, "Sexual Harassment and Race."
9. Kimberlé Crenshaw, "Race, Gender, and Sexual Harassment," *Southern California Law Review* 65 (1992): 1467, 1469–70; Crenshaw, "Mapping the Margins," 93–118.
10. John Beckwith and Barbara Beckwith, "Sexual Harassment: Your Body or Your Job," *Science for the People* (July/August 1980): 6.
11. Yla Eason, "When Your Boss Wants Sex," *Essence*, March 1981, 82. Eason also argued that, as the last hired and the first fired, African-American women have the least to lose, noting that the most oppressed people tended to be in the forefront of civil uprisings.
12. Brief for Appellant, *Miller v. Bank of America*, 600 F. 2d 211.
13. Joint Pre-Trial Statement at 7, *Munford v. James T. Barnes and Co.*, 441 F. Supp. 459 (E.D. Mich. 1977).
14. *Continental Can Company*, 297 N.W.2d at 246.
15. Crenshaw, "Whose Story Is It Anyway?" 421–34.
16. The Merit System Protection Board studies on sexual harassment in 1981, 1988, and 1995 produced similar rates of sexual harassment. Merit Systems Protection Board, *Sexual Harassment in the Federal Workplace: Is It A Problem*; Merit System Protection Board, *Sexual Harassment of Federal Workers: An Update*; Merit System Protection Board, *Sexual Harassment in the Federal Workplace: Trends, Progress, Continuing Challenges* (Washington, D.C.: Government Printing Office, 1995). Rates of sexual harassment at educational institutions remain high also. Michelle L. Kelley and Beth Parsons, "Sexual Harassment in the 1990s: A University-Wide Survey of Faculty, Administrators, Staff, and Students," *Journal of Higher*

Education 71 (2000): 548–69 (between 19% and 43% of females at Ohio State University reported sexual harassment). Despite these high rates of harassment, Freada Klein believes that sexual harassment is generally not as egregious today as it was in the 1970s. Klein, telephone interview, 26 March 2001.

17. Mary F. Rogers, "Clarence Thomas, Patriarchal Discourse and Public/Private Spheres," *Sociological Quarterly* 39 (1998): 289–308 (describing how Thomas used arguments about privacy to avoid inquiries into whether he sexually harassed Anita Hill). Bill Clinton did the same thing. Both men also attributed political motives to their accusers.

18. Mink, *Hostile Environment*, 77, 115.

19. See, for example, Geoghegan, *Which Side Are You On?*.

20. Hoff, *Law, Gender, and Injustice*, 255. She noted that the treatment of the female employee in *Meritor* was so blatant that it would be difficult to apply to "'normal,' on-the-job examples of gender-biased harassment of female employees in the workplace." Ibid., 258–59.

21. Pamela Paul, *Pornified: How Pornography is Transforming Our Lives, Our Relationships, and Our Families* (New York: Times Books, 2005); Ariel Levy, *Female Chauvinist Pigs: Women and the Rise of Raunch Culture* (New York: Free Press, 2005).

22. Nan Stein, "Bullying or Sexual Harassment? The Missing Discourse of Rights in an Era of Zero Tolerance," *Arizona Law Review* 45 (Fall 2003): 783–99; James E. Gruber and Phoebe Morgan, eds., *In the Company of Men: Male Dominance and Sexual Harassment* (Boston: Northeastern University Press, 2005), x.

Bibliography

Books and Articles

Abrams, Kathryn. "The New Jurisprudence of Sexual Harassment." *Cornell Law Review.* 83 (1998): 1169–230.

Alliance Against Sexual Coercion. *Combatiendo El Hostigamiento Sexual.* Cambridge: Alliance Against Sexual Coercion, 1982.

——. *Fighting Sexual Harassment: An Advocacy Handbook.* Boston: Alliance Against Sexual Coercion, 1979.

——. *Mitos y realidades sobre el hostigemiento sexual.* Cambridge: Alliance Against Sexual Coercion, 1981.

——. "Organizing Against Sexual Harassment." *Radical America.* 15 (July/August 1981): 17–34.

——. *Sexual Harassment: An Annotated Bibliography.* Cambridge: Alliance Against Sexual Coercion, 1980.

——. *Sexual Harassment at the Workplace.* Cambridge: Alliance Against Sexual Coercion, 1977.

——. *Strategies for Change: Working Women and Sexual Harassment.* Cambridge: Alliance Against Sexual Coercion, 1981.

——. University Grievance Procedures, Title IX and Sexual Harassment on Campus. Cambridge: Alliance Against Sexual Coercion, 1980.

——. Who's Hurt and Who's Liable: Sexual Harassment in Massachusetts Schools. A Curriculum and Guide for School Personnel. Cambridge: Alliance Against Sexual Coercion, 1981.

——. *Why Men Harass.* Cambridge: Alliance Against Sexual Coercion, 1979.

American Association of University Women Educational Foundation. *Hostile Hallways: The AAUW Survey on Sexual Harassment in America's Schools.* Washington, D.C.: AAUW Educational Foundation, June 1993.

American Federation of State, County and Municipal Employees. *On the Job Sexual Harassment: What the Union Can Do.* Washington, D.C.: American Federation of State, County and Municipal Employees, 1981.

Amott, Teresa and Julie Matthaei. Race, Gender, and Work: A Multicultural Economic History of Women in the United States. Boston: South End Press, 1991.

Arriola, Elvia R. "'What's the Big Deal?' Women in the New York City Construction Industry and Sexual Harassment Law, 1970–1985." *Columbia Human Rights Law Review.* 22 (1990): 21–71.

Atkinson, Jr., Joseph and Diane R. Layden. "A Federal Response to Sexual Harassment: Policy-Making at Johnson Space Center, NASA." In *Sexuality Organizations: Romantic and Coercive Behavior at Work*, eds. Dail Ann Neugarten and Jay M. Shafritz, 100–106. Oak Park, Ill.: Moore Publishing Company, Inc., 1980.

Backhouse, Constance, et al. *Fighting Sexual Harassment: An Advocacy Handbook.* Cambridge: Alliance Against Sexual Coercion, 1979.

Backhouse, Constance and Leah Cohen. *The Secret Oppression: Sexual Harassment of Working Women.* Toronto: Macmillan of Canada, 1978.

Baer, Judith. The Chains of Protection: The Judicial Response to Women's Labor Legislation. Westport, CT: Greenwood Press, 1978.

Baker, N.L. "Sexual Harassment and Job Satisfaction in Traditional and Nontraditional Industrial Occupations." Ph.D. diss., California School of Professional Psychology, 1989.

Banaszak, Lee Ann. "Women's Movements and Women in Movements: Influencing American Democracy from the 'Outside'?" Presented at the annual meeting of the Midwest Political Science Association. Chicago, IL , 20–23 April 2006.

Baxandall, Rosalyn and Linda Gordon, eds. *Dear Sisters: Dispatches from the Women's Liberation Movement.* New York: Basic Books, 2000.

Baxter, Jr., Ralph H. *Sexual Harassment in the Workplace: A Guide to the Law.* New York: Executive Enterprises Publications Co., Inc., 1981.

Beckwith, John and Barbara Beckwith. "Sexual Harassment: Your Body or Your Job." *Science for the People.* (July/August 1980): 6.

Benson, Donna J. and Gregg E. Thomson. "Sexual Harassment on a University Campus: The Confluence of Authority Relations, Sexual Interest, and Gender Stratification." *Social Problems.* 29 (February 1982): 236–51.

Bernstein, Anita. "Treating Sexual Harassment with Respect." *Harvard Law Review.* 111 (1997): 446–527.

Bevacqua, Maria. "Anti-Rape Coalitions: Radical, Liberal, Black, and White Feminists Challenging Boundaries." In *Forcing Radical Alliances Across Difference: Coalition Politics for the New Millennium,* eds. Jill Bystydzienski & Steven P. Schacht, 163–76. New York: Rowman & Littlefield, 2001.

"Beyond Nine to Five: Sexual Harassment on the Job." *Journal of Social Issues.* (Winter 1982): 1–148.

Bingham, Clara and Laura Leedy Gansler. Class Action: The Story of Lois Jenson and the Landmark Case that Changed Sexual Harassment Law. New York: Doubleday, 2002.

Bloustein, Edward J., President, Rutgers University. "Memorandum to All University Personnel, Regarding Issue of Sexual Harassment." 5 February 1979.

Borgida, Eugene and Susan T. Fiske, eds. "Gender Stereotyping, Sexual Harassment, and the Law." *Journal of Social Issues.* 51 (1995): 1–207.

Bowman, Cynthia Grant. "Street Harassment and the Informal Ghettoization of Women." *Harvard Law Review.* 106 (January 1993): 517–80.

Breines, Winifred. The Trouble Between Us: An Uneasy History of White and Black Women in the Feminist Movement. New York: Oxford University Press, 2006.

Brodsky, Carroll M. *The Harassed Worker.* Lexington, Mass.: Lexington Books, 1976.

Brown, Helen Gurley. *Sex and the Office.* New York: Random House, 1964.

Brownmiller, Susan. *In Our Time: Memoir of a Revolution.* New York: Dial Press, 1999.

Buek, Alexandra. *Sexual Harassment: A Fact of Life or Violation of Law? University Liability Under Title IX.* Washington, D.C.: National Advisory Council on Women's Educational Programs, 1 July, 1978.

Bularzik, Mary. "Sexual Harassment at the Workplace: Historical Notes." *Radical America.* 12 (June 1978): 25–43.

Bureau of National Affairs, Inc. *Sexual Harassment and Labor Relations.* Washington, D.C.: Bureau of National Affairs, Inc., 1981.

Cahan, Regina."Home Is No Haven: An Analysis of Sexual Harassment in Housing." *Wisconsin Law Review.* 6 (November–December 1987): 1061–83.

Campbell, Helen. *Women Wage-Earners, Their Trades and Their Lives.* Boston: Roberts Brothers, 1887; reprinted as *Prisoners of Poverty.* Westport, CT.: Greenwood Press, 1970, 1975.

Carothers, Suzanne C. and Peggy Crull. "Contrasting Sexual Harassment in Female and Male-Dominated Occupations." In *My Troubles Are Going to Have Trouble With Me: Everyday Trials and Triumphs of Women Workers,* eds. Karen Sacks and Dorothy Remy, 219–28. Brunswick, NJ: Rutgers University Press, 1984.

——. "Understanding Sexual Harassment: A Way For Women to Gain Control of the Conditions of Their Work." New York: Working Women's Institute, 1982.

Center for Sex Equity in Schools. *Title IX Line.* Ann Arbor, MI.: Center for Sex Equity in Schools, Fall 1983.

Center for Women's Policy Studies. *Harassment and Discrimination in Employment.* Washington, D.C.: Center for Women's Policy Studies, 1981.

Chamallas, Martha. "Feminist Construction of Objectivity: Multiple Perspectives in Sexual and Racial Harassment Litigation." *Texas Journal of Women and Law.* 1 (1992): 95.

——. "Writing About Sexual Harassment: A Guide to the Literature." *UCLA Women's Law Journal* 4 (1993): 37–58.

Chudacoff, Nancy Fisher. "New EEOC Guidelines on Discrimination Because of Sex: Employer Liability for Sexual Harassment Under Title VII." *Boston University Law Review.* 61 (1981): 535–62.

Clarke, Elissa, et al. *Stopping Sexual Harassment: A Handbook.* Detroit: Labor and Education Research Project, 1980.

Coal Employment Project. *Sexual Harassment in the Mines – Bringing the Issue to Light.* Oak Ridge, TN: Coal Employment Project, 1981.

Coalition Against Sexual Harassment. *Checklist and Position Paper.* Minneapolis: Coalition Against Sexual Harassment, 1981.

Cobble, Dorothy Sue. The Other Women's Movement: Workplace Justice and Social Rights in Modern America. Princeton: Princeton University Press, 2004.

Cochran, Augustus B. *Sexual Harassment and the Law: The Mechelle Vinson Case.* Lawrence: University Press of Kansas, 2004.

Collins, Eliza G. C. and Timothy Blodgett. "Sexual Harassment: Some See It ... Some Won't." *Harvard Business Review.* (March/April 1981): 76–95.

Collins, Patricia Hill. Black Feminist Thought: Knowledge, Consciousness, and the Politics of Empowerment. New York: Routledge, Chapman, and Hall, 1991.

Columbus Committee Against Sexual Harassment. *Combating Sexual Harassment.* Columbus, OH: Committee Against Sexual Harassment, 1981.

Conte, Robert F. and David L. Gregory. "Sexual Harassment in Employment – Some Proposals Toward More Realistic Standards of Liability." *Drake Law Review.* 32 (1982–83): 407–39.

Cott, Nancy. *Public Vows: A History of Marriage and the Nation.* Cambridge: Harvard University Press, 2000.

——. The Bonds of Womanhood: 'Woman's Sphere' in New England, 1780–1835. New Haven: Yale University Press, 1977.

Crenshaw, Kimberlé Williams. "Mapping the Margins: Intersectionality, Identity Politics, and Violence Against Women of Color." In *The Public Nature of Private Violence*, eds. Martha Albertson Fineman and Fixanne Mykitiuk. New York: Routledge, 1994.

——. "Race, Gender, and Sexual Harassment." *Southern California Law Review.* 65 (1992): 1467–76.

——. "Whose Story Is It Anyway? Feminist and Antiracist Appropriation of Anita Hill." In *Race-ing Justice, Engendering Power,* ed. Toni Morrison. New York: Pantheon Books, 1992.

Crocker, Phyllis L. "Annotated Bibliography on Sexual Harassment in Education." *Women's Rights Law Reporter* 7 (Winter 1982): 91–106.

Crull, Peggy. *The Impact of Sexual Harassment on the Job: A Profile of the Experiences of 92 Women.* Research Series, Report No. 3. New York: Working Women's Institute, 1979.

——. "Responses to Fair Employment Practices Agencies to Sexual Harassment Complaints: A Report and Recommendation." Research Series, Report No. 2. New York: Working Women's Institute, 1978.

——. "Searching for the Causes of Sexual Harassment: An Examination of Two Proto-types." In *Hidden Aspects of Women's Work*, eds. Christine Bose, Roslyn Feldberg, and Natalie Sokoloff, 225–44. New York: Praeger Publishing Company, 1987.

——. "Sexual Harassment and Male Control of Women's Work." Research Series, Report No. 5, Fall 1982. New York: Working Women's Institute, 1981. Published in *Women: A Journal of Liberation* 8 (1982): 3–7.

——. "Sexual Harassment and Women's Health." In *Double Exposure: Women's Health Hazards on the Job and in the Home*, ed. Wendy Chavkin, 100–120. New York: Monthly Review Press, 1983.

——. "The Stress Effects of Sexual Harassment on the Job." *Am J Orthopsychiatry.* 52(July 1982): 539–44.

Crull, Peggy and Marilyn Cohen. "Expanding the Definition of Sexual Harassment." Research Series, Report No. 4, Winter 1982. New York: Working Women's Institute, 1981.

Davis, Flora. *Moving the Mountain: The Women's Movement in America Since 1960.* Chicago: University of Illinois Press, 1999.

Davis, Kathy. "Feminist Body/Politics as World Traveller: Translating Our Bodies, Ourselves." *The European Journal of Women's Studies.* 9(3): 223–47.

D'Emilio, John and Estelle Freedman. *Intimate Matters: A History of Sexuality in America.* New York: Harper & Row, 1988.

Derthick, Martha and Paul J. Quirk. *The Politics of Deregulation.* Washington, D.C.: The Brookings Institute, 1985.

Deslippe Dennis A. "Rights, Not Roses": Unions and the Rise of Working-Class Feminism, 1945–1980. Urbana: University of Illinois Press, 2000.

"Development, New EEOC Guidelines on Discrimination Because of Sex: Employer Liability for Sexual Harassment Under Title VII." *Boston University Law Review.* 61 (1981): 535–62.

Diamond, Robin, Lynn Feller, and Nancy Felipe Russo. *Sexual Harassment Action Kit.* Washington, D.C.: Federation of Organizations for Professional Women, 1981.

Dollinger, Sol and Genora Johnson Dollinger. *Not Automatic: Women and the Left in the Forging of the Auto Workers' Union.* Monthly Review Press, 2000.

Dubrow, Laurie. *Sexual Harassment and the Law.* Cambridge: Alliance Against Sexual Coercion, 1980.

Dye, Nancy Schrom. *As Equals and as Sisters.* University of Missouri Press, 1980.

Dziech, Billie Wright Linda Weiner. *The Lecherous Professor: Sexual Harassment on Campus.* Boston: Beacon Press, 1984.

Eisenberg, Susan. We'll Call You If We Need You: Experiences of Women Working Construction. Ithaca, NY: Cornell University Press, 1999.

Ellis, Judy Trent. "Sexual Harassment and Race: A Legal Analysis of Discrimination." *Journal of Legislation.* 8(1981): 30–45.

Elshtain, Jean Bethke. *Public Man, Private Woman.* Princeton: Princeton University Press, 1981.

Enke, Anne. "Smuggling Sex Through the Gates: Race, Sexuality, and the Politics of Space in Second Wave Feminism." *American Quarterly.* 55.4(2003): 634–67.

Estrich Susan R. "Sex at Work." *Stanford Law Review.* 43(1991): 813–61.

Evans, Laura J. "Sexual Harassment: Women's Hidden Occupational Hazard." In *The Victimization of Women,* eds. Jane Roberts Chapman and Margaret Gates, 203–23. Beverly Hills: SAGE Publications, 1978.

Evans, Sara M. Tidal Wave: How Women Changed America at Century's End. New York: Free Press, 2003.

——, "Beyond Declension: Feminist Radicalism in the 1970s and 1980s." In *The World the 60s Made: Politics and Culture in Recent America,* eds. Van Gosse and Richard Moser, 52–66. Philadelphia: Temple University Press, 2003.

——. "Re-Viewing the Second Wave". *Feminist Studies.* 28:2 (Summer 2002): 259–67.

——. Born for Liberty: A History of Women in America. New York: Free Press,1989.

Ezekiel, Judith. *Feminism in the Heartland.* Columbus: Ohio State University Press, 2002.

Farley, Lin. Sexual Shakedown: The Sexual Harassment of Women on the Job. New York: McGraw-Hill, 1978.

Farrell, Amy. "'Like a Tarantula on a Banana Boat': Ms. Magazine, 1972–1989." In *Feminist Organizations: Harvest of the New Women's Movement,* eds. Myra Marx Ferree and Patricia Yancey Martin, 53–68. Philadelphia: Temple University Press, 1995.

Faucher, Mary D. and Kenneth J. McCulloch. "Sexual Harassment in the Workplace: What Should the Employer Do?" *EEO Today.* (Spring 1978): 38–44.

Ferree, Myra Marx and Beth B. Hess. *Controversy and Coalition: The New Feminist Movement.* Boston: G.K. Hall & Company, 1985.

Fitzgerald, Louise F. and Sandra L .Shullman. "Sexual Harassment: A Research Analysis and Agenda for the 1990s." *Journal of Vocational Behavior.* 42(1993): 5–27.

Foner, Philip S. Women and the American Labor Movement: From Colonial Times to the Eve of World War I. New York: Free Press, 1979.

Fox-Genovese, Elizabeth."Rethinking Sexual Harassment". *Partisan Review.* (1996) 366–74.

Franke, Katherine. "What's Wrong With Sexual Harassment?" *Stanford Law Review.* 49 (1997): 691–772.

Franklin, Phyllis, Helene Moglen, Phyllis Zatlin-Boring, and Ruth Angress. *Sexual and Gender Harassment in the Academy: A Guide for Faculty, Students, and Administrators.* New York: Modern Language Association of America, 1981.

Gallop, Jane. *Feminist Accused of Sexual Harassment.* Durham, NC: Duke University Press, 1997.

Geoghegan, Thomas. Which Side Are You On? Trying To Be For Labor When It's Flat On Its Back. New York: Farrar, Straus, Giroux, 1991.

Gillespie, Dair and AnnLeffler. "The Politics of Research Methodology in Claims-Making Activities: Social Science and Sexual Harassment." *Social Problems.* 34 (1987): 490–508.

Gilmore, Stephanie. "The Dynamics of the Second-Wave Feminist Activism in Memphis, 1971–1982: Rethinking the Liberal/Radical Divide." *NWSA Journal.* 15.1 (2003): 94–117.

Ginsburg, Gilbert J. and Jean Galloway Koreski. "Sexual Advances by an Employee's Supervisor: A Sex-Discrimination Violation of Title VII?" *Employee Relations Law Journal.* 3 (Summer 1977): 83–93.

Gomez, S., R. Brown and L. Martin. "Public Hearings on Sexual Harassment in the Workplace: Analysis of Testimony." Office of Women and Work, Michigan Department of Labor, November 1979.

Goodman, Jill Laurie. "Sexual Demands on the Job: Women's Work." *Civil Liberties Review.* (March/April 1978): 55–8.

Gordon, Linda. "The Politics of Sexual Harassment". *Radical America.* 15 (July/August): 7–14.

——. Heroes of Their Own Lives: The Politics and History Violence. New York: Penguin Books, 1988.

Greenbaum Marcia L. and Bruce Fraser. "Sexual Harassment in the Workplace". *Arbitration Journal.* 36:4 (December 1981): 30–41.

Greene, Kimberly K. and Susan B. Tatnall. *Sexual Harassment of Working Women in Kentucky: "She Gave at the Office": A Handbook.* Louisville: Kentucky Commission on Women, no date.

Groeber, Ronald X. "A Survey of Sexual Harassment: A Wrong Redressable Under Title VII Only When Discrimination is Shown." *Northern Kentucky Law Review.* 8 (1981): 397–410.

Gruber, James E. Phoebe Morgan, eds. *In the Company of Men: Male Dominance and Sexual Harassment.* Boston: Northeastern University Press, 2005.

Gruber, James E. "Methodological Problems and Policy Implications in Sexual Harassment Research." *Population Research and Policy Review.* 9 (1990): 235–54.

Gruber, James E. and Lars Bjorn. "Blue-Collar Blues: The Sexual Harassment of Women Autoworkers". *Work and Occupations.* 9 (August 1982): 271–98.

Guinier, Lani. The Tyranny of the Majority: Fundamental Fairness in Representative Democracy. New York: Free Press, 1994.

Gutek, Barbara A. Sex and the Workplace: The Impact of Sexual Behavior and Harassment on Women, Men, and Organizations. San Francisco: Jossey-Bass Publishers, 1985.

——. Experiences of Sexual Harassment: Results from a Representative Survey. Bethesda, MD: National Institute of Mental Health, 1981.

Gutek, Barbara and Bruce Morasch. "Sex Roles, Sex-Role Spillover, and Sexual Harassment of Women at Work." *Journal of Social Issues.* (Winter 1982): 30–48.

Gutek, Barbara, Bruce Morasch, and Aaron G .Cohen. "Interpreting Social-Sexual Behavior in a Work Setting." *Journal of Vocational Behavior.* 22 (1983): 30–48.

Gutek, Barbara, and C. Nakamura. "Gender Roles and Sexuality in the World of Work." In *Changing Boundaries*, eds. Elizabeth Allgeier and Naomi McCormick, 182–201. Palo Alto, CA: Mayfield Publishing Company, 1983.

Gutek, Barbara, et al. "Sexuality and the Workplace." *Basic and Applied Social Psychology*. (September 1980): 255–65.

Gutman, Herbert G. *The Black Family in Slavery and Freedom, 1750–1925*. New York: Pantheon Books, 1976.

Harel, Gedaliahu and Karen Cottledge. "Combatting Sexual Harassment: The Michigan Experience." *Human Resource Management*. 21 (Spring 1982): 2–21.

Harragan, Betty Lehan. Games Mother Never Taught You: Corporate Gamesmanship for Women. New York: Warner Books, 1977.

Harrison, Cynthia. "Creating a National Feminist Agenda: The Women's Action Alliance and Feminist Coalition Building in the 1970s." In *Feminist Coalitions: Historical Perspectives on Second-Wave Feminism in the United States*, ed. Stephanie Gilmore. Urbana: University of Illinois Press, 2007.

Hartmann, Susan M . *The Other Feminists: Activists in the Liberal Establishment*. New Haven: Yale University Press, 2000.

Hill, Anita. *Speaking Truth to Power*. New York: Doubleday, 1997.

Hill, Anita Faye and Emma Coleman Jordan, eds .*Race, Gender and Power in America: The Legacy of the Hill-Thomas Hearings*. New York: Oxford University Press, 1995.

Hoff, Joan. Law, Gender, and Injustice: A Legal History of U.S. Women. New York: New York University Press, 1991.

Howard, Susan. *Title VII Sexual Harassment Guidelines and Educational Employment*. Washington, D.C.: Association of American Colleges Project on Status and Education of Women, August 1980.

Hughes, Jean O. and Bernice R. Sandler. *In Case of Sexual Harassment – A Guide for Women Students*. Washington, D.C.: Center for Women Policy Studies, 1986.

Irmina, Wawrzyczek. "The Women of Accomack Versus Henry Smith: Gender, Legal Recourse, and the Social Order in Seventeenth Century Virginia." *Virginia Magazine of History and Biography*. 105 (1997): 5–26.

Jacobs, Harriet A. *Incidents in the Life of a Slave Girl*, ed. Jean Fagan Yellin. Cambridge: Harvard University Press, 1987.

Jensen, Inger W. and Barbara Gutek. "Attributions and Assignment of Responsibility in Sexual Harassment." *Journal of Social Issues*. (Winter 1982): 121–36.

Johnson, William Dean. "Administrative Law – *Continental Can Co., Inc. v. State of Minnesota*: A Cause of Action for Sexual Harassment by Co-workers." *North Carolina Law Review*. 59 (April 1981): 803–17.

Joint Committee to Study Sexual Harassment. *Final Report*. Tempe: Arizona State University, 1980.

Kelley, Michelle L . and Beth Parsons. "Sexual Harassment in the 1990s: A University-Wide Survey of Faculty, Administrators, Staff, and Students." *Journal of Higher Education*. 71 (2000): 548–69.

Kentucky Commission on Human Rights. *Sexual Harassment on the Job Is Against the Law*. Louisville: Kentucky Commission on Human Rights, June 1980.

Kentucky Commission on Human Rights. *Stop Sexual Harassment on the Job*. Louisville: Kentucky Commission on Human Rights, no date.

Kessler-Harris Alice. In Pursuit of Equity: Women, Men, and the Quest for Economic Citizenship in 20th-Century America. New York: Oxford, 2001.

Klein, Freada, and Nancy Wilber. Who's Hurt and Who's Liable: Sexual Harassment in Massachusetts Schools. A Curriculum and Guide for School Personnel. Boston: Massachusetts State Dept. of Education, 1981.

Kline, Wendy. "'Please Include This in Your Book': Readers Respond to *Our Bodies, Ourselves.*" *Bulletin of the History of Medicine.* 79 (2005): 81–110.

Konrad, A.M. and Barbara Gutek. "Impact of Work Experiences on Attitudes Toward Sexual Harassment". *Administrative Science Quarterly.* 31 (1986): 422–38.

Korda, Michael. *Male Chauvinism: How It Works.* New York: Random House, 1972.

LaFontaine, Edward and Leslie Tredeau. "The Frequency, Sources and Correlates of Sexual Harassment Among Women in Traditional Male Occupations." *Sex Roles.* 15 (1986): 423–32.

Largen, Mary Ann. *What to Do If You're Sexually Harassed.* Arlington, VA: New Responses, Inc., 1980.

——. Report on Sexual Harassment in Federal Employment, November 1978–July 1979. Arlington, VA: New Responses, Inc., 1979.

Largen, Mary Ann and Alyce McAdam, *The Sexually Harassed Woman: A Counselor's Guide.* Arlington, VA: New Responses, Inc., 1980.

Lehrer, Susan. Origins of Protective Labor Legislation for Women, 1905–1925. Albany: State University of New York, 1987.

Lembright, Muriet Faltz, and Jeffrey W. Riemer. "Women Truckers' Problems and the Impact of Sponsorship." *Work and Occupations.* 9 (November 1982): 457–74.

Leventer, Jan C. "Sexual Harassment and Title VII: EEOC Guidelines, Conditions Litigation, and the United States Supreme Court." *Capital University Law Review.* 10 (1981): 484–85.

Levy, Ariel. Female Chauvinist Pigs: Women and the Rise of Raunch Culture. New York: Free Press, 2005.

Lindemann, BarbaraSchlei, and David D. Kadue. *Sexual Harassment in Employment Law.* Washington, D.C.: Bureau of National Affairs, 1992.

Livingston, Jo Ann., "Sexual Harassment of Working Women." Master's Thesis, University of Vermont, 1979.

Lloyd R. "Research Problems in the Study of Sexual Harassment." Paper presented at the annual meetings of the American Sociological Association, Chicago, IL, August 1987.

Lott, Bernice. "Assessment of Sexual Harassment Within the University of Rhode Island Community." Paper presented at the Eighth Annual Conference of the Association for Women in Psychology, Boston, MA, 5–8 March 1981.

MacKinnon, Catharine A. *Feminism Unmodified: Discourses on Life and Law.* Cambridge: Harvard University Press, 1987.

——. "Introduction." *Capital University Law Review.* 10 (1981): ii.

——. *Sexual Harassment of Working Women.* New Haven: Yale University Press, 1979.

——. *Toward a Feminist Theory of the State.* Cambridge: Harvard University Press, 1989.

MacKinnon, Catharine A. and Reva B. Siegel, eds. *Directions in Sexual Harassment Law.* New Haven: Yale University Press, 2004.

MacLean, Nancy. *Freedom is Not Enough: The Opening of the American Workplace.* Cambridge: Harvard University Press, 2006.

Maihoff, Nancy and Linda Forrest. "Sexual Harassment in Higher Education: An Assessment Study." *Journal of the National Association for Women Deans, Administrators and Counselors* 46, no. 2 (Winter 1982): 3–8.

Markson, Elizabeth. "Sexual Harassment: Self-Reports by Women Members of the Eastern Sociological Society." *New England Sociologist.* 1 (Fall 1978):45–57.

Marmo, Michael. "Arbitrating Sex Harassment Cases." *Arbitration Journal* 35, no. 1 (March 1980): 35–40.

Marshall, Anna-Marie. "Closing the Gaps: Plaintiffs in Pivotal Sexual Harassment Cases." *Law and Social Inquiry.* 23 (Fall 1998):761–92.

Martin, John R., Vice President for University Personnel, Rutgers University. "Memorandum to Members of the University Community, Regarding Sexual Harassment: Procedures for the Handling of Complaints." 28 June 1980.

Martin, Molly, ed. *Hard-Hatted Women: Life on the Job.* Seattle: Seal Press, 1988.

Martin, Robert. "EEOC's New Sexual Harassment Guidelines: Civility in the Workplace." *Nova Law Journal.* 5 (Spring 1981): 405–19.

Martindale, M. *Sexual Harassment in the Military: 1988.* Arlington, VA: Defense Manpower Data Center, 1988.

Matthews, Glenna. The Rise of Public Woman: Woman's Power and Woman's Place in the United States, 1630–1970. New York: Oxford University Press, 1992.

Mayer, Jane and Jill Abramson. *Strange Justice: The Selling of Clarence Thomas.* Boston: Houghton Mifflin, 1994.

Maypole, Donald E. and Rosemarie Skaine. "Sexual Harassment of Blue Collar Workers." *Journal of Sociology and Social Welfare.* 9 (1982):682–95.

McAdam, Doug. Political Process and the Development of Black Insurgency, 1930–1970, 2nd ed. Chicago: University of Chicago Press, 1999.

McAdam, Doug, John D. McCarthy, and Mayer N. Zald. *Comparative Perspectives on Social Movements.* New York: Cambridge University Press, 1996.

McCaghy, M. Dawn. *Sexual Harassment: A Guide to Resources.* Boston: G. K. Hall & Co., 1985.

McGee, Jr., Jack I. "Casenote – Civil Rights: Sexual Advances by Male Supervisory Personnel as Actionable under Title VII of the Civil Rights Act of 1964: *Corne v. Bausch & Lomb, Inc., Williams v. Saxbe.*" *South Texas Law Journal.* 17(1976): 409–15.

Meyer, Mary Coeli and Jeanenne Oestreich. The Power Pinch: Sexual Harassment at the Workplace, Film, Leader's Guide for Conducting a Sexual Harassment Workshop and Manager's Handbook for Handling Sexual Harassment in the Workplace. Northbrook, IL: MTI Teleprograms, Inc., 1981.

Meyer, Mary Coeli, Inge M. Berchtold, Jeannenne L. Oestreich, and Frederick J. Collins. *Sexual Harassment.* New York: Petrocelli Books, Inc., 1981.

Michigan Task Force on Sexual Harassment in the Workplace. *Conference Report: Sexual Harassment at the Workplace.* Ann Arbor: Program on Women and Work, 1979.

Milkman, Ruth. Women, Work and Protest – A Century of U.S. Women's Labor History. Boston: Routledge & Kegan Paul, 1985.

Miller, III, James. Introduction to *A Conversation with Commissioner Eleanor Holmes Norton.* Washington, D.C.: American Enterprise Institute, 1979.

Mink, Gwendolyn. Hostile Environment: The Political Betrayal of Sexually Harassed Women. Ithaca, NY: Cornell University Press, 2000.

Miranda Associates, Inc. Sexual Harassment: It's Not Academic! A Workshop for Higher Education Administrators, Faculty and Students; Participants' Notebook. Bethesda: Miranda Associates, Inc., and Office for Civil Rights, U.S. Department of Education, 1983.

Moore, Marat and Connie White. *Sexual Harassment in the Mines – Legal Rights, Legal Remedies*. Oak Ridge, TN: Coal Employment Project, 1981.

Morewitz, Stephen J. *Sexual Harassment & Social Change in American Society*. Bethesda: Austin & Winfield, 1996.

Nadasen, Premilla. "Expanding the Boundaries of the Women's Movement: Black Feminism and the Struggle for Welfare Rights." *Feminist Studies*. 28(2002):271–301.

Naples, Nancy. Grassroots Warriors: Activist Mothering, Community Work, and the War on Poverty. New York: Routledge, 1998.

Nardino, Marie. "Note: Discrimination: Sex – Title VII – Cause of Action Under Title VII Arises When Supervisor, With Employer's Knowledge and Acquiescence, Makes Sexual Advances Toward Subordinate Employee and Conditions Employee's Job Status on Favorable Response – *Tomkins v. Public Service Electric & Gas Co.*, 568 F.2d 1044 (3d Cir. 1977)." *Seton Hall Law Review*. 9(1978):108–129.

Nathan, Maud. *The Story of an Epoch-Making Movement*. New York: Doubleday, 1926.

National Council on Research on Women. *Sexual Harassment: Research and Resources*, 3rd ed. New York: National Council for Research on Women, 1995.

New Hampshire Advisory Committee to the U.S. Commission on Civil Rights. *Sexual Harassment on the Job: A Guide for Employers*. Boston: New Hampshire Advisory Committee to the U.S. Commission on Civil Rights, September 1982.

"Note: Legal Remedies for Employment-Related Sexual Harassment." *Minnesota Law Review*. 64 (1979): 151–81.

"Note: Sexual Harassment and Title VII: The Foundation for the Elimination of Sexual Cooperation as an Employment Condition." *Michigan Law Review*. 76 (1978): 1007–35.

NOW Legal Defense and Education Fund, Women's Legal Defense Fund, et al. Comments on the Equal Employment Opportunity Commission's Interim Guidelines on Sexual Harassment. 10 June, 1980.

O'Farrell, Brigid and Sharon Harlan. *Craftworkers and Clerks: The Effect of Male Co-worker Hostility on Women's Satisfaction with Nontraditional Jobs*. Working Paper No. 62. Wellesley, MA: Wellesley College Center for Research on Women, 1980.

Olson, Jack. *The Girls in the Office*. New York: Simon and Schuster, 1972.

Orlando, Jeannette. *Sexual Harassment in the Workplace: A Practical Guide to What It Is and What to Do About It*. Los Angeles: Women's Legal Clinic, Center Against Sexual Harassment, 1981.

Oshinsky, Judy Charla. "Sexual Harassment of Women Students in Higher Education." Ph.D. diss., University of Florida, 1980.

Paludi, Michele, ed. *Ivory Power: Sexual Harassment on Campus*. Albany: State University of New York Press, 1990.

Patai, Daphne. *Heterophobia: Sexual Harassment and the Future of Feminism*. Lanham, MD: Rowman and Littlefield Publishers, 1998.

Paul, Ellen Frankel. "Sexual Harassment as Sex Discrimination: A Defective Paradigm." *Yale Law and Policy Review*. 8 (1990): 333.

Paul, Pamela. Pornified: How Pornography is Transforming Our Lives, Our Relationships, and Our Families. New York: Times Books, 2005.

Pennsylvania Commission on Women. *Not for Fun, Not for Profit: Strategies for Ending Sexual Harassment on the Job*. Harrisburg: Pennsylvania Commission for Women, 1981.

Pope, Kenneth S., Hanna Levenson, and Leslie R. Schover. "Sexual Behavior Between Clinical Supervisors and Trainees: Implications for Professional Standards." *Professional Psychological*. 11 (February 1980): 157–62.

——. "Sexual Intimacy in Psychology Training: Results and Implications of a National Survey." *American Psychologist.* 34 (August 1979): 682–89.

Project on the Status and Education of Women. *Sexual Harassment on Campus.* Washington, D.C.: Association of American Colleges, 1985.

——. *Title VII Sexual Harassment Guidelines and Educational Employment.* Washington, D.C.: Project on the Status and Education of Women, Association of American Colleges, 1980.

——. *Sexual Harassment: A Hidden Issue.* Washington, D.C.: Project on the Status and Education of Women, June 1978.

Quinn, Robert. "Coping with Cupid: The Formation, Impact, and Management of Romantic Relationships in Organizations." *Administrative Scientific Quarterly.* (March 1977): 40–45.

Rhoden, Nancy K. "Comment – Employment Discrimination – Sexual Harassment and Title VII – Female Employees' Claim Alleging Verbal and Physical Advances by a Male Supervisor Dismissed as Nonactionable – *Corne v. Bausch and Lomb, Inc.*" *New York University Law Review.* 51 (April 1976): 148–67.

Robnett, Belinda. How Long? How Long? African-American Women in the Sturggle for Civil Rights. New York: Oxford University Press, 1997.

Rogers, Mary F. "Clarence Thomas, Patriarchal Discourse and Public/Private Spheres." *Sociological Quarterly.* 39(1998):289–308.

Rosen, Ruth. The World Split Open: How the Modern Women's Movement Changed America. New York: Penguin Books, 2000.

Ross, Susan C. The Rights of Women, An American Civil Liberties Handbook. New York: Avon Books, 1973.

Rossein, Merrick T. "Sex Discrimination and the Sexually Charged Work Environment." *NYU Review of Law and Social Change.* 9 (1979–1980): 271–305.

Roth, Benita. Separate Roads to Feminism: Black, Chicana, and White Feminist Movements in the Second Wave. New York: Cambridge University Press, 2004.

Rubinett, Lynn. "Sex and Economics: The Tie That Binds. Judicial Approaches to Sexual Harassment as a Title VII Violation." *Journal of Law and Inequality.* 4 (July 1986): 245–93.

Sandler, Bernice R. *Writing a Letter to the Sexual Harasser: Another Way of Dealing With the Problem.* Washington, D.C.: Project on the Status and Education of Women, 1983.

Sauvigné, Karen. *Digest of Leading Sexual Harassment Cases*, Policy Series, Report No. 4. New York: Working Women's Institute and Center for Women in Government, 1981.

——. *Sexual Harassment: Discussion of Policies and Procedures.* New York: Working Women's Institute and Center for Women in Government, 1981.

——. *Sexual Harassment Is Against the Law.* New York: Working Women's Institute, 1982.

——. What's a Supervisor to Do: Handling Sexual Harassment Complaints. New York: Working Women's Institute, 1982.

Scalia, Eugene. "The Strange Career of Quid Pro Quo Harassment." *Harvard Journal of Law and Public Policy.* 21 (1999): 307–25.

Schnabel, Marta-Ann. "Sexual Harassment in the Workplace: New Guidelines from the EEOC." *Loyola Law Review.* 27 (1981): 512–31.

Schneider, Ann. "Sexual Harassment Brief Bank and Bibliography." *Women's Rights Law Reporter.* 8 (Fall 1985): 294–98.

Schneider, Beth E . "Consciousness About Sexual Harassment Among Heterosexual and Lesbian Women Workers." *Journal of Social Issues* (Winter 1982): 75–98.

Schroedel, Jean Reith, *Alone in the Crowd: Women in the Trades Tell Their Studies.* Philadelphia, PA: Temple University Press, 1986.

Schultz, Vicki, "Reconceptualizing Sexual Harassment." *Yale Law Journal.* 107(1998): 1683–1805.

Schupp, Robert W., Joyce Windham, and Scott Draughn. "Sexual Harassment Under Title VII: The Legal Status." *Labor Law Journal.* 32 (1981): 238–52.

Scott, Robert E. "The Pleasures and Pitfalls of a Non-Traditional Occupation." Paper presented at the American Vocational Association Annual Convention, New Orleans, LA, 7 December, 1980 (ERIC, ED 195729).

Segrave, Kerry. *The Sexual Harassment of Women in the Workplace, 1600 to 1993.* Jefferson, NC: McFarland and Company, Inc., 1994.

"Sexual Harassment Brief Bank and Bibliography," *Women's Rights Law Reporter.* 8 (Fall 1985): 267–98.

"Sexual Harassment on Campus." Journal of the National Association for Women Deans, Administrators, and Counselors. (Winter 1983): 1–50.

Sexual Harassment on the Job: A Fact Sheet. Arlington, VA: New Responses, Inc., 1978.

"Sexual Harassment Symposium." *Capital University Law Review.* 10 (Spring 1981): 445–606.

Seymour, William C. "Sexual Harassment: Finding a Cause of Action Under Title VII." *Labor Law Journal.* (March 1979): 139–56.

Shepard, Martin. The Love Treatment: Sexual Intimacy Between Patients and Psychotherapists. New York: P. H. Wyden, 1971.

Short, Jodi L. "Creating Peer Sexual Harassment: Mobilizing Schools to Throw the Book at Themselves." *Law and Policy.* 28 (January 2006): 31–59.

Sigworth, Heather. "Abortion Laws in the Federal Courts: The Supreme Court as Supreme Platonic Guardian." *Indiana Law Review.* 5 (1971): 130.

———. "The Legal Status of Antinepotism Regulations." *AAUP Bulletin.* (Spring 1972): 31–34.

Silverman, Dierdre. "Sexual Harassment: Working Women's Dilemma." *Quest: A Feminist Quarterly* 3, no. 3 (1976–77): 15–24.

Siniscalco, Gary R. "Sexual Harassment and Employer Liability: The Flirtation that Could Cost a Fortune." *Employee Relations Law Journal.* 6 (1980–1981) 277–93.

Smith, J. Clay, Jr. "Prologue to the EEOC Guidelines on Sexual Harassment." *Capital University Law Review.* 10(1981): 472.

Sporkin, Stanley. "In Memoriam: Charles R. Richey." *George Washington Law Review.* 66 (April 1998): 744.

Springer, Kimberly. Living for the Revolution: Black Feminist Organizations, 1968–1980. Durham, NC: Duke University Press, 2005.

Spruill, Julia Cherry. *Women's Life and Work in the Southern Colonies.* New York: Norton, 1998.

Stanley-Elliott, Lynne. "Sexual Harassment in the Workplace: Title VII's Imperfect Relief." *Journal of Corporation Law.* 6 (Spring 1981): 625–56.

Stein, Laura W. *"Sexual Harassment in America: A Documentary History.* Westport, CT: Greenwood Press, 1999.

Stein, Nan. "Bullying or Sexual Harassment? The Missing Discourse of Rights in an Era of Zero Tolerance." *Arizona Law Review.* 45 (Fall 2003): 783–99.

Strossen, Nadine. "The Tensions Between Regulating Workplace Harassment and the First Amendment: No Trump." *Chicago Kent Law Review.* 71(1995): 701–27.

"Symposium: Gender, Race, and the Politics of Supreme Court Appointments: The Import of the Anita Hill/Clarence Thomas Hearings." *Southern California Law Review.* 65 (March 1992): 1279–1582.

Taub, Nadine. "Keeping Women in Their Place: Stereotyping *Per Se* as a Form of Employment Discrimination." *Boston College Law Review.* 21 (January 1980): 345–418.

Taub, Nadine and Elizabeth M. Schneider. "Women's Subordination and the Role of Law." In *Feminist Legal Theory: Foundations,* ed. D. Kelly Weisbert, 9–21. Philadelphia: Temple University Press, 1993. Originally published in *Politics of Law,* ed. David Kairys. New York: Pantheon Books, 1982.

Taylor, Verta A. "How To Avoid Taking Sexual Harassment Seriously: A New Book That Perpetuates Old Myths: A Review of *Sexual Harassment* – by Mary Coeli Meyer, Inge M. Berchtold, Jeannenne L. Oestreich, and Frederick J. Collins." *Capital University Law Review.* 10(1981): 673–84.

Tell Someone! A Program for Combatting Sexual Harassment. Ann Arbor: University of Michigan, Affirmative Action Office, 1981.

Till, Frank. *Sexual Harassment: A Report on Sexual Harassment of Students.* Washington, D.C.: National Advisory Council on Women's Educational Programs, August 1980.

Tillar, Darrel Long. *Sexual Harassment in Employment: Legal Perspectives for University Administrators.* Charlottesville, VA: Center for the Study of Higher Education, 1980.

Tomkins, Adrienne. "Sex Discrimination: Adrienne Tomkins, Stenographer." *Civil Liberties Review.* (September/October 1978): 19–23.

Valk, Anne M. "'Mother Power': The Movement for Welfare Rights in Washington, D.C., 1966–1972," *Journal of Women's History.* 11.4 (2000): 34–58.

Vermeulen, Joan. "Comments on the Equal Employment Opportunity Commission's Proposed Amendment Adding Section 1604.11, Sexual Harassment, to Its Guidelines on Discrimination." *Women's Rights Law Reporter.* 6 (Summer 1980): 285–94.

Wagner K. C. "A Socialist Feminist Perspective." In *Not for Women Only: Social Work Practice for a Feminist Future,* eds. Mary Bricker-Jenkins and Nancy R. Hooyman, 64–68. Silver Spring, MD: National Association of Social Workers, 1986.

Weeks, Elaine Lunsford, Jacqueline M. Boles, Albeno P. Garbin, and John Blount. "The Transformation of Sexual Harassment from a Private Trouble into a Public Issue." *Sociological Inquiry.* 56 (1986): 432–55.

Wehrli, Lynn. "Sexual Harassment at the Workplace: A Feminist Analysis and Strategy for Social Change." Master's Thesis, Massachusetts Institute of Technology, 1976.

Weisel, Kerry. "Title VII: Legal Protection Against Sexual Harassment." *Washington Law Review.* 53(1977): 123–44.

Whalen, Charles and Barbara Whalen. *The Longest Debate: A Legislative History of the 1964 Civil Rights Act.* Washington, D.C.: Seven Locks Press, 1985.

White, Connie, Barbara Angle, and Marat Moore. *Sexual Harassment in the Coal Industry: A Survey of Women Miners.* Oak Ridge, TN: Coal Employment Project, 1981.

Whitelegg, Drew. "Cabin Pressure: The Dialectics of Emotional Labour in the Airline Industry." *Journal of Transport History.* 23 (2002): 73–86.

Whittier, Nancy. "Meaning and Structure in Social Movements." In *Social Movements: Identity, Culture, and the State,* eds. David S. Meyer, Nancy Whittier, and Belinda Robnett (New York: Oxford University Press, 2002).

Wider Opportunities for Women and the Center for National Policy Review. *A Territorial Issue: A Study of Women in the Construction Trades*. Washington, D.C.: Wider Opportunities for Women and the Center for National Policy Review, 1982.

Williams, Kimberlé Crenshaw. "Mapping the Margins: Intersectionality, Identity Politics, and Violence Against Women of Color." In *The Public Nature of Private Violence*, eds. Martha Albertson Fineman and Rixanne Mykitiuk, 93–118. New York: Routledge, 1994.

Wilson, Kenneth R. and Linda A. Kraus. "Sexual Harassment in the University." *Journal of College Student Personnel*. (May 1983).

Women in the Work Force. *What Every Working Woman Should Know About Sexual Harassment*. High Point, NC: American Friends Service Committee, 1980.

Women Organized Against Sexual Harassment. *Conditions for a Title IX Grievance Procedure*. Berkeley, CA: Women Organized Against Sexual Harassment, 1980.

——. *Sexual Harassment: What Is It, What To Do About It*. Berkeley, CA: Women Organized Against Sexual Harassment, 1979.

Women's Labor Project. Bargaining for Equality: A Guide to Legal and Collective Bargaining Solutions for Workplace Problems that Particularly Affect Women, 2nd ed. San Francisco: Women's Labor Project, 1981.

Women's Legal Defense Fund. *Legal Remedies for Sexual Harassment*. Washington, D.C.: Women's Legal Defense Fund, 1983.

Working Women's Institute. Equal Employment Opportunity Commission: How to File a Job-Related Sexual Harassment Complaint. New York: Working Women's Institute, 1983.

——. National Labor Relations Board: How to File an Unfair Labor Practice Charge for Job-Related Sexual Harassment. New York: Working Women's Institute, 1983.

——. New York City Commission on Human Rights and New York State Division of Human Rights: How To File a Job-Related Sexual Harassment Complaint. New York: Working Women's Institute, 1983.

——. Sexual Harassment on the Job and in Education: A Comprehensive Bibliography. New York: Working Women's Institute, Fall 1979.

——. "Sexual Harassment on the Job: Results of Preliminary Survey." Research Series, Report No. 1, Fall 1975.

——. Tort and Contract Law: How to File a Job-Related Sexual Harassment Complaint. New York: Working Women's Institute, 1983.

Federal Statutes, Regulations, and Administrative Guidelines

Civil Rights Act of 1991, 42 U.S.C. § 1981a(a)(1), (b), (c)(1) (Supp. III 1991).

Construction Contractors, Affirmative Action Requirements, 42 Fed. Reg. 41381 (1977), codified at 41 C.F.R. Ch. 60.

Department of Labor, Office of Federal Contract Compliance Programs, Final Rule, 45 Fed. Reg. 86216 (30 December 1980).

Department of Labor, Office of Federal Contract Compliance Programs, Final Rule, 46 Fed. Reg. 42968 (1981).

Equal Employment Opportunity Commission Guidelines on Discrimination Because of Sex, 29 C.F.R. Ch. XIV, Sec. 1604.11 Sexual Harassment (1980).

Equal Employment Opportunity Commission, Policy Guidance on Current Issues of Sexual Harassment, 19 March 1990.

Equal Opportunity in Apprenticeship, 43 Federal Register 20760 (12 May 1978), codified at 29 C.F.R. § 30 (1978).

Title IX of the Education Amendments of 1972, 20 U.S.C. § 1681.

Title VII of the Civil Rights Act of 1964, as amended by the Equal Employment Opportunity Act of 1972 and the Civil Rights Act of 1991, 42 U.S.C. Sec. 2000e.

Women in Construction, 43 Federal Register 14888–91 (7 April 1978), codified at 41 C.F.R. § 60-4 (1978).

Federal Government Hearings and Documents

Califa, Antonio J. Memorandum to Regional Civil Rights Directors, Regions I-X, Office for Civil Rights, United States Department of Education, Re: Title IX and Sexual Harassment Complaints 31 August 1981.

Campbell, Alan K . Director, U.S. Office of Personnel Management to Heads of Departments and Independent Agencies, Re: Policy Statement and Definition of Sexual Harassment, 12 December 1979.

Memorandum from Commissioner R. Gaull Silberman to Chairman Clarence Thomas, Commissioner Tony Gallegos, Commissioner William Webb, and Commissioner Fred Alvarez, Dated 28 October 1985, Subject: Commission Participation as Amicus Curiae in PSFS Savings Bank, FSB v. Vinson, No. 84–1979 (S. Ct.), reprinted in *Daily Labor Report* 210 (30 October 1985): E–1.

Memorandum from Johnny J. Butler, General Counsel (Acting), to Chairman Clarence Thomas, Commissioner Tony Gallegos, Commissioner William Webb, Commissioner Fred Alvarez, and Commissioner R. Gaull Silberman, Dated 24 October 1984, Subject: *PSFS Savings, FSB v. Mechelle Vinson, et al. (Vinson v. Taylor,* 753 F.2d 141 [D.C. Cir. 1985]), reprinted in *Daily Labor Report* 210 (30 October 1985): E–2.

National Commission on Unemployment Compensation, *Consideration of the Issue of Sexual Harassment and Disqualification: Hearings.* 28 June 1979. (Unemployment Compensation Hearings).

U.S. Congress. House. Subcommittee on Investigations of the Committee on Post Office and Civil Service. *Sexual Harassment in the Federal Government.* 96th Congress, 1st Session, 23 October 1979, 1, 13 November 1979. (1979 Hanley Hearings on Sexual Harassment).

U.S. Congress. House. Military Personnel Subcommittee of the Committee on Armed Services. *Women in the Military.* 96th Congress, 1st and 2nd Sessions, 13–16 November 1979 and 11 February 1980.

U.S. Congress. House. Subcommittee on Labor-Management Relations of the Committee on Education and Labor. *Pressures in Today's Workplace (Vol. II).* 96th Congress, 1st Session, 4 and 6 December 1979.

U.S. Congress. House. Subcommittee on Investigations of the Committee on Post Office and Civil Service. *Sexual Harassment in the Federal Government.* 96th Congress, 2nd Session, 30 April 1980. (Sexual Harassment Report).

U.S. Congress. House. Subcommittee on Investigations of the Committee on Post Office and Civil Service. *Sexual Harassment in the Federal Government (Part II).* 96th Congress, 2nd Session, 25 September 1980. (Hanley Hearings on Sexual Harassment [Part II]).

U.S. Congress. House. Committee on Post Office and Civil Service. *Equal Employment Opportunity and Sexual Harassment in the Postal Service.* 96th Congress, 2nd Session, 27 October 1980.

U.S. Congress. House. Subcommittee on Postal Personnel and Modernizations of the Committee on Post Office and Civil Service. *Racial Discrimination and Sexual Harassment in the U.S. Postal Service.* 97th Congress, First Session, 1 July 1981. (Racial Discrimination and Sexual Harassment in the U.S. Postal Service Hearings).

U.S. Congress. Senate. *Report on Conditions of Women and Child Wage Earners in the United States*, 19 vols., 61st Congress, 2nd Session, Document #645 (Conyington, Mary. "Relations Between Occupations and Criminality of Women"). Washington, D.C.; Government Printing Office, 1911.

U.S. Congress. Senate. Committee on Labor and Human Resources. *Sex Discrimination in the Workplace, 1981.* 97th Congress, 1st Session, 28 January 1981 and 21 April 1981. (1981 Hatch Hearings on Sex Discrimination).

U.S. Merit Systems Protection Board. *Sexual Harassment in the Federal Workplace: Is It A Problem?: A Report of the U.S. Merit Systems Protection Board, Office of Merit Systems Review and Studies.* Washington, D.C.: Government Printing Office, 1981.

U.S. Merit Systems Protection Board. *Sexual Harassment of Federal Workers: An Update.* Washington, D.C.: United States Government Printing Office, 1987.

U.S. Merit Systems Protection Board. *Sexual Harassment in the Federal Workplace: Trends, Progress, Continuing Challenges.* Washington, D.C.: Government Printing Office, 1995.

U.S. Office of Personnel Management. *Workshop on Sexual Harassment: Trainer's Manual.* Washington, D.C.: Government Printing Office, 1980.

Case Records Including Briefs and Pleadings

Alexander v. Yale University, Case No. 79–7547, United States Court of Appeals for the Second Circuit, University of Iowa Law Library, Iowa City, IA.

Barnes v. Train, Case No. 73–1828, United States District Court for the District of Columbia, Federal Records Center, Washington, D.C.

Bundy v. Delbert Jackson, Case No. 79–1693, United States Court of Appeals for the District of Columbia, University of Iowa Law Library, Iowa City, IA.

Corne and Geneva DeVane v. Bausch and Lomb, Inc., Case No. 74–173-TUC-WCF, United States District Court for the District of Arizona, National Archives and Records Administration, Pacific Region, Laguna Niguel, CA.

Corne and Geneva DeVane v. Bausch and Lomb, Inc., Case No. 75–1857, United States Court of Appeals for the Ninth Circuit, National Archives and Records Administration, Pacific Region-San Francisco, San Bruno, CA.

In re Carmita Wood, Case No. 75–92437, New York State Department of Labor, Unemployment Insurance Referee Section.

Meritor Savings Bank v. Vinson, Case No. 84–1979, Supreme Court of the United States (microfiche), Emory University Law Library, Atlanta, GA.

Meritor Savings Bank v. Vinson, Case No. 80–2369, United States Court of Appeals for the District of Columbia, Emory University Law Library, Atlanta, GA.

Miller v. Bank of America, Case No. 76–3344, United States Court of Appeals of the Ninth Circuit, National Archives and Records Administration, Pacific Region-San Francisco, San Bruno, CA.

Munford v. James T. Barnes and Co., Case No. 79–1120, United States Court of Appeals for the Sixth Circuit, Library of Congress, Washington, D.C.

Saxon Industries, Inc., Case No. 76–1610, United States Court of Appeals for the Fourth Circuit, University of North Carolina Law Library, Chapel Hill, NC.

Tomkins v. Public Service Electric and Gas Co., Case No. 75–1673, United States District Court for the District of New Jersey, National Archives and Records Administration, Central Plains Region, Lee's Summit, MO.

Tomkins v. Public Service Electric and Gas Co., Case No. 77–1212, United States Court of Appeals for the Third Circuit, National Archives and Records Administration, Philadelphia, PA.

Williams v. William B. Saxbe, Case No. 79–7547, United States Circuit Court for the District of Columbia, University of Iowa Law Library, Iowa City, IA.

Interviews

Arditti, Rita, 10 June 2005, Orlando, FL
Cooper, Maudine Rice, 24 February 2000, Washington, D.C.
Crull, Peggy, 27 February 2001, New York, NY
Disch, Estelle, 10 June 2005, Orlando, FL
Graff, Joan, 14 February 2001, San Francisco, CA
Klein, Freada, 26 March 2001, 1 April 2001, 13 April 2001, San Francisco, CA; 25 June 2001, New York, NY
Levy, Trudi, 14 February 2001, Washington, D.C.
Mazzaferri, Katherine, 10 February 2001, Bethesda, MD
Meyer, Susan, 17 February 2001, New York, NY
Rubinett, Lynn, 23 June 2001, Austin, TX
Sauvigné, Karen, 4, 12 February 2001, 25, 26 June 2001, Brooklyn, NY
Simon, Anne E., 26 April 2001, Oakland, CA
Taub, Nadine, 21 March 2001, Newark, NJ
Wagner, K. C., 28 February 2000, 25 June 2001, New York, NY

Manuscript Collections

Alexander v. Yale: Collected Documents from the Yale Undergraduate Women's Caucus and Grievance Committee. New Haven: Yale University, 1978 (ERIC No.: ED180385). (Alexander v. Yale: Collected Documents).

Alliance Against Sexual Coercion Ephemeral Materials, 1976–1977, Wilcox Collection of Contemporary Political Movements, Schlesinger Library, Radcliffe College, Cambridge, MA. (AASC Materials at Schlesinger).

Coal Employment Project Records. Archives of Appalachia, Sherrod Library, East Tennessee State University, Johnson City, TN. (Coal Employment Project Collection).

Equal Employment Opportunity Commission Records, Washington, D.C.

Judge Charles R. Richey Papers. Ohio Wesleyan University Manuscript Collection #2.

Karen Sauvigné Papers, Brooklyn, New York. Private Collection. (Karen Sauvigné), Private Papers).

Katherine Mazzaferri Papers, Bethesda, MD. Private Collection.

National Organization for Women (NOW) Records. Schlesinger Library, Radcliffe College. (NOW Collection).

NOW Legal Defense and Education Fund Records. Schlesinger Library, Radcliffe College.

Trudy Levy Papers, Falls Church, VA. Private Collection.

Working Women's Institute Records. Barnard Center for Research on Women, New York, NY. (Working Women's Institute Collection).

Periodicals

Aegis: Magazine on Ending Violence Against Women, 1978–1987.
Equal Rights Advocate, December 1980–Winter 1985.
Feminist Alliance Against Rape Newsletter, 1974–1978.
Labor Pains, vol. 1, no. 1 (May 1975), no. 2 (November 1975), no. 3 (March 1976).
Life and Labor, vol. 4, no. 8 (August 1914) (publication of the National Women's Trade Union League).
On Campus With Women, June 1978–Spring 1985.
On the Job, Summer 1982, Winter/Spring 1983.

Index